American Corruption Talk

Robert G. Boatright and
Molly Brigid McGrath

American Corruption Talk

A Political Etymology

TEMPLE UNIVERSITY PRESS
Philadelphia • *Rome* • *Tokyo*

TEMPLE UNIVERSITY PRESS
Philadelphia, Pennsylvania 19122
tupress.temple.edu

Library of Congress Cataloging-in-Publication Data

Names: Boatright, Robert G. author | McGrath, Molly Brigid, 1977– author
Title: American corruption talk : a political etymology / Robert G.
   Boatright and Molly Brigid McGrath.
Description: Philadelphia : Temple University Press, 2025. | Includes
   bibliographical references and index. | Summary: "Explores the topic of
   corruption in American political discourse, including what claims of
   corruption mean, why those claims are made, whether the contemporary
   American preoccupation with corruption has any historical precedent, and
   how discussions of corruption might be improved"— Provided by publisher.
Identifiers: LCCN 2024054014 (print) | LCCN 2024054015 (ebook) | ISBN
   9781439916889 cloth | ISBN 9781439916896 paperback | ISBN 9781439916902 pdf
Subjects: LCSH: Political corruption—United States—Public opinion |
   Political culture—United States | Discourse analysis—Political
   aspects—United States | Rhetoric—Political aspects—United States
Classification: LCC JK2249 .B63 2025 (print) | LCC JK2249 (ebook) | DDC
   306.20973—dc23/eng/20250416
LC record available at https://lccn.loc.gov/2024054014
LC ebook record available at https://lccn.loc.gov/2024054015

The manufacturer's authorized representative in the EU for product safety is
Temple University Rome, Via di San Sebastianello, 16, 00187 Rome RM, Italy
(https://rome.temple.edu/).
tempress@temple.edu

9 8 7 6 5 4 3 2 1

Contents

List of Figures and Tables

FIGURES

TABLES

Acknowledgments

This book grew out of a series of heated discussions we had in the summer of 2014 while watching our kids swim at the local pool. It is in part a consequence of a lengthy debate we had about Jill Lepore's 2014 *New Yorker* article about corruption; it is also in part an experiment in seeing whether two people who disagree vigorously (but always cheerfully) about many things could find sufficient common ground to write a (vigorous yet, despite the subject matter, cheerful) book together. We hope we have succeeded in that.

It seems like everyone we know has something valuable to say about corruption. Many of our colleagues have helped us think about the ideas we explore in this book. The Early Modernists Unite! Collective at Clark University—and in particular, Nina Kushner, Lisa Kasmer, Wiebke Deimling, Meredith Neumann, Wim Klooster, and Ben Korstvedt—provided detailed commentary and support for our dabbling in medieval political theory. We received many comments on our efforts to link populism and corruption talk from Amit Ron, Majia Nadesan, and other participants in the Arizona State University Populism conference; from Mark Navin, Richard Nunan, Joan McGregor, and other participants in the 2018 AMINTAPHIL conference on corruption; and from audience members and fellow panelists at the American Political Science Association/Political Studies Association conference on populism. We also thank the participants in the National Institute for Civil Discourse's research symposium in September 2022 for their helpful feedback. Several of the chapters here received their first airings at the past few meetings of the International Political Science Association Research Committee on Party Finance and Political Corruption (RC 20); we thank the organizers of these events—and in particular, Jonathan Mendilow, Eric Phelippeau, Paulo Roberto Neves Costa, Ezequiel Martins Paz, and Fernando Jiménez Sánchez—for supporting our efforts to understand and critique contemporary scholarship on corruption. We also received valuable comments along the way from David Schmidtz, John Searle, Jennifer Hudin and the Berkeley Social Ontology Group, Greg Weiner, Anne Baker, David Ricci, Vickie Sullivan, Diana Schaub, Nancy Rosenblum, Joseph Reisert, and Romulus Maier. In addition to the conferences mentioned above, we have also benefited from the opportunity to present this research at meetings of the Midwest, Northeast, and New England Political Science Associations. Heidi Peltier helped with innumerable conversations as well as with the cover. We extend our apologies to anyone else we talked about corruption with but have failed to mention here.

We received research support for this project from the National Institute for Civil Discourse's "Creating Research Projects Across Disciplinary and Ideological Lines" project, through the Stand Together Courageous Collaborations initiative. We acknowledge the Francis A. Harrington Fund at Clark University for support for indexing and travel related to this book. And we thank Clark University students Brittany Klug and Rebecca Hadik for their help with the coding in the presidential rhetoric chapter.

We owe a special thanks to Aaron Javsicas, Gary Kramer, and the rest of the editorial staff at Temple University Press. We greatly appreciate Aaron's advice and his patience with our frequent delays in completing this manuscript. We also thank Robin Kolodny for recommending that we publish with Temple.

An earlier version of Chapter 9 was published as "The Poverty of 'Corruption': Confusions and Disagreements about the Rotten in Politics," in *Corruption and Governmental Legitimacy: A Twenty-First Century Perspective*, ed. Jonathan Mendilow and Ilan Peleg (Lanham, MD: Rowman & Littlefield, 2016), 287–308. Chapter 11 incorporates material from two previously published pieces: "Populist Corruption Talk," in *Mapping Populism: A Guide to Understanding and Studying Populism*, ed. Majia Nadesan and Amit Ron (New York: Routledge, 2020), 176–184, and "Corruption, Populism, and Sloth," in *Democracy, Populism, and Truth*, ed. Mark C. Navin and Richard Nunan (New York: Springer, 2020), 47–59. We thank the publishers for permission to reprint that material here.

Finally, we thank our colleagues at Clark University, Assumption University, and the National Institute for Civil Discourse at the University of Arizona. Most of all, of course, we thank our families for putting up with this whole endeavor.

American Corruption Talk

1

Introduction

In the Swedish film *Force Majeure* (Östlund 2014), Tomas and Ebba, a happily married couple, are dining outdoors at a Swiss ski resort with their children. When an avalanche threatens the outdoor restaurant, Ebba instinctively shields her children. Tomas grabs his cell phone and runs off, leaving his family to fend for themselves. Although everyone is ultimately safe, and the husband had until then always acted as a loving partner and father, he has revealed a heretofore hidden truth about his character. Subsequently, the marriage unravels. Nothing Tomas can do or say could ever undo what has been shown about who he really is.

As husband and father, Tomas had a job to do. In this difficult moment he did not merely fail to do his job. Rather, he did not even try. Failure is a common enough human experience, and failure after effort is easily forgiven. Had Tomas tried but failed to protect his wife and children, the event would have aroused viewers' pity, not their indignation. When Tomas abdicated his duties in order to serve himself, he failed not merely to protect his family. He failed, more seriously, at a basic orientation toward the good that defines his job, the good to which he was, as husband and father, supposed to aim. This lack of trying is less easily forgiven. After all, even if Ebba forgives that isolated action, it must seem in general that Tomas, as husband and father, is not all that interested in his job but is really, despite his outward performance, underneath it all, up to something else.

A similar story could be told regarding corruption. Individual acts of corruption may be egregiously unjust, or not. They come in all shapes and sizes.

Some are quite petty and inconsequential—as isolated incidents. The individual action, however, appears a symptom of something more troubling: In the case of someone who holds public office, for instance, it is not merely that the officeholder is not trying to do his or her job; it is that the person is trying to do something else entirely. When the public discovers an act of corruption, the officeholder and perhaps the whole system are cast in a shadow: Is that who they really are? Is that what all this is really about?

But, then again, perhaps corruption is more easily forgiven than Tomas's desertion. Many times, politicians caught in corruption scandals find fervent defenders—those constituencies, especially local beneficiaries, who feel like the corrupt representative has looked out for them, or those who have gained from the politician's policies or spoils. Those defenders sometimes insist on the politician's innocence, even in the face of evidence, perhaps out of personal affection or loyalty to a group identity. But they may defend the politician because they feel that this person—despite the act of corruption— has in fact done quite well in the job of a politician, precisely in providing goods and services they value, regardless of the cost to others or to the integrity of the system. Such stories could be told about former Boston mayor James Michael Curley or longtime Ohio congressman James Traficant.

Such examples force us to ask, what actually is the officeholder's job? That is, discussions of corruption lead us, after just a bit of reflection, into discussions of what officeholders are supposed to be, and what the institutions in which they act are supposed to be all about. Corruption talk, we would contend, is always explicitly or implicitly about what roles we assign in our society, which goods and whose goods those roles are meant to serve, and how we expect those roles to be fulfilled. While this book explores the messiness and vagueness of the word "corruption," it also seeks to remind us that lurking underneath our corruption talk are serious claims and concerns about how we organize our common life.

1.1: Corruption and Corruption Talk in the Contemporary United States

It is easy for us to assume that corruption is a problem somewhere else—in other cities, in other countries—but that it is not a pressing problem in our own lives or communities. Or, as is perhaps the case for some Americans today, we might assume that corruption is a temporary and easily reversible condition—we may occasionally pick the wrong politicians to lead us, but in time they will be voted out of power and we will return to the way we were. Many times, those who make such assumptions are correct. Even when we know corruption is afoot in our government, how it impinges upon our own day-to-day lives is often difficult to see. Yet numerous political writers have emphasized that the potential for corruption is present in all manner of political systems, and that even when it is not manifest it is still, in some ways, latent. Hence, while the academic literature on corruption often takes on cases of rampant fraud and bribery (particularly in undemocratic regimes), corruption remains a lively subject of political chatter or partisan attack even in stable democratic regimes where cases of individual transactional corruption tend to be more easily prosecuted. Such insights might promote, at the extremes, paranoia or complacency, or anything in between.

That corruption is always possible does not merely suggest that we should be vigilant. It suggests, as well, that the corrupt walk among us. Even when we cannot see instances of corruption, we may well have gathered insights that suggest that corrupt actions have taken place or that corrupt actors are in a position to subvert our democratic institutions.

It means something, then, when we accuse each other of corruption. There are public consequences of corruption talk. It may become the stuff of conspiracy theories. There is, after all, always a chance that we do not see corruption simply because we are not looking closely enough, or in the right places, just as there is always a new way to explain the September 11 cover-up, the hidden truth regarding Barack Obama's birth certificate, how Trump managed to win the 2016 election (or lose the 2020 election), our failure to find UFOs, or the ultimate possibility that the QAnon predictions will transpire. It is difficult to conclusively disprove corruption claims, just as it is difficult to debunk conspiracy theories, because by their nature they suggest a cover-up perpetrated by people with devious, self-serving motives (see, e.g., Uscinski and Parent 2016, chap. 1). And, as we shall show here, arguments about corruption tend to wax and wane across time, often in tandem with political unrest or with dislocating social change. That is, perhaps the prevalence of corruption talk does not reliably correlate with the prevalence of corruption but with other challenges. We may wonder, then, how much we should worry about corruption versus how much we should worry about corruption talk in those political systems where officeholder corruption does not run rampant.

In this book we present a study of corruption and corruption talk. These are, we argue, two different things. There are all manner of taxonomies of officeholder corruption, and there has been debate for centuries about the relationship between different types of corruption. We are skeptical that there is much to be gained by developing our own taxonomy or by taking sides in the debates over which taxonomy is preferable. We are more concerned, then, with distinguishing between different types of corruption talk—different styles or modes of describing corruption to the public. Corruption has typically been spun in one of two ways. First, corruption may be spoken of in a purifying mode, as something akin to rot, in which corruption is seen as something that evokes disgust and is a potentially contagious or contaminating, alien presence in the body politic. Such an attitude calls for a sort of cleansing or casting out. Second, corruption may be spun in a mending mode, as something akin to crookedness—as something that does not disgust but does prompt concern for replacing or repairing a broken part.

We dabble in different types of literatures here, because political corruption and our discourse about it must be put into broader contexts. Corruption is not exclusively a political phenomenon. However, this study is primarily concerned with politics and with the role that corruption talk plays in American political discourse. Our reason for this is simple—we believe (and hope to demonstrate) that the United States is in the midst of a particularly interesting, and sometimes heated, debate over political corruption. This debate has perhaps become more visible since the 2016 election, but it had been picking up steam for some time before that. It is a debate that has been going on seemingly independently of any actual increase in textbook corruption in America. That is, if Americans are talking more about corruption when bribery and extortion seem not to have increased, we might wonder, fruitfully, whether the issue is not really corruption in these textbook senses. Our corruption talk might indicate other concerns, deeper worries.

Scholars have noted many consequential changes in American politics over the past decade. Even before the tumultuous 2016 and 2020 elections (about which we talk more later in this introduction), American voters were, according to a variety of measures, unhappy with their government. Trust in government and in political institutions has been in decline for over four decades (Dalton 2004). American politicians and political elites are far more ideologically polarized today than they have been since the late nineteenth century. The distribution of incomes in the United States is the most unequal it has been since before the Great Depression. The amount of money spent in American elections is greater than it has been at any time in American history. And, perhaps coincidentally or perhaps not, both major American parties were roiled by populist movements in 2016: An avowed socialist vilifying "the one percent," running on a platform calling for, among other things, free college education, nearly won one party's nomination; and a candidate who campaigned against free trade, against liberalized immigration laws, against elite norms of civility, and against many issues where there had traditionally been bipartisan consensus won the nomination of the other party and, ultimately, the presidency.

A variety of quantitative historical studies have sought to make sense of these changes. Many studies of political polarization in the United States have plotted the growing gap between Republicans and Democrats in Congress and in the electorate. Among these, Thomas Mann and Norman Ornstein (2016, 107–11) call our attention to a period of time in the 1890s where our political parties were similarly distant, and they ask what happened to bring the parties closer together. Mann and Ornstein suggest a number of institutional fixes, while admitting that we have no solid evidence that these fixes would work. Nolan McCarty, Keith Poole, and Howard Rosenthal (2006) explore the relationship between political polarization and income inequality; despite the absence of a compelling causal story about the relationship between the two, the correlation here suggests that perhaps reducing one might reduce the other. Since the 2016 election, there has also been a burgeoning literature connecting populism, in the United States and worldwide, to these same patterns. For instance, Julia Azari and Mark Hetherington (2016) compare the nature of the political issues motivating outsider or populist candidates today to the issues that motivated arguably similar candidates in the 1890s. J. Eric Oliver and Wendy Rahn (2016) note changes in the words that presidential candidates use in their speeches over time, seeing an increase in simplistic and what they called "people-centric" words in recent elections and, more generally, at times of rapid economic change and dislocation. And Jan-Werner Müller (2016) has explored the links between populist rhetoric across a variety of Western democracies. Collectively, accounts such as these all add up to a larger claim: Many people feel our government isn't working very well, many people (and many politicians) are very exercised about this, and the problems we face are not easily legislated away.

To these accountings, we propose to add another: a tracing of what we call "corruption talk" in the United States. It is our contention that the words Americans use intimate a great deal about their state of mind. Many neo-pluralist writers, such as Bruce Cain (2015), argue that the decline in public confidence is related to the declining power of civic and governmental institutions in our lives. We argue here that as our politics has become more contentious, as the ideological purists at the extremes increasingly dominate public discourse and attention, as our political institutions seem to many to fail to function, the language we use to talk about politics changes—the word "corruption," with its strong moral overtones and its hint of a hidden systemic problem, captures something, however vaguely, that people are worried about.

We make this argument in a few ways. To get us started, however, here is a simple depiction of changes in corruption talk. The Google Ngram in Figure 1.1 shows that references to "corrupt politicians" have steadily increased in the United States over the past thirty years, despite a lack of any obvious increase in textbook transactional corruption or an overwhelmingly newsworthy event.[1] Data for other nations show a similar increase.

We can subsume any number of claims about corruption into this framework; the Ngram, after all, measures all uses of the term in American books.

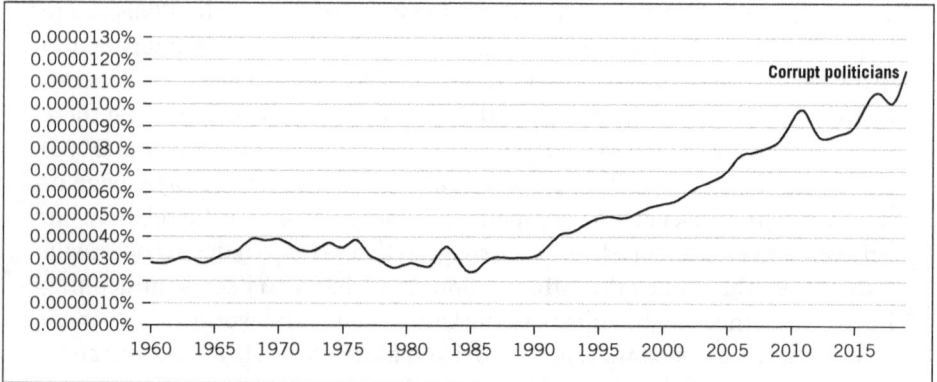

Figure 1.1 References to "Corrupt Politicians" in U.S. Nonfiction Books, 1960–2020. *(Source: Google Ngram.)*
Note: This figure shows changes in the frequency of the term in all English-language books published in the United States over this time period. For an explanation of the methodology, see https://books.google.com/ngrams/info.

Some of these references to corruption, we presume, are to documented cases of malfeasance: corrupt transactions, perhaps, between individual politicians and nefarious special interests. Others are to broader critiques: Congress is corrupt, the political system is corrupt, the justice system is corrupt, the high-profile leaders of the other side are all corrupt. Some are larger cultural broadsides: The morals of our citizens have been corrupted, by the media, by popular culture, or by other pernicious influences. And some are historical studies: We may have been prompted to revisit sensational scandals of the past, or to indulge in melodramatic stories of organized crime.

Are all of these stories of corruption about the same thing? What does this increase mean? And where, in our society, has it taken place? These are the questions we address here. The twofold argument of this book is straightforward. At the empirical level of analysis, there has been an increase in "corruption talk" in American public discourse for the past two decades. Despite this increase, however, it is not at all clear what we are talking about. The increase in corruption talk has not taken place in tandem with an obvious increase in corruption in the standard sense. We appear to be talking about many different things, to be simultaneously using various conceptions of corruption mixed together. As a consequence, in day-to-day politics we often talk past each other. The heat of such here-today partisan arguments obscures what we actually agree and disagree about. Political philosophy as well as empirical political science help us bring these agreements and disagreements to light.

At the theoretical level of analysis, corruption—despite its various uses and connotations throughout the history of political theory and across contemporary partisan debates—retains a core identity, but one that usually is only vaguely intended. But this same meaning must be applied differently when different assumptions are made—by people from different political points of view—about the purpose and structure of our institutions and officeholders. Therefore, this meaning, when clarified, helps us recognize the more fundamental issues, questions of perennial controversy, fueling our contemporary contests.

The goal of this book is to unravel different types of corruption allegation: their origins, the places in public life where they are most commonly found, and the purposes people use claims about corruption to pursue. As we show, claims about corruption inevitably depend upon beliefs about what sort of political order, or what sort of uncorrupted human condition, would exist if corruption had not set in. Arguments about corruption, then, are really arguments about perennial human questions such as what a just government and society are, what we have in common with our fellow citizens, or what our shared aspirations are or should be. This reflection on corruption talk is, therefore, intended both to clarify what corruption itself is and to show how such a clarification might illuminate the nature of our political life together. We hope that this book can foster a more honest and productive discussion of what corruption is and also foster some restraint in our tendency to label as corruption things that we merely disagree with.

1.2: Why Write about a Word?

We are hardly the first to write a book on corruption; indeed, as we explain in some detail, corruption studies are experiencing something of a moment of late. In just the past decade or so, Lawrence Lessig's *Republic, Lost* (2012), Zephyr Teachout's *Corruption in America* (2014), and Laura Underkuffler's *Captured by Evil* (2013) have considered corruption from a legal standpoint; Sarah Chayes's *Thieves of State: Why Corruption Threatens Global Security* (2015) and Michael Johnston's *Corruption, Contention, and Reform* (2014) have explored how one identifies and measures political corruption; Bruce Buchan and Lisa Hill's *An Intellectual History of Political Corruption* (2014) considers how philosophers have treated corruption over time. Oxford University Press's Very Short Introductions series includes a volume on corruption (Holmes 2015), and there are, as far as we know, two academic handbooks on political corruption (Rose-Ackerman and Søreide 2011; Heywood 2014).

Many of these books are valuable, and we draw upon several of them here. We part ways with these authors, however, in that we don't focus on corruption per se; rather, we want to talk about how other people talk about corruption. In short, the very existence of such books is part of our object of inquiry here. When people express concern about corruption, what are they worried about? What types of responses are they trying to elicit? What do they suggest is wrong with corruption, and what measures do they urge on us to prevent or combat it?

One of our preferred comparisons here, then, is not to the oeuvre of books about corruption, but to the genre of books about particular words. This is, we confess, not a genre that is universally recognized within any academic discipline. Yet without thinking too hard, it is easy to identify many books that are focused upon words—how their meanings change over time, how they become popular or unpopular, and how the decision to use them can shape political debates.

Consider, for instance, four such books. In *Ghetto: The Invention of a Place, the History of an Idea*, sociologist Mitchell Duneier (2016) argues that Americans, and Europeans as well, have used the word "ghetto" at different times to describe different circumstances and different racial groups or nationalities. Our willingness to use (or cease to use) the term can reflect social mores, but its application can also serve as a rhetorical tool to influence our willingness to support antipoverty efforts. Siegfried Wenzel's 1967 book *The Sin of Sloth* (which we discuss in Chapter 11) is an inquiry into how the word "sloth" has come to mean something very different than it did during the Middle Ages, and how as a result our common understandings of the moral implications of sloth have changed. Similarly, in *Boredom: A Lively History* (2011), philosopher Peter Toohey has explored the appearance of the word "boredom" in the English lexicon and the different normative connotations of the word. And finally, Jan-Werner Müller's 2016 book *What Is Populism?* (which we also say more about in Chapter 11) confronts the imprecise ways in which the term "populism" is used and the frequently unsuccessful attempts of democratic political analysts to attach the term to different ideological viewpoints.

All books of this type explore the slipperiness and malleability of language, the manner in which words acquire or lose particular moral overtones, and the ways in which they can be deployed in order to pursue certain ends. Our effort here documents the ways in which talk about corruption fits this pattern.

It is possible to situate such talk with reference to an academic disagreement that took place several decades ago over classifying words. Raymond Williams's (1976) Keywords Project sought to clarify, or at least explore, the meanings of several different commonly used terms. In the introduction to his book, Williams pondered the question of whether this sort of clarification would bring about any larger social consensus on what we humans are doing together; he concluded that this was perhaps too ambitious, but he did suggest that by clarifying the meaning of these terms we might achieve "not resolution but perhaps, at times, just that extra edge of consciousness" (Williams 1976, 21). Williams's book is still widely emulated by scholars seeking to engage in discussions of what the foundational terms are within their disciplines. In the introduction to the 1989 book *Political Innovation and Conceptual Change*, however, Quentin Skinner argues that Williams's approach downplays the political aspect of language. Politicians redefine language to suit their own needs and strategies. The meanings of words change over time, as Williams notes, but sometimes the meanings change because individual speakers seek to change them. Conceptual history, not definition, is required for us to understand how political beliefs, actions, and practices are partly constituted by these concepts, and how changes in these concepts themselves change political behavior (see also Farr 1989).

The Williams and Skinner approaches are ambitious efforts to plot the relationship between language and action or behavior. Given the choice, we would attach our effort more closely to the conceptual history approach. At the same time, however, we do not purport to offer a history of the concept of corruption. Rather, we are interested in the discourse that surrounds corruption—the context of corruption claims, the possibility that different types of meanings can become attached to the term "corruption" at the same time, albeit by different actors. As we see again and again in this book, different languages—different styles of corruption talk—can coexist or can confront each other.

This, then, is a book about language—what we mean when we use particular words, and how the meaning of words shifts depending on the goals of the speaker, the context of the speech, and the background beliefs of the author and of the community. Language is the basic human institution because human beings use it to invent, structure, and operate other social institutions. Words are not just powerful in themselves; in addition, words are the tools we use to create other interpersonal powers—rights, expectations, responsibilities, roles, and rules. Of course, sometimes words are used merely to express some fact in the world or some feeling in ourselves that we want others to recognize. But words can also function like enormous power generators, fueled by the meanings we have given them. It is with words that human beings create presidents and processes, citizens and convicts, laws and lawyers—in short, political systems from top to bottom. So, the meaning of our political words and the way we use them in operating our institutions matter. Language is the basic *political* institution.

We propose to investigate corruption talk not as linguists or etymologists or intellectual historians—we are none of these. Rather, we investigate corruption talk from the point of view of political science and philosophy, in order to clarify the phenomenon of corruption—corruption and allegations of it as they show up in political life, structured as it is by our words (and even more generally in what political theorist Michael Oakeshott [1991, 488] called "the conversation of mankind").

Ultimately, we hope that by going through our language about corruption, the analyses offered here will contribute not only to a deeper understanding of our contemporary political life but also to our understanding of what it means to live as human beings and citizens more generally.

One concern in this book is with the corruption allegation as a political (not just legal) *speech act*. That is, we do not deny that corruption in the legal sense exists, and that it is the goal of a wide range of governmental institutions and nongovernmental organizations to identify, discourage, and penalize corrupt acts. Yet much of what is said to be corrupt is often not necessarily corrupt by legal standards, and even legally defined categories of corruption often have ambiguities. Many of those who talk about corruption, however, are not exactly concerned with such legalistic niceties. They talk about corruption in a more abstract sense—because something bothers them, because they seek political advantage, because they feel something in the system is out of joint, or just because they are careless with their language. Yet this language has effects.

Language has a triangular structure. As a speech act, an accusation or complaint of corruption is used by some speaker to categorize some target (some action, person, or institution); and the speaker does so for an audience, the auditors, often to suggest a change that is seemingly justified by the alleged fact of corruption. But what is that feature in the world warranting the categorization and response?

People speak the word "corruption" in different ways that bleed into each other. Sometimes these uses of the word have quite clear meanings; for example, when a bribe or a bribed judge is called corrupt, we point to certain public, legally adjudicative facts and suggest to the audience that certain legal actions should be taken. Sometimes the meaning is a bit more vague, for example, if someone calls Congress corrupt. It may not be clear whether this means that some quantitative threshold has been met—that too many of its members are corrupt in the legal sense—or whether the entire structure, not merely the individuals involved, has gone awry. This type of usage urges the auditors less toward legal action than toward political action, either personnel changes or institutional structuring. Sometimes the word seems vaguer about what features of the world warrant the categorization: The word seems to be used less to capture certain public facts than to express feelings that the speaker wants others to recognize—feelings of condemnation and alienation from an entire system. The system somehow seems all wrong, even if the exasperated speaker can't spell out how.

The word is used to talk about and critique power—officeholders and their particular actions, the institutions in which they hold their offices. But it also is used as an attempt to build or exert or restructure power—to urge a change in officeholders, to punish their actions, or to transform institutions.

This study does not seek to "fix" or correct corruption talk, but to notice it and how it works, and what it indicates. We intend to use this talk for leverage to help us reflect on where we are and what we might properly condemn and hope for.

1.3: The Structure of Our Argument

This book is broken into two major sections: first, an inquiry into how the concept of political corruption has been developed by philosophers and political thinkers, leading up to how it has been understood in the American context especially in the Progressive Era; and second, a comparison of contemporary corruption talk in the United States across different areas of public life. Within each of these sections, we present disagreements about what corruption is and what our attitude and response to it should be.

In Chapters 2 through 6, we discuss the development of the concept of political corruption in political thought. We do so in roughly chronological order. Chapters 2 and 3 provide an ontology of corruption, tracing its roots back to Greek philosophy, where corruption was often held to be an inevitable process of decay affecting earthly things and an analogous decay or ruin of moral character. To call officeholder corruption "corrupt" appears as a metaphorical application of these meanings. We also explore various recurring motives or narratives about social, political, and moral corruption, such as The Fall from an Edenic state, the suspicion of money and commerce, and the prejudice against all politics as inherently corrupt. Chapters 4 and 5 explore the more overtly political definitions of corruption that are present in modern political thought, and in particular in the political writings of Montesquieu (Chapter 4) and Rousseau (Chapter 5). These modern theories lend themselves to comparisons of different political constitutions and to big-picture reflection on their stability or economic success over time, but these theories have not always been part of the repertoire of American political theorists. We argue in Chapter 6 that early American writers followed the Montesquieuian model, particularly as it pertained to the corruption they saw in the European colonial powers and as it inspired an attempt to diffuse power to prevent its abuse. However, the understanding of corruption that gained prominence in the United States in the late nineteenth and early twentieth centuries is more Rousseauian and inextricably linked to the Progressive movement's effort to improve the quality and fairness of American government. The Progressive project established a quintessentially American way of deploying corruption talk, one that subsumed many political practices that had been widely accepted elsewhere. For the Progressives, the transactional, balancing, and moderating nature of politics is itself a form of corruption, one that can be solved by a turn away from politics and toward government as administration. The Progressives framed progress as a natural evolution of society toward a more democratic and more scientific social life, but also as susceptible to derailment by corruption. Yet they shied away from a full-throated argument for cleansing in response, something like a revolution, and instead advocated stepwise fixes, hoping for some blend of Rousseau's general will with a politics-free bureaucracy of experts.

In the second part of the book, we address four contemporary venues in which corruption talk has played a prominent role. In each venue, we explore the blending of different types of corruption talk, and the confusions that result. We also show how different speakers draw from different styles of corruption talk in order to pursue their goals. In Chapter 7, we consider the growth of social scientific research on political corruption. Although the social scientific literature often begins with an acknowledgment that corruption is difficult to define precisely, its emphasis on measurement often leads to a focus either on demonstrable instances of legal wrongdoing or on public beliefs, two distinct categories that are both limited in their ability to capture what is expressed in political corruption talk. The social scientific approach is thus limited to a focus on bright-line instances of officeholder corruption and tends to a Mender's approach to corruption, which is sometimes a poor fit for the public and political ways corruption talk is used. In Chapter 8, we explore how American presidents and presidential candidates discuss corruption in their official statements. We show that there are identifiable eras in which one style or another of corruption talk becomes more prevalent, but we caution that those who hold power and those who seek power will adopt different styles according to their status. And in Chapter 9, we discuss ways in which corruption talk can be misapplied. There, we consider the explosion of contemporary work by legal scholars on the role of corruption in Supreme Court jurisprudence, with a particular focus on lobbying and campaign finance. The language the court has used in holding corruption as relevant to the constitutionality of some types of regulation invites proponents of regulation to seek to broaden or reinterpret the court's legal conception of corruption, a tendency that is understandable yet can also be deceptive. We close this section in Chapter 10 by considering the views of American citizens about what corruption is and how prevalent it is. Drawing upon recent surveys about political corruption, we also explore the ways in which citizens vary in their conceptions of corruption—that is, whether liberals understand corruption to be a different thing than do conservatives, or whether more politically engaged Americans see corruption differently than do less engaged citizens. What we show here suggests that it is entirely possible (perhaps rational) for politicians to describe corruption differently to different types of citizens.

For each of these considerations of contemporary corruption talk, we draw on diverse quantitative data sources to document changes over time, across nations, and across different American political actors in their language and concerns about corruption. Despite variations in the purpose of corruption talk and the conceptions of corruption used in these different settings, we show in this book that references to corruption are substantially more common today than they have been in recent years. This increase in "corruption talk" raises a host of empirical issues that unite these different chapters. For instance, we ask whether Americans talk about corruption in a different fashion than do citizens of other countries, and what the import of the difference between American corruption talk and international research on corruption is. Allegations of corruption in the United States are more frequently used as a tool for political attack, and conceptions of corruption also differ according to the ideology or partisanship of those engaged in corruption talk. References to corruption also do not necessarily become more common when legally corrupt things happen; the increase in corruption talk over the past twenty years does not seem to be the consequence of particular scandals or events. In this regard, contemporary references to corruption are different from past ones; as we show in the time series in this chapter, past concern with corruption tended to be prompted by events such as Watergate or other well-known scandals. Contemporary American concerns with corruption, on the other hand, appear to track closely with the increase in elite political polarization. This suggests to us that allegations of corruption are tools of political combat, but there is rarely any agreed-upon content to them.

There is value to exploring empirical questions such as these. Corruption as a word can have different meaning at different levels, but words are not completely malleable—those who speak of corruption can say one thing, yet still be aware that the audience hears another. For anyone concerned with precision in language, the empirical work here suggests that, at a minimum, many Americans fail to understand each other when they talk about corruption because their meanings and reference points are often quite different. "Corruption" is hardly the only term with such contested meanings, but it is different from other such contested terms in that efforts to address corruption—in the narrow, legal sense—are often held not only to be part of a legitimate governing agenda but also to be efforts on which ideological foes might collaborate.

In the final chapter of the book, we offer our thoughts on how Americans might find a better way to talk about political corruption. We argue that framing corruption as a consequence of "sloth," or inattention to institutional roles, can result in a more civil and constructive discussion of corruption than is the case in contemporary political discourse. It can also offer an alternative to the populist's tendency to deploy corruption talk as a way to accuse those inside institutions of betraying the people.

1.4: The Proverbial Elephant in the Room

We have noted a few times that we feel compelled to talk about corruption in part because Americans have seemed to us compelled to talk about corruption a lot lately. We began this project in the summer of 2014, well before the 2016 presidential election campaign had cast its shadow. As the project unfolded, we were witness to a presidential campaign that featured one major party nominee, Hillary Clinton, who was regularly pilloried by her primary and general election opponents for her alleged corruption, and another major party nominee, Donald Trump, who has been dogged by allegations—during his campaign, during his first presidency, and beyond—that the byzantine nature of his family's real estate empire and his personal finances posed, at a minimum, the risk of corruption. In a way, the nature of these claims makes our point here: Everybody talks about corruption, but not everybody is talking about the same things. Corruption claims were part of the stew of ill will that characterized that election, and they certainly have not gone away since. The first Trump presidency, the Biden presidency, and the 2020 and 2024 presidential campaigns have also featured allegations of corruption coming from both sides.

Many recent books have sought to explain what has happened to American politics since 2016, and some of these books have had passages about corruption. It would be tempting to make our book part of this genre, and perhaps, to a degree, we have. In Chapter 8 we talk a bit about some of the corruption claims from 2016, we comment elsewhere on the contemporary populist impulse that is said by some to be part of Donald Trump's appeal to voters, and we briefly discuss current affairs in the conclusion to this book. It would be possible to find in these discussions views of the Trump election, administration, and the 2020–2024 interregnum. We have tried, however, not to emphasize 2016 and the Trump presidency as anything more than one data point in a much larger story.

In this spirit, then, we do not aim to point fingers at anyone, but we do hope that when the term is used—as it certainly will continue to be—by our nation's leaders, by investigative committees, and in the media, this book will prompt readers to pause and ask questions: Is this thing that is being talked about really corruption? What is the structure and goal of the claim? What type of corruption is it? What understanding of our shared life does it assume and what type of action is it urging on us? And, most importantly, what is the consequence, for all of us, of using this word, in this circumstance?

I

The Origins of American Corruption Talk

2

Types of Corruption and Types of Corruption Talk

2.1: Two Styles of Corruption Talk

Talk about corruption often features metaphors. There are several recurrent images that play a prominent role in corruption discourse. Corrupt behavior is condemned as rotten. A corrupted group is considered contaminated. A corrupt person is called dirty.

These metaphors express emotions. Something rotten provokes disgust. Dirtiness suggests disease. Contamination elicits fear. At the most basic, biological level, these metaphors imply things that are dangerous to eat or drink or handle, things that could make us sick. Corruption can be feared as something contagious. One may fear to be (or fear to seem to be) party to a corrupt action, or one may be hesitant to engage with a corrupt official. One gets dirty when dealing with dirty people, losing one's purity by proximity or interaction.

Employing a less emotion-laden metaphor, we commonly call corrupt officials "crooked." A tool that has been bent or disfigured becomes less useful, or maybe even useless. It no longer does its job well. A person who is crooked is not upright—the metaphor is between physical posture and moral character. Just as the crooked or disfigured body is less capable physically, calling an official crooked implies that the official is morally incapacitated. In contrast to the more visceral metaphors rooted in rot, contamination, or dirtiness, the "crooked" metaphor suggests something broken or less functional, dishonest but not disgusting and not necessarily dangerous.

Just as the various metaphors express different emotions, they also suggest different sources, and they evoke thoughts of different remedies. Whereas contamination comes in from the outside, rot happens to a thing naturally—one may postpone it with proper care, but ultimately it may not be preventable. Something could simply come crooked or may grow crookedly by its own natural disposition, but it could also become crooked through damage or pressure. Rot, disease, and contamination spread; brokenness does not. Though brokenness is not contagious, it may yet be dangerous: When the job that needs to be done is important, a broken tool or a weak person may do more harm than good. There are risks to misplaced trust. In response to the disgust-evoking metaphors of rot, dirtiness, disease, and contamination, we reestablish a hygienic purity in an organization when we "clean house" or "drain the swamp" by punishing or purging perpetrators. The response to something crooked is to straighten it out or to replace it, but emotionally the metaphor calls not for purification but for avoidance.

Thus, the metaphors used for corrupt actions or agents within an institution draw us in two emotional directions. Should we respond with repulsion and purification, or should we adopt a more problem-solving approach that involves regular maintenance, prevention, replacement, and ad hoc punishment? Perhaps the answer depends in part on circumstance, on the type and prevalence of the corruption. Still, these two attitudes are profoundly different: seeing corruption as evidence of rottenness or of crookedness—evoking disgust and cleansing in the first instance, or eliciting problem-solving strategies in the second. Let us represent those who hold these two types of attitudes—who engage in these two types of responses—as the Purists and the Menders.

Not only do we see the two attitudes in common talk about corruption. These attitudes also mark different styles of politics and different philosophical approaches to corruption. Yet the metaphors we use are often mixed together. So are the attitudes. These two general styles of corruption talk are not neatly separable. They are two directions or tendencies, two poles of corruption discourse, like north and south, and few people live on the poles. People rarely stick rigorously to using one set of metaphors and not the other, or one attitude and not the other. The Purist style and the Mender style shade into one another.

Political corruption talk comes from a tradition that is not only political. Rather, corruption is also spoken about in ontological and moral terms. We cannot understand contemporary corruption talk without reflecting on these other senses of the word and the tradition behind us that has shaped our current assumptions. In this chapter, we survey the textual tradition in order to distinguish between three types of corruption, and we show how these senses are related. We begin with ontological corruption because we believe it is conceptually primary, not just etymologically primary. We then show how the ontological concept is applied to human agency: Moral corruption occurs when human beings are rotten or crooked. The third type, office-holder corruption, has obvious political implications, but it is understood as corruption only given the context set up by the ontological and moral types of corruption. These three types of corruption are distinct from the two different attitudes of corruption talk we presented two paragraphs ago. As we survey this textual background, we see that the two attitudes of discourse—the Purists' sense of rottenness with the desire to purge and the Menders' sense of crookedness and the desire to punish the person and repair the system—cut across the types of corruption and surface in thinkers who are otherwise quite different.

2.2: Three Types of Corruption

It is common for those who write or talk about corruption to make distinctions, to develop categories of different kinds of corruption. These categories of types of corruption are distinct from the two styles of corruption talk we have noted earlier—they have to do with what corruption is, not with how we talk about it or how it should be addressed. In fact, there are as many kinds of corruption as there are categories of things that can be corrupted. In this section, we distinguish three broad categories of corruption: ontological corruption, moral corruption, and officeholder corruption (focusing on bribery). As we have seen, the primary metaphors by which we speak about corruption are physical and bodily. In political discourse, "corruption" is usually used to refer to either moral corruption or official corruption, but the root concept, we believe, is physical, or—better—ontological. *Corruption is, at root, an ontological event.* That is, moral corruption and officeholder corruption are best understood as extensions of corruption understood simply and basically as the ruin of a thing's being, its falling apart, its rot, decay, spoiling, breaking, corrosion, or contamination such that it can no longer be what it is supposed to be or do what it is supposed to do.

2.2a: Ontological Corruption: Things Fall Apart

Ontology is the study of what makes particular beings be what they are. Ontologically, corruption refers to the ruin or destruction of a thing.

The earliest Greek philosophers wondered about the ultimate material out of which things are formed. Various pre-Socratic thinkers championed water or air or the unbounded, for example, as that out of which all things were made; but it was Aristotle who advocated what was to become for millennia the canonical view of premodern Western science that earth, fire, air, and water are the four material elements out of which all sublunary, nonheavenly things are composed. Simultaneously, he argues that these material elements are only part of the story. After all, the same wood could become part of a tree, a bookshelf, or a boat. The material elements only potentially make up a particular thing depending on how they are formed together. Arranged differently, the same material could be made into something else or could be scattered and made into many different things. Thus, Aristotle concludes, a thing's form or arrangement causes material stuff to cohere into a thing that is unified as one determinate kind of thing: By taking on a form, shape, or arrangement, the wood moves from potentially being a boat or bookshelf, for example, into actually being one.

We should put aside the quibble about whether earth, fire, air, and water are in fact the basic elements (rather than, say, leptons and quarks). Aristotle should be understood as describing something more basic and commonsensical. Ontologically, material and form—stuff and arrangement—both matter. Only together do they explain what makes a particular thing what it is, and we experience this in everyday life when we see things made or see things fall apart.

This implies a view of corruption. Corruption occurs when material is no longer properly organized and integrated into a whole. This can happen because of internal forces or external forces. For example, the boat gets ruined if its material rots, falling apart into dirt and water, or if the wood it is made from disintegrates because it's infected with termites; the boat gets ruined also if it's rammed in battle and its shape is thus damaged. While Seumas Miller (2011) distinguishes, when speaking of institutional corruption, between passive corrosion and agent-caused corruption, ontological corruption encompasses both the intransitive *falling apart* and the transitive *being damaged*.

It turns out that the metaphor by which we call a corrupt politician "rotten" is as old as dirt. In many languages (including, for instance, Greek, Latin, Hebrew, Arabic, and Hindi), the root of many words for moral or political corruption suggests that corruption shows up fundamentally in these physical ways: as a "de-composition," a rot, spoiling, or decay, or as a destruction or "dis-integration."

The thing's ceasing to be is a total loss of the unifying and organizing form. When the material is informed by its proper arrangement or shape, a thing is able to do what it is supposed to do. A tree can nourish itself and grow, a ship can sail, a bookshelf can hold books. By losing its proper form or shape, the thing can no longer do what it is supposed to do—it can no longer engage in the activities that define it and make it what it is. But not all corruption is total. A thing can begin to fall apart without being totally destroyed. An apple with a rotten spot is still an apple. Corruption might refer to the complete loss of identity, a ceasing to be what the thing was, but corruption may also refer to stages in a process tending toward destruction; a damaged thing may simply have diminished ability to function as the kind of thing the thing is.

A thing is made worse as the kind of thing it is, becoming a less excellent instance of its kind, as its ability to function as that type of thing is diminished. To be corrupted in this sense is to become worse per se. We can still recognize, for example, broken spectacles as spectacles, though they are worse as spectacles since they are no longer functional, and at a certain point of damage we would say they are no longer spectacles at all, but bits of metal and plastic. Ontological corruption includes passing away or being destroyed (total loss of identity) as well as damage (loss of excellence).

The ontological sense of corruption is used, for example, when we speak of a corrupt text: Sometimes a manuscript is untrustworthy either through material damage or copying error. We commonly speak of corrupt data on a computer drive when it is unreadable, and, likewise, sometimes biologists or medical researchers refer to a corrupt chromosome. Linguistic corruption occurs when a word or an idiom derives from another, often as the result of a mistake or sloppiness, as "goodbye" resulted from "God be with ye" or "Cajun" from "Arcadian." Sickness of the body and the body's decomposition in the grave are forms of ontological corruption. Traditional Christianity teaches that, when resurrected in heaven, saints receive "incorruptible bodies," no longer subject to aging, disease, or rot.

Aristotle's ancient and influential account implies something important—that all earthly things are not only corruptible also but are destined for corruption. Things composed of the four elements are doomed for destruction, rot, and decay. Things fall apart. It is just what they do. Traditionally understood, all earthly or composite things are given to this destructive process, as we read in the King James version of the Bible at Matthew 6:19: "Lay not up for yourselves treasures upon earth, where moth and rust doth corrupt."

We can underline this point with a contrast with the heavily bodies. It was thought, prior to Galilean astronomy, that the stars were composed of something else—pure *aether*, a fifth element. They were not admixtures of several elements needing to be arranged together. Incorruptible, images of perfection, purity, and permanence, the stars cannot fall apart, or so it was thought. After Galileo demystified the stars, we still set up ideals for ourselves. In having an ideal we project a sense of uncorrupted perfection that contrasts with the imperfect and corruptible things, people, and institutions of our ordinary experience.

2.2b: Moral Corruption: Human Ruin

It may be tempting to think that the ontological sense of corruption is irrelevant to morality, politics, and institutions, that it is a play on words, a mere accident of linguistic history that we may call both computer data and a society "corrupt." After all, ontological corruption is not a matter of morality—there is no culpability behind the corruption of a phrase, the rotting of wood, a damaged tool, or the sickness or malformation of a body. Still, whenever corruption is spoken of, even nonmorally, there is a norm implicitly at work. There is an implicit reference to what the thing is supposed to be or do—a proper, healthy, typical, or previous form in comparison to which the corruption is recognized.

It is no mere equivocation when we use the word "corruption" in both of these senses. Just as sickness can be understood as a form of ontological corruption, so can vice. In the case of moral corruption, what is corrupted is a person's *character* as an agent, the person's propensity to feel and act correctly.

When we speak of morality, we mean people's affective and practical orientation to the human good—our ability to want and do good actions. A good person both acts well and has appropriate emotions about life's events, whereas a bad person not only acts badly but also has emotions that draw the person toward bad actions. Moral corruption occurs when an individual is no longer affectively and practically oriented toward the good. This admits of degrees. We project moral ideals, but all people we have met fall somewhere in the middle—morally neither all good nor all bad.

When Socrates is accused of corrupting the youth, for example, moral corruption is at issue. Socrates is allegedly making the youth worse human beings and worse citizens by eroding their commitment to the civic religion. In Plato's *Crito*, Socrates describes the loss of health that occurs when one disobeys a doctor as bodily corruption or destruction, and he then makes an analogy between this and the corruption that results from performing bad, unjust, or shameful actions; such actions ruin that part of oneself by which one discerns the good and bad, just and unjust, noble and shameful (47b). Disease or injury cause deterioration or incapacitation of the body; unjust action causes deterioration or incapacitation of one's character and practical judgment. The body literally decays, but metaphorically the soul also can become rotten.

In the *Nicomachean Ethics* (VII.1, 1145a), Aristotle distinguishes vice from weak character by explaining that vice corrupts or destroys knowledge of the good, that for the sake of which we act. Here, systematic moral failure is explained in terms of a type of ontological corruption, or destruction, of an aspect of the person, namely, one's ability to identify the good to be accomplished through action. Along these lines, we might call someone "a complete degenerate," implying that vice is a degeneration, akin to something falling apart and, ultimately, passing away. Put in another way, if what each person is, most of all, is his or her character—one's practical judgment, one's habituated reason as oriented toward good action—then a deterioration of that character would be corruption of one's self, one's person, in the most humanly relevant sense. Or again, if we take moral virtue to be a person's characteristic excellence, what allows one to function well as a person, then moral corruption is simply one application of ontological corruption—diminished ability to function as the determinate kind of thing that human beings are. Moral corruption is a special type of ontological corruption, namely, corruption applied to the human being *as an agent of good, as a source of choices*. Moral corruption is an event that moves a person away from virtue.

In addition to being likened to rotting, moral corruption is often also analogized to a turning or twisting. Many words for moral corruption in English carry the sense ultimately of the person erring, turning from the correct path, or the person becoming twisted or crooked (e.g., deviant, devious, perverted, depraved, warped, debauched). Moral corruption appears as a turning away or turning aside or as being distracted from the good. Instances of crooked behavior, then, may imply moral rot of character. The crooked act is not merely wrong in itself. It is symptomatic of something dispositional.

Along these lines, in the Allegory of the Cave (*Republic* VII, 514a), Socrates portrays both philosophy and ethics as depending upon which way the soul *turns* its attention—toward the light of the Good or toward the lesser objects and lesser goods of the cave. In Aristotle, moral corruption likewise involves a turning of one's desires toward lesser goods, such as external possessions, honor, or pleasure, and away from true human flourishing. In the *Nicomachean Ethics* (II.9, 1109b) he describes human beings as like "sticks that are bent": We come slightly crooked, and to unwarp ourselves we must push ourselves in the opposite direction, away from the errors to which we are prone. He then warns us to be especially wary of pleasure, which we do not judge "unbribed." It is as though human beings all have a job to do or as though being human is an office we all hold, and not-so-great actions bribe us away from this with the pleasure they promise. A partial moral corruption seems commonly human and is cast here as a warping or turning, analogous to the turning of attention, affection, and allegiance that occurs in officeholder corruption. Moral corruption is loss of the ability to function decently as a human being, and it involves a turning away from the human good.

But what is the human good? All talk of corruption implies a norm or an ideal—a standard of goodness or proper form compared to which the corruption comes into relief as corrupt. Therefore, all talk of moral corruption as corruption of the person's character or of society's mores refers at least implicitly and vaguely to a standard of morality, a sense of the human good and what it means to be an excellent human agent. But that standard is disputed—to some extent, it always has been. No society has ever been so monolithic as to be free of moral disagreements. Reflect, for example, on the accusation against Socrates that he corrupts the young men of Athens. Plato's account in *The Apology of Socrates* shows Socrates defending himself by challenging his accusers, and even Athens as a whole, on their vision of what makes an excellent human being and citizen. He seems guilty by their standards—yet they honor the wrong standards.

Given this analytic connection—like a photo and its film negative—between one's ideal and one's idea of corruption, thinkers often indicate what they think is morally pure and perfect by how they speak of corruption. Immanuel Kant (2001), for example, believes that we "corrupt [the laws of morality] at their very source" and "destroy their worth" when we rationalize exceptions to the moral rule, trying to conform the demands of duty to our wishes rather than the reverse (21). The Purist tells us that there may be no negotiation with the desires. Kant believes that reason, independent of all inclination, desire, or feeling, determines what is right: "Reason issues its commands unyieldingly, without promising anything to the inclinations, and, as it were, with disregard and contempt for these claims" (20). According to this account, feelings and desires are the source of corruption, the root of evil, turning us away from the good, which is the unconditional command of reason. Kant's view of the root of moral corruption follows from his view of moral rectitude.

Likewise, in his work *A Discourse on the Sciences and the Arts*, Jean-Jacques Rousseau (2012, 15) says as much about his own view of the excellence of a human being and citizen as he does about the sciences and arts of his day, in arguing that popularized arts and sciences corrupt morals: "Born in idleness, they nourish it in turn." He valorizes, instead, the virtues of patriotism, useful skills, and moral simplicity for common citizens. When identifying "the dissolution of morals" as a "necessary consequence of luxury" (17), he expressed a common motif in the history of reflection of civilizational degeneration. When Rousseau laments a theater opening in his home of Geneva, he is worried about its corrupting influence, about how it will draw people's emotional attachments away from civic concerns and encourage bad morals. About such decadent entertainments as "gambling, theaters, comedies, opera," he says, "All that makes men effeminate, all that distracts them, makes them forget their fatherland and their duty" (1997, 186). Notice that human corruption, moral as well as political, appears here as a kind of distraction from the good. We see a similar—albeit more puritan, less civic republican—concern in Pennsylvania's 1911 law to censor movie theaters, which was copied by several other states. The law aimed to restrict those films that were "sacrilegious, obscene, indecent, or immoral, or such as tend, in the judgment of the board, to debase or corrupt morals" (quoted in Wittern-Keller 2008, 25–26). What counted as corrupting of morals, in the judgment of the board, would necessarily be determined by the board's judgment of the moral good.

Whereas the comparison between sickness of the body and corruption of the soul is, in Plato's *Crito*, an analogy, sometimes people talk as though the connection were more direct, more than metaphor. Not only are physical decay and moral decay both forms of ontological corruption (corrupting different aspects of the person: body and character), they are often taken to be linked causally. In medieval medicine, for example, certain sicknesses were thought to result from certain sins. And this belief continued beyond medieval medicine. One need not go back to the medieval or early modern periods to find links being made between moral and bodily corruption. It surfaced brutally, for example, in some early responses to the AIDS epidemic. Jerry Falwell evoked the standard corruption metaphor of rot by calling AIDS "tangible proof of society's moral decay" (quoted in Stearns 2007). Of course, because most illness is not the result of moral failure, one cannot take any illness as proof of immorality. Falwell was, in fact, reasoning the other way around. He wasn't convinced by the advent of AIDS that homosexual activity was morally corrupt; he needed no proof, because he started with this belief, and his reasoning here is an instance of confirmation bias. Corruption talk implies, always, the speaker's underlying ideas about what is good and what is bad.

It is not difficult to define moral corruption at a formal level—it is the ruin of the person's character, the decay of one's ability to want and do the human good. To *fully* define human corruption, however, one would have to identify the human good. So, the problem in defining moral corruption is that the good is a matter of dispute. Sickness of the body is, and has always been, more evident and obvious than sickness of character.

2.2c: Officeholder Corruption

Officeholder corruption has become the standard sense, such that people think of it as the literal or central meaning of "corruption." There are many individual actions that might be construed as instances of corruption in this sense. The concepts of corruption and bribery, for instance, are closely linked, and they have been since antiquity. It is worth wondering why. Is bribery called "corrupt" because it tends to damage or destroy something, perhaps the community? Or is it inherently wrong, and thus simply a form of moral corruption? The same might be asked about other corrupt acts engaged in by officeholders—nepotism, graft, or embezzlement, for instance—but let us keep our focus on bribery as the model to illustrate some of the characteristics of officeholder corruption.

In Plato's *Laws* (955c–d) the Athenian Stranger condemns "gifts" or bribes. He suggests that good people will do good, even if not paid, and will not do bad, even if paid:

> Those who serve their country ought to serve without receiving gifts, and there ought to be no excusing or approving the saying, "Men should receive gifts as the reward of good, but not of evil deeds"; for to know which we are doing, and to stand fast by our knowledge, is no easy matter. The safest course is to obey the law which says, "Do no service for a bribe," and let him who disobeys, if he be convicted, simply die.

The line between a gift and a bribe is inherently fuzzy, and that makes not just bribes but gifts *unsafe*. This is why, for example, we have developed rules about what types of goods members of Congress are allowed to accept, even when no quid pro quo is alleged. Our ability to discern right from wrong is finite and fragile, Plato suggests, and gifts undermine the agent's moral knowledge. In this way, what might seem to be minor transgressions can have consequences for one's character. Bribery is bad because it corrupts judgment about right and wrong. It seems in this instance to be a subtype of moral corruption. The anticorruption policy implied by Plato is intolerance: Outlaw gifts to officeholders and kill the offenders.

While not quite disagreeing with Plato, Aristotle adopts a different attitude. Consider the following passage—one of Aristotle's scant references to bribery. He criticizes how the structure of a Spartan institution, the overseers, incentivized bribery:

> Also poorly handled [in the Spartan constitution] is the matter of the overseers. This office has authority by itself over the greatest matters among them, yet it is filled entirely from the people, so that the board is often entered by very poor men who because of their poverty can be bought. They have often made this clear both in the past and now in the Andros matter, where some of them, having been corrupted by silver, did all that was in them to ruin the city as a whole. (*Politics* II.9 1470b6–10)

Aristotle uses one of the typical corruption words, rooted in rot or spoilage, for the buying of the overseers, and then connects this to the city's destruction. Bribery is corrupt because it tends toward the damage (ontological corruption) of the community. There is no moral commentary here. While not absolving the persons involved, Aristotle focuses blame on the institution. Crooked acts are in this case symptomatic of an unwisely configured institution; they can be ruinous, even when they are not the only root of the problem.

Later in the *Politics*, Aristotle weaves in the moral element and illuminates the connections among disloyalty of an official, ethical failure, and political ruin. The three qualifications of an official are affection for the regime, skill at the task, and virtue. The first two are not enough, he says, for a decent officeholder. The third is needed because a man, when distracted by desire, may do something he otherwise believes is bad. Virtue is the only protection against that, because a man who lacks self-control is not loyal even to himself, let alone to the city (V.9; 1309a33–b14). In his account of lack of self-control in the *Ethics*, Aristotle notes that in the presence of a temptation, one might do what one otherwise wouldn't do, just as drunkenness undermines one's judgment. Aristotle's comments suggest that being susceptible to bribes or other distractions is itself a moral weakness and that it draws officials to decisions that can harm the political community. Thus, preventing corruption or ruin of the *polis* requires preventing morally weak persons from becoming officials and preventing situations in which moral weakness might be tried or easily exploitable. We need strategies to deal with officeholder corruption beyond outlawing bad behavior. For Aristotle, this requires a combination of wisely designed institutions, education of the citizens, careful appointment of officials, and individual virtue in those officials.

Plato and Aristotle both suggest that what bribery corrupts is judgment. A similar explanation is found in Exodus 23:8, which warns, "Neither shalt thou take bribes, which even blind the wise, and pervert the words of the just."[1] The problem with gifts or bribes is that they distort moral vision, leading to bad decisions by otherwise adequate people. Deuteronomy 16:18–20 puts this in a judicial context: Judges must avoid gifts, "for gifts blind the eyes of the wise, and change the words of the just. Thou shalt follow justly after that which is just: that thou mayst live and possess the land, which the Lord thy God shall give thee." The passage shows an outright rejection of bribery as morally corrupting, while also employing a strategy to reduce it: the promise of a reward! It may seem ironic that the passage ends with something of a bribe. Yet the Promised Land is not, in the biblical context, a corrupting gift, because it clarifies, rather than distorts, our moral vision. By using the Promised Land to orient human beings toward justice, the Bible establishes a cosmic incentive structure that might be strong enough to override a given situation's perverse incentives to cheat.

The basic idea at work behind such corruption talk is that officials are functionaries. They have a job to do. Their power has been entrusted to them for the sake of that job, and exercising their power appropriately requires that they be reliably oriented toward the good or the goal of that job, and not toward some other goal. Good officeholders must be people whose desires are not easily distractable. Corruption of the officeholders consists in disorienting them, affectively and cognitively, from the goods or goals of the office they hold.

John Locke, for example, comments in the *Second Treatise* on how the chief executive might—whether through bribe, favoritism, threat, or much else—disorient the legislators, whose job is to represent the people, by directing them away from their true goals and toward the executive's own distinct goals. Locke (1988) writes that the executive acts *"contrary to his Trust*, when he ... imploys the Force, Treasure, and Offices of his Society, to corrupt the *Representatives*, and gain them to his purposes"* (13). Such actions by the executive disorient the representatives from their proper ends and turn them toward other purposes, just as we have seen in moral corruption that people are turned, made crooked, twisted away from the true human good. By understanding offices as trusts of power for the sake of certain purposes, we can see that disorientation from those purposes is a violation of a promise. Trust is a bond that, when breached, can no longer function—it is corrupted in the sense of being *broken*. One cannot trust a crooked agent. For Locke, such actions are wrong both in themselves, as violations of a fiduciary responsibility, and in that they hasten the decay of a healthy political system as a whole.

In general, then, corrupting officeholders consists in undermining their knowledge or judgment about what they are supposed to do with their office; distracted by bribes or other temptations or pressures, corrupt officials are disorientated from their proper ends and thus do not do their job.

The medieval writer John of Salisbury (1990) provides an example of the attitude that focuses on bribery as simply wrong in itself, thus inherently a kind of moral corruption. In discussing those rulers and judges "who are corrupted by presents," John argues, "Justice is to be served in all matters and none of the things which they are to do are to be done for a price. . . . For what is unjust is at no time permitted; injustice is not to be done, even for the price of one's temporal life. Yet what is just does not need the aid of remuneration, since it must be done for itself and it is iniquitous to offer for sale that to which one is obligated" (93). Like Plato, John focuses on bribery being, in itself, a form of moral corruption: Do justice, and do not do injustice—period.

Hobbes, in contrast, provides in *Leviathan* an example of someone who identifies bribes as bad because they destroy the political community:

> No man in any Cause ought to be received for Arbitrator, to whom greater profit, or honour, or pleasure apparently ariseth out of the victory of one part, than of the other: for hee hath taken (though an un-

avoidable bribe, yet) a bribe; and no man be obliged to trust him. And thus also the controversie, and the condition of War remaineth, contrary to the Natural Law. (1994, 109)

To return to "the condition of War" simply means, for Hobbes, to destroy sovereignty. Therefore, the reason bribery is wrong (i.e., the reason it violates the natural law to procure the conditions of one's own survival) is that it ontologically corrupts the body politic. Hobbes here uses "bribery" not narrowly, but broadly, to cover both quid pro quos and any self-interest undermining impartiality. Literal bribes are avoidable, but Hobbes labels these metaphysical bribes as "unavoidable." This is because, he thinks, everyone always wills one's own self-interest: "The proper object of every mans Will, is some Good to himself" (176).

Hobbes also uses bribery metaphorically when discussing corrupt counselors. Exhortation and dehortation (i.e., dissuasion), he says, occur when advice is given vehemently, betraying that the advice serves the advice-giver, rather than serving the one who is being advised. "They that Exhort and Dehort, where they are required to give Counsell, are corrupt Counsellours, and as it were bribed by their own self-interest" (Hobbes 178). A judge or counselor's judgment is corrupted, therefore, by any situation—it may be caused by a bribe or something else—in which one's own self-interest is at odds with the interest of the case. "Where the publique and private interest are most closely united, there is the publique most advanced" (178). This is a main reason why Hobbes favors monarchy, which (in theory) makes the private interest of one individual the very same thing as the public interest.

If Hobbes were right that people always will their own self-interest, corrupt acts would be not a form of moral failure but a necessary and predictable result of a badly structured situation. The remedy would be to avoid counselors and judges who are operating when they have interests diverging from their roles as counselors or judges. "The first condition of a good Counsellour," according to Hobbes, is "that his Ends, and Interest, be not inconsistent with the Ends and Interest of him he Counselleth" (179). Whereas Plato and John of Salisbury focus on the moral failing of corruption, and Aristotle and Locke focus both on the moral failure and on the need for wise institutional arrangements, Hobbes must focus exclusively on institutional arrangements, on setting up the right situation. One might say that for Plato and John of Salisbury, a corrupt official is rotten; for Aristotle and Locke, that official is both rotten and crooked; for Hobbes, the official—or rather, the situation the official is in—is just broken. Either the situation should be rearranged or the part should be replaced.

It should be clear that, for all of these thinkers, bribery is only one cause of officeholder corruption. The key is that such officials are not what they are supposed to be, that they do not do what they are supposed to do because their desires are distracted. In other words, officeholder corruption is another application of ontological corruption. As officials, such persons are functionaries; as corrupt officials, they are functionaries who do not function, the cause being an affective alienation from the goods that one's office is supposed to seek. To the extent that the officials' function is clear or unclear—What are their duties? What end are they serving?—what constitutes corruption of these officials should be correspondingly clear or unclear.

Officeholder corruption can be rather broad and vague—something like not doing one's job. The opposite is the type of professionalism that is dedicated to doing the work at hand honestly and well. In one sense, transactional corruption—extortion, embezzling, bribery, selling of favors—is just one subtype of a failure of professionalism. Officeholder corruption might be a consequence of avarice or greed, but it might also result from sloppiness, laziness, or carelessness, boredom with the job, or being a shirker who expects others to take up the slack. Transactional corruption sticks out from other forms of officeholder corruption because it can be forbidden in "bright-line" rules. While the fundamental anticorruption principle may be professionalism, "do your job well" is not a bright-line standard. It is too vague. The standards of law and criminal punishment require bright-line rules, given in advance and with minimal ambiguity. Though such rules are very valuable, they cannot capture entirely what we mean by officeholder corruption.

2.3: Clarifying a Contested Concept: Decontesting and Recontesting Corruption

We have presented this typology because in discussing corruption in a political context, it helps to remember that the word has a broader and more basic meaning, from which its political meaning is derived. Corruption is, at root, an ontological event. A thing is corrupted when it is ruined—broken, rotted, disintegrated, when it falls apart or comes to pieces. When that happens, the thing can no longer do what it is supposed to do because it can no longer be what it is, once was, or is supposed to be. We also speak about corruption when we discuss matters of morality or misbehavior of an officeholder. Institutional corruption can be read as a straightforward version of ontological corruption: Sometimes institutions stop working. But when speaking of "institutional corruption," people confuse the issue with officeholder corruption—since that has become the dominant usage of the word. Because of this, people may assume that officeholder corruption is the primary or only way an institution might fall apart or go bad.

Political corruption has to do with all of these three types. An institutional office is a thing with a function, and the person who holds the office takes on the function of the office. That person holding the office can be ruined such that the person can no longer do what he or she are supposed to do, and thus can no longer be what the officer is supposed to be. And then the office itself, the institution itself, is less able to function. Officeholder corruption is thus a moral corruption that tends to the ontological corruption of both the office and the institution. This is because institutions live not just by the rules they explicitly promulgate but more so by the norms and ideals they honor. Corrupt behavior corrodes such norms and ideals. Patterns of corrupt action disorient the institution. Corruption confuses the institution's officeholders and its subjects about the ideals it honors and which goods it is supposed to seek. Remember, however, that transactional officeholder corruption is not the only way that institutions can fall apart or stop working.

As we see in the coming discussion, contemporary literature on political corruption often begins by noting that such corruption lacks a clear, agreed-upon definition: It is a contested concept. Skirting rather than solving this problem, empirical studies of corruption merely begin by stipulating a working metric, focusing on transactional officeholder corruption, while acknowledging that there are other possible metrics and definitions. Our point is that by recalling its root in ontological corruption, we can elucidate political corruption, decontesting it. But, like all philosophical elucidations, this clarifying decontestation will reveal deeper, more interesting contests. Our disagreements will be clarified but not resolved. The contest returns, this time more interestingly, for we often disagree about what the function of an institution or an office actually is. What ideals should we honor? What goods shall we pursue? And what attitude should we take toward corruption—shall we be Menders, or Purifiers?

There are cases of clear-cut corruption, when the office is well constituted by a broad and clear view of its functions, its duties. Yet such clear cases can be rare in politics; there is often no clear and widely shared view of an office's function and duties. In such circumstances, disagreements will more frequently occur. A judge taking bribes in a criminal sentence would be an uncontroversial example. On the other hand, are members of Congress corrupt for supporting bills they otherwise would not support in order to secure spending in their districts? Does that make them good—or bad—representatives? What counts as corruption will be unclear when what counts as faithful service is unclear. The disagreements about what counts are symptoms of deeper disagreements about what it is that we are supposed to be doing in the first place. Though indispensable as a means of defense for keeping an institution and its agents more or less honest and more or less on task, bright-line rules against transactional corruption skirt, rather than solve, these deeper dis-agreements about the ultimate goals of our institutions. Bright-line rules are a matter of *legal* codes or explicit rules. In contrast, those deeper disagree-ments are, and must always be, *political*. Corruption talk in our political lives is, we suggest, usually a way of talking about how things might fall apart, or how we fear they are.

3

Corruption Narratives and Motifs

Who or What Tends to Be Corrupted?

ontemporary corruption talk draws upon several motifs—repeated patterns of ideas, ideals, and images, ways that the corruption story has been told. In Chapter 2 we discussed types of corruption and styles of corruption talk. Here, we want to focus on who, or what, has historically been the subject of corruption accusations. Are all politicians corrupt? Are money and commerce inherently corrupting? Can "the people" be corrupt, or is this a term we would use to describe only the wealthy and the powerful? Is inequality a symptom, or perhaps a cause, of corruption? Does disobedience make an official corrupt? Is corruption sinful? Will it bring disorder—perhaps portending death—to the community?

There is nothing new about these questions. Corruption has often been framed with reference to religious conceptions of morality and of the cosmos, and often to a vision of the community as an organic, bodily unity. Other common motifs include the suspicion of trade, commerce, inequality, elites, and foreigners. These remain common touchpoints for contemporary rhetoric. Each of these motifs, as we show in this chapter, blends the styles of corruption talk and the definitions of corruption that we explored in the previous chapter. Our purpose here is, first, to show this blending. Also, understanding the way corruption is spoken about today requires recognizing these motifs—which carry almost subconscious force over us, just as all traditions do. We want to be able to spot these motifs when they are employed. These are surely not the only corruption motifs, but they are sufficiently common that most people encounter them, and most people draw upon them when they hear contemporary references to corruption.

3.1: The Wages of Sin: The Biblical Corruption Narrative

Corruption is spoken of throughout the Hebrew and Christian testaments. What makes biblical corruption talk especially interesting is the way in which it suggests that the different types of corruption are linked causally. The Bible weaves different types of corruption together and into a broader story about human nature, human failure, and human recovery.

The Bible presents moral corruption not merely as vice as Aristotle would, that is, as a set of bad habits and a disorientation from an ideal of human excellence. Rather, moral corruption is presented as sin, that is, as an offense against God or a rupture with God or a breaking apart of our covenantal relationship with the Divine.

The first corruption in the Bible is an inferior's act of disobedience to a superior. God grants Adam and Eve authority and discretionary power within Eden (Genesis 2), but the serpent—with something like a bribe—lures them into violating the rules, to break out of the roles given them (Genesis 3). Corrupt action often involves the agent grasping for illicit wages or gains. Adam and Eve's plan backfires. For, it turns out, "the wages of sin is death" (Romans 6:23).

Moral corruption is paid for with physical corruptibility. The original sin of Adam and Eve leads God to exile them from Eden and to curse them with mortality, the decomposition of the body: "For dust thou art, and unto dust thou shalt return." The moral and spiritual corruption also infects the natural order of the world—for God curses the ground itself, such that the human relationship with the earth becomes labored and difficult. Human sins affect the very being of nature as a whole. Adam and Eve's posterity share in their mortality—and immorality; it is as though these spread generationally like an inherited disease. Within a few generations, the human world seems dominated by sin. In Genesis 6, leading up to the earth's destruction and rebirth in the flood, the whole earth is said to have been corrupted by human iniquity: "And the Lord God saw the earth, and it was corrupted; because all flesh had corrupted its way upon the earth." There seemed no way to fix or mend this ubiquitous rot. The deadly flood, God's response, is a cleansing purge.

What is implied by Genesis is that the entire natural order has been damaged. What we see and experience around us now is a degraded version of an original state, Eden, which had been properly ordered. Moreover, this corruption of natural and social order resulted from a moral corruption, understood as an act of disobedience and a breaking of trust, elicited by a bribe.

The striking feature of biblical corruption talk is how all the major types of corruption become intertwined. References to different kinds of corruption are piled next to each other and tend to connote each other.

For example, in Malachi 2, the prophet, in a very compact statement, connects officeholder corruption (of the Levites, or priests) with the turning or twisting commonly used to symbolize moral corruption, while tying these also to social degradation and to a violation of an agreement and disobedience of a superior. The prophet addresses the priests: "But ye have turned aside from the way, and caused many to fail in [following] the law: ye have corrupted the covenant of Levi, saith the Lord Almighty." Again, Wisdom of Solomon 14 displays several senses of corruption linked together. Unlike God, worldly objects are perishable—they fall apart. Idolatry, which stupidly calls such objects by the holy name, is "the beginning, the cause, and the end of all evil." The text links the ontological corruptibility of the idol to a moral corruption of the idolater: "For the devising of idols was the beginning of spiritual fornication, and the invention of them the corruption of life. For neither were they from the beginning, nor shall they be forever." The corruptibility of the idol, which renders it unworthy of worship, spreads to the idolater, and in turn the moral corruption of the idolater spreads into a general corruption of society involving a plague of evils, which the text then enumerates: adultery, perjury, theft, lying, child sacrifice, etc.

The Bible tells a story that links, causally, the major types of corruption: physical, moral, and social corruption, as well as bribery, insubordination, and breach of trust. The Bible also has an account of how to recover from this plague of failure and death: Returning to the covenant with the Lord, the covenant initiated with Noah after God has drained the swamp and has started the world anew. God makes the promise signified by "the bow in the cloud" that "neither shall there any more be a flood to destroy the earth" (Genesis 9). So, while the Purist style is certainly present in the Bible and epitomized by the brutal flood, the Mender style is also present and symbolized by the rainbow. The way seems open to repair, rather than purging and purifying, as a response to human corruption.

This theme is amplified in the Christian (New) Testament, in which the world is redeemed from corruptibility and restored through the resurrection of the Christ. Thus, though the world has been damaged, ontologically and morally, God as redeemer is the means by which the corruption is overcome and the world is repaired. And for classical Christians, this means a healing recovery even from the corruptibility of our material bodies. As St. Paul puts it, "For the trumpet shall sound, and the dead shall be raised incorruptible, and we shall be changed. For this corruptible must put on incorruption, and this mortal must put on immortality. So when this corruptible shall have put on incorruption, and this mortal shall have put on immortality, then shall be brought to pass the saying that is written, Death is swallowed up in victory. O death, where is thy sting? O grave, where is thy victory?" (1 Corinthians 15).

In subsequent theological reflection, biblical corruption talk appears in different ways, according to the theological styles and leanings of the various thinkers. Aquinas (2006) explicitly blames the original sin of Adam for two forms of corruption now endemic to human life—mortality and immorality:

> In [an incidental] way, the sin of our first parent is the cause of death and all such like defects in human nature, in so far as by the sin of our first parent original justice was taken away, whereby not only were the lower powers of the soul held together under the control of reason, without any disorder whatever, but also the whole body was held together in subjection to the soul, without any defect. . . . Wherefore, original justice being forfeited through the sin of our first parent, just as human nature was stricken in the soul by the disorder among the powers . . . , so also it became subject to corruption, by reason of disorder in the body. (*ST* I-II Q 85 a 5)

Here, Aquinas says that after Eden the new normal is a fallen state, a state susceptible to moral corruption—the disordering of the powers of the soul. But he also blames Adam's fall for our bodily corruptibility—our susceptibility to sickness and death.

Though Aquinas claims that the *original* fall causes our species-wide vulnerability to sickness, in the same article he denies that a person's particular sins cause, by their sinfulness, any actual sicknesses. Whereas an act that happens to be sinful (like eating too much) may cause sickness, he says, it is not the sinfulness of the act that causes sickness: "Actual sin does not cause [bodily] defects" (*ST* I-II Q 85, a 6, ad 3).

Different theological traditions interpret both the Bible and the world differently. As we saw in the previous chapter—in the suggestion that AIDS is proof of society's moral rot—some corruption talk implies that immoral actions induce sickness by natural causality; other talk implies, further, that sin causes maladies or misfortunes by way of divine punishment. This is one, but not the only, strain of the theological tradition. This style of interpreting biblical corruption talk has political consequences—consequences for how we interpret and respond to the moral, social, and political world around us and how we treat those we judge to be corrupt.

In contrast to Aquinas, Martin Luther viewed the world as comprehensively warped by sin's corruption—except that true Christians (and only true Christians) were free of it. It was this corruption that requires government, for sinners at least, and this is a punishment from God: "The world is too wicked to deserve princes" who are wise or just, Luther says. "As a rule, princes are the greatest fools or the worst criminals on earth. . . . For these are God's jailers and hangmen, and his divine wrath makes use of them to punish the wicked and to maintain outward peace" (Luther and Calvin 1991, 30). Similarly, John Calvin concludes, "Those who govern unjustly or intemperately have been raised up by [God] to punish the iniquity of the people" (76–77). According to this line of interpretation, corruption of political orders results from the moral corruption of the people, not by natural propensity, but by divine design. Luther and Calvin's Purist stance was, perhaps, a natural response to the contemporary, recalcitrant corruption of the ecclesiastical hierarchy; it is not, generally, shared by those who inherited membership in the religious communities that Luther and Calvin founded. Just as corruption is an equal opportunity danger, the Purist/Mender distinction cuts across the Catholic, Orthodox, and Protestant divisions between Christian churches.

Aquinas claims that a people can become so corrupt that it is no longer capable of sharing in government, thus requiring rule by a smaller group. But this is quite different from Luther's idea that the few elect of true Cristians should either govern the corrupted many for their own safety, or let the doomed suffer their proper punishment of bad government. About the unsaved among his fellow men, punished by God with despotism, Luther comments, "Frogs need storks" (Luther and Calvin 1991, 30)—referring to a fable of Aesop's in which the king, a stork, devours his subjects.

What type of attitude does biblical corruption talk elicit? One can go in either of the two general directions we have already encountered in distinguishing between Purist Corruption Talk and Mender Corruption Talk.

One response is suggested by the flood. If one believes that the corruption is thorough and that those who are corrupt are incurable, one might respond by purging and purifying. And if the corrupt cannot be purged or purified, perhaps they should rot in the hell on earth they deserve, or perhaps the pure should establish a paternalistic government over them. The problem with this type of response is that it implies that the purgers, purifiers, and paternalists are not themselves complicit in the corruption. This requires a belief in the purity of the elect. The biblical corruption narrative lays in back of that feeling—which some, Left and Right, express in jeremiads according to which other people's corruption will be the ruin of us all—the feeling that *those* people are not just tempting fate but courting cataclysmic disaster for *our* society.

Another response is suggested by God's covenant with Noah after the flood and God's promise that there would not be another flood. After all, never-ending waves of purges do not seem an appealing option. If the corruption of the fall is understood to be partial, rather than complete, and if all human beings are complicit in it, then a different response would make more sense: repeated repentance, return to the covenant, and regular repair of creation.

In contemporary work on corruption, Laura Underkuffler (2013) suggests that the connotations of corruption involve a person being "captured by evil." It is a vivid image. Underkuffler's wording reminds us of Dante's idea in the *Inferno* that some people are, while still alive, captured by hell. Upon committing certain sins, their souls leave their living bodies on earth to a devil: "When a soul betrays as I did, it falls from flesh and a demon takes its place," one condemned soul reports (Canto 333:128–29). According to Underkuffler, this capture becomes manifest in corrupt actions when the person is given power. Unless contained, this capture by evil ruins the person's character and the trustworthiness of the institution within which the person acts. These connotations are illuminated by the roots of the concept in classical treatments of corruption as ruin and moral decay, but Underkuffler's account makes the most sense in the light of biblical corruption talk. In the biblical tradition, the term "corruption" describes not merely occasional, particular actions but also an evil state of the human soul that infects other humans and wreaks havoc on our earthly existence. Underkuffler is correct that this conception of corruption is not a proper legal category. It would be dangerous as a legal category—for legal justice requires that people be punished only for particular actions, not for states of being. Still, it forms part of the deeper context of our accusations of corruption and infuses much of our talk about it.

3.2: Sickness of the Body Politic

A perennial way to conceptualize a political community is to analogize it to a living body. This analogy is in the background of much corruption talk. Corruption can be understood, metaphorically, as a disease—not of this or that official only, but of the social system and agents within it. What makes this narrative mode of corruption talk especially interesting is its explanatory power to link officeholder corruption with a community's ontological corruption naturalistically (not by divine intervention). Given this background, there can be something large—even civilizational—at stake in accusations of corruption. As members of one body, we will all perish together.

In this analogy, we are all, by nature, members of the "body politic." As organs of this body, we are interdependent parts, each having tasks to do for maintenance and flourishing of the whole. A part's failure to do its job undermines the good functioning, maybe even the survival, of the community. So, it is not merely "officials" but all members who have offices, dutiful roles for the common good. We have these roles not merely by choice or appointment but just by being parts, just by being there in the community. Also, in the context of this analogy, it is not only particular people but large groups like the ruling class, the craftsmen, the merchants, or the farmers who have functions and can be called corrupt when they are not operating correctly. Dysfunction of the body politic can be traced to any of its members.

This analogy focuses our attention on how the parts are supposed to work together, each making its own special contributions to the common good. The analogy reminds us also of the fragility of the body politic. Animals die. For a while, new cells replace older ones, just as generations replace generations in a community, but eventually the body fails. Though death by disease or damage may come at any age, organisms have a natural life span, and in old age an animal is more susceptible to sickness and less able to resist or recover from injury. By suggesting that communities, too, grow old, the analogy contributes to decline narratives. Just as individuals indulge in "glory days" stories of youth, communities tell "golden age" tales, leading to belief in decline. Eventually, the analogy implies, internal corruption—disease—will destroy the community, if some predator doesn't get it first.

The metaphor begins in the Western tradition with Aesop's fable "The Belly and Its Members" (1909, 22), but versions are found in many other writers:

> One fine day it occurred to the Members of the Body that they were doing all the work and the Belly was having all the food. So they held a meeting, and after a long discussion, decided to strike work till the Belly consented to take its proper share of the work. So for a day or two, the Hands refused to take the food, the Mouth refused to receive it, and the Teeth had no work to do. But after a day or two the Members began to find that they themselves were not in a very active condition: the Hands could hardly move, and the Mouth was all parched and dry, while the Legs were unable to support the rest. So thus they found that even the Belly in its dull quiet way was doing necessary work for the Body, and that all must work together or the Body will go to pieces.

The fable starts with something of an accusation of greed-motivated corruption against the rulers, represented by the stomach, but this accusation is misplaced: Each part has a different job, and each part should do its job on penalty of a shared demise. The original fable is more about corruption talk than about corruption. It cautions against loose accusations of corruption against the ruling group, which only seems to be leisured and unproductive.

The analogy's emphasis on interdependence can, however, cut the other way. The stomach is, after all, tyrannically self-serving at least sometimes.

Medieval philosopher Christine de Pizan's version of the fable begins, instead, with gluttonous demands from the stomach for more. The moral she draws places blame on the Belly: "When a prince requires more than a people can bear, then the people complain against their prince and rebel by disobedience. In such discord, they all perish together" (Pizan 1994, 91).

The story begins with an accusation of self-serving failure to do one's duty, either from greed or from a resentment resulting from a failure to understand the system. The story ends with ontological corruption of the whole. The complaint against the rulers of selfish abuse of power may sometimes be correct. In other cases, it is not correct but is an easy mistake to make because the stomach's hidden work seems less laborious, and yet the stomach enjoys all the food for which the other organs work. In either case, mutual destruction follows. In Pizan's words: "To spite one another, the whole body died" (1994, 91). Corruption talk in the narrative mode of the body politic, therefore, clearly connects partial, officeholder corruption with ontological corruption of the whole.

Marsiglio of Padua also uses the body politic metaphor, making health analogous to tranquility in the city and sickness analogous to "discord and quarrels" (1993, 176). "Intranquility will be the diseased disposition of a city or kingdom, in the manner of an illness of an animal, in which all or some of its parts are impeded from performing their appropriate functions." In Marsiglio's diagnosis, the "pernicious disease" underlying the sicknesses of politics in his day was the pope's desire to exercise civil power. Some members of the ecclesiastical hierarchy took themselves to be the organ objectively possessing a sovereign function in the whole civilization order—and Marsiglio challenges this view of the natural, proper ordering of the body politic. The error resulted, according to Marsiglio, in the civil powers not being able to fulfill their function of providing tranquility; the "decay of the city" eventuates. Marsiglio uses the dominant image of proper communal order in his challenge to the status quo order. Our point in juxtaposing Aesop, Christine, and Marsiglio, is that it isn't always clear what the functions of our offices are, or who should hold more powerful or less prestigious roles. This is true even if we accept and continue to use the body politic metaphor of organs with natural duties to the common good. We build our sense of the body politic partly by labeling organs and their roles in it, and by labeling some events as corruption of it. Corruption talk, in general, is one way in which we defend and reinforce the public order—or contest and reconfigure it.

3.3: Politics as a Corrupt Business

Niccolò Machiavelli advocates a political style that is not shy about getting dirty to deal with a dirty world. What looks pretty bad by the standards of conventional morality is, rather, the strength to respond to reality. For this reason, Machiavelli is associated with the cynical conviction—sometimes advocated by those who stay out of politics, sometimes advocated by those knee-deep in it—that politics is inherently corrupt.

Machiavelli doesn't engage in either Purist Corruption Talk or Mender Corruption Talk—after all, both types condemn corruption. He is definitely not a Purist, even if he occasionally suggests (literal) purges to control the corrupt nobles, who grow like weeds. Perhaps a type of Mender, he would better be called a "fixer"—a word carrying its own connotations of corruption. Where others might see corruption, political life being broken or rotten by the standards of conventional morality or ideals of traditional political philosophy, Machiavelli sees that that's just how things are. A good politician should grow up and cope. Of course, cynics view themselves as realists. Like a skilled aggressive driver cursing other, less skilled, aggressive drivers who get in his way, some people feel justified, or even forced of necessity, to respond in kind and with escalation to the behavior of others they complain of.

Taking Marsiglio's challenge further, Machiavelli's discussion of corruption both builds on and upends the tradition that precedes him. Machiavelli uses, though less obviously, the body politic metaphor. In an analogy to the dominant medicine of his day, in which the body has "humors" or liquids functioning anatomically and emotionally, he discusses the two humors found in the city: The nobles want to dominate, while the people want not to be dominated (1985, chap. 9). These are humors, not organs, and it is not the cooperative harmony but the balanced discord between these two contrary humors that must be used, according to Machiavelli, to secure a state. The humors must be limited, partially satisfied, vented, and played against one another. In another departure from the classical body politic metaphor, Machiavelli holds that this happens not by nature but by the audacity of a good ruler. In a system properly ordered by human cleverness, none of the humors can ruin the whole.

While accepting as part of political reality things that other thinkers might condemn as corrupt, Machiavelli maintains some sense of good and bad political action, and therefore some sense of corruption. For Machiavelli, corruption is manifested differently for different strata of society. Corruption of the nobles consists in their unfettered and imprudent desire to dominate, while the corruption of the people consists in the desire to live without authority—that is, their inability to live freely, where living freely means obeying law, fighting for their patria, and abiding by their agreements. One can do little with corrupt material; so to institute good orders, someone who wants to found a solid republic or principality must remake the material—for example, by killing all the gentlemen or by returning the people to the original principles by demanding terrifying periodic executions to check the "ambitions and insolence of men" (Machiavelli 1996, 3.1). While this may seem excessive, perhaps even evil, Machiavelli endorses a strategy of accommodating ourselves to the times—and all human times are corrupt. Virtue knows how to respond to necessity for the sake of accomplishing what needs to be done; it does not, and perhaps cannot, remedy the root cause of corruption.

Clearly, Machiavelli is upending traditional moral assumptions. Virtue comes to mean, from his pen, something like efficacy or effective industriousness—the ability to get what you want. This is opposed most of all to idleness or leisure (*ozio*), which wants but cannot or will not get, and to ambition, which wants more than it can get or can keep. Machiavelli frequently refers to the political problem of a corrupt people—a people who wants the freedom of not being dominated but cannot live freely because it does not want to live under proper orders. He also speaks of the corruption of the gentlemen or the powerful who, in ambitious idleness, want preeminence and luxury but are not industrious, prudent, or bold enough to actually rule.

The proper orders that Machiavelli endorses are any that preserve the life and liberty of the patria: "Where one deliberates on the safety of his fatherland, there ought not to enter any consideration of either just or unjust, merciful or cruel, praiseworthy or ignominious; indeed every other concern put aside, one ought to follow entirely the policy that saves its life and maintains its liberty" (1996, 3.42). Political effectiveness transcends moral categories. Here Machiavelli justifies a new sense of virtue—one emancipated from morality—in the name of the traditional virtue of patriotism. But this is in name only. In fact, what is being served—and also checked and vented—by Machiavelli's system is the insatiable desire of human beings for acquisition. "Nature has created men so that they are able to desire everything and unable to attain everything" (1.37).

Human beings may, most of all, wish to keep what they have, to prevent loss. But this is not a stable limit to desire: "For it does not appear to men that they possess securely what a man has unless he acquires something else" (Machiavelli 1996, 1.5). It would be best, Machiavelli suggests, if we could remain within limits, accomplishing the "true political way of life and the true quiet of a city" (1.7). But that best is impossible. It is so impossible as not even to be the right goal or standard. Nothing human stays still. The man or state wanting merely to maintain himself or itself will be overcome by others. Thus, security necessitates acquisition—expansion limited only by what one can get and keep. Good political orders encourage the gentlemen and the people to vent their desires for ambition and freedom through the petty acquisition of commerce and through the glory and expansion of the state, in which they participate by obeying its laws, serving militarily, and adding to its wealth.

At the same time as Machiavelli seems to think it is better for the nobility or gentlemen to be engaged in trade (1996, 1.55), he also sees it as a possible source of a dangerous type of inequality in a republic. A well-ordered republic, he suggests, prevents people from becoming tyrants because the laws would prevent them from acquiring the type of preeminence that would allow them to buy favors or gather a following:

> If a citizen wishes to be able to offend and to seize extraordinary authority for himself, he must have many qualities that in a noncorrupt republic he can never have. For he needs to be very rich and to have very many adherents and partisans, which he cannot have where the laws are observed. (1996, 3.8)

In general, Machiavelli fears the corruption—the idle ambition—of the rich and powerful much more than he fears the corruption of the people. In a republic, corruption starts with inequality.

This is no longer a matter of a body politic with cooperative organs, where nature provides a model for proper roles within a whole. Rather, Machiavelli rejects the assumption that nature provides a system of cooperative roles rather than a set of regularities to game, and he thereby also resists decline narratives. Through the bold virtue of those who order and reorder a state for continual change, we can create new orders. We can surpass the ancients and the status quo, as well as what are falsely taken to be the natural limits.

If corruption can be understood only in the light of a good or proper form that is corrupted, Machiavelli contests not only the traditional views of political and moral corruption but the concepts themselves. This is because he discards the very idea of "the good" as imaginary or so distant as to be irrelevant and distracting:

> I depart from the orders of others. But since my intent is to write something useful to whoever understands it, it has appeared to me more fitting to go directly to the effectual truth of the thing than to the imagination of it. And many have imagined republics and principalities that have never been seen or known to exist in truth; for it is so far from how one lives to how one should live that he who lets go of what is done for what should be done learns his ruin rather than his preservation. For a man who wants to make a profession of good in all regards must come to ruin among so many who are not good. (1985, chap. 15)

In politics, dedication to "the good" is in fact corrupt, ruinous. The ideals previously honored are unmasked as unreal. As Ambrose Bierce (1999) defines it, in Machiavellian style, a cynic is "a blackguard whose faulty vision sees things as they are, not as they ought to be" (32). Of course, he cannot do without a conception of the good and thus a standard for corruption.

George Carlin better captures the truth when he says, "Inside every cynical person there is a disappointed idealist."[1] One danger of purist ideals is that they set us up for disillusionment, and the fall is often hard, leading to a rejection of all ideals. Machiavellian realism reinforces the suspicion that all politics is essentially corrupt by traditional standards and then decides to judge politicians by a different standard—effectiveness.

One might mark the end of the medieval period with the discovery that the stars are corruptible. The ideal we had admired turned out to be not so ideal after all. The disillusion about the physical cosmos was accompanied also by the disillusion of moral ideals. When thinking about corruption, the Purists seem to shoot for the stars, while the Menders labor in the light of the stars but without aiming for them. Machiavellians debunk others' stars and are determined to judge things by only their own lights. Machiavelli suggests a system in which human desires, however insatiable, can be better fulfilled—putting aside the question of whether or not they are "truly" good. With desires replacing the good, the standards become subjectivized. The whole world is corrupt. What, then, can provide a *public* standard for moral and political corruption?

3.4: Obedience and Professionalism

Though this exaggerates the influence of theorists, one might say—rather symbolically—that Machiavelli destroys some of the false ideals that were fettering the late-medieval world, and by doing so clears more space in which the human will can operate. The question becomes, then, What should we do with this space created by the destruction of past ideals? Many modern theorists after Machiavelli attempt to understand the human good procedurally, rather than substantially, as freedom—and thus corruption, too, comes to be understood procedurally.

In the seventeenth century, Hobbes uses the body politic metaphor liberally, correlating different maladies of civil life with specific diseases, such as syphilis, epilepsy, rabies, and consumption.[2] Hobbes's body politic metaphor is not the traditional one. He makes it clear that this is an artificial animal, and the only members are sovereign and subject. The diseases all share the same form: They undermine the power of the sovereign.

Hobbes wrote *Leviathan* in a time of civil war and communal crisis. With old standards in disarray, it was clear to him that desires liberated from the good are dangerous—producing a war of all against all. He attempts in a post-Machiavellian mode to provide objective and public standards based on the most universal and lowest human desire. While there is no highest good for Hobbes, there is an ultimate bad—death. The ontological corruption of the body becomes the only true evil, and on it he bases a system of complete and unlimited power of the sovereign, a power that includes the power to define good and bad themselves. Corruption, for political purposes, becomes insubordination. It makes no sense to ask whether the sovereign is right or wrong substantially. Hobbes is attempting an account of communal order free from such substantial conceptions. The roles of the body's members are determined by the sovereign. Corruption is any violation of the form of the social contract, which creates sovereignty. The proper desire of a subject is obedience. Corruption of an official is disobedience.

We find a similar formalization of the political problem in Kant. In ethics, he argues, we do not need a substantial conception of the good in order to define morality; we need only the rational form of the will. Likewise in politics, we can find the proper republican form "merely by organizing the nation well." We do not need virtue to avoid corruption. "The problem of organizing a nation is solvable even for a people comprised of devils (if only they possess understanding)," he comments. This "does not require the moral improvement of man" but is rather a matter of organizing men so that "they compel one another to submit to coercive laws and thus to enter into a state of peace" (1983, 124). It follows that, politically, corruption is formalized as a lack of submission to sovereignty.

Max Weber provides another important example. Weber distinguishes between fact and value in a way that demotes the good as completely unknowable: In the polytheistic war of value-drenched worldviews, it must be a raw decision for each of us which value to worship, a matter of the will and not of truth or correctness. Politically, this means that corruption cannot be defined based on a substantive conception of the common good that the body politic is meant to achieve. Rather, politics must have leaders, and leaders must have causes—which can be neither right nor wrong. Leaders must also have followers, functionaries. Corruption is proceduralized as disobedience. What prevents "terrible corruption and vulgar philistinism" in a political system, according to Weber (2004, 54), is "a highly developed sense of professional honor" among officials:

> When an official receives an order, his honor lies in his ability to carry it out, on his superior's responsibility, conscientiously and exactly as if it corresponded to his own convictions. This remains the case even if the order seems wrong to him and if, despite his protests, his superior insists on his compliance. Without this discipline and self-denial, which is ethical in the highest degree, the entire edifice would collapse. In contrast, the point of honor of the political leader, that

is, the leading statesman, is that he acts exclusively on his *own* responsibility.

What is most remarkable in this quotation is the idea that an official—out of honor and ethics—should act in a way he believes wrong and should be absolved of all responsibility for his actions. Corruption, here understood as disobedience by officeholders, brings ruin in its wake: "The entire edifice would collapse." Weber here follows Hobbes. As Hobbes has it, an agent acting under orders from the person he represents takes no responsibility for the action, which belongs entirely to the person on whose authority he acts. Defining officeholder corruption procedurally can give us procedural purity, but only at the cost of requiring officeholders to pass the buck morally to their superiors whose causes are—ultimately—beyond morality.

In the body politic metaphor, corruption appears primarily as a case of people not doing their part for the common good. The metaphor becomes less common as post-Machiavellians cease to think of the community as a natural ordering of organs with cooperative roles for an objective good. One result of this decline is that corruption becomes increasingly defined as being merely procedural. This, of course, poses the danger of denying people the ability to judge the superior's orders as, sometimes, plain wrong, bad, or evil.

From the point of view of someone holding a substantive conception of the human and common good, this change in the understanding of corruption is itself a corruption. What Weber means by "professional honor" is just expert servitude. But Weber's meaning of professionalism or professional honor isn't the normal one. Rather, in its everyday meaning, professionalism implies a strong sense of the good of the task to be done and a dedication to doing it well in principle. People acting professionally sincerely endeavor to do their job well—not merely because it is commanded but because it is good, it is worth doing, and it is their own responsibility.

3.5: The Love of Money Is the Root of All Evil

Another motif that continues to surface in corruption talk is the suspicion of money and commerce. Wherever money and power are, we naturally suspect, people will too often give in to the temptation of injustice.

Commerce, like politics, is often suspected of being inherently corrupt and corrupting. In both, people often see results they don't like—laws or prices, for instance, that make their life harder—while the inner workings and the benefits of the larger system are less visible. How and why the laws were made, or why the price of something is so high, is less obvious than the inconvenience caused by the laws or the price. As Aesop's version of "The Belly and Its Members" suggests, the system is hard to understand. Resentment is easy.

Moreover, commerce, like politics, requires compromise. This can be frustrating to Purists. The activities of politicking and of trading are particularly susceptible to corruption because there will be more opportunities for corruption whenever fiduciary trust is required, as they are in politics and commerce. Though both politics and commerce may achieve great goods, they can also encourage bitterness and suspicion. The groups of people involved in commerce are often set apart and therefore are easy to blame. The prejudice against merchants and middlemen, who are often foreigners or ethnic minorities, is likely older than the civilizations they helped build. The suspicion of commerce is linked, also, to a concern that luxury corrupts social mores—it softens people and draws their concern away from public duties to private enjoyments.

The English politician Charles Davenant in 1699 nicely summarizes this motif of corruption talk: "Trade, without doubt, is in its nature a pernicious thing; it brings in that wealth which introduces luxury; it gives rise to fraud and avarice, and extinguishes virtue and simplicity of manners; it depraves a people, and makes way for that corruption which never fails to end in slavery, foreign or domestic. Lycurgus, in the most perfect model of government that was ever framed, did banish it from his commonwealth" (quoted in Muller 2002, 3).

This suspicion of commerce and the merchants who engage in it sometimes has a populist tone (for instance, when it overlaps with resentment either of the rich or of ethnic minorities or foreigners). But it sometimes has an elitist motivation. In the *Laws*, Plato's Athenian Stranger seems to lament that a city should have a harbor at all:

> For a city to have the sea nearby is pleasant enough for the purpose of everyday life, but in fact it is a 'salty-sharp and bitter neighbor' in more senses than one. It fills the land with wholesaling and retailing, breeds shifty and deceitful habit in a man's soul, and makes the citizens distrustful and hostile. (1961, 704–5a)

In addition to stating his disapproval of avarice, the Athenian Stranger condemns the desire for money because it lures people to engage in immoral activities and diverts them from civic concerns to private ones: "A passion for wealth . . . makes men unwilling to devote a minute of their time to anything except their own personal property. This is what every single citizen concentrates on with all his heart and soul; his ruling passion is his daily profit and he's quite incapable of worrying about anything else" (1961, 831c–d).

Aquinas summarizes, and endorses, the traditional arguments against trade, asserting that a city should be as self-sufficient and economically isolated as possible. Trade means foreigners, which means change, and therefore corruption, of the community's indigenous mores. "A city which must engage in much trade in order to supply its needs also has to put up with the continuous presence of foreigners," he comments, which is "particularly harmful to civic customs." Moreover, it is bad for the citizens if they engage in trade themselves:

> If the citizens themselves devote their life to matters of trade, the way will be opened to many vices. Since the foremost tendency of tradesmen is to make money, greed is awakened in the hearts of the citizens through the pursuit of trade. The result is that everything in the city will become venal; good faith will be destroyed and the way opened to all kinds of trickery; each one will work only for his own benefit, despising the public good; the cultivation of virtue will fail since honour, virtue's reward, will be bestowed on the rich. Thus, in such a city, civic life will necessarily be corrupted.

For a moment here Aquinas sounds like a Purist, yet in the end he returns to a Mender's approach, reluctantly admitting that no city can be completely self-sufficient, so that "the perfect city will make moderate use of merchants" (1949, 76–78).

In Thomas More's *Utopia* (2016), a Purist character named Raphael Hythloday (whose name implies that he is an angelic talker of nonsense) takes the extreme Purist position, arguing that money is the sole cause of all corruption and civic problems: "Everyone knows that if money were abolished fraud, theft, robbery, quarrels, brawls, altercations, seditions, murders, treasons, poisonings and a whole set of crimes which are avenged but not prevented by the hangman would at once die out" (111).

There are others who resist this prejudice against merchants and commerce. Bernard Mandeville (like Machiavelli, an anti-Purist fixer) in his allegorical poem "The Grumbling Hive" takes the position at the other extreme from Hythloday, approaching the "greed is good" idea advocated later by the cartoonish villain of the movie *Wall Street*. In contrast, the medieval Christine de Pizan (1994, 241–42) takes a moderate, Mending attitude. She celebrates how "by the industry of [merchants'] labor, all kinds of people are provided for, without having to make these things themselves, because, if they have money, merchants bring from afar all things necessary and proper for human beings to live. For it is a good thing that in the world people can have different duties. For otherwise, one would be so busy with trying to make a living that no one could attend to other aspects of knowledge." That is, she sees in the wealth that commerce provides not a corrupting luxury, but a leisure that liberates for higher activities. This does not mean, however, that all commerce is good or that all merchants are upright. Christine's praise of merchants is balanced by an admonition for honest professionalism among them. Avoiding the corrupting influence of commerce, for her, requires rejecting the corruption of commerce. Virtue is needed. Merchants "ought to be honest in their work. . . . And those who practice deception ought not to be called merchants but rather deceivers and bad people. Above all, merchants should be truthful in words and in promises" (241–42). By her very admonition, she admits that commerce and money can be corrupting, even if they are not inherently so.

3.6: Cleanse the Foul Body of the Infected World: A Conclusion of Sorts

All the different corruption motifs we have explored are capable of standing by themselves. That is, we can think of the corrupting effects of commerce without necessarily thinking about corruption in biblical terms. Or, we can consider corruption of the body politic without necessarily assuming that disobedience might also be corrupt. Yet it is often the case that these different motifs are woven together. We can see many instances where more than one motif is drawn upon. Part of the goal of this chapter is to enhance our ability to recognize in the corruption discourse that we each hear or read the various metaphors for corruptions, types of corruption, and motifs about corruption. Here we present Shakespeare as an example of this blending.

It should not be surprising that Shakespeare would be able to weave together many of the topics covered in these previous chapters: the metaphors of rot, disease, dirt, and crookedness; the connections between ontological, moral, and official corruption; the theological temptation toward puritanical cleansing; the body politic analogy; and the dangers of rejecting the good itself. And of course, he manages to do all this in a way that both enhances our perception of the world and counsels us on how to, and how not to, respond. Shakespeare is, in our terms, a Mender, and he is interested in warning us against the Purists and against those who fall off the Purist/Mender continuum into cynicism.

Consider the following lines spoken by the hunchbacked Duke of Gloucester, later Richard III, one of the most villainous characters in Shakespeare's corpus—a sovereign with foul and unchecked desires:

Why, love forswore me in my mother's womb:
And, for I should not deal in her soft laws,

She did corrupt frail nature with some bribe,
To shrink mine arm up like a wither'd shrub;
To make an envious mountain on my back,
Where sits deformity to mock my body;
To shape my legs of an unequal size;
To disproportion me in every part,
Like to a chaos . . .

This passage (from *Henry VI*, part 3, act 3, scene 2) explicitly links quid pro quo corruption to bodily disfigurement—nature was metaphorically bribed in the womb to disfigure Richard's body. Further, Richard's physical crookedness symbolizes his moral crookedness. The result of nature's corruption is that Richard takes himself to be unlovable; most importantly, he will not love himself ("I rather hate myself") and will not love the world. Richard is thus "determined to prove a villain" (from *Richard III*, 5.2, 1.1). The ontological corruption of his body is symbolically linked with his corruption as a moral and political agent. Chaos or disorder, in his own soul and in the body politic, results.

The whole world, it seems, is crooked and unlovable, and so Richard is left with nothing to do but serve himself and his own desires. Shakespeare here shows, psychologically, how dangerous it is to believe that it's all corrupt. To completely reject a naturally good order, to buy into cosmic chaos, may motivate even more corruption—rationalizing the most villainous and selfish behavior. As the novelist Marilynne Robinson (2019) puts it, "Cynicism is the great enabler of corruption, normalizing and universalizing it so that any particular instance of wrongdoing can be left to fester and metastasize as the world wags."

Shakespeare, again with the body politic metaphor in the background, wishes to make a different point about corruption in *Hamlet*. "Something is rotten in the state of Denmark," and indeed the problem is that people can be "rotten before [they] die" (1.4, 5.1). Hamlet's uncle has killed his father, the king, and married his mother, the queen. In pleading to her to repent, Hamlet links the corruptibility of the body in disease with the sexual, moral, and political corruption of leaders of the body politic: "Mother, for love of grace, lay not that flattering unction [i.e., a salve] to your soul. . . . It will but skin and film the ulcerous place, whilst rank corruption, mining all within, infects unseen" (3.4). Superficial responses only cover up corruption, while they exacerbate the interior rot that is destined to destroy everything from the inside out. Yet we should resist the temptation to make Hamlet a hero here. The disturbed Hamlet's moral crusade to purify ceases only in death (and not his alone), spurring us to wonder whether an unction might have worked better than a purge.

It is not like Shakespeare to endorse a theory of complete irremediable corruption or a policy of intolerance and purification. In *As You Like It* (2.7) the misanthropic Jaques begs the duke: "Invest me in my motley; give me leave / To speak my mind, and I will through and through / Cleanse the foul body of the infected world, / If they will patiently receive my medicine." Jaques is requesting to be court jester, but he is not quite benevolent or insightful enough for it—or for the job of inquisitor, we might add. No body can be completely cleansed, and so no body should ever be placed in the care of anyone who is afraid of a little dirt. Shakespeare warns us against the idea that the whole world is a corrupt moral chaos, while also cautioning against the temptation to think that corruption can be eradicated. Doing good in the world requires both a belief in its good and a loving recognition of its failures.

4

Montesquieu

A Mender's Approach to Corruption

In the previous chapters we have noted three basic senses of "corruption"—ontological, moral, and officeholder; we have discussed two styles of corruption talk—the Purist and the Mender; and we have outlined several motifs or narratives common in corruption talk. Each of these helps us understand the way corruption is spoken about in politics, but none of it maps onto contemporary divisions in political outlook. In this chapter and the next, we connect the distinction between a Mender's approach to corruption and a Purifier's approach to corruption, to contemporary politics. We do so by introducing the distinction between a politics of faith and a politics of skepticism. Although our source for this dichotomy is relatively recent (the work of twentieth-century philosopher Michael Oakeshott), we think this distinction is analogous to the Purifier/Mender distinction in many ways, and we use two older political theorists, the Baron de Montesquieu (this chapter) and Jean-Jacques Rousseau (the next chapter), to illustrate the two distinct approaches to corruption.

4.1: Oakeshott's Distinction: Faith and Skepticism

In *The Politics of Faith and the Politics of Scepticism*, Michael Oakeshott distinguishes between two types of politics. The politics of faith, in his accounting, loosely accords with a sort of hopeful ideology, but one with totalitarian tendencies. A politics of faith entails an articulation of who a people is and what the values of that people are, and such a politics can have particular appeal in large, contemporary societies where the natural bonds of community have frayed. In the context of the 1950s (when the essay was written), this framing echoes concerns voiced by Hannah Arendt and others about the susceptibility of the "mass man" to demagoguery. Yet even though Oakeshott is concerned about the consequences of a politics of faith, he argues that it is an ineradicable aspect of political life—that it is, to an extent, needed. He declines to connect the politics of faith with any concrete political movement, party, or outlook. It is, rather, a style of politics. It proposes a knowledge of the future: "We know the direction in which the world is moving and we must bow to it or perish" (Oakeshott 1996, 66).

Oakeshott's politics of skepticism is less developed in the essay, but it is easy enough to fill in what it might be from his comments there and in his other works. Oakeshott suggests that government, in this style, is like garlic in cooking; if it is done right, we notice its absence but not necessarily its presence (1996, 36). This type of politics, Oakeshott notes, is humbler in its aims, orderly, and unobtrusive, but also unsatisfying of ultimate desires, or desires for ultimates. It skirts big questions and can become a sort of ritualized "play" within well-understood confines. Disputes take place without hatred, rules and conventions govern political actions, and friends and enemies change depending on the issues at stake. In his essay "Political Education," Oakeshott (1991, 43–70) argues that a politics of this sort does not create a community but presupposes it. To have this sort of politics, there must already be an agreed-upon set of existing arrangements, customs, institutions, and patterns. Or to put matters in other words, this politics operates within a tradition that is not being subject to radical contention.

Left and Right, in our contemporary sense, can both operate within the politics of skepticism; and Left and Right sometimes mobilize in a style of the politics of faith. The politics of skepticism is a sort of conservatism, but one in which many liberals, too, participate. (Just as most conservatives in the West often advocate a type of liberalism, whether they know it or not.) Oakeshott's conservatism is, like the politics of faith, a style—not a political ideology or a location on the American Left/Right continuum. Oakeshott discusses this at length in his essay "On Being Conservative" (1991, 407–38). There, he defines conservatism as a disposition, not a set of policy positions or ethical or political principles. The merits of conservatism are relative to the particular state or government in question; if the laws of that state are functioning and if the adjudication of conflicts is proceeding smoothly, the conservative disposition will be strong and healthy. Conservatism, as Oakeshott defines it, is not dismissively definable as a willingness to accept the status quo; it entails, rather, a sort of pragmatic inclination to use available political tools to adjust appropriately to changing circumstances. It views the politician's task as akin to that of an artisan or a craftsman (not so much to that of the modern artist or radical inventor). This sort of approach to politics need not seek to roll back change nor to, for instance, minimize the size of government. It entails, rather, a reluctance either to articulate a sort of utopian view of society or to use the tools at government's disposal to inflame public sentiment or to rigorously define friend and foe.

These two styles of the politics of faith and of skepticism nicely, if loosely, map onto the distinction we suggested earlier in this book between Purists and Menders—between those who take up the urge to purify in response to the rotten and those who take up the impulse to repair or mend in response to the crooked. We can see this contrast in two pivotal accounts of the relationship between corruption and the modern political project: the political theory of Montesquieu and of Rousseau. For Montesquieu and Rousseau as well as their successors, corruption in a political context names three distinct but often linked things: first, the falling apart, failure, rot, or brokenness of the political system itself (the regime, the constitutional order, body politic, etc.); second, the deterioration of morals or mores; and third, any particular, often transactional, malfeasance of an officeholder. Both thinkers focus, however, on the first of these—on how the essential institutions of a political system become ruined.

We focus here on Montesquieu and Rousseau because they have influenced American discourse about corruption and because they continue to serve as touchstones for those reflecting on what corruption means in a democracy or in a checks-and-balances republic such as our own. In this sense, they serve as a bridge between discourses that precede the American republic and those that have characterized and continue to characterize the many different levels and venues of American corruption talk.

Moreover, these two thinkers instantiate the two styles that Oakeshott identifies. À la the politics of skepticism, Montesquieu is what one might call an imperfectionist. He has been an inspiration for Menders who think about calibrating institutional arrangements to create and preserve liberty and who tend to identify corruption of the constitutional system with miscalibrations of these institutional arrangements. Montesquieuians often talk about corruption as though there were a piece of the system that needs to be fixed, adjusted, or straightened out. À la the politics of faith, in contrast, Rousseauians tend to talk about corruption as though nefarious, contaminating forces need to be purged lest they infect and spoil the whole. Rousseau has been and continues to be an inspiration for Purists, who hope for a government that channels the voice of the people and who tend to identify corruption of a truly democratic system with private interests running amok.

4.2: How Corruption Happens

Montesquieu (1989) treats corruption most directly in Book 8 of *The Spirit of the Laws*, entitled "On the Corruption of the Principles of the Three Governments." The three types of government here are republics, monarchies, and despotisms. In Montesquieu's account, corruption of a government occurs when that government can no longer function, or function well, as the type of government it is, and perhaps changes its nature entirely. That is to say, Montesquieu focuses here on ontological corruption of governments, and he often uses the verb "to be ruined" in place of "corrupted." Moral corruption of the people or the rulers, officeholder corruption, and transactional corruption appear as possible causes or symptoms of this ontological corruption, but they are not focused upon independently. Particular acts of corruption or particular corrupt individuals, of course, may just be an anomaly in an otherwise healthy government; they are mentioned by Montesquieu primarily to discuss a broader corruption of the system as a whole.

Particular corrupt acts, then, are reason for concern about a regime. But the regime is the real concern. Montesquieu implies this in his comment about how harsh or slack punishment might corrupt the mores of the people (1989, 86): "There are two kinds of corruption: one, when the people do not observe the laws, the other, when they become corrupted by the laws; the latter is an incurable ill because it lies in the remedy itself." Montesquieu is interested here in the health or unhealth of a system and is less concerned about particular actions. Overly harsh punishments corrupt the mores of the people by habituating them to despotism.

Different things undergo different processes of corruption. For Montesquieu, the changes that corrupt a republic differ from the changes that corrupt a monarchy, because republics and monarchies have different structures, purposes, and ways of working. The corruption of government that Montesquieu focuses on is relative to the type of government that is being corrupted. This point requires emphasis so as to avoid absolutizing one of the three processes of corruption—that is, the processes endemic to a republic, a monarchy, or a despotism, his three government types—as definitive of corruption generally. This might be particularly tempting for us regarding republics. Given that our contemporary Western prejudices might regard a republic or a democracy as the singly correct form, we might be tempted to look at its corruption as the real thing, missing Montesquieu's deeper insights.

For this reason, Montesquieu's descriptive approach should be appreciated: If he were simply offering an endorsement of one of the three basic types of government, corruption of that favored type would be corruption simply speaking, and the other governments might appear as corruptions of that uniquely correct type. With some philosophical detachment, Montesquieu in Book 8 wishes rather to note and categorize the ways in which each of the three is ruined per se, as the type of government it is. Rather than starting with an external norm by which to diagnose the corruption of all governments, Montesquieu initially describes corruption of a government relative to the norms inherent to the type. A general theory of corruption also shines through. To understand it, first we must look at Montesquieu's theory of the corruption of the basic types.

4.2a: Corruption of Different Types of Government

Montesquieu's account of corruption forms part of his theory of the types of government. In his terminology, the three basic regimes have both "natures" and "principles," where the natures are manifest in institutional structures and the principles serve as the emotional fuel of the regime. The "nature" is the constitutional system, and the "principle" is the principal passion that moves the system. He identifies "the general idea" of Book 8 as the claim "The corruption of each government almost always begins with that of its principles" (1989, 112). That is to say, corruption of a republic, a monarchy, or a despotism begins, usually, with the spirit—the emotional dispositions and values—that actuates the system. Corruption usually starts when the people acting within the system learn and adopt passions that cannot sustain the system, given its nature.

Each of the three basic types, therefore, has a passion or feeling that animates it. For republics, this principle or main passion is what Montesquieu calls "political virtue"—love of the homeland, thus love of the republican form, thus love of equality (1989, xli, 43). This may seem an array of passions, rather than one, but they belong together, he implies. And we do see it, for example, in a traditional form of American patriotism: To love America is to love that it is ruled by the people and dedicated to equality. For monarchies, this main passion is honor. For despotisms, it is fear. He emphasizes that all three passions are present in all governments, but that each government depends in particular on people being motivated by its special passion. These basic types become complicated, however, as Montesquieu elaborates his description. Governments can be mixed; indeed, Montesquieu seems to prefer them mixed. These are basic but not exclusive types. They are like the primary colors.

Corruption of a democracy begins with the loss of political virtue. Political virtue involves love of equality and "a continuous preference for the public interest over one's own" (Montesquieu 1989, 36). This fits into contemporary attempts to define the root of corruption as prioritization of private gain over public gain. But notice that this would apply specifically only to democracies, and Montesquieu does not endorse democracies (or republics generally) as uniquely legitimate governments. If we read into Montesquieu an assumption that republics, particularly democracies, are good and legitimate and that monarchies are illegitimate, we might falsely simplify his account of corruption as loss of political virtue—that is, as a reduction of the people's quasi-religious dedication to equality and prioritization of the common good over individual goods. But this would be to miss what Montesquieu is trying to tell us. Montesquieu's descriptions of republics and of political virtue make it clear that the passion of political virtue is not a pure good, to be maximized without cost. In fact, corruption of republics happens not only in the diminution of its animating passion but also in the increase of this passion. *Excessive* love of equality or dedication to rule by the people can also ruin republics.

Honor involves placing concern with oneself above public goods, but the government it animates—monarchy—is not portrayed by Montesquieu as essentially corrupt. This might be obscured by two points. First, a republic is fueled by political virtue, whereas a monarchy is not, perhaps implying that it essentially lacks the virtues definitive of a decent politics. But "political virtue" does not name what we might naturally think it does name, the excellence of a person as a citizen of a political system. Political virtue is not really a virtue in Montesquieu's terminology; it is, rather, a *passion*, possessed more or less by the people and rulers to love equality and the community above oneself and one's own. And it is a passion with an ugly side.

> The less we can satisfy our particular passions, the more we give ourselves up to passions for the general order. Why do monks so love their order? Their love comes from the same thing that makes their order intolerable to them. Their rule deprives them of everything upon which ordinary passions rest, what remains, therefore, is the passion for the very rule that afflicts them. (Montesquieu 1989, 42–43)

We should not read this as a celebration of the public-spiritedness of citizens in a pure republic. This "political virtue" is a painful passion, involving a great deal of self-abnegation and demands from others for the same. Montesquieu is not condemning monarchy for not being animated by virtue. His point is merely that monarchy manages to function while relying on this difficult and expensive passion less than a republic does; he thus describes monarchies as more efficient (Montesquieu 1989, 25).

Second, the fact that a monarchy is not essentially corrupt as a form of government may be obscured also by the fact that Montesquieu portrays *the morals* of a monarchy as more corrupt than those of a republic. He expresses this judgment, however, rather matter-of-factly, even approvingly, not moralistically. The purity of the morals of a republic and a republic's methods of maintaining those morals are mixed blessings, or even just bad sometimes. "Who would think it! Even virtue has need of limits" (Montesquieu 1989, 155). What people often call "morals," he implies, or what we would better call *moralism*, may not always be good for people.

This coheres with Montesquieu's comment in Book 20, chapter 1, that commerce renders mores "less fierce" and more "gentle." "Good things have resulted from" the exposure to other cultures' mores through commerce: "One can say that the laws of commerce perfect mores for the same reason that these same laws ruin mores. Commerce corrupts pure mores, and this was the subject of Plato's complaints; it polishes and softens barbarous mores, as we see every day" (Montesquieu 1989, 338). In this sense, according to Montesquieu some degree of corruption would actually be a normative improvement. Notice here that he playfully upholds, and then reverses, the traditional motif (discussed in Chapter 3 of our book) that money and commerce are the root of corruption. One might, furthermore, link this observation to the long line of arguments regarding the potential economic benefits of corruption (e.g., Rose-Ackerman 1999), although such arguments generally have to do with transactional corruption. Montesquieu (1989, 48) also mentions Plato in the context of anticommercial laws, when describing which institutions one might adopt to maximize a republic's political virtue—but he makes clear repeatedly that one should not want to maximize this passion.

Corruption of a monarchy usually begins with corruption of honor as the animating passion of those sharing in rule, the king and nobility. Montesquieu describes this as a "false honor" and as in some ways morally ugly, but he emphasizes that it is easier to maintain than political virtue and that a decent monarchy manages to harness it for the benefit of the political community. "It can inspire the finest actions; joined with the force of laws, it can lead to the goal of government as does [political] virtue itself" (1989, 26). In a Mandevillean turn, Montesquieu comments that with honor "each person works for the common good, believing he works for his individual interests" (27).

Montesquieu's account of despotism is especially important for understanding his general theory of corruption. This is so because he orients his account of politics not so much by an ideal regime to shoot for, as by a bad regime—despotism—to avoid. In some sense, despotism just is the ultimate political corruption, according to Montesquieu. To understand the health and corruption of other regimes requires understanding how they would become despotic.

Corruption of a despotism would begin with a corruption of its main passion, fear, but such corruption is essentially paradoxical, because by the very power of the passion that maintains it, despotism is self-destructive. To procure its goal of tranquility, despotism seeks subservience, using fear to get it. It inculcates fear through destabilization of people's lives, and the regime is not immune from the destabilization with which it rules. Though despotisms require and aim for tranquility (Montesquieu 1989, 320, 493, 617), this is a tranquility without security. The despotic façade of peace (270) resembles perhaps the quiet stretches of compliance between—and enforced by—the eruptions of an abusive parent or spouse. A dreadful contemporary example can be found in North Korea. Discussing the practice there of regular public and extrajudicial killings, the researcher Sarah Son at Transitional Justice Working Group explains, "Public executions are to remind people of particular policy positions that the state has, but the second and more powerful reason is it instills a culture of fear among ordinary people" (quoted in McCurry 2019). We might also think here of the social control exercised by the practice of lynching, which made the American South of 1903, in W. E. B. Du Bois's judgment, little more than "an armed camp for intimidating black folk" (Du Bois 1903, 105).

Whereas moderate versions of the animating passions of the other governments have a homeostatic function, the animating passion of despotism is more like a disease on the body politic. "The principle of despotic government is endlessly corrupted because it is corrupt by its nature" (Montesquieu 1989, 119). We might be tempted to read this corruption "by its nature" as a moral corruption, or as a judgment by Montesquieu of despotism according to a norm that is external to despotism, but it should be read, rather, as ontological description: Despotisms are inherently unstable, tending to their own ruin by the very thing that makes them work. (For example, despots rule by making *others* fear, but the person who must fear the most in a despotism is the despot himself, followed closely by those closest to him.) This feature of despotism becomes clear in Montesquieu's next sentence: "Other governments are destroyed because particular accidents violate their principles; this one is destroyed by its own internal vice if accidental causes do not prevent its principle from becoming corrupt" (119). While republics and monarchies possess an internal force that maintains them against external accidents—a positive passion to maintain the regime—a despotism, feared but never loved, is maintained by external accidents (climate or religion, for example) that lend some stability and regularity to it, in spite of itself.

If we assume despotism is bad, the corruption of a despotism is paradoxical normatively—because the destruction of a bad would likely be good. But a despotism is also paradoxical ontologically, because despotism seems not really a thing, with a stable identity, structure, and functioning proper to it. Despotism might seem to be a government, and we might call it one, but it is really an absence. A pure despotism would cease to exist. In *Considerations* (1999), Montesquieu comments that an absolutely despotic power cannot exist, because there is always some external, limiting force: The external forces that permit its perdurance also prevent its true instantiation. Whereas republics and monarchies are animated and maintained by a moderate version of their dominant passions, if the despotism were to moderate the fear by which it rules its subjects, fear would no longer be the dominant passion, and the despotism could no longer be a despotism (1999, 28), but something else—there would have to be shared and limited power. At the same time, increasing the fear tends only to more self-destruction. Because despotism is inherently corrupt, broken as a government, there is no way, it seems, to both serve and save the government.

4.2b: The Processes of Corruption and Their Terminus

Within this theory of corruption relative to the regime, Montesquieu nestles many examples of how these governments can be corrupted.

A democracy is corrupted both by the weakening and the exaggeration of the spirit of equality. Montesquieu (1989) comments about republics in Book 5, chapter 2, that "corruption seldom begins with the people." They do not have the inclination toward corruption, because those individuals with "middling enlightenment" tend to have an "attachment to that which is established" (42). Later, Montesquieu suggests that the people's corruption in democracy begins with their rulers, who may encourage the people's corruption in order to excuse and hide their own: "The people fall into this misfortune" of rejecting rule and of expecting to be supported by the government "when those to whom they entrust themselves, wanting to hide their own corruption, seek to corrupt the people. To keep the people from seeing their own ambition, they speak only of the people's greatness; to keep the people from perceiving their avarice, they constantly encourage that of the people" (113). This leads to the people abusing the public treasury. This process likely results in a change in the nature of the government into an aristocracy or a despotism. In this narrative, distortion of the principle leads to the ontological corruption of the government by way of what we today more naturally call corruption—that is, misuse of institutional power for private gain.

For Montesquieu (1989), such corruption is committed by the rulers *and by the people*. It is a cooperative corruption in which someone else's misdeeds enable one's own. He makes a similar observation in Book 2, chapter 2: "The misfortune of a republic is to be without intrigues, and this happens when the people have been corrupted by silver; they become cool, they grow fond of silver, and they are no longer fond of public affairs; without concern for the government or for what is proposed there, they quietly await their payments" (14). This comment recalls the concern we discussed earlier in Chapter 2, voiced by Plato's Athenean Stranger in the *Laws*: that commerce distracts people from the common good. Unlike Plato, however, Montesquieu values the softening that commerce brings and fears this effect that comes instead from government distributions.

It may be tempting to think that a republic is corrupted primarily through the corrupt actions of public officials, who use the prerogatives of their offices for themselves rather than for the people. This is where much contemporary discourse on corruption stops, but for Montesquieu this is merely corruption's beginning in a republic. The thorough corruption of the government occurs only with corruption of the people themselves, and this corruption consists in the people's becoming convinced—and this point should seem ironic given how contrary it is to contemporary assumptions about corruption—that every public thing is rightly under the people's power (undermining mediating bodies) and is there to serve what the people perceive as good for them. It is not unusual for corruption talk, in a Rousseauian mode, to imply that the people are supposed to be in charge of everything and that corruption gets in the way of the people getting what they want. For Montesquieu, this is a dangerous corruption of republicanism.

Just as corruption in a republic can happen when the power of the people and their demand for equality is exaggerated, corruption of an aristocracy occurs when the ideas of nobility are exaggerated. Corruption of an aristocracy occurs when "the power of the nobles becomes arbitrary," which especially happens when their nobility is hereditary, since they can "scarcely remain moderate," and moderation is the animating passion of aristocracy (Montesquieu 1989, 115). Likewise, a monarchy becomes corrupted when the king undermines the power of intermediate bodies such that his power is increased and increasingly concentrated in his office. Just as the people of a republic are sometimes corrupted by the flattery of their ministers, the king may be corrupted by the flattery of his servants who think they "owe everything to the prince" and "nothing to their homeland." Importantly, Montesquieu suggests that such intense devotion to the sovereign amounts, ironically, to "high treason" since it "corrupts" the sovereign's power "to the extent of changing its nature" (118). That is, ruin or corruption of the king's power occurs especially by strengthening that power, pushing it toward despotism.

Treason can take the form of an excessive, misplaced devotion to the regime. In kingship, this is the desire to increase the power of the king, undermining the system of powers in which he is a king and not a despot. In a republic, as we saw earlier, this is shown when corrupt public figures claim to be speaking or acting on behalf of the people but in fact are buying the people with profligate spending and are casting any opposition to themselves as opposition to the people—a situation which, if accepted by the people, corrupts them as well. (It seems relevant here to note that partisans in contemporary America tend to do both at once: While partisans tend to object to the expansion of presidential power when the opposing party holds the office, this expansion, when their own party holds the presidency, is often supported in the name of the power of the people.)

We are led by these details of Montesquieu's discourse on corruption to recognize two things. First, the principles or norms emphasized by each species of government are partial and incomplete. And second, a government becomes corrupt either when it loses its principal passion or when there is an emphasis on its purity—that is, then there is an unmoderated dedication to the passion or norm that is the standard for corruption within each species. Anticorruption purism can be just as corrupting as a turning away from the principles. Though Montesquieu says that the cure for corruption is a return to the principles of the regime, he does not mean a maximization of those principles.

Our contemporary American republic would be classified by Montesquieu as a mixed regime, and so applying his theory of corruption to our own case requires understanding his views of republics and monarchies—how they work, their drawbacks, and how they go bad when they go bad. Applying his theory of corruption to our own case, or to any case, requires understanding also that despotism, because that is the ultimate bad for Montesquieu, is the terminus of ruin in all types of government. One common feature of the corruptions of republics and monarchies is that both processes tend toward despotism. Montesquieu (1989) defends neither republics nor monarchies unequivocally. He unequivocally defends moderate government against despotism, and he emphasizes that both republics and monarchies (and mixtures) can be moderate (or fail to be). In Book 8, chapter 8, he comments on the danger of the corruption of his contemporary monarchies: "It is not a drawback when the state passes from a moderate government to a moderate government, as from a republic to a monarchy or from monarchy to republic, but rather when it falls and collapses from moderate government into despotism" (118). Despotism is, for Montesquieu, the epitome of the corruption of a political system.

4.3: Beneficial Corruptions

This basic picture of Montesquieu's three forms of government and their respective processes of ruin is complicated by two points. First, these three basic types do not adequately describe all regimes, since they can be blended. Second, Montesquieu does not seem to view corruption of a government as inherently bad.

Indeed, corruption or ruin of the government can be good, and not only when the government is a despotism. The "best republics" of ancient Greece were democracies that arose "through the corruption of the ancient governments," which had been aristocracies (Montesquieu 1989, 40, n. 17). Because of the mixed structures and the play of forces at work in a gradual change of government, "states are often more flourishing during the imperceptible shift from one constitution to another than they are under either constitution" (173). The purest form of a government may not be its best form, in which case some corruption may prove beneficial. This point coheres with Montesquieu's general ethic: Flaws can be beautiful, and we should learn to appreciate, or at least tolerate, the imperfections that naturally accompany the goods we value (310–11).

Montesquieu's starkest and most suggestive comment on corruption comes in Book 11, chapter 8, which discusses "Why the ancients had no clear idea of monarchy." This seems not to be the simpler monarchy described in Part I of *Spirit of the Laws* (and discussed earlier), but some new and mixed form especially conducive to liberty (1989, 166). He celebrates in Book 11, chapter 8, a government of one that is founded on a nobility or "on a legislative body formed of the representatives of a nation"—and by "representatives" he means geographical "deputies to an assembly" (167). This is, in fact, a government mixed of kingship, aristocracy, and representational democracy. He explains "the origin of Gothic government among us": The practice of regional representatives to an assembly arose in the breakdown of the Roman Empire. Because the Germanic conquerors "spread out across the country," "they could no longer assemble" all in person; instead, they "did so by representatives." At first, "the common people were slaves," so the government was "a mixture of aristocracy and monarchy" only. But the democratic element was added once the slaves were emancipated. "Soon the civil liberty of the people, the prerogatives of the nobility and of the clergy, and the power of the kings, were in such concert that there has never been, I believe, a government on earth as well tempered as that of each part of Europe during the time that this government continued to exist" (167).

Montesquieu perhaps implies here that his European contemporaries possess only corrupt or derivative remnants of such a government, but he concludes with a superlative compliment: "It is remarkable that the corruption of the government of a conquering people should have formed the best kind of government men have been able to devise" (1989, 167–68).

To some, mixtures of the basic types will appear to be corruptions—as mutts appear to dog-show enthusiasts. But Montesquieu admires mixed and moderate government. And he is skeptical of purism and absolutization of any single principle—rule by any single person, group, or passion is bound to be despotic. We should not be surprised that corruption of a government should be regarded so positively. Montesquieu is a Mender, and he thinks Purists are dangerous.

One may glean from this same admiration and skepticism a general account of good or uncorrupted institutional agency. In any nondespotic government, good institutional agency—whether of an official or a citizen—would involve maintaining and bolstering its moderation. One would support the government, its laws, and its lawful character. One would seek to relax its immoderate aspects, rejecting any purism that would imbalance the government or possibly upset society's good aspects (which must coexist with imperfections, see Montesquieu 1989, 310–11).

Indeed, if we are looking for clues regarding Montesquieu's view of corrupted institutions and corrupt use of institutional roles, we might look for his views of its opposite. What should the citizens, subjects, and rulers be like in the various states? Particularly telling is Montesquieu's (1989) conclusion to Book 4, which is on education. After recounting the need to inculcate the passion animating each type of government, he changes course by suggesting that this passion be moderated as well. He comments on the ancient Greek use of music in education. Because the Greek ruling groups were prejudiced against the manual arts, and even against commerce (which Montesquieu praises for moderating mores), citizens were educated primarily through gymnastic and martial exercises, rendering them too rough. "Now these exercises, so appropriate for making people harsh and savage, needed to be tempered by others that might soften the mores"—a function fulfilled for the Greeks by music (40–41). Thus, Montesquieu approaches something like Aristotle's "education relative to the regime" in *The Politics* (1989, V. 9). For Aristotle, a citizen should be educated not only to be a good citizen according to the standards emphasized by the regime but especially to *temper* the regime's proclivities toward seeking its standards single-mindedly. To the principled purist, a truly good citizen may look like a compromising corruptor. But for both Aristotle and Montesquieu, a purist dedication to maximizing the partial goods or standards of the regime would be self-destructive. Perhaps it is a curse of good citizens to be seen as bad citizens by the most passionate citizens.

This account of uncorrupted institutional agency finds verification in Montesquieu's account of the paradox of being a good citizen in a despotism. Despotism requires fear, extreme submission, and ignorance. "Education is, in a way, null there," with the goal of "making a bad subject in order to create a good slave." It is nonsensical in a despotism to attempt to form a "good citizen," since that person could only participate "in the public unhappiness." Were such a citizen to arise in a despotism, "if he loved the state, he would be tempted to relax the springs of the government; if he failed, he would be ruined; if he succeeded, he would run the risk of ruining himself, the prince, and the empire" (Montesquieu 1989, 35). In a bad government, there is no way to save and serve the state.

We need not look only to contemporary despotic regimes to see this paradox. Elements of despotism can exist in nongovernmental organizations as well. There are organizations that cannot tolerate professionals who want to do their job correctly, for this threatens their colleagues' ability not to do so. There are organizations that do not tolerate members who would moderate the group's actions and principles, even when moderation is needed for survival and for the flourishing of the group itself. This suggests that corruption of a state simply speaking—not merely relative to one type or another—*is* ruin of the political system's ability to survive uncorrupt officeholders and cultivate good citizens. Uncorrupt officeholders and citizens serve the moderation and maintenance of the government and, by doing so, serve the well-being of the people. And this makes sense: The ontological corruption of any instrument occurs when it can no longer function, or function well, as the type of thing it is—that is, when it can no longer be used well by those who would use it for its proper ends. And this can happen to an institution or an organization through either an anemic or a purist dedication to a principle.

Thus, Montesquieu begins his account by describing corruption of each government relative to the norms inherent to its species. As his account develops, however, it becomes clear that there are also generic norms inherent to all as types of government. He may at times appear to approach a value-free analysis, and his claim in the preface may, given the subsequent development of the social sciences, be taken as implying this: "I did not draw my principles from my prejudices but from the nature of things" (Montesquieu 1989, xliii). But this would be to read Montesquieu anachronistically: It is a contemporary prejudice that norms are prejudices, and that an objective description of the nature of things would be nonnormative. He aims not for a value-free recording of naked facts, but rather for a prejudice-free description of things intrinsically value-laden. (Whether he uniquely achieves a vision uncolored by prejudices is a different question [Montesquieu 1989, 618].)

Each government has the end of maintaining itself (Montesquieu 1989, 156) and the political community it governs, and every system of political and civil laws is measured by how well it secures "the well-being of the people" (516). Although Montesquieu begins his account of corruption by sketching corruption of each regime type relative to the values inherent to its type, the driving spirit and the dominating passion of its species, he does not stop there. Each government should be judged by norms or values going beyond its principles. What this allows us to see is that the norms that each type might take as supreme are merely relative to their type, and may, if pressed too far, undermine the generic norms inherent to all governments as such. And it seems that it is mixed governments—not any of the basic types, but "corruptions" of the basic types—that would be best able to achieve these inherent purposes of government.

Montesquieu playfully undermines the way purists within any given government may talk about corruption by praising some corruptions. But in the end he also offers a theory of political corruption in which despotism is truly, objectively bad, the epitome of true corruption. Even his playful praise for certain corruptions is in the service of avoiding real corruption. His is at once a morally serious and an imperfectionist account of corruption, a Mender's theory aiming for the better, not the best—strategizing to avoid the worst.

4.4: The Corruption of Liberty: "Power Must Check Power"

Montesquieu famously praises the constitution of England—a mixed government that has "political liberty for its direct purpose" (Montesquieu 1989, 156). It is not that he thinks that liberty is the unique end of government. "Liberty" is a slippery word, and it is easily confused with each doing as one pleases or the people having power over everything (154–55), either of which can destroy true liberty. Even the passion for liberty needs moderating (166), lest it consume its beloved, because the liberty we want is possible only under law (155). It requires at the constitutional level a division of powers, and it requires at the personal level both a willingness to live under rule by one's equals (114) and also—especially—just procedures of criminal law. About the latter, Montesquieu comments that the knowledge about the rules that should guide criminal judgments "is of more concern to mankind than anything else in the world" (188), because it is a basic condition of personal liberty—a condition of that sense of tranquility that we have at being secure from other citizens. (It makes sense, then, that people are usually more alarmed at officeholder corruption in the courts than corruption in other branches of government.)

The chapter on England (Montesquieu 1989, 156–66) is especially important in the American context, as Montesquieu's discussion of the checks and balances in his rather idealized version of England influenced how Americans adapted their inheritance of an English-style mixed constitution, and how Americans continue to view that adaptation. What he says about the threats of corruption to this system of liberty should speak to us rather directly.

In this system, representatives of the people hold a legislative power that is checked by a solitary executive. Montesquieu emphasizes that this government dedicated to liberty requires a constitutional structure in which the executive and legislative powers are separated and thus limited. The key is the constitutional arrangement:

> Democracy and aristocracy [the two forms of republican government] are not free states by their nature. Political liberty is found only in

moderate governments. But it is not always in moderate states. It is present only when power is not abused, but it has eternally been observed that any man who has power is led to abuse it; he continues until he finds limits.

Therefore, Montesquieu reasons, "So that one cannot abuse power, power must check power by the arrangement of things" (Montesquieu 1989, 155). He lays out specific mechanisms that allow this. For example, the executive must not be able to raise his own money, but must depend on yearly funding by the legislature. The people must have a voice not directly but through representatives in the legislature. The legislature must be checked by an executive veto. The executive must not be able to author legislation (164). Corruption of this system of political liberty would occur, and the system would move toward despotism, when such nitpicky-sounding rules are evaded. The devil is in the constitutional details.

Montesquieu predicts that it is corruption of the legislative assembly that will ultimately be the ruin of this system he admires. "Since all human things have an end, the state of which we are speaking will lose its liberty; it will perish.... This state will perish when legislative power is more corrupt than executive power" (1989, 166). He does not specify what this corruption of the legislature would look like, and one supposes that it could take several forms. This corruption might occur when the legislature no longer controls the executive through its annual power of taxing and spending—for example, if the executive can make major expenditures without legislative approval. Or it might occur when the legislature no longer authors laws itself and fails to prevent the executive from authoring such laws in its stead, or when it destroys executive or judicial powers.

Montesquieu gives a few intriguing hints about what this corruption of the legislature would look like. For instance,

When various legislative bodies follow each other, the people, holding a poor opinion of the current legislative body, put their hopes, reasonably enough, in the one that will follow; but if the legislative body were always the same, the people, seeing it corrupted, would expect nothing further from its laws; they would become furious, or would sink into indolence. (1989, 162)

The threat here is that the people would grow either rebellious or cynical due to lost hope in an unresponsive legislature. It doesn't take much imagination to see that these emotions of fury and indolence could lead to decreased checks on the power of the legislature or, perhaps, to the opposite—to empowering a stronger executive.

One can imagine that the legislature might grow corrupt in the opposite direction as well—by being too responsive to what the people want, by being too democratic and thus not checked enough by other forces. The legislature, likely flattering the people and casting itself as the voice of the people, could become despotic.

This system he praises is a mixed system, a mixture of aristocracy, monarchy, and democracy—so perhaps it could give way to corruption in any of the ways discussed for those three systems. In this mixed government, the democratic aspect is legislative, so perhaps this system's corruption through the legislature would follow the processes he describes in democracies. About corruption in democracy, Montesquieu tells us, as discussed earlier, that representatives or officers may corrupt the people (1989, 113). Their representatives may feed the ambition and avarice of the people in order to hide their own ambition and avarice:

> The people fall into this misfortune when those to whom they entrust themselves, wanting to hide their own corruption, seek to corrupt the people. To keep the people from seeing their own ambition, they speak only of the people's greatness; to keep the people from perceiving their avarice, they constantly encourage that of the people. Corruption will increase among those who corrupt, and it will increase among those who are already corrupted. The people will distribute among themselves all the public funds; and, just as they will join the management of business to their laziness, they will want to join the amusement of their luxury to their poverty. But given their laziness and their luxury, only the public treasure can be their object. . . . The more the people appear to take advantage of their liberty, the nearer they approach the moment they are to lose it. Petty tyrants are formed, having all the vices of a single one. What remains of liberty soon becomes intolerable. A single tyrant rises up, and the people lose everything, even the advantages of their corruption. (1989, 113)

What Montesquieu would seem to suggest about mixed systems like the one Americans have adapted from England is that the corruption toward despotism would become manifest ultimately in an executive power—a single tyrant rising up. However, this process will have started with a corrupt legislative branch that chose to feed, rather than check, the avarice and ambition of the people and the executive because corrupting those others fed its own laziness and luxury, avarice, and ambition.

Montesquieu is an imperfectionist, a skeptic, and a Mender, but that is not because he thinks that "good enough" is easy. The balances necessary for political liberty are complex and fragile. And despotism, of one sort or another, is the fallback system that is more common than not.

4.5: The Diversity of Corruption Discourses

Montesquieu's discourse on corruption is sophisticated and layered. It leads us not only to reflect on corruption and how governments can go bad but also to understand different discourses on corruption. By telling us what corruption appears to be from within different political systems, Montesquieu helps us see that, quite naturally, people with different political starting points will engage in different types of corruption talk. Individual acts of corruption in these various systems will appear, to those within the system, soaked in the significance given by the context of government's type.

In a republic, for instance, a discourse on officeholder corruption will focus not merely on whether someone has broken this or that law, or even on whether this or that law or institution is proper or improper to a republic. Discourse on corruption within a republic will focus on political virtue, on prioritizing love of the public over the private, and on equality. To someone within a republic and dedicated to it, corruption means loss of political virtue, public spiritedness, and equality. It is natural for someone with this political starting point to see in instances of transactional corruption selfish violations of the moral imperative to prioritize the public good over one's own. This discourse will likely explain that the problem with such acts is that they violate principles of equality. Also, it is natural for someone with a democratic starting point to see it as a corruption of the whole system, the regime itself, when the ability of the people to get what they want from government is frustrated.

Likewise, the discourse on corruption within a monarchy will focus on honor. To someone with such a starting point, the primary thing wrong with instances of officeholder corruption will be its vulgarity, its baseness. It is dishonorable. We can extrapolate here to something that might apply to us. Having rejected great-chain-of-being hierarchies of birth and church, today we sometimes hear a bourgeois echo of this concern with honor: People who take pride in their work condemn transactional corruption as unprofessional.

It is hard to imagine a discourse on corruption in a despotism. Montesquieu tells us that despotisms suffer a poverty of political discourse: "One is less communicative in countries where each man, whether a superior or inferior, exercises an arbitrary power" (Montesquieu 1989, 314). It would make sense, though, that the discourse on corruption within a despotism (to the extent there can be one) would focus on obedience and fear of the despot and the despot's lieutenants. Montesquieu comments that officials receiving presents for doing favors goes against the spirit of both republics and monarchies, but coheres with the spirit of despotism (67). Despots and their servants enjoy gifts as expressions of servility. Yet, if a servant acts corruptly to violate the despot's will, it would be seen as insolence, an affront to the despot's power, a failure to be animated by the proper fear. In despotism, corruption would be confused with disobedience, virtue confused with compliance.

In a mixed system, corruption discourse will sometimes take the shape of condemning corrupt behavior because it imbalances the blend. Corrupt action means that someone's power is not being properly checked by other actors in the system. Under a government dedicated to personal liberty, corruption discourse will take this as its theme. Instances of officeholder corruption—think, for instance, of corrupt police forces, judges, or building permit offices—will be seen as undermining the ability of individuals to feel safe from improper punishment and to trust that they can exercise their legal liberties.

Though political virtue and equality, honor, fear—and even liberty—are necessary in any decent state, their exaggerations undermine the system, so they should not be taken as the standard against which to measure corruption *simpliciter*. Montesquieu is a pluralist and an imperfectionist. He is a Mender, not a Purist. He recognizes the possibility of several types of decent government while not succumbing to a relativism according to which just any system is as good as any other. Thus, Montesquieu's own discourse on corruption allows us to see the relative validity of these multiple discourses, and to place them within a context that relativizes them as partial and limited, the context of the norms applicable to governments generically. Those norms are, for Montesquieu, the survival of the political community and the well-being of the people. Montesquieu also helps us appreciate that it is different assumptions about what government should be—what does it mean to serve the well-being of the people?—that are at the root of our disagreements about corruption.

5

Rousseau and the Limits of
the Purifier's Approach

5.1: Rousseau, Faith, and Despair

If Montesquieu can be seen as an articulator of Oakeshott's politics of skepticism, Jean-Jacques Rousseau might be understood as a proponent of a politics of faith. Rousseau's description of an idealized form of government that would channel the public will without intermediary institutions is often presented as the polar opposite of the sort of pluralistic, institutional form of government championed by, among others, Montesquieu.

Montesquieu and Rousseau present contrasting accounts of how governments—and, indeed, human beings—become corrupted. These two accounts differ in their understanding of what corruption is in two important ways. First, they differ in regard to whether corruption takes as its reference point one single ideal (and, therefore whether corruption is essentially the same whatever regime one inhabits), or whether there are multiples goods, orders, and ideals at stake (such that corruption must be understood derivatively and relatively to the regime and to particular situations, which are diverse and always complicated). Second, they differ in regard to the paths that corruption takes: Is it inevitable, or can it be contained or even reversed? When one takes into account Rousseau's belief that corruption is inevitable, irreversible, and independent of regime type, it becomes clear that rather than being the articulator of a grand vision where the popular will triumphs, Rousseau is a critic of such populist inclinations. Rousseau explains the romantic appeal of this vision, but he also shows us how any reform movement will inevitably become corrupted. He seems to start in a politics of faith, but he then shows, we argue, how people who adopt that faith will end in a politics of despair.

5.2: Corruption and Human Alienation

Rousseau's account of corruption differs from that of Montesquieu, first, because it is rooted in a single, ontological definition. This definition is developed consistently across his major political works—from the First and Second Discourses (1750, 1755) to *On the Social Contract* (1762) and his later "Considerations on the Government of Poland and on Its Proposed Reformation" (1772). Corruption for Rousseau remains a disintegration that prevents something from fulfilling its function. In the human realm, it is made manifest in alienation—alienation of the citizen from his duties, alienation of the human animal from himself, alienation of the government from legitimate sovereign authority, or alienation of individuals from the folk identity of their patria.

In the First Discourse, Rousseau presents corruption as an alienation of the citizen from his duties. Rousseau revels in being a contrarian. While his contemporaries were optimistically assuming that the forces of enlightenment would also be sources of improvement, Rousseau argues that the arts and sciences are morally and politically corrupting: "The effect is certain, the depravity real, and our souls have been corrupted in proportion to the advancement of our sciences and arts toward perfection" (1964, 39). The arts and sciences produce luxury and soften people; they enervate and effeminize. They develop some goods that most people don't need anyway (for example, scientific knowledge, charming luxuries, and social pleasantries) at the expense of more important ones. Ultimately, the spread of enlightenment disorients citizens from their simple duties: "Who would want to spend his life in sterile speculations," Rousseau asks, "if each of us, consulting only the duties of man and the needs of nature, had time for nothing except his fatherland, the unfortunate, and his friends?" (48).

What is especially corrupted by the arts and sciences is political virtue, the realm of manly citizenship. Rousseau laments in the First Discourse, "We have physicists, geometers, chemists, astronomers, poets, musicians, painters; we no longer have citizens" (1964, 59). Some thirty years later, in "Considerations on the Government of Poland and on Its Proposed Reformation," he similarly complains, "There are no more Frenchmen, Germans, Spaniards, even Englishmen, nowadays, regardless of what people may say; there are only Europeans. All have the same tastes, the same passions, the same morals, because none has been given a national form by a distinctive institution" (1985, 184). Citizenship calls for a rooted, narrow, and practical devotion to a particular community with its own ways, however peculiar. Rousseau concludes the First Discourse by confessing that there will always be "a few men" who are not only "tempted to learn" but strong enough to overcome the natural and social obstacles to doing so. As these few pursue their own, individual passion, they should keep it to themselves—they should neither undermine the good of the society to which they owe public loyalty nor seek to define themselves according to this passion. The people need "the old-fashioned words of fatherland and religion," but the naïve enlighteners debase these sacred things (1964, 50) by encouraging the luxuries of a soft, naïve, and ultimately vain cosmopolitanism.

In the Second Discourse, Rousseau presents corruption in a broader fashion, as alienation of the human animal from himself. Although this is not as explicitly political a conception as he provides in the First Discourse, this inner alienation has, as we shall see, more substantial political ramifications. Rousseau's later account of political corruption builds upon his claim that human beings, as we know them (and ourselves) today, are corruptions of a more innocent human animal.

Mischievously adjusting the state-of-nature tales told by prior political theorists, Rousseau presents a playful, speculative vision of human beings in their "natural" condition—it was, he thinks, a state of happiness, strength, equality, freedom, and integrity. Contrary to reputation, Rousseau's early man was not really a noble savage. Early man was, in fact, just another animal, albeit one with more potential. The potential comes from his ability to observe and imitate, and that means to change himself. Our species possesses "perfectibility" or "the faculty of self-perfection" (1964, 114–15): We can make ourselves something different than what nature made us. This is "the specific characteristic of the human species," distinguishing us from other animals (208).

Within the state of nature, the human animal was happy because he was easy to please, wanting only "nourishment, a female, and repose" (Rousseau 1964, 116). In other words, his function was obvious and easily obtainable, and his organism was naturally suited to fulfill it. Those humans who were inferior to the rest—the sickly, the injured, the weak—died, naturally and no less happily, since they died without anticipating it (106, 116). Those remaining would have been more or less equal, just as all wild chipmunks surviving to adulthood are more or less the same. Pain and hunger being his only evils, savage man could undergo only physical corruption.

Man's "perfectibility"—that is, his adaptability—serves him well in his savage state as he mimics useful behaviors of other human and nonhuman animals. In a social situation, the effects of this ability multiply in all directions. We observe others, we make comparisons, we imitate. New skills, new desires, new needs appear and quickly compound. Through cooperation and invention, the animal becomes softer, less robust—thus more dependent. This is a physical degeneration. Worse is the moral corruption. A healthy and natural self-concern mutates into vanity (Rousseau 1964, 221–22). This is a loss of integrity: "For one's advantage, it was necessary to appear to be other than what one in fact was. To be and to seem to be become two altogether different things" (155). Social life sparks and unrelentingly stokes the desire to appear—the desire to be seen by others not only as keeping up, but as superior, and thus to seem so to oneself.

Savage man's happiness consists in a tranquility undisturbed by civilization's myriad artificial passions. Comparing ourselves with others and copying them yield the desire to compare favorably with them and to enjoy many new things unnecessary from the point of view of the original human animal—conveniences that both weaken our survival fitness and make us unhappy by drawing our desires further outside of ourselves, further and further from mere nourishment, copulation, and repose. The simplicity of animal consciousness is destroyed by social life. The animal carries himself entirely within himself, Rousseau says (1964, 107). Civil man's consciousness is dispersed, distracted, his happiness disturbed.

The nature of this first corruption—a corruption that has become our nature—comes to light when we note the major distinction between savage man and man in civil society. Savage man enjoyed a simple unity with himself. Civil man lacks integrity. The corruption at issue is a corruption of consciousness—an inner alienation, a placing of one's self outside of oneself. Rousseau boils down the essential difference between savage and civil man to this: "The savage lives within himself; the sociable man, always outside himself, knows how to live only in the opinion of others" (Rousseau 1964, 179).

A large part of this corruption stems from the creation of artificial inequalities (on this point see Dobel 1978; Shklar 1969, 110), but it is not merely inequality that matters. We have lost our animal ignorance permanently, and with it our innocence and contentment. The fall is a mixed blessing. Many of the things that people most value come as a result of this corruption, but it is impossible for a civilized adult to be, as the saying goes, "as happy as a clam." Instead, we spend our time vainly chasing things others have and society makes us think we want. It is not so much that inequality is inherently wrong, according to Rousseau. Inequality matters because it fuels vain desires, and vanity causes social and political problems. The hatred of others, envy, and the desires for more property or power spring, ultimately, from vanity—which is a corruption of consciousness and which consists in the inner alienation of the person from himself.

For the Rousseau of the Second Discourse, then, corruption is primarily ontological: It is the loss of integrity or simple unity, a falling to pieces, that makes the animal unable to satisfy his function. Our primeval integrity, equality, happiness, and strength have been destroyed by society. Rousseau recognizes this loss both as permanent and as the source of many things that we enjoy, but still casts it a loss. Human beings should be understood as corrupted animals.

Naturally, this account of human corruption has political implications. First, Rousseau points out that now human beings primarily pursue two things: ever more commodities, and the approval of others (Rousseau 1964, 223). Second, property and money are necessary to society, yet they are also the source of crime and misery. Rousseau seems to assume a zero-sum supply of property such that some people's possession of more causes other people to have not enough. Third, Rousseau thinks of luxury as something like an addictive drug, requiring ever higher doses, damaging self and others. "It is first of all a question of providing for the necessary, and then for the superfluous; next come delights, then immense wealth, and then subjects, and then slaves" (195). Luxury is "the worst of all evils in any State whatever, whether large or small, and in order to feed the crowds of lackeys and miserable people it has created, it crushes and ruins the farmer and the citizen" (199). Corruption talk influenced by Rousseau often emphasizes these motifs.

Fourth and finally, it is not unusual for corruption talk to be marked by a politically potent nostalgia for an uncorrupted past. Rousseau's account explains this desire to return to what people may imagine as an earlier and simpler age. He says as much in the preface:

> The times of which I am going to speak are very far off: how you have changed from what you were! . . . There is, I feel, an age at which the individual man would want to stop: you will seek the age at which you would desire your species had stopped. Discontented with your present state for reasons that foretell even greater discontents for your unhappy posterity, perhaps you would want to be able to go backward in time. (Rousseau 1964, 104)

Rousseau suggests that there was a moment in human history in which the species reached its peak. It occurred after the formation of basic societies or nomadic villages, but before the division of labor, the development of agriculture, and the institution of government. This "happiest and most durable epoch" was the "best for man": "This state was the veritable prime of the world" (1964, 150–51).

Before paleodiets and paleofitness became trendy, there was paleopolitics, and Rousseau helps us understand it. Corruption talk influenced by Rousseau often betrays a nostalgia for the communal, the precommercial village; it often displays a distrust or antipathy toward the increasingly globalized, extended society of strangers constructed through travel and trade. Many people vaguely inspired by Rousseau imagine that humans in this earlier, uncorrupted age were less greedy. Such people may imagine an idyllic life before "capitalism" rather than before Rousseau's "civil society." Perhaps, simply because there were fewer commodities, humans spent less time chasing after them. Moreover, because property creates opposed interests, greed, rotten behavior, and others' poverty, people in this earlier, less corrupted age would have been more virtuous, more unified, and less poor, even if they also had less stuff. There would be greater social solidarity, equality, and cohesion. Such images tap into a deep desire for wholeness and simplicity at both the personal level and the political level. We recognize here strong reverberations of two traditional corruption motifs: the loss of an Edenic garden of delights, and the incriminating attitude toward money and commerce (discussed in Chapter 3, above).

Imaginatively remembering the childlike simplicity of the human animal or the communal feeling-at-home of the tribe or village, we feel alienated—as though we have lost something. Can we recover it? Politically, the question becomes whether we can get the best of both nature and society: Can we find a form of social life that allows civilized adults to participate in the contentment, equality, strength, freedom, and integrity of the savage and childlike state of nature? What would an uncorrupted civil life look like?

5.3: How Good Governments Go Bad

5.3a: What Uncorrupted Political Integrity Looks Like

In *On the Social Contract*, Rousseau takes up this question. His driving concern here is to define the conditions of a valid government, one exercising a right to govern. Political corruption as Rousseau presents it here is simply the loss of this validity—in other words, corruption entails the alienation of the government from sovereign authority. Corruption undermines the legitimacy of government. To understand Rousseau's account of political corruption, then, we must first look to his discussion of legitimacy. *On the Social Contract*'s account of corruption of the body politic builds on the Second Discourse's picture of the corruption of the species. The ideal, uncorrupted political association would also, by its very legitimacy, recover and protect our natural freedom, equality, strength, and integrity.

The difference between illegitimate government and legitimate government is the difference between being forced to obey and being obligated to obey. It may be smart to obey a ruler (or a highwayman, for that matter) because he is powerful, whether or not he is right, but "one is only obligated to obey legitimate powers" (Rousseau 1978, 49). What, then, makes political power legitimate? Where does the obligation to obey originate? This obligation cannot be natural, because by nature we are all free.

The duty to obey must come from each person obliging himself. Rousseau puts the driving question of *On the Social Contract* as follows—as though he were posing a mathematical problem:

> Find the form of association that defends and protects the person and goods of each associate with all the common force, and by means of which each one, united with all, nevertheless obeys only himself and remains as free as before. (1978, 53)

Find a truly legitimate political power. *Solve for x.* Elsewhere Rousseau claims that "the great problem of Politics" is "to find a form of Government that might place the law above man" (1997, 270)—notice he says *law* and not *force*; right is more difficult than might. These two are in fact the same problem, differently phrased. Both formulations ask what the value of the variable "sovereignty" must be if power is to be legitimate and the citizens obligated to obey. Rousseau solves the problem by equating "the sovereign" with "the people." When the laws radiate from the people, legitimacy of rule is guaranteed a priori, because, in Rousseau's accounting, no one submits to anyone except himself. The law—the will of the people—would rule justly over all particular persons because it would derive from them all.

If we conceive of the law as a contract in which every citizen joins, then in the rule of law, I am free because I obey only myself. As Jacob Klein comments, "It is important to understand that what this theory of lawgiving is primarily interested in, is not the giving of good laws but securing the lawfulness of the law itself. . . . The content of the law, its goodness or badness in terms of human welfare, in terms of the common good, is not the ultimate concern" (Klein 1969, 4). The ultimate concern is the legitimacy—not the wisdom—of a political order. According to Rousseau, because each citizen "obeys only himself" he "remains as free as before" (Rousseau 1978, 53), even when he is being forced to obey the law he helped create (55).

Each citizen helps to create the laws by joining into the social contract, which is "the total alienation of each associate, with all his rights, to the whole community" (Rousseau 1978, 53). That is, the contract necessary to build a decent political society requires that the members give their all to it. In such a society, no private person can ever possess authority to rule over anyone else. Rather, it is the "public person" of the state created by this implicit social contract—in other words, the community as a whole—that possesses sovereign authority.

> This public person, formed thus by the union of all the others [i.e., all the private persons], formerly took the name *City*, and now takes that of *Republic* or *body politic*, which its members call *State* when it

is passive, *Sovereign* when active, *Power* when comparing it to similar bodies. As for the associates, they collectively take the name *people*; and individually are called *Citizens* as participants in sovereign authority, and *Subjects* as subject to the laws of the State. (1978, 54)

These italicized terms have different connotations, Rousseau says, but they all refer to the same thing—like "Clark Kent" and "Superman." They are variables with the same value or meaning. Notice that "government" is not one of these terms. The people are, by composing the republic, at once sovereign and subjects, and they manage this seemingly oxymoronic feat by being citizens (Rousseau 1978, 101). As citizens people have complete authority, and none at all. Individually, citizens surrender over to the community all of their rights without remainder. Collectively, citizens govern over the community without limitation.

Therefore, legitimate laws come from the people. Whether or not the government looks monarchical or aristocratic structurally, it is legitimate if and only if it rules according to the will of the people. This means that "every legitimate government is republican" (Rousseau 1978, 67). Rousseau adds, "By this word ['republic'] I do not mean only an aristocracy or a democracy, but in general any government guided by the general will, which is the law. In order to be legitimate, the government must not be confounded with the sovereign, but must be its minister" (67n).

The government is supposed to be merely the agent of the people and the executor of the people's will. The true sovereign is the people. So the law, if it is to have obliging force, must be the will of the people, what Rousseau calls "the general will." This will of the people must be general—that is, common, not particular—in two ways: both in its subject and in its object (1978, 62). First, the will of the people is possessed corporately by the community. The whole people united together is the subject that knows and expresses the law. Second, the people's will is about only general objects, not about particulars, such that it applies commonly and equally to all. The law—the expression of the will of the people—consists in general rules, but makes no decisions about facts, details, or applications. Such decisions about particulars are the government's job.

A community governed like this—the law comes from the will of the people, and the government faithfully applies it—would be marked by freedom, equality, strength, and integrity. In other words, a legitimate political association would, felicitously, heal the corruption of the species. It seems that after the fall described in the Second Discourse, we can now get a new and improved version of the things we lost.

Natural equality is not quite preserved, but it is transformed and perfected in the social contract. In the state of nature, savage men are all, more or less, equal—the way that wild animals of the same species are more or less the same. But they are not perfectly equal, and their differences in physique and mind are exacerbated and turned to ill by the social forces of vanity and greed. The social contract recovers this loss, with interest: "Rather than destroying natural equality, the fundamental compact on the contrary substitutes a moral and legitimate equality for whatever physical inequality nature may have placed between men, and . . . although they may be unequal in force or in genius, they all become equal by convention and right" (Rousseau 1978, 58).

This improving recovery of natural equality happens also with natural freedom and strength. It is, Rousseau says, "false that the social contract involves any true renunciation on the part of private individuals"—even though he defines the social contract as requiring "total alienation" by all the citizens of all their rights (1978, 53). They do not lose, but gain, in freedom and strength: "Instead of alienation, they have exchanged to their advantage an uncertain, precarious mode of existence for another that is better and safer; natural independence for freedom; the power to harm others for their personal safety; and their force, which others could overcome, for a right which the social union makes invincible" (64).

In addition to recovering a new and improved equality, freedom, and strength, the members of this community also regain integrity or wholeness, the loss of which constituted the corruption of the species—the alienation of the human animal from himself. It is important to ask in what way this can happen, however. Human consciousness remains changed forever, of course. People are irreversibly shaped by social life and the dispersions and distortions of desire and self that result from social living. There is no going back (Rousseau 1964, 202). It is not that each individual regains the self-contained, simple-minded integrity of the wild animal. Rather, in the social contract, people *participate* in a new *public* integrity. It is a new kind of being-at-one with oneself. Citizens share in the solidarity of the political community. Rousseau for this reason emphasizes political unity: "As the association is made without reservation, the union is perfect as can be" (1978, 53). That is, legitimacy of the political association consists in the strongest type of unity—identity—between ruler and ruled, sovereign and subject, and thereby the union of all associates with each other and themselves. In the political community we "receive each member as an indivisible part of the whole" (53). Human beings regain wholeness only as citizens, parts or members of the body politic, rather than by recovering the individually possessed integrity of the presocial human animal.

The body politic thus seems to promise to reverse the corruption of the species that we inflicted upon ourselves by quitting nature. As was mentioned earlier, some of those influenced by Rousseau have dreamt of going back toward nature to recover some primeval community—convinced that civilization is corrupt. Others' imaginations project perfection not backward but forward. Perhaps by reforming, by harkening to the voice of the people, we can attain a form of social life marked by freedom, equality, and solidarity. The founding, or refounding, of a government can be a response to corruption. Some romantically inclined people are drawn to join social movements that aim at such a refounding, imagining that membership will allow them at once both to fight society's outer corruption and to heal their individual inner alienation. By surrendering themselves to what they take to be the general will, these joiners seek a home that can soothe their homelessness.

5.3b: What Corruption Looks Like: Partiality and Alienation from the General Will

After forming a republic in a social contract, the people appoints a government to be its minister. The government's job is to apply the general will—which is the law—to the people that has expressed it. Thus, two things must happen to maintain legitimacy of the political system. First, the people must express the general will to create law. Second, the government must harken to the general will, applying it (and nothing else) as the law. With this backdrop, we can see two ways that the political system in Rousseau's account could be corrupted. First, it could entail some fault in expressing the general will. Second, it could happen in disobedience by the government.

In our discussion of the Second Discourse, we argued (in Section 4.2 of this chapter) that corruption of the human animal occurs through vanity and consists in an alienation within consciousness of the human animal from himself. Exactly parallel to this, Rousseauian political corruption occurs through partiality and consists in an alienation of the body politic from the general will—that is to say, from its true self. Political corruption implies a loss of legitimacy of government, and this can be blamed on corruption of those in the government, but it can also sometimes be blamed, according to Rousseau, on corruption of the citizens. In either case, corruption occurs through partiality, which is the political analogue to vanity—improper self-love. We might observe here some individual or governmental acts that we could label as corrupt in the colloquial sense, but these are only symptoms of corruption as alienation or loss of legitimacy.

To illustrate this, let us begin with the corruption of those in government. The government (called in the following passage "the prince") should have no will apart from the will of the people (called here "the State"):

> The essential difference between these two bodies [the government and the State] is that the State exists by itself, but the government exists only through the sovereign. Thus the dominant will of the prince [the

government] is not or should not be anything except the general will or the law; his force is only the public force concentrated in him. *As soon as he wants to derive from himself some absolute and independent act, the bond tying the whole together begins to loosen.* (Rousseau 1978, 81, emphasis added)

The government is a subgroup or social body within the republic that is tasked with applying the laws expressed by the people in assembly. The government is to have no legislative authority at all; it cannot be the source of any new, independent act. The government that exercises a will of its own alienates itself from its source, the sovereign people, on which it depends.

The effect of the government having a will of its own is that the unity of the body politic is weakened. In fact, the bond may loosen to the point of dissolution. Rousseau continues the previous passage by pointing out that the terminus of this process is the passing away of the body politic:

If it finally came about that the prince [the government] had a private will more active than that of the sovereign [the people], and that he used some of the public force at his discretion to obey that private will, so that there were, so to speak, two sovereigns—the one by right, the other in fact—*at that moment the social union would vanish and the body politic would be dissolved.* (1978, 81, emphasis added)

"At that moment" of corruption, Rousseau claims here, the body politic dies. This is simple ontological corruption of the body politic. Yet this death may not be obvious. It likely looks like there are still a people and a government and things are probably proceeding as before in most observable ways. For Rousseau, the body politic dies when normative legitimacy has been lost even though it may look, to empirical observers, like it is still a walking, talking, living, functioning republic. This reminds us, again, of Dante's image of betrayers in the ninth circle of the Inferno; while their souls were sent to hell, their bodies looked quite alive on earth, controlled by demons. Partial interests have captured the government of the now dead republic. It may be a while before people notice the government is puppeteering a corpse politic.

Rousseau claims, in fact, that this decomposition of the body politic ends in the growth of a new body politic. The people of the original social union no longer exists as a people (that republic is dead). Those in the government now form a republic of their own, constituting a new people, excluding the former citizens:

When the prince no longer administers the State in accordance with the laws and usurps the sovereign power[,] then a remarkable change takes place, which is not that the government but the State shrinks. I mean that the large State dissolves and another is formed within it that is composed solely of the members of the government and is no longer anything for the rest of the people except its master and tyrant. So that the instant the government usurps sovereignty, the social compact is broken, and all the ordinary citizens, by right recovering their natural freedom, are forced but not obligated to obey. (1978, 97–98)

A corrupt government undermines its connection to its source, the sovereign will of the people, like a boy sitting on the tree, sawing off the branch he is sitting on. Extending our analogy, it is as though Rousseau says here that it is not the boy, but the tree, that dies when he falls. It is the republic, the body politic, the people that corrupts ontologically—not the government. The government lives on, now as a self-contained state. The individuals who were the citizens of the old body politic are now slaves of a new one, mastered by but not obligated to the government.

Rousseau's account of citizenly corruption runs parallel to this account of corruption starting in the government. In *On the Social Contract* he asserts, "The people is never corrupted" and "the general will is always right." But that doesn't mean that *the citizens* are never corrupted or that *what they say they want* is always right.

The general will is always right and always tends toward the public utility. But it does not follow that the people's deliberations always have the same rectitude. One always wants what is good for oneself, but one does not always see it. The people is never corrupted, but it is often fooled, and only then does it appear to want what is bad. (1978, 61)

The question is how to get the people to express the general will clearly. Given that the general will is not guaranteed by a majority vote, or even a unanimous vote, this is a challenge. The citizens while voting will be distracted by private interests, and most individuals are not capable of understanding what is good for the whole (1978, 69). Rousseau suggests that if the people vote without deliberation or communication, without forming subgroups conspiring to win, then these opposing partial interests among the citizens will "cancel each other out" (61). By something like the statistician's "law of large numbers," these mistakes by individual citizens will come out in the wash, and the general, shared interest will emerge clean and clear. "In order for the general will to be well expressed, it is therefore important that there be no partial society in the State, and that each citizen give only his own opinion" (61).

The first way in which the citizenry can be corrupted, then, is by the citizens forming partial associations within the state. Rousseau does not seem to be indicting the sorts of social movements we described in the previous section. Nor does he seem to mean civic associations like Alcoholics Anonymous, bowling leagues, Jewish Community Centers, or neighborhood book clubs—although an excessive preoccupation with such pursuits, at the expense of engaging with politics, can (as we document in the next paragraph) be a symptom of corruption. Rather, what he has in mind are voting blocs, individuals connected by "a common interest." As he makes clear in *A Discourse on Political Economy* (2009), some of these will be visible, formal groups, like the Better Business Bureau and the National Corn Growers Association. Others are "no less real for being less apparent" or less organized. For instance, consider a set of citizens who benefit from the mortgage interest tax deduction. Such subgroups distort the voice of the people, obscuring the expression of the general will: "All these tacit or formal associations . . . modify . . . *the appearance* of the public will by the influence of their own" (212, emphasis added). When people vote in blocs, the total number of real votes is smaller, and this means that the outliers in the data aren't smoothed out. There is no process by which the private interests cancel each other out, and thus the competition of private interests produces "a result that is less general," according to *On the Social Contract* (1978, 61). The general will can no longer appear as clearly. Furthermore, when any one of these subgroups becomes predominant, the result is even more dire: "There is no longer a general will, and the opinion that prevails is merely a private opinion" (61). Partiality among the citizens, especially the citizens congealing into interests, first obscures and then destroys the general will. And where there is no general will, there is no republic.

There is a second way in which the citizens can be corrupted, and that is by loss of public spirit—no longer caring about the general will or about doing their part in public business. It might happen that out of laziness or greed, the people no longer want to do their basic citizenly duties: "As soon as public service ceases to be the main business of the citizens, and they prefer to serve with their pocketbooks rather than with their persons, the State is already close to its ruin." When the citizens prefer to delegate defense and deliberation to professionals rather than do the work themselves, "by dint of laziness and money, they finally have soldiers to enslave the country and representatives to sell it" (Rousseau 1978, 101–2). It might also happen simply because people have come to enjoy private or partial pursuits more than they enjoy public service. What might appear to the outsider to be a thriving, pluralist civil society can in fact be a corrupt, decaying polity.

Notice that this second form of corruption occurs especially through representation. Those in the government are executors of the people's will, but they cannot legislate. The law must come from the people. In order for legitimacy to be maintained, the people must express the general will in regular live assemblies, not through representatives. "The lawgiver as a body is impossible to corrupt, but easy to deceive," Rousseau says. "Its representatives are difficult to deceive, but easily corrupted, and it rarely happens that they are not corrupted" (Rousseau 1985, 201). Presumably, these two facts work together to the detriment of legitimate government: Corrupt representatives exploit the gullibility of the people.

This way of putting it focuses blame on the representatives, and it raises the possibility that the general will might be better articulated by those who are unelected or who otherwise stand outside of government. But it must be remembered that the corruption of representatives can happen only consequent to a corruption of the citizenry. After all, the choice by the citizens to name representatives at all, and then not to supervise them well, must be the result of a lack of citizenly virtue. The citizens should themselves do the work of expressing the general will. Those in government are naturally "terrified" of direct democracy, and they put up obstacles and discouragements to it. The ultimate corruption of the citizenry occurs when they give in to these efforts, not caring enough to exercise their sovereignty over the government: "When they [the citizens] are greedy, cowardly, pusillanimous, fonder of repose than of freedom, they don't hold out long against the redoubled efforts of the government. So it is that with the force of resistance constantly increasing, the sovereign authority finally vanishes, and most Cities fall and perish prematurely" (Rousseau 1985, 101). The official cause of death is a corrupt government alienating itself from the source of its authority. That malady could arise only given a failure of the immune system: insufficient citizenly virtue.

Notice that Rousseau's understanding of political corruption remains first and foremost ontological. It is the rotting, falling apart, or going to pieces of the body politic. In this sense it resembles his larger discussion of human corruption in the Discourses. This ontological event—the falling apart of a republic—is also a form of alienation. It consists in the growing gap between the will of the government and the will of the people and results in the loss of legitimacy. It results from partiality, the political equivalent of vanity.

Thus we find in Rousseau a claim that colors much of contemporary discourse: the notion that corruption entails undue influence of or bias toward private—that is, partial—interests, interests of the part rather than of the whole. Obviously, this may take the form of transactional corruption or quid pro quos, but these are hardly the only forms of partiality. Rousseau describes a process of political corruption in which there is no single bogeyman. It can be caused by partiality of those in government. It can be caused, also, by the partiality of the citizens—an alienation of individuals from the communal will of their republic because they are lazy, distracted by factional interests, or preoccupied with private concerns. The root cause is a turning away from the public, or, as Joseph Reisert (2003, 187–88) argues, a manifestation of excessive *amour propre*.

5.3c: Rousseau's Anticorruption Program

Based on Rousseau's vision of legitimate government and of how it goes bad, we are now in a position to better understand Rousseau's practical suggestions to prevent corruption of a republic. This list summarizes his suggestions, especially as found in *On the Social Contract* (Rousseau 1978) and "Considerations on the Government of Poland and Its Proposed Reformation" (Rousseau 1985):

(a) *Hold frequent popular assemblies:* Frequent and regular assemblies of the citizens, with minimal campaigning or organization of subgroups, are needed to express the general will clearly, and they are needed also in order for the government to be kept in line, faithful to the general will. "All the governments of the world, once they are invested with the public force, sooner or later usurp the sovereign authority," but frequent popular assemblies can "postpone this misfortune" (Rousseau 1978, 106; 1985, 201).

(b) *Make and keep the country small:* Larger countries need more concentrated, more powerful governments, which will necessarily be more distant and more disconnected from the general will. Smaller countries can have governments that are more local and more organically aligned with the general will (Rousseau 1978, 83).

(c) *Maintain equality of conditions and do not allow luxury:* Luxury "corrupts both rich and poor, the one by possessing, the other by coveting" (Rousseau 1978, 85). Citizens need not be exactly equal, but they should be roughly equivalent in power and possessions, so that there are no concentrations of influence or of vulnerability to influence. No one should be able, apart from government office, to control others or be susceptible to being bought (75). Rousseau advocates this not for the sake of economic or social justice but for political reasons: "Do you then want to give stability to the State? Bring the extremes as close together as possible: tolerate neither opulent people nor beggars. These two conditions, naturally inseparable, are equally fatal to the common good. From the one come those who foment tyranny and from the other the tyrants. It is always between them that trafficking in public freedom takes place. The one buys it and the other sells it" (75n).

(d) *Keep the citizens busy with public affairs:* The citizen should be "constantly occupied with the fatherland" (Rousseau 1985, 185). Because the freedom and social coherence require that the citizens do the public work themselves, "freedom and repose" are "incompatible"; one has to choose (Rousseau 1985, 178). The citizens should devote the bulk of their time and emotional energy to public life. "The better constituted the State, the more public affairs dominate private ones in the minds of the citizens" (1978, 102). Otherwise, subgroups and private interests will capture public life.

(e) *Minimize commerce, trade, and the use of money:* Money produces inequality of conditions and also, because of its secrecy, invites corruption, "putting the public good and freedom on the auction block" (Rousseau 1978, 226). Rousseau wishes for an economic system that is not based on money or finance, and he even suggests that taxes be paid by service rather than in currency (230). He realizes this will make the citizens poorer economically, but politically his goal is freedom, not economic growth or prosperity. Moreover, the occupation with money, along with the inequality it produces, distorts the citizens' desires, such that "being rich" becomes "the dominant passion," which is "a major source of corruption" (Rousseau 1985, 188).

(f) *Maximize folkish unity and distinction:* In order to maintain social coherence and dedication to the general will, a people should possess distinctive folkways (like dress) and should minimize interaction with outsiders, even having "a natural revulsion to mingling with foreigners" (Rousseau 1985, 185; see also 180, 184).

(g) *Maximize patriotic passion:* "Upon opening its eyes, a child should see the fatherland, and see only it until his dying day" (Rousseau 1985, 189). To maintain a distinctive folk identity, to prevent preoccupation with private interests, and to motivate public involvement, Rousseau suggests a system to "raise patriotism and the virtues inseparable from it to their highest possible pitch" (Rousseau 1985, 184). Without such "patriotic intoxication which alone is capable of raising men above themselves . . . freedom is but an empty word and legislation but a chimera" (Rousseau 1978, 239).

For those who see Rousseau as a "back to nature" primitivist, it may be tempting to deny that Rousseau has a comprehensive anticorruption agenda, yet when taken together, these suggestions comprise a relatively coherent, and perhaps even pragmatic, political program. The key suggestions really are the last two—a xenophobic solidarity and patriotic inebriation. If political corruption and ruin of the republic are rooted in partiality and private vanity, according to Rousseau, then the key way to avoid them is to foster a passionate devotion within the society toward the republic as the expression of the unity of the people.

5.4: The Impossibility of Uncorrupt Politics

Given Rousseau's description of an uncorrupt democratic republic and of how it goes bad, those inspired by his vision may feel they have enough to sketch an anticorruption program, a plan to attain a legitimate political system, a genuine, uncorrupted republic. We are skeptical that this is the case, however. For Rousseau, given what government really is, corruption will always come with it. That is, we believe, Rousseau has described for us a government he believes to be ideal but knows to be impossible.

This is so because uncorrupt politics would require a unity—even an identity—between ruler and ruled, in order for obedience to be obligatory. But government, according to Rousseau, is just an intermediary separating these two. It is "a new body in the State, distinct from both the people and the sovereign, and intermediate between them" (Rousseau 1978, 81). By being a third thing between sovereign and subject, government by its mere existence proves that these two are really not identical. And if ruler and ruled are not the same—identically the same—then Rousseau's conditions of legitimate rule are not met.

We can see this if we look again at the justification for government in the first place. Why do we need it at all, according to Rousseau? Because justice, the law, does not apply itself. The law, to be legitimate, must be the general will. But the general will, to have force, needs to be applied to particulars. At the same time, it ceases to be general when it is applied to particulars; thus "it loses its natural rectitude when it is directed toward any individual, determinate object" (Rousseau 1978, 62). Applying the general will to particulars is what good government would consist of, but according to Rousseau that is an essentially corrupting activity because all particulars involve implications for private interests rather than the general interest. It is because dealing with particulars is corrupting that the sovereign should not rule: "It is not good . . . for the body of the people to turn its attention away from the general considerations to particular objects. Nothing is more dangerous than the influence of private interests on public affairs; and the abuse of laws by the government is a lesser evil than the corruption of the legislator [the people], which is the inevitable consequence of private considerations" (84–85). It is as though the general will cannot dirty its hands with particulars and so must hire someone else—the government—to do this work. But it is dirty work, and anyone involved in ruling must do it. The particularism, the distribution and redistribution that are the task of the professional politician are all essentially corrupt, and Rousseau wants to protect the people from it.

For example, the general will can say "Murder is wrong" or "Don't drive too fast," but the law's concrete applicability requires judgments about details, facts, and persons that always carry implications for private interests such that partiality will be a temptation. In a word, the only legitimate rule in principle is rule by the general will, and the general will cannot rule in fact because it is general. Rousseau has built an antinomy—an absurdity—into his account: Only the sovereign can justly rule, and the sovereign cannot rule.

This antinomy will seem less surprising when we think through what Rousseau claims about how government can be instituted. We already know that the general will cannot decide about particulars and that deciding about particulars is a corrupting activity. The designation of a government is just such a decision—after all, in government, particular people possess roles, duties, and prerogatives. According to the social contract, Rousseau tells us, "No one has the right to require another to do what he himself does not do. Now it is precisely this right, indispensable for giving life and motion to the body politic, that the sovereign gives to the prince by instituting government" (Rousseau 1978, 104). This right is both indispensable and impossible. The life of the body politic requires government, and instituting government involves designating some particular person or group as having a "right" to rule that violates the equality of the social contract.

Legitimate government would have to be a transparent medium, a mere executor of the general will, with no distortion. Yet Rousseau emphasizes that government "must have a separate self, a sensibility shared by its members, a force or will of its own" (Rousseau 1978, 81). Rather than being merely an organ of the whole, the government in fact is its own group, with its own will and interests—perhaps we should think of it as something of its own organism within another organism, like a parasite at best symbiotic with its host. Consequently, Rousseau says that each governmental officer possesses, in fact, three warring wills within himself—first, the general will of the body politic (which he is supposed to follow), second, the general will of the ruling party or subgroup, and third, his own private will.

A given member of Congress, for example, may be a patriot dedicated to the will of the people, but that person is also a Democrat or a Republican, a member of the House, a part of the ruling class, and also, don't forget, a person from somewhere with a family and with all manner of desires and concerns. Given the complexity of real (nontheoretical) human beings, government cannot be a transparent medium. We cannot know why legislators do what they do, but social scientists have shown that we can explain legislators' voting behavior pretty accurately if we assume that these types of partiality tend to prevail.

Rousseau is certainly aware of this. Of these three internally conflicting wills in the government official, "the general will is always the weakest," he says pessimistically: "The corporate will [of the governing group] has second place, and the private will is the first of all" (1978, 82). Thus, the actual order is "exactly opposite to the one required" by justice (1978, 82). Partiality reigns in the person, and thus in the government. The opposition between private wills and the general will—within both rulers and citizens—"is the inherent and inevitable defect which, from the very birth of the body politic, tends ceaselessly to destroy it, as age and death eventually destroy the human body" (1978, 96). Corruption as partiality, as alienation of the government from the general will, as disintegration of the body politic, is ubiquitous and inevitable.

Although Rousseau articulates an inspirational vision of legitimate government in the first part of On the Social Contract (1762), his underlying point is that legitimate government as he has defined it is impossible. This point coincides with the pessimism he shows in his later writing, in the "Considerations" as well as his earlier Second Discourse (1755). In the Second Discourse, for instance, he avers that an uncorrupt government would prove its own uselessness: "For the vices that make social institutions necessary are the same ones that make their abuse inevitable. And . . . it would be easy to prove that any government that, without being corrupted or altered, always worked exactly according to the ends of its institution, would have been instituted unnecessarily, and that a country where no one eluded the laws and abused the magistracy would need neither magistracy nor laws" (1964, 173).

After the fall from Rousseau's savage Eden, the act of constituting the body politic, united and animated by the general will, initially appears to be our chance to recover integrity—this time corporately rather than individually. And although we may never be able to recover the naïve simplicity of savage man, social unity can transform savage individual rights and powers to elevate and secure them. This uplifting and unifying work of the general will functions as a kind of grace—just as, according to Christian doctrine, human beings need grace to recover from the fall, in which recovery we may even surpass the goods of Eden. For Rousseau, this recovery, the social integrity in which we participate, lasts but for a moment, because instituting and operating government essentially entails disintegration and partiality. With the social contract, the body politic is pregnant with the general will, but she always dies in childbirth and the government she delivers is always illegitimate.

This is how Rousseau presents the problem in "Considerations on the Government of Poland and on Its Proposed Reformation" (written in 1772):

> Granted that it is easy to make better laws. It is impossible to make laws which men's passions do not abuse, as they have abused earlier ones. To anticipate and to weigh all these future abuses is something which perhaps even the most consummate Statesman may find it impossible to do. Putting the law above man is a problem in politics which I liken to that of squaring the circle in geometry. Solve this problem satisfactorily, and the government based on this solution will be good and free of abuses. But until then, you may be sure that wherever you believe you have made laws rule, it will be men who will be ruling. (1985, 179)

Squaring the circle is an ancient math problem in which one tries to find a square of equal area to that of a given circle. Occasionally hopes have arisen for a solution, only to be repeatedly disappointed. Though not proven impossible to solve until a century after Rousseau's death, "squaring the circle" was a cliché for a futile task, akin to our saying about "trying to fit a square peg into a round hole." In this case, Rousseau is claiming that one cannot get legitimacy and rulers to occupy the same space (see also the Letter to Mirabeau, 1997, 270). Glancing back to the straightforward mathematical directive early in *On the Social Contract*, "uncorrupt government" is now seen as a contradiction in terms, a problem with no solution.

When the parts begin to follow their own natural forces, the whole can no longer maintain its unity. Things fall apart—it's just what things do. Here Rousseau echoes premodern metaphysics, according to which every composite body—everything sublunary—eventually comes to pieces. Disintegration—corruption—is an inevitable, natural process. Some commentators have linked Rousseau's discussion to the common medieval and early modern framing of corruption as a disease (e.g., Friedrich 1972; Rothstein and Varraich 2017, 35). Yet the disease metaphor carries with it, at least for contemporary readers, the implication that corruption can be "treated" and maybe even "cured." Rousseau offers his readers no such palliatives.

The model Rousseau has provided—based on the infallibility of the general will and the simple identity between ruler and ruled—is an idealization that is impossible of realization. Because men (a government), and not laws (the general will), always rule, uncorrupted politics is impossible. An uncorrupted body politic, being incapable of realization, is, perhaps, a myth (1978, 69–70) or political religion (1978, 124–32) of the type Rousseau says is necessary to the founding of stable governments. Or one might say that it is just Rousseau's ideal, a powerful rhetorical construct, and that a claim such as this can be deployed as a weapon against the status quo, but one might doubt whether it provides practical guidance on how to produce something better.

5.5: Conclusion

One rather simplified account of the difference between Montesquieu and Rousseau might play upon contemporary distinctions between pluralism and populism. There is some logic to this, if one merely considers the ends of these two theories: Montesquieu's account presumes a plurality of acceptable political regimes, and a plurality of types of corruption that plague such regimes. If one seeks to ameliorate corruption, one must take into account the preexisting features of government and the ways in which they give rise to corrupt behaviors. Because Rousseau supposes a social unity that precedes government—and therefore limits the possible types of legitimate government far more radically than is the case for Montesquieu—corruption has a singular form and the instances of it do not vary in politically meaningful ways.

One might place Rousseau's exaltation of the people united within Oakeshott's politics of faith, whereas Montesquieu's pluralistic imperfectionism belongs to the politics of skepticism. This is arguably the way in which contemporary pluralists and populists (regardless of where they fall on a contemporary Left/Right spectrum) might conceptualize the nature of the disagreements about corruption here. To do this, however, would require that one understand Rousseau to be a believer in the model or myth he articulates. As we have argued here, we doubt that this is an adequate characterization of Rousseau. He projects a vision of an uncorrupted, truly legitimate republic; he sets it up as a standard, however impossible, presumably with the hope that we might endeavor to do better or worse in light of this standard. At the same time, it has generally been Rousseau's ideal, and not his suggestion that it is impossible, that has been influential politically.

Rousseau presents an argument about corruption that captures a sort of human longing, an emotional expression of corruption that is not satisfied in the Montesquieuian account. Rather than becoming skeptical of this faith, when realizing the perennial failure of the world to implement his ideals, many following Rousseau fall into the dejection possible only for those still enraptured by faith. While Montesquieu helps us understand discourses of corruption within regimes and why it might behoove us to focus on institutional checks and balances, Rousseau helps us understand why so much of our corruption discourse is, instead, tinged with the populist pendulum swing between a hopeful politics of faith and the bitter politics of despair that inevitably follows upon its heels.

This is a bleak conclusion, and it is one that requires one to set aside the sort of romantic vision of a politics of faith that some have taken from Montesquieu. Or to put matters more bluntly, it is easy to get swept up in a political movement to fight corruption. It is harder to imagine an exciting movement centered around reform pluralism, around the sort of tinkering that Montesquieu recommends. As we see in the next chapter, the most serious American anticorruption movement sought to blend these approaches, with decidedly mixed results.

6

American Progressive Corruption Talk

Are the people honest? Are the people better than Tammany?
Are they better than the merchant and the politician? Isn't
our corrupt government, after all, representative? . . . No,
the contemned methods of our despised politics are the
mast methods of our braggart business, and the corruption
that shocks us in public affairs we practice ourselves in our
private concerns.

—LINCOLN STEFFENS, *THE SHAME OF THE CITIES*

As the previous chapters of this book suggest, accounts of corruption
are often theories about political constitutions, their foundings, and
their basic principles or ideals. In particular, one can read our discussion of Montesquieu and Rousseau in Chapters 4 and 5 as being about the
establishment of first principles, the spirit that animates different political
orders. Corruption is a derivative concept pointing back to what the system
is supposed to be, its principles or ideals, often expressed in stories of founding or origin. Yet corruption is also a subject of concern in regimes that have
traveled far from their founding and for those less reverent in the face of historical origins or past principles. In such a context, is there room to talk about
corruption without also calling for a full refounding, and for an entirely new
constitution or new ideals and principles? The Progressive Era in the United
States, the period from roughly the late 1890s to the late 1910s, serves as a
starting point for a new way of talking about corruption in American discourse. We suggest that it sought, perhaps unsuccessfully, to navigate between
the Mender and Purifier types we have presented in the prior chapters, and
to use corruption talk as a way to motivate changes to the fundamental principles of the system but to do so progressively, stepwise, that is, without a
revolution or sudden overhaul. Although the Progressive reforms had decidedly mixed results, the corruption rhetoric they employed has broadly shaped
how Americans talk about corruption since then.

In this chapter we seek to establish four claims about American corruption talk during the Progressive Era and beyond. First, rhetoric during the

Progressive Era regarding corruption represented a break with American discussions of corruption during the previous century. While corruption in eighteenth- and nineteenth-century America was framed as a manifestation of foreign influences in American politics—as an imposition of the corrupt mores of aristocratic European society into American republican governance—Progressives viewed corruption as it occurs in America as a distinctly American problem, rooted in the flaws of the founding.

Second, Progressive rhetoric surrounding corruption was more expansive and less precise than much of the philosophical discussion outlined in the previous chapters. As others have pointed out, less intellectual Progressive activists—in particular, the muckraking journalists of the early 1900s—viewed a wide array of entirely traditional and legal acts and arrangements as manifestations of corruption.

Third, the more intellectual Progressive accounts of corruption represent an attempted synthesis of our two styles of corruption talk. The Progressives viewed corruption, in a broadly Rousseauian way, as a moral decay that took place in the citizens as well as their officials and as an alienation of government from the public or the people. Unlike Rousseau's pessimism that the species as well as society has passed its prime, they viewed the future as an open-ended opportunity for an undefined progress or social evolution—if the people and the experts in power are properly aligned toward the public interest. At the same time, Progressives prescribed a set of procedural reforms or adjustments as a remedy for corruption. These were not quite, as Montesquieu would have it, a return to foundational principles that animate the system; nor were they, as Montesquieu would also have it, attempts to dilute power by distributing it. But the Progressive reforms were still attempts to mend, being technical fixes designed to serve as a moderate (nonradical) political remedy. Progressives did not see corruption as something that inevitably befalls humans, nor did they see radical restructuring as a practical goal. They also put great hopes both in empowering uncorrupted expertise and in having an uncorrupted people or public.

And fourth, this Progressive synthesis was ultimately deemed unsatisfactory by the erstwhile Progressive reformers themselves. Although the more philosophical Progressives ultimately despaired of their efforts to act upon this synthesis, the Progressive way of leveraging corruption rhetoric nonetheless has endured in American politics, creating a scolding rhetorical tradition that is often unmoored from the compromising and piecemeal practical tasks of governmental reform. Also enduring in American political rhetoric from Progressive Era corruption talk is the pointing to corruption as the thing to blame when one's hopes for democracy or scientific administration get thwarted—when the ballot box or expert policies frustrate rather than confirm one's expectations.

We begin here by outlining some of the ways in which American corruption talk was framed in the eighteenth and nineteenth centuries. We then turn to two accounts of Progressive corruption talk. We briefly summarize the Progressive project, with particular attention to the ways in which the concept of corruption was used not only by the more philosophically inclined but also by journalists, politicians, and even novelists to describe the American political and social condition at the end of the nineteenth century. This discussion serves as context for establishing the milieu of more theoretical accounts of corruption. Following this context-setting, we then summarize the role that corruption plays in the theories of four of the most consequential Progressive theorists—Edward A. Ross, Herbert Croly, Walter Weyl, and the early Walter Lippmann. After this discussion, we explore the tensions within this Progressive account, paying particular attention to the later writings of Lippmann. Finally, we comment, as a means of setting up the subsequent more empirical and contemporary chapters, on the ways in which we see the Progressive project as the origin of twentieth- and twenty-first-century American confusions about what corruption is.

6.1: Corruption Talk in Eighteenth- and Nineteenth-Century America

As Zephyr Teachout (2014, 18) notes, early American discourse about corruption largely had to do with the threat posed by corrupt foreign powers. The French were seen as being corrupt because of the prerevolutionary French aristocracy's pursuit of luxury, while the British were seen as being an example of what a corrupt Republic looks like—British institutions themselves were generally admired, but the civic virtue of the British subjects had declined, and the system was not republican or free enough, creating a nation whose actions did not reflect its foundational principles. In both accounts, we see an association of corruption with otherness—with an improper insertion into our debates of the values of those who did not subscribe to the American republican project. This was not the xenophobic concern with foreigners that one sees in looser descriptions of corruption in the Progressive Era and later, but it does involve two suspicions. In a narrow sense, foreign governments might corrupt American officeholders into treasonous behavior by means of appealing to their self-interest. In a broader sense, those who do not subscribe to, were not accustomed to, or are not governed by the United States' founding principles cannot be expected to play a suitably public-spirited role in the creation of the American government. America was trying something new, and European culture and habits threatened that.

The combating of corruption was initially seen mostly as a matter of constitutional design. This meant early American discussions about corruption fit into the basic Montesquieuian framework. In the *Federalist Papers*, for instance, corruption in Britain tends to be framed as a falling away in spirit from constitutional principles:

> This peculiar felicity of situation [the fact that England is an island nation and thus protected from the problems of other European nations] has, in a great degree, contributed to preserve the liberty which that country to this day enjoys, in spite of the prevalent venality and corruption. (Publius 1961, *Federalist #8*)

Likewise, *Federalist #55* addresses the question of whether "foreign gold" can corrupt. Here, corruption tends to be framed as the pursuit of individual self-interest (often in the service of alliance with a foreign power) or of factional advantage against the good of the whole; the goal in several of the *Federalist Papers* (Publius 1961, Federalist #10, 22, 55, 56, 63) is to explain why a large and complex republic will mitigate such problems. A legislature will have within it corrupt individuals, but the size of the legislature may ensure that these individuals will not predominate. A bicameral system will ensure that even if corrupt individuals prevail in one they will not prevail in the other, and even if they prevail in one branch of government they will not prevail in the other. A nation of thirteen states will be sufficiently large that one state, or one group of states, will not have the power to corrupt the others.

The *Federalist Papers* do not provide lengthy consideration of how regimes other than republics might be corrupted, but corruption is treated as an inevitable threat in republics, particularly in unmixed ones. Political parties and factions are inevitable within republics, and they pose a threat insofar as they act upon particular or factional interests. It might be too much to say that partisanship or party spirit is by definition corrupt (although Joseph Ellis [2000, 186] notes that this was a common conception at the time), but the establishment of parties does tend to lead to corruption both of individuals and of institutional structures. The solution to this, as *Federalist #10* points out, is to create overlapping forms of government, or to establish a mixed rather than pure form of republicanism, so as to slow corruption. One cannot expect the constitutional structure to prevent all corrupt behavior of democratically elected politicians, but it can make successful corrupt behavior harder and can help encourage the virtuous and uncorrupt to accept political office. Furthermore, corruption can be discouraged through transparency. *Federalist #68* links corruption to a range of clandestine behaviors, such as "cabal and intrigue." The virtue of a republic—a virtue which would seem to distinguish republican government from other forms—is that the actions of politicians are subject to scrutiny and public evaluation.

These constitutional design issues were also at play in the Hamiltonian-Jeffersonian debate, where Hamilton is closer to Montesquieu and Jefferson is closer to Rousseau. Hamilton, of course, favors a commercial republic, and we are reminded of Montesquieu's line that commerce corrupts mores in a good way by softening them. Jefferson, of course, was on board with the idea of Montesquieu-style checks on power, and he personally was quite cosmopolitan. Yet, closer to Rousseau, he suggests a sentimental faith in an uncorrupted, noncommercial people. It is one thing to establish a structure of overlapping institutions to check each other, but there are also matters of regional balance to be considered; these are not just matters of geographic representation but matters regarding the kind of people who reside in different regions of the country. In *Notes on the State of Virginia* (Query XIX), Thomas Jefferson ([1780] 1998) argues that

> those who labour in the earth are the chosen people of God, if ever he had a chosen people, whose breasts he has made his peculiar deposit for substantial and genuine virtue. It is the focus in which he keeps alive that sacred fire, which otherwise might escape from the face of the earth. Corruption of morals in the mass of cultivators is a phaenomenon of which no age nor nation has furnished an example. It is the mark set on those, who not looking up to heaven, to their own soil and industry, as does the husbandman, for their subsistence, depend for it on casualties and caprice of customers. Dependance begets subservience and venality, suffocates the germ of virtue, and prepares fit tools for the designs of ambition.

Here, as Eric MacGilvray (2011, 107) points out, Jefferson is making two claims. He is making a sectional claim that the planter class is morally virtuous and less susceptible to foreign influence than the mercantile class. Yet it is not merely foreign influence that is of concern here; rather, interaction with and economic dependence upon others will lead people to stray from the national interest and from republican virtue.

Even after the constitutional debates had ended, concerns about corruption lingered. In John R. Howe's (1967) recounting of conflicts during the 1790s over how best to organize postrevolutionary America, the real concern that the American republic would fail—a concern rooted in the common argument in classical and modern political thought that republics inevitably tended to become corrupt—resulted in a fear that any manifestation of self-interested behavior, however mild, was a sign that the republic itself was in danger. Howe quotes Theophilus Parsons, a Massachusetts judge and Federalist ally of James Madison and John Hancock, arguing as follows:

> The morals of all people, in all ages, have been shockingly corrupt-ed. . . . Shall we alone boast an exemption from the general fate of mankind? Are our private and political virtues to be transmitted un-tainted from generation to generation, through a course of ages?[1]

Parsons here expresses a pessimism about moral corruption of the populace, and then turns toward the importance of institutional design as discourag-ing corruption by guiding people toward virtuous behavior, or at least en-suring that private interests counter each other so as to ensure that no indi-vidual or factional interest dominates. Howe goes on to note, however, that this concern was rooted both in a lack of confidence that American institu-tions would survive, and in the sense that the threat posed to them was best understood by looking at the corrupt mores of European regimes. Should America fail, it would fail because of its involvement in the intrigues of the French and the British, because of the failure of institutional arrangements to block the abuse of power, or because of American emulation of the deca-dent customs of those countries.

J. G. A. Pocock (1975, 526) argues that during the nineteenth century ar-guments about corruption largely disappeared from American political thought—in part because the era of constitutional design had passed but also because discussions of corruption tend also to involve discussions of politi-cal virtue, and there was perhaps less intense concern about political virtue during that era. This is a big claim, and as we see in our discussion of presi-dential rhetoric, it is not entirely accurate. In American politics, Andrew Jackson and his successors spoke frequently of economic corruption, and northerners and southerners alike tended to brand their opponents as being morally corrupt. There are also scattered references in nineteenth-century literature to corruption as a perennial political problem in republics; witness, for instance, James Fenimore Cooper's ([1838] 1981) oft-quoted assertion in *The American Democrat* that "contact with the affairs of state is one of the most corrupting of the influences to which men are exposed."

Yet Pocock seems to us to be correct that corruption played less of a role during this time given the growing security that the American national proj-ect would not be co-opted by foreign powers and the growing sense that the American Constitution was relatively safe from a full-scale reevaluation. As John Wallis (2006) asserts, by the mid-nineteenth century Americans ap-pear to have begun to trust their government, and thus references to corrup-tion tended to be less political in nature; rather, they tended to be about drunk-enness, sexual peccadillos, or moral failings rather than about matters related to the holding of public office. Remarkably, Wallis claims, "corruption" was not even a term typically used to characterize slavery. (It should be noted that Frederick Douglass does use the term in this way. In his *Narrative of the Life of Frederick Douglass* [first published in 1845], he discusses slavery as corrupting the Christianity of the South, and in his response to the *Dred Scott* decision he comments, "Step by step, we have seen the slave power advancing, poisoning, corrupting, and perverting the institutions of the country." Likewise, he explains the practice of slavery as "corrupting to the morals" of both enslaving and enslaved persons in *My Bondage and My Freedom* [first published in 1855], where he calls slavery a "monster of corruption.")

Arguably the most comprehensive discussion of corruption in American during the nineteenth century was that of Alexis de Tocqueville who, in *Democracy in America* ([1848] 1969, 220–21) sought not to question or amend foundational principles but to describe their effects on American political culture. Tocqueville there presents a relatively standard modern-era European view of corruption: Democratic rulers tend to be of lower character than aristocratic ones, and therefore are easier to corrupt. The size of the American republic and the complicated mixed regime, however, limit the spread of corruption. The true danger of corruption lies in the example that is set: Corruption can easily become contagious.

Tocqueville (1969, 221) goes on to make two claims that are specific to the American circumstances of the 1800s. First, he argues that the presumption of equality that characterizes American democracy makes the perception of corruption widespread; because citizens are equal, they assume that those who succeeded in political roles have done so because of corruption, not because they have been better or more virtuous than other citizens. This presumption of equality exists in all democracies, but the lack of a hereditary aristocracy makes it particularly noteworthy in America.

Second (Tocqueville 1969, 233–35), however, the lack of a history of class in the aristocratic sense and the weakness of class conflict in the United States also have created a politics that is largely bereft of enduring ideological elements. This all leads Tocqueville to suggest that American politicians are of inferior quality to the politicians of other countries, which means that they are prone to become corrupt, but their corruption is more limited in scope. Their corrupt actions are undertaken in an incompetent fashion, and their corruption is aimed at short-term individual profit, not at creating an enduring advantage for a durable political faction: "In this way it may come about that under aristocratic governments public men do evil without intending it, and in democracies they bring about good results of which they have never thought" (Tocqueville 1969, 235).

If Tocqueville and Pocock are correct, then, Americans may well have felt during the early 1800s that the sort of corruption that preoccupied the founding generation was no longer a pressing concern. With foreign intrigue no longer a principal fear, corruption may have come to be seen as an expected and manageable problem. The proper constitutional safeguards would ensure that while we might still suspect politicians of having corrupt motives, their corruption was unlikely to dramatically alter the constitutional structure or determine the issues at stake in our larger political conflicts.

6.2: The Progressive Redefinition of Corruption?

The Progressive Era thus arrives at a historical moment where concerns about corruption could be framed in a different manner than had been the case during the eighteenth and nineteenth centuries. The conventional understanding, as explained in contemporary discussions such as those by Rosenblum (2008), Achen and Bartels (2016, 67–68), Howell and Moe (2016, 187), and Sitaraman (2017, chap. 3), is that the Progressives began with a relatively accurate assessment of corruption within particular industries or on the part of particular politicians, but expanded this into a system-wide critique. This critique identified corruption as effectively synonymous with interest group politics, and expanded from there, convinced that interest group politics were, in effect, encouraged by the structure of American institutions and business culture. Progressives sought to critique and reform flaws in the American founding, but they sought to do so not through revolt but in a stepwise, gradual fashion. Their approach was therefore an unstable mixture between a rhetoric about purification and a set of proposed reforms that appeared closer to Montesquieu-style mending.

In order for us to understand the ways in which corruption was redefined by Progressive Era theorists, four pieces of context are necessary: (a) an account of the journalistic inquiries into corruption at the time, (b) an account of the public "mood" regarding corruption at the time, (c) an account of the political problems confronted by Progressives and their proposed reforms, and (d) an account of how Progressive intellectuals deploy corruption talk. We take these up in turn here, and then briefly summarize the ways in which they reveal a larger Progressive project. It should be noted that these four pieces of context loosely parallel (although not in the same order) the four strands of contemporary corruption talk that we consider in Chapters 7 through 10 and that we argue are indebted, for better or worse, to Progressive Era political rhetoric about corruption.

6.2a: Journalistic Context: The Muckrakers

American national politics during the late nineteenth century was characterized by many easily documentable instances of officeholder corruption.

The presidency of Ulysses S. Grant, for instance, was hobbled by rampant corruption (see Chernow 2017, chaps. 31–32), and the 1880s were punctuated by patronage scandals, by the assassination of newly elected president James A. Garfield by a disgruntled patronage seeker, and ultimately by the Pendleton Act and other steps taken to reform what were widely seen as corrupt practices in allocating federal jobs. Yet American journalists in the late nineteenth and early twentieth centuries took aim not at corruption at the national level but at documenting the corruption of American cities. "Muckrakers" such as Josiah Flynt and Lincoln Steffens undertook an expansive, and often sensationalistic, exploration of corrupt ties between public and private interests. The muckrakers did not fancy themselves objective researchers. Their writings can be seen as a market-driven effort to draw attention to corruption in areas where it had not been documented before, as a test of commonly held assumptions about where and why corruption flourished, sometimes as ideological pot-stirring, and ultimately as a partial reorientation of Americans' beliefs about what corruption is.

Louis Filler's (1976) account of the muckrakers, *Crusaders for American Liberalism* (originally published in 1939), emphasizes the relationship between muckraking and new forms of American media. The muckrakers, in his account, were not an organized movement, but were interested in distinguishing themselves as pioneers of a new genre of American journalism—one which uncovered sensational stories about routine and immediate aspects of American life. A good muckraking book or article combined personal experience with emerging patterns of urban life, a moralistic concern about social conditions and inequalities, at least implicit agitation for social or government action, and a sympathy for the downtrodden. Because there was no significant national media, Americans knew little about governance in cities other than their own. By comparing the activities of machine politicians in cities such as St. Louis, Philadelphia, and Chicago, the more enterprising muckraking journalists such as Steffens sought to demonstrate that political corruption was far more pervasive than the average citizen might assume.

To write a good exposé of municipal corruption did not require a deep understanding of what corruption is or what appropriate norms of government are; as a result, Filler characterizes the muckrakers as "sentimentalists of democracy." An anecdotal account of the cozy relationship between a business titan and a bought politician was far more effective at stirring up outrage than any theoretical argument. In addition, such efforts were effective in selling newspapers. Some of the patterns we have noted in nineteenth-century corruption accounts—a tendency of native-born citizens to blame foreigners, for rural citizens to blame big cities, or for urban dwellers to blame rural politicians—are present in the muckrakers' work. Muckrakers tended to focus their attention on particular industries (for instance, on the ties between railroad interests and the politicians of cities dependent on the railroads) and to adopt terminology (such as "graft") previously used in describing organized crime. In this regard, they operated largely outside of partisan politics. Theirs was a critique of a certain form of democracy. Lawrence Lessig (2012, 161) and Nancy Rosenblum (2008), for instance, recount Lincoln Steffens's query "Isn't our corrupt government, after all, democratic?" and then go on to explore the implications: Doesn't choosing self-interested politicians mean that politicians will be indebted to those who got them there, whether they are business supporters, the media, organized interests, or voters? And doesn't this mean that the self-interest common in the pursuit of public office is a sort of corruption? In this framework, the call for "clean government" was a call not just for less partisan government but for a different form of democracy altogether—one that we would be unlikely to achieve through piecemeal or technical adjustments to our current regime.

A widespread view of the muckrakers, then and now, has been that they sought to characterize politics itself as being corrupt. John Chamberlain (1932, 132) notes that Steffens and W. A. White (1910) did draw attention to the lack of constitutional provision for political parties, or for other actors who informally dominated politics at the time. In "The Treason of the Senate," David Graham Phillips (1906), likewise, defined political corruption as the effort to simultaneously serve two masters—the people and the "interests." This situation was not what the Founders intended, but it resulted from our imperfect founding.

The muckrakers' effort to provide an expansive understanding of corruption undermined some commonly held beliefs about the origins of corruption. One argument that emerges from Steffens's studies of American cities, for instance, is that corruption is not a result of foreign interests or values. Philadelphia, a city with, at the time, a greater percentage of native-born residents than any other major American city, was just as corrupt as cities controlled by immigrants (Steffens 1957, 135). Steffens did not provide a direct theoretical account of corruption, although he did claim in his study of St. Louis that corruption is a dereliction of citizens' responsibility to rule; when the people refuse to govern themselves, to take a proper interest in politics, they implicitly accept self-interested, corrupt rulers (69). (It is worth noting that this is close to a point that Rousseau makes, and which we discussed in Chapter 5: that representative government—government through representatives rather than rule by the common will expressed by the people directly—is essentially corrupt.) In many of his articles, Steffens sought to show that there was little difference between public corruption and private corruption, that compromises we make in our own private lives are connected to the corrupt behavior we observe among the politicians we elect. He wanted rule by the people but was also concerned about corruption of the people.

We might, then, extract some lessons about how the muckrakers defined and explained corruption. Yet, the primary relevance of the muckrakers to our project lies elsewhere. Namely, their popularity sets the stage for Progressives to use corruption as a rallying cry. Arguments about corruption were popular, in the same way that contemporary investigative journalism can be popular. This could lead to abuses—to a general hostility toward governing institutions or successful entrepreneurs, for instance. As Richard Hofstadter (1955, 187) notes, most of the people who owned the magazines that published muckraking work were not as concerned with accuracy as they were with profit. This led some of the more serious muckraking journalists, such as Ida Tarbell, to disown the label, but it also led to flare-ups of outrage and then to many industry-specific reforms—for instance, to changes in the regulation of the meatpacking industry. The muckrakers also created a template that has been said to have inspired later social scientists such as David Riesman and C. Wright Mills (Forcey 1961, 309).

In sum, the muckrakers popularized a rather unspecific, sensational, and moralistic way of talking about corruption, and they sought to describe corruption not for political gain but usually out of both sincere political beliefs and the desire to establish themselves—that is, to make a profit and build a career. The muckrakers' attack on corruption was tied to an agenda of political, economic, and social proposals for change, and this was an agenda that was not tied to any one political party or politician, yet neither was it free of the interests and ambitions they lambasted. And they did this with a purist rhetoric and a populist flair that the Progressives would appropriate and build on.

6.2b: Corruption and American Literature

As market-driven as the muckrakers' discussions of corruption may have been, however, they did not come from nowhere. They came from preexisting conditions and preestablished worries. Even before the muckrakers appeared on the scene, there were concerns that the arts, and American culture more generally, were being corrupted by oligarchic politics, and that there was a need for novelists, artists, and other defenders of American culture to speak out against this corruption. This sentiment is perhaps best described in Henry George's *Progress and Poverty*, a quasi-Marxist critique of American economic decline that was first published in 1879. George argued that American civilization was on an almost irreversible path toward corruption. George argued that America was undergoing a form of republican corruption, in that the "worst" individuals had been given power (1949, 532–40). In other forms of government, corrupt leaders might be "fenced off" from the public, but in a democracy they mix with them, corrupting the citizens. Once citizens had seen that individual corruption can lead to political gain, they would lose faith in politics entirely, and there could be no "resurrection" of public faith. George forecast that over the next few decades, public spirit, patriotism, and respect for law would be lost; "in the festering mass will be generated volcanic forces," he prophesied, but the rulers brought to power will be no better than those they replace. "Carnivals of brute force" would alternate with "the lethargy of a declining civilization." George purported to see this in the decline of Protestantism, in the rise of Mormonism and "even grosser 'isms,'" and, most notably in the decline in the quality of American literature and the unwillingness of American artists and writers to acknowledge the corruption that was taking place.

George's take on American decline may strike some readers as overwrought, but *Progress and Poverty* was one of the best-selling books of the 1890s and became a foundational text for the Progressive movement (see Frederick 1976). As a popular treatment of the effects of inequality, one might analogize it to Thomas Piketty's *Capital in the Twenty-First Century* (2013), although George's book was much more widely read. George's emphasis on the role of writers and artists was followed by an outpouring of social criticism by American novelists such as Frank Norris, Theodore Dreiser, Jack London, and, slightly later, Sinclair Lewis and John Dos Passos. Many of these novelists were trained as journalists and used some of the same techniques as the muckrakers to dramatize the corruption of American urban life (see Hofstadter 1955, 199). Some writers of the era, such as Upton Sinclair, did the reverse, using literary techniques to write nonfiction. The novels that were most directly about corruption, such as Norris's *McTeague* (1899), *The Octopus* (1901) and *The Pit* (1903), and Dreiser's *The Financier* (1912) and *An American Tragedy* (1925) portray corrupt ties between businessmen and politicians. While the villains of these novels are corrupt, the protagonists are often decent and simple people who have to come to the cities, and corruption is presented as a danger for anyone.

In *Farewell to Reform* (1932, 86, 107), John Chamberlain notes the similarities between novelists of the era and muckrakers, but he emphasizes as well the element of tragedy that appeared in these works. The protagonists of Norris's novels, he argues, are caught in "a tragic economic situation" where individual lives are "a cruel, grim joke." They have the misfortune of living at a time of rapid economic change and cultural disruption. There is little that they can do to combat the corruption that they see; at best they can avoid being swept up in it. Chamberlain notes, as well, the implicit appeal to rural simplicity, describing the novels of Booth Tarkington as efforts to emphasize rural and small-town values as an antidote to urban corruption.

There are three main points of distinction between the role of the novelists and that of the muckrakers. First, the classic novels of the era frame corruption in a more explicitly moral fashion than do the journalistic accounts. That is, corruption is a perennial temptation, but it is an individual failing, not an inevitability, and not exclusively a problem of politics. Second, the novelists' account of corruption is less nuanced and more nostalgic than that of the muckrakers. While journalists like Steffens and Tarbell were careful to directly explore the urban/rural distinctions or the implications of linking corruption to immigrants or foreign values, the novels of this era did not, perhaps because of their medium, do this directly, although they often did feature a clash between people from what appeared to be more characteristically nineteenth-century American milieus confronting urban life. The naïve but well-meaning rural or small-town characters play a role akin to Rousseau's prepolitical man. And third, while these novelists may well have sought to profit from their sensational and sentimental fiction, subsequent discussions of their approach to corruption emphasize their role as shapers and interpreters of American cultural values of the time.

6.2c: *The Progressive Political Project*

It is possible to trace much of the practical political reform agenda of the Progressives back to Henry George. George's argument, writes Stanley Caine (1974, 11–34), fused the argument of the Social Gospel movement about inequality with a call for incremental government reform. As Progressives developed their agenda during the 1890s, the defining characteristic of their efforts was the belief that changes in the mechanisms of democratic government could yield more just policy outcomes. This required, however, that democratic citizens be educated in how to take their responsibilities more seriously—how to exercise their political power as Progressives thought responsible. The major Progressive reforms thus had the potential to substantially change the direction of public policy, but the Progressives were not always clear about what a more democratic sort of public policy would look like.

There are many different ways to categorize Progressive political reforms. Rosenblum (2008, 189–202) divides the chronology of reform efforts into four stages: civil service reforms, which mostly involved reducing the number of patronage positions and elected positions in government (notice that for the Progressives, these two belong together as corrupt); changes to municipal governance, such as the establishment of nonpartisan or off-cycle elections; the establishment of primary elections; and direct democracy reforms such as the initiative, referendum, and recall. Notice the tension between two goals of Progressive reforms. They wanted more power to the people but also they wanted decisions to be made in a nonpolitical way by experts or science. The Progressives generally did not see the tension here, although it explains why many of their direct democracy reforms ended up yielding results that disappointed them.

Rosenblum's list accommodates much of the institutional reform agenda but does not include the economic reform agenda. Robert La Follette, the architect of the Progressive movement in Wisconsin, presented a broader view of the Progressive agenda, stressing the "shift from pure individualism to social control," which included expansion of government power to regulate business practices, increased trust in popular majorities, and an expansion of government functions to meet social needs (Nye 1951, 199–200). La Follette's vision emphasized the importance of insulating the administration of policies from the process of creating them. This expansive agenda included all of the mechanisms cited by Rosenblum, but it framed them as an economic or social tool as much as a political one.

Another way to go about explaining the Progressive political agenda is to focus not so much on what was done, but on shared principles. Thomas McCraw (1974, 181–201) lists nine areas of agreement among Progressives: (1) industrialization has undermined shared values; (2) the task of reform is urgent; (3) morals need to be improved, and Protestantism is the best model for this; (4) the American political situation requires novel political remedies; (5) government should be more *directly* democratic (less republican or representative); (6) reform should follow scientific principles; (7) the population should become more homogeneous; (8) "certain abstractions—'the trusts,' 'the Negro,' 'the public interest'—closely resembled reality"; and (9) the uncertainties of life must be mitigated through professionalization, insurance, and other administrative remedies. McCraw's listing encompasses a variety of clearly identifiable reforms, but it also includes beliefs about how social life should be changed and how the political project assumed a set of moral beliefs that underpinned Progressive rhetoric in other spheres of public life also. Hofstadter (1955, 145–151) also notes the relationship between Progressive politicians and the rising middle class, the growing distance between professionals and the business elites, and the rise of professional norms in journalism, the academy, and social service occupations. It is easy to frame some of the moralizing aspects of Progressivism—such as the establishment of service providers like Hull House and the nascent Prohibition movement—as middle-class responses to immigration and as backlash against immigrants' social values and habits. Yet most of the political reforms were rooted in more theoretical understandings of the proper role of government.

Many of the ideas of reformers were not new; the direct primary, for instance, was framed as a response to the corruption of party bosses, but some political scientists and historians at the time (e.g., Dallinger 1897; Merriam 1908) and since (Reynolds 2006) have noted that things that looked like primary elections had in fact developed gradually over the course of the nineteenth century, and many political party leaders supported them even though they were not sympathetic to the rest of the Progressive agenda. The same can be said for the direct democracy proposals.

There were also important distinctions between types of Progressives. Eastern urban Progressives, such as Robert Luce and Butler Ames in Massachusetts or Tom Johnson in Cleveland, initially focused their attention on municipal reform and avoided class-based or religious rhetoric (Abrams 1964; Warner 1964). Midwestern Progressives, on the other hand, often drew greater inspiration from the Populist movement and inequalities between farmers and the business elites who controlled commodity grading and pricing. While these two groups found common cause in their advocacy for direct democracy and other such political reforms, they differed in the particular policy outcomes they believed would follow such reforms. Western Progressives ultimately took more of an interest in developing Progressivism as a national movement (Wiebe 1967, 198–99), and Easterners did not know what to make of phenomena such as the development of the Nonpartisan League in Minnesota and North Dakota (Lansing 2015, chap. 5).

Along with the moralizing element of the Progressive movement came a suspicion of politicians' sincerity in adopting the Progressive agenda. It was pragmatic politics for elected politicians to use public sentiment in their own campaigns, so it was natural for Progressives to regard these politicians' rhetoric with caution. At the presidential level, this meant that Theodore Roosevelt, despite his emphasis on corruption throughout his presidency, may have had greater success in making the case for these reforms after he had left office and sought to return as an outsider. And since most Progressives, especially in the Midwest, were Republicans, this made Progressives even more suspicious of Woodrow Wilson's enthusiasm for Progressivism (Link 1954, 79–80; Levy 1985, 237). Some Progressives endorsed the Nonpartisan League's strategy of recruiting political neophytes to run for office (see Morlan 1955), on the grounds that they had no existing stake in the political system—but this approach may well have only postponed disillusionment, since these people, of course, became politicians once they had won office. If the assumption is that politics is inherently corrupt, then replacing current politicians with new ones is not a promising fix.

The unifying thread to all of these efforts was corruption. Within this focus on political corruption, different types of Progressives modified their explanation of who was corrupt, or of what a less corrupt polity would look like. Where there was agreement on first steps, as was the case for the direct primary or the initiative and referendum, Progressive reforms were highly successful. The direct primary, for instance, was adopted in all but three states by the early 1920s. As V. O. Key (1956, 92) was to note decades later, advocacy for the direct primary took on "an evangelical tone" in which any opponent "was made to appear to be, ipso facto, an enemy of democracy." As long as the frame was corruption, opponents lost because no one could make an effective case in favor of corruption. Those who were skeptical of Progressivism might question the ability or interest of citizens to use the tools that Progressives designed for them, and many empirical studies of these electoral reforms have borne out the contention—after a period of public enthusiasm, the system adapted and little of substance changed. One way to think about this is that, as Cain (2015, 40; see also Hofstadter 1955, 265) notes, the proponents of any governmental reform always overpromise about the results (and the opponents tend to exaggerate the negative consequences), and in the end everyone is disillusioned—or calls for more reforms. Or, a bit more in keeping with the theoretical arguments we consider below, all of these reforms depended upon assumptions about the public and about policy. The reforms could only ever work with an informed, politically engaged public that would express what the Progressives believed was the public interest and that would empower the experts whom the Progressives believed could practically pursue that public interest. From a Progressive point of view, perhaps the American people were simply not up to the task.

6.2d: Unifying Themes

All of the writers considered earlier may well have had comprehensive theoretical understandings of what corruption is. Yet it is not the role of a novelist, a journalist, or a politician to fully articulate such views—each has more immediate personal and professional goals. Indeed, any attempt to frame a literary, descriptive, or political movement with reference to a philosophy of government, let alone of a governmental characteristic such as corruption, runs the risk of oversimplifying such theoretical referents to the point of caricature. Yet the summary above indicates that corruption in America was a large enough social concern that it perhaps called for a more thoughtful treatment. The summary indicates that the lens that early Americans had used to understand corruption was, by the late nineteenth century, no longer sufficient for understanding the problems faced by the sort of mature representational democracy and modern economy that America had developed. The circumstances of American political life—the massive increase in population, the development of industrial economy within a federated republican democracy, the reconsideration of the nation's founding principles, and the relationship between the American Constitution and these developments—called for a new articulation of what corruption was. It is to these efforts by Progressive theorists that we now turn.

6.3: Corruption Talk in Progressive Political Theory: Four Exemplars

As the preceding discussion shows, America during the late nineteenth and early twentieth centuries was involved in a complex discussion of what corruption in the American context was. In this section we focus on four Progressive intellectuals who develop a clear account of corruption.

The authors we have selected to consider below—Edward A. Ross, Walter Weyl, Herbert Croly, and Walter Lippmann—use extended discussions of political corruption as a grounding for their larger arguments. All were highly influential—Ross for his role in the establishment of the American social sciences, and Weyl, Croly, and Lippmann for their role in establishing *The New Republic* magazine as the principal forum for Progressive political and social thought. Although each of these writers, and *The New Republic* as an entity, would eventually stray from these narrow confines, their influence in providing a popular philosophy of Progressivism is undeniable. Some contemporary writers (e.g., Noel 2013) provide persuasive evidence that *The New Republic* framed the ideology of the American Left for much of the twentieth century. These writers offered a view of corruption that was richer than that given by the Progressive journalists, novelists, and activists we discussed previously, that was different from the prevailing American and European views of the eighteenth and nineteenth centuries, and that laid the groundwork for discussions of corruption in America in the years to come.

We draw the reader's attention as well to our decision to break the arguments of our fourth exemplar, Walter Lippmann, into an early period and a later period. All of the theoretical accounts we discuss below have their problems, and there is a substantial body of late-twentieth-century literature that is critical of the Progressive project. Ross's concerns changed over the course of his career (he lived until 1951),[2] and Weyl died in 1919, too early for him to have had the space to reflect on the effect of Progressive changes. Herbert Croly turned his attention to religion and mysticism in the 1920s and by many accounts was disenchanted with what had become of the Progressive movement, without publicly articulating what he thought had happened (Levy 1985). It is only in the writings of Walter Lippmann in the 1920s that we see one of the major articulators of the Progressive view of corruption take stock of the limits of his earlier arguments and of the tensions within the Progressive view.

6.3a: Edward A. Ross: Corruption and "New Sins"

Perhaps the most succinct account of the Progressive concern about corruption can be found in Edward A. Ross's *Sin and Society,* published in 1907. Ross was one of the founders of the field of sociology, and his concern with corruption is less tied to the reform of political institutions than is the case for more political Progressive writers. Ross's arguments about sin, however, found an eager audience among Progressives; Theodore Roosevelt, for instance, provided an enthusiastic introduction to Ross's book. Ross was to become controversial, however, for a number of reasons. His effort to develop a scientific understanding of noneconomic forces—to develop a social science that was clearly separate from economics—was to prove highly influential, but it also veered into a pseudoscientific biological racism that was to dog later Progressives and led Lippmann, Weyl, and Croly to disavow some elements of Ross's teachings (Forcey 1961, 214). By 1907, Ross had already been removed from a teaching position at Stanford (for reasons not unrelated to his racial views but linked also to his criticism of the business practices of the Stanford family [Dorothy Ross 1991, 230–39]). While Ross's connection to subsequent Progressive writers was tenuous—and Ross himself likely would not have seen himself as an unequivocal ally of the other writers we consider below—Ross's effort to forge a "new liberalism" and to create "social minds" serves as an important articulation of what was to become a project that not only shaped the development of the social sciences but reached beyond the academy as well.

In *Sin and Society*, Ross (1907) attributes corruption to the growing complexity of society. In simpler times, it was easy for the average person to recognize the sins of others and to identify evil people. But times have changed, and ethics, Ross argues, must catch up to social progress. Activities that have traditionally been seen as sinful—murder or adultery, for instance—have well-defined victims, and sinners know, or should know, what they have done. Ross distinguishes between "old sins" and "new sins," and he contends that the public is and always has been adept at recognizing and punishing old sins (chap. 3). Corruption, however, counts as a "new sin." Those who engage in corruption (in the transactional, individual sense) do not necessarily do so out of deliberate malice or attempt to harm, and they may not even be aware that they have harmed others. "The hurt" of corruption and other new sins "passes into that vague mass, the 'public,' and is there lost to view" (11). It is thus harder to label corrupt actors as evil: "Often there are no victims. . . . Many sins, in fact, simply augment risk. Evil does not dog their footsteps with relentless and heart-shaking certainty" (12). Ross goes on to say that in many instances, the "victim" here is not even an individual but an institution, be it a formal one such as a legislature or an informal one such as a social practice or societal norm.

We might interpret Ross's claim in two ways. First, perhaps corrupt actions are undertaken without enough thought—one might engage in a particular practice that is harmful to the body politic, yet fail to recognize it as

such. For instance, a politician might justify doing favors for a wealthy supporter without appealing to any sort of general principle (i.e., what would
happen if every legislator did favors for wealthy supporters?). Alternately, perhaps a corrupt action is chosen knowingly, but one might be sufficiently removed from those who are harmed that one does not know the others have
been harmed. A building contractor who takes a bribe to allow the construc-
tion of a building that does not meet code requirements may never find out
that residents of this building ultimately suffered. In this second circumstance, the corrupt actor may know he is doing something wrong but will not
know that his wrong action had consequences. In both cases, corruption, in
Ross's view, becomes a collective action problem.

Both circumstances make corruption a particularly insidious problem,
and it requires a governmental solution. Ross devotes much attention to what
he calls the "grading of sinners" (1907, chap. 2). At one level, we might imagine "old sins" to be worse than "new sins" in a moral sense—they are manifestations of evil, and they are committed by people who know they are harm-
ing others yet do so anyway. But for most old sins, identifying the victim is
easy. With the new sins, we have more trouble identifying the evildoers.

As a consequence, moral exhortation will be of limited use for the new
sins. We have a harder time connecting corruption to one's character, singling out the culprits, or clearly explaining to them, or the public, what the
link is between their actions and the consequences of those actions. The connection seems abstract. A call for "fair play" will not have the drama that
would be present in the singling out of a person who has more obviously committed an old sin (Ross 1907, 94). We also cannot resort to existing laws for
guidance, because as society becomes more complicated, the laws will fail to
keep up with the opportunities for corruption. New technologies, for instance, may be exploited, deliberately or not, in ways that are harmful to the
public. For the contemporary reader, this may bring to mind the complexity of developing laws to regulate cybercrime, artificial intelligence, or intellectual property rights.

Instead of relying on existing laws or moral exhortation, then, the prevention of corruption must be placed in the hands of a class of experts—those
who have the imagination or expertise to understand the link between corruption and its consequences: "If the public does not speedily become far
shrewder in the grading and grilling of sinners, there is nothing for it but to
turn over the defense of society to professionals" (Ross 1907, 41–42). These
professionals must be "neutrals"—they must be able to make dispassionate
judgments about the link between actions and the harm that comes from
them, and their judgment must not be clouded by the possibility that they
themselves will be directly harmed. The people still have a role to play in the

identification of old sins, but it is the duty of these experts both to identify new sins and to educate the public so that it can be aroused to understand and object to ever-emerging transgressions.

In this sense, Ross has located the core mission of the Progressive movement as a response to changes in the size and structure of society, changes that have created new ways to sin. The growing complexity of American society creates both a need for more direct democracy—the appeal to the public to identify transgressions—and a need for an expert class that will understand the inability of the public to do so without expert guidance and that will therefore train the public to identify sins and will direct the public's frustrations into appropriate legal and institutional policies.

In Ross's framing, this was a particularly American problem, at least at that historical moment. Economic growth in America since the Civil War, he thought, had created the opportunity for widespread corruption, and many of the agents of this corruption—corporations and political bosses, to name but two—acquired power in the United States to an extent that they did not in other nations. The corporation is, Ross argues, particularly vulnerable to corruption because of its separation of shareholders from the provision of goods and because of the difficulty in observing the externalities that derive from corporations' practices. Identifying corruption in the early American sense—as the import of corrupt European norms and values, as the holdover of antidemocratic values—will not be of use in large part because it does not recognize the economic development of America and the roots of this development in American political decisions. The origins of this form of corruption are rooted in American institutional practices, perhaps in our Constitution itself, and in the individualism that is part of the American character.

At the same time, Ross (1907) contends, Americans are particularly ill-equipped to confront corruption because of the country's size and diversity. The American public, he argues, is "too incoherent to make a good policeman" (85). We are fragmented, he says, by race, nationality, and class in a much more complicated manner than are European countries, and we simply do not have a strong sense of national purpose. Hence, in a fashion similar to other Progressives who were more policy-minded, such as Herbert Croly, Ross would argue that we also need to develop a new American form of nationalism or a new sense of national purpose.

Finally, Ross also provides, implicitly, a distinction between the Progressive agenda and the populist agenda. The widespread anger about corruption manifested in the work of Lincoln Steffens, the muckrakers, and other popular writers of the era showed that many citizens could be aroused by allegations of corruption. But, for Ross, populist outrage won't solve the problems. Without guidance by experts, there is the risk that the "cheated class" will use government merely to shift the scales, to pursue its own interests as opposed to developing neutral means of pursuing the public interest (1907, chap. 6). Populist appeals and sensational stories alone, then, may change the identities of the corrupt actors but will not reduce corruption. The Progressives add rule by experts to their populism.

What, then, is corruption for Ross? Corruption is inextricably linked to sin, and its origins ultimately lie in the actions of individuals. In this sense, most instances of corruption are transactional in nature. Although the language of Ross's account invites the reader to consider corruption in biblical terms—sin, evil, and so forth—he is not interested in discussing or reforming the character of the sinners themselves. He is more concerned with training the purportedly disinterested parties, be they the bureaucratic "neutrals" or the citizens. Ross rarely speaks of corruption as a sort of societal state of being, and he holds out hope that laws can be devised to identify and regulate corruption. At the same time, however, Ross holds out little hope that corruption can be addressed, à la Montesquieu, by recalling Americans to any preexisting understanding or to the true purpose of our institutions or by adjusting our institutions to limit the use of power. There is no such understanding, and our institutions are part of the problem. A new national character must be created; new laws are part of this but a broader program of moral uplift and education is also needed.

6.3b: *Walter Weyl and Herbert Croly: Corruption, American Style*

Walter Weyl and Herbert Croly are generally considered (along with Walter Lippmann) to have provided the most consequential explanations of Progressive political thought (e.g., Forcey 1961; Nye 1951; Sitaraman 2017). While Croly's landmark works, *Progressive Democracy* (1915) and *The Promise of American Life* (1919), have received more scholarly attention, Weyl's *The New Democracy* (1912) tends to be seen as providing a more applied road map for Progressive policy (Forcey 1961, 83; Moore 1974). Although the two authors differ in their understanding of the relationship between corruption and American political culture and institutions, the two men's views on the causes of and remedies for corruption have enough in common that their thoughts are best considered together. Although neither of these authors places political corruption at the center of their theories (as opposed to Ross), both saw corruption as something endemic to the sort of American ethos of individualism and democracy that Tocqueville discussed, and both rejected the idea that corruption could be addressed either by moral exhortation or by the sort of constitutional principles that a follower of Montesquieu might recommend. On the contrary, Croly and Weyl both called for institutional changes that would encourage centralized power and a greater role for the informed public.

Weyl (1912) spends much of *The New Democracy* exploring the corruption of politicians by business interests—by what he calls "the plutocracy." For Weyl, corruption by the plutocracy entails the crafting of laws to serve the self-interest of business. Americans have tended to turn a blind eye to such practices simply because they have not tended to impose substantial burdens upon the public. The American ethos, he argues, entails optimism and tolerance. The fluidity of American life—economic and geographic mobility, the free exchange of ideas, and a lack of rigidity in political outlook—has led to a belief that the downtrodden will eventually triumph, or at least will acquire the means to support themselves (42). This optimism is not in itself a bad thing, and it may even be salutary to political development. Yet it has led to the view that corruption is not a major problem. Individual instances of corruption are not seen as signs of a systemic problem. As Weyl puts it, for much of American history "the 'practical' man saw monopolies, but he did not see Monopoly. He saw corrupt politicians, but he did not see Corruption. He saw evils, but he did not see Evil" (49; capitalization in original).

Americans have also tended to hold politicians in low esteem, but this low esteem has resulted in an inability to understand changes in the degree of corruption among politicians. For much of our history, Weyl (1912) claims, "we had no traditions of public service" (57), no high standards that we might apply to politicians. "Our legislators," he argues, "were not all uncorrupted creatures of God before the fall" (98). We thus lack both the inclination to worry about corruption and the ability to measure it against anything in particular. When corruption is pervasive, we often lose sight of its boundaries, and we fail to recognize and reward politicians who are not corrupt, or more broadly, we fail to see and appreciate areas of public life where corruption is not the norm.

Weyl, like Croly, argues that corruption has been most prevalent at the state and local levels (Weyl 1912, 97). We have become used to corrupt state and municipal politics. Indeed, we have perhaps become so used to it that we barely see it anymore. Three related changes of the late nineteenth century have caused corruption to become a greater problem. First, in the wake of the Civil War, America has become more of a nation—we look to the federal government to solve our problems, and increased immigration has led to a critical mass among the citizenry who think of themselves as citizens of the nation, as opposed to being citizens of a particular state. This has created greater expectations for the national government.

These expectations (again, not necessarily bad, and even salutary in themselves) have appeared at the same time, however, as the plutocracy has acquired the inclination and means to attempt to corrupt federal officeholders. The second change, then, is an increase in the prevalence of corruption, but also a change in kind.

The peculiar significance of our present-day American political corruption lies not in its novelty, but in its change of character and source. It has become subtle, scientific, organized. It has become a pendant to large businesses, which is also subtle, scientific, organized. Today political corruption is menacing, not only because all corruption is immoral and antidemocratic but because it represents the intrusion into politics of a disciplined and aggressive plutocracy. (Weyl 1912, 97)

Weyl refers to the Ulysses S. Grant administration (generally seen as one of the more corrupt presidential administrations) as the initial moment where this sort of systemic corruption first appeared, but he is not interested in condemning Grant, or any individual politician; this is, rather, a process that might well have been inevitable.

And third, the growing power of political parties has provided a conduit for corruption. Weyl does not, like other Progressives, spend very much time discussing the evils of partisanship or party bosses. Rather, he worries that a two-step dynamic has taken place. The belief that parties are private, nongovernmental institutions may have made sense in the early American republic, but by the early twentieth century political leadership had become centralized within political parties—first at the state and local levels, then at the national level—such that the nation was faced with "irresponsible" (in the political, representative sense) leaders. Business leaders, unlike the mass public, have not exhibited strong partisan allegiances and have corrupted both parties. The political system has become beholden to party leaders, and party leaders have become beholden to business. Parties are used for private gain, and party platforms have become meaningless as tools for the public to use in voting.

The sort of corruption Weyl discusses, then, involves a gradual movement from individual corrupt acts to systemic efforts to corrupt government, and it has happened so imperceptibly that the public has not been able to respond. There was no master plan here; despite the "subtle, scientific, organized" process Weyl (1912) described in the earlier quote, he admits that no one in particular mapped out a plan for organized corruption (105–6). Because of this, there is little that can be done short of substantial governmental reform. Moral exhortation will not work, because there is no one in particular to exhort—the people themselves are not corrupt, and even the politicians and business leaders Weyl singles out do not seem to have the agency to change this process. We also cannot be called back to any sort of uncorrupted state of affairs, because the process Weyl describes is rooted in our national character and in the institutions that previously served us reasonably well.

In his lengthy explanation of the corruption of newspapers, Weyl begins by describing the accumulation of rather pedestrian instances of corruption—a business that purchases advertisements might request some sort of quid pro quo in the newspaper's coverage of said advertiser's actions, but even absent an explicit quid pro quo the newspaper might be cautious in how it discusses an advertiser or a potential advertiser. Weyl moves on from there, however, to describe how newspapers might shape public opinion more broadly:

> The influence of the plutocracy on the newspaper, even on the newspaper which it secretly owns, is thus so circumscribed that its teachings are necessarily subtle, and its suggestions indirect. The plutocracy does not proclaim that political corruption, misery, slums, unequal distribution of wealth, and other present-day evils are good. We could not be made to believe it. Nor are we taught that democracy is bad. We could not be made to believe that. We are rather taught that while evil exists, proposed remedies are always worse. We are cautioned against flying to evils that we know not of; against following our natural leaders; against adopting any of the means necessary to attain the democratic ends so grudgingly approved. (1912, 130)

Public opinion is thus controlled in a "covert" way, where precedent, patriotism, liberty, and American values more broadly are presented as being consistent with acceptance of the political status quo and the role of business. We are not pushed to disregard flagrant abuses, but we are taught to attach ourselves to a somewhat perverted description of American ideals. This sort of rhetoric "may corrode our national morals, or at least tend[s] to maintain them on a low level" (Weyl 1912, 154).

In the end, then, the people may not be corrupted themselves, but our moral development is degraded by a corrupting context. This makes it hard for Weyl—as for other Progressives—to exalt a raw populism, a simple appeal to public opinion, as a solution to the problem of corruption. He does, however, have faith that the Progressive program of institutional reform—direct primaries, direct election of senators, the initiative and referendum, recall elections, nonpartisan elections, and such—will serve as a check on plutocratic power. Like other Progressives, he seems to share a vaguely Rousseauian faith that the people can express the general will if given the right context and mechanisms, and the idea that Madisonian mechanisms to filter opinion or limit the ability of government to act are bad. These changes may in the end contain corruption, by restoring the impulse for businesses toward efficiency that originally prompted American to ignore corruption. And in the long run, the exercise of this sort of democracy may create a sufficiently large number of informed citizens that public opinion might prevail in encouraging responsible party government and political leadership.

Like Weyl, Herbert Croly pays particular attention to corruption at the state and local levels, but he uses this starting point to develop a much more detailed explanation of the relationship between corruption and institutional change. Croly agrees that the corruption he saw around him was a distinctly American phenomenon—in the conclusion to *The Promise of American Life* he rejects the notion that Americans have ever been at risk of corruption by "European values" (1919, 426). The nation long ago achieved its "moral and intellectual emancipation" from undemocratic views and created its own distinctive culture. American democracy, however, has never been fully realized—it is a "young enterprise" and requires "a long and slow process of social reorganization and individual emancipation" (452). In his emphasis on the "individual," Croly provides a less process-oriented account than Weyl of how corruption happens and how it might be solved. People with "moral values" are needed. The sorts of moral appeals to fight corruption that Theodore Roosevelt and (to a slightly lesser extent) Woodrow Wilson espoused might not in themselves be enough, but they likely will do more good than harm (12–15).

Corruption, for Croly, has been endemic in state and local government. The reason for this, however, is that these governments have limited power. They are organized by corrupt individuals, but this is the case because people of stronger moral values have little interest in state government. State legislatures have been prevented from doing anything of consequence, and as a result they have become a vehicle for the provision of small favors. Corruption stems, then, not from having too much power but from having too little. Public cynicism about these governments has yielded a paradoxical result, he contends in *Progressive Democracy*: State governments have "abandoned themselves to legalism" (Croly 1915, 252). They pass more laws that constrain their own actions, which results in more corrupt behavior by legislators as these legislators are reduced to merely conferring privileges on those who petition them.

Weyl's concerns about corruption are focused almost exclusively upon "the plutocracy," while Croly's conception of corruption seems broader.[3] Any instance in which the public will is compromised in the name of self-interest is corrupt. Judges are corrupted when they are overly reliant on the legislature. Legislators are corrupted when their power to enact laws that address public needs is compromised. Governors are corrupted, likewise, when legislatures restrain them. Legislatures are a particular problem because they do not have the centralization necessary to speak on behalf of the public, and there are no procedural safeguards that prevent unchecked state legislatures from actively destroying democracy.

On the one hand, Croly embraces a more modest reform program than does Weyl. His major concern is state and local government, not only because he thinks it is more corrupt than the federal government but also because he has more respect for the U.S. Constitution than he has for state constitutions. More consequential, however, are Croly's practical concerns. The U.S.

Constitution is hard to amend, so efforts to reform the federal government will be more difficult. State constitutions, on the other hand, are less coherent documents and they command little public allegiance. In both of the books considered here, Croly endorses a dramatic centralization of power at the state level—governors should have more power, they and their parties should be prompted to provide clearer platforms so that the public can hold them responsible, and governors should have the ability to introduce legislation. The public, as well, should be provided with more direct means of making law, through the usual Progressive projects.

A return to founding principles would simply be impractical—our polity and our economy have changed too much. The rise of corrupt actors in politics and the economy is rooted in American individualism. Yet Croly is not a revolutionary, but a gradualist. Seeking either restoration or an abandonment of revered federal institutions entirely would entail indiscriminate harm—we cannot have a full understanding of what is good and what is not good, or of the relationship between different mechanisms or practices. But Croly seems ambivalent about the idea that our polity is emblematic of any sort of virtue of which we might be reminded. Croly closes *The Promise of American Life* with a direct reference to Montesquieu—he contends that Montesquieu's claim that "the principle of democracy is virtue" is one that "may be more ominous than flattering" (1919, 454). How shall we cultivate virtue? If we cannot necessarily find it in our past, and if we are ambivalent about the abilities of the public to see and combat corruption, then there is no obvious cure.

What is most odd about Croly's brief reference to Montesquieu is that his reform program for state and local politics seems drawn much more from the spirit of Rousseau. The notion that corruption is best addressed through appealing more directly to the public (either through an empowered chief executive or through direct democracy) is closer to Rousseau's description of the genuine social contract. Corruption is also addressed by isolating governmental tasks from politics—through the appeal to specialists. Croly does not take on the question of whether the people are corrupt, or corruptible. One might infer from his ambivalence at the close of *The Promise of American Life* that he is inclined to see whether they can rise to the challenge. He lacks faith, it seems, but has some hope.

Both Weyl and Croly take a less moralistic and more political approach to understanding corruption than does Ross. Their arguments are not entirely bereft of moral claims; they, like Lippmann, occasionally show concern for individual, nonpolitical choices with regard to alcohol, marriage, or the work ethic. But their focus on institutions suggests that democratic reform is a more practical, immediate goal and might lead to broader social reform. Modest governmental reform is achievable, and seemingly modest changes, incrementally pursued, can amount to big changes. It would be up to Walter Lippmann, then, to reflect on whether in fact this attempt might have negative consequences.

6.3c: Early Walter Lippmann

The primary significance of Walter Lippmann's arguments about corruption lies in Lippmann's initial hope for and ultimate disillusionment with key aspects of the Progressive project. Lippmann's early works—*A Preface to Politics* (1913) and *Drift and Mastery* (1914)—present an understanding of corruption that fuses some of the moral claims raised by Ross with a description of American political and economic development similar to what appears in Croly's and Weyl's works. Lippmann, like these other authors, emphasizes the uniqueness of a form of corruption that has emerged in the American context. Throughout his early writings, however, he retains some detachment from the Progressive political agenda. This detachment would ultimately lead to Lippmann's abandonment of Progressive faith in "the people" by the 1920s. His later writings, from *Public Opinion* (1921) through *The Public Philosophy* (1955), show a pessimism that neither a Rousseauian turn to a prepolitical notion of the general will nor a Montesquieuian revivification of founding principles was feasible. Corruption remained an abiding concern throughout Lippmann's career, but once the Progressive movement had splintered it is possible to see both a concern on Lippmann's part about the danger of corruption rhetoric, on the one hand, and a skepticism about emerging social scientific tools for quantifying and defining public opinion, on the other. These concerns are, as we shall see, complementary.

In *A Preface to Politics*, Lippmann begins with an account of the corruption inherent in American institutions. The Constitution, he argues, is a "scaffold" derived from Montesquieu and erected by the founders to establish some measure of democratic governance (1913, 18). "It has become part of our national piety," he contends, "to pretend that they succeeded." They did not, he argues. Political parties and political machines have been established precisely because of the Constitution's inadequacy. The creation of party machines was the only way by which economic interests could press their demands upon politicians. There is nothing morally wrong or "monstrous" about this development (21), and hence the "corruption of which we heard so much" in discussions of American machine politics is not evil, either, although it is a real thing. Corrupt political actions are, he says, "the odor of a decaying political system done to death by economic growth" (23).

It is easy to mischaracterize corruption as a moral phenomenon. This is what the muckrakers have done, Lippmann argues. Although Lippmann has a strong moralistic bent himself (he is, for instance, drawn frequently to discussions of sexual promiscuity), he believes that immoral acts are a second-ary symptom of political corruption, and that muckrakers who focus on urban vice do so in order to titillate, not to diagnose actual problems. The corruption they describe, he claims in *A Preface to Politics*, is a way in which the American political system has been modified to provide for the wants and needs of urban residents:

> The demand for pleasure, adventure, romance has been left to the devil's catering for so long a time that most people think he inspires the demand. He doesn't. Our neglect is the devil's opportunity. What we should use, we let him abuse, and the corruption of the best things, as Hume remarked, produces the worst. (1913, 42)

Muckrakers, Lippmann goes on to say, characterize far too many things as corrupt, including normal political deliberation. They also fail to adequately distinguish between political corruption and economic corruption. The preoccupation with so many different forms of corruption can lead one to be confused about what corruption really is, how it might be combated, or who is to blame. It is inevitable, he argues in *Drift and Mastery* (1914, 23–27), that the public appetite for stories about corruption will lead people to assume that it is all part of an elaborate conspiracy.

This does not mean that corruption is not endemic to American politics. It is true, Lippmann argues, that government is by and large a "petty and partisan, slavish and blind, clumsy and rusty instrument" (1914, 31). Like Weyl, Lippmann argues that corruption has historically existed within American government precisely because it was never a major problem. Partisanship and other political problems are not synonymous with corruption, but transactionally corrupt acts, such as taking payoffs from special interests, have always existed within the American system. As long as the scope of American government was limited, Americans tended to assume corrupt politicians were inevitable and containable. It has only been with the expansion in the size of government during the late nineteenth century that corruption has become an important concern. Likewise, the economic dislocation that occurred in the late nineteenth century created an appetite among the people for hearing about and reading about corruption.

Lippmann is skeptical about cures for corruption. In his two early books he does close with a somewhat ambivalent call to better educate the public for democracy—a typical Progressive concern. But beyond this, he does not have a clear agenda. In *A Preface to Politics* Lippmann (1913) disavows "moralizing" for the same reasons that Croly did. He also, however, disavows procedural tools for addressing corruption. There is, he says, a "curious sterility" to the solutions proffered by Progressive reformers, such as the direct primary, recall elections, and the sort (252–53). People are told that these tools will enable them to regain control of government, but they will have no idea what to do should they actually gain more control. These tools will be vulnerable to capture by opportunists, and after these changes have been enacted and have failed to change anything noticeable, people will be disillusioned. In short, all of these changes are neither adequate for dealing with corruption nor plausible ends in themselves.

At the end of *Drift and Mastery*, Lippmann (1914) casts his net a bit wider. Not only can we not address corruption through procedural reforms, we also cannot do so through any sort of backward-looking reference to shared norms. The understandings that undergirded the Constitution, and which undergirded all other social and political institutions, have been wiped away through economic changes. "We have lost authority," he argued. "We are 'emancipated' from an ordered world. We drift" (111).

In what sense, then, do Lippmann's early works count as "Progressive"? While they articulate a skepticism about focusing too much on corruption, in them Lippmann shares with Croly and Weyl a belief that corruption has increased and that the sort of corruption that exists is endemic to American politics. Perhaps more than the other Progressives, however, Lippmann worried that the term "corruption" was being used too expansively. Although he does not style himself as a political philosopher, Lippmann mentions both Montesquieu and Rousseau regularly. We cannot use the Montesquieuian vision, he argues, because American government has become too complex, too dependent on an "invisible" government of party machines (Lippmann 1913, 18). However, the sort of world Rousseau envisions is also probably not a possibility—it probably never existed in the first place, and it is seductive in part because we have caricaturized Rousseau to the point that his work is more useful as a symbol than as a practical guide (Lippmann 1913, 226). Also, as Lippmann would say later in *A Preface to Morals* (1931, 154), Rousseau was largely a creature of his time. Things really were so bad, human nature was trusted so little, in mid-eighteenth-century France that Rousseau is better seen as offering an overcorrection, as an example of what happens to people under such circumstances than as a more broadly useful articulation of how one might address elite or societal corruption.

There are two components of Lippmann's early arguments about corruption that would be useful to him in later writings. More so than other Progressives, he recognizes the seductiveness of the Rousseauian argument and, more broadly, of using an expansive conception corruption. He also would go on to agonize a bit more than other Progressives over what "the public" is. One can see this in *Drift and Mastery*. There, Lippmann goes further than either Croly or Weyl in articulating a clear definition of what corruption is: "The attempt to serve at the same time two antagonistic interests is what constitutes 'corruption.' . . . The crime is serious in proportion to the degree of loyalty that we expect" (1914, 28). The two interests here, he argues, are the public and the private. He makes this distinction with reference to the difference between governmental corruption and business corruption—we judge corrupt politicians more harshly than business executives because we have higher expectations for politicians to consider the public interest. Likewise, we judge corrupt presidents more harshly than corrupt city councilors because the president is expected to be more representative than local officials of the public interest.

6.3d: Later Walter Lippmann

Lippmann's early account of corruption suggests the question of what the public interest is. This is a question Lippmann would take up in *Public Opinion* (1921) and *The Phantom Public* (1925). In both of these works, Lippmann explores the limitations of relying on references to "the public" as justification for political actions. Lippmann's indictment—controversial at the time but today largely accepted by quantitative researchers—has two components. First, citizens do not have perfect views of reality; rather, they have partial understandings of particular phenomena, which are not always stable and are often based on personal experiences (1925, 146), and while some of their opinions are true, others are not. Politicians can use these understandings and misunderstandings to further their own ends; they can play upon stereotypes, frame matters in moral terms, or use symbols to characterize political choices. However, nowhere in there, hidden in the citizen body, "the people" or "the public," is there an informed, deliberative conviction to guide political action.

Second, just as there is no such thing as stable and consistent "public opinion" to use as a North Star, there is also no clear body called "the public" (Lippmann 1921, 16–19). We are all enmeshed in a variety of different social interactions and are only intermittently concerned at all with governmental matters. When politicians argue that "the public" has been engaged, they have really engaged only a particular, often carefully selected, sliver of the population. Lippmann's claims about the public are partial, but they would be seconded in 1926 by John Dewey. Dewey contends in *The Public and Its Problems* (1927, 35) that the public is something that is entirely constituted by the state—it exists only as a function of government regulation of the externalities caused by private behaviors. There are thus, in Dewey's formulation, many different publics. But "the public" or "the people" in the romantic sense vaguely inspired by Rousseau simply does not exist, according to Dewey or Lippmann. It is a construct that is used to explain and justify governmental action. Unlike Dewey, however, Lippmann (1921, 229–30) argues that it is not only the state that creates publics; intermediary institutions such as schools, churches, or the media can also do so, and are perhaps better equipped to do so. Lippmann contends that the liberal worldview presupposes a complex array of such things—commissions, boards, agencies, and the like. The state can evaluate all of these things, but the process of doing so has little to do with democratic governance, particularly the sort of governance that might spring from Rousseauian social contract theory. Progressivism seemed to presume that there is a general will of an independently existing social community, and government is supposed to discover it, obey it, and expertly administer it. Lippmann comes to reject that sharply.

Even more so than in his early works, Lippmann seeks here both to explain the appeal of the Rousseauian conception of the popular will and to reject its existence. In *Public Opinion* (1921, 169–70) Lippmann discusses the early American understanding of corruption—the Founders saw corruption in European, cosmopolitan societies and, following Rousseau, he says, proposed that its antidote lay in American rural towns. As evidence, Lippmann presents Thomas Jefferson's aforementioned claim (in our Chapter 6) that there had never been instances of "corruption of morals in the mass of cultivators." Jefferson was wrong, however—in these towns, it was churches, schools, and families that established democratic values. There was, again, no public—there were institutions that created different publics. Institutions organize publics.

This conception of intermediary institutions that create and shape publics thus develops naturally from Lippmann's prior skepticism that political reforms could enable the public to engage in democracy in a meaningful way, coupled with his interest in shaping the public and educating it for some sort of democratic role. Democracy should not, in the end, be defined by its inputs, but rather by its outputs—a system that improved the social and economic circumstances of its citizens might count as democratic even if the people did not meaningfully instruct it to do so. Schools and the like might enable the people to realize this, to accept governmental actions, or at the least to reduce the sort of corruption panics that had animated the Progressive Era and threatened to fuel totalitarian movements.

By the 1930s, Lippmann's concern with totalitarianism had in fact come to dominate his writings about corruption. By the time he wrote *The Good Society* (1936), Lippmann had reached the point where he argued that the Progressive impulse was now manifest in a belief that government power should be used coercively for the goals of a particular group—those who saw themselves as Progressives and were convinced they understood the public interest. The Purifiers had won, with disturbing results. Corruption talk, Lippmann (1936, 71, 83) now argued, was a tool for those seeking social control. Dropping the gradualism of Progressives, other groups were also making antiliberal corruption claims to justify greater governmental control for social change.

Communists argued that society and democracy had been corrupted by private property; fascists argued that national spirit and solidarity had been corrupted by liberalism. All three were against both the individualism said to be part of the national character, and all three were against the limitations of power espoused by the Founders—limitations that made the government "moderate" in Montesquieu's sense, but also made it inefficient and somewhat ineffectual from the point of view of frustrated reformers. There was a sort of pure human nature that preceded government, and the pettiness and compromise endemic to the politics of democratic government were seen as corrupt in themselves. They were symptoms of the weakness of government, an admission that the state could not articulate what was best for society. Of course, a decision by the state to stay out of petty decision-making—to allow private citizens to resolve their own disputes—also appeared corrupt to such groups, in that the government stood by and allowed private gain to dictate interactions. Either way, the sorts of decisions made by liberal governments appeared unsatisfying to those whom Lippmann dubbed "romantic democrats" (1925, 265)—those who believed that the people could exist in an uncorrupted state.

Thus, Lippmann discards the notion that the public exists, but emphasizes its power as a rhetorical concept in totalizing worldviews. We can identify instances of transactional, individual corruption—there still may be politicians who clearly place private gain ahead of any plausible conception of common good—but building upon them to posit any grand scheme of corruption is a dangerous endeavor.

In his last major work, *The Public Philosophy* (1955), however, Lippmann argues that in fact American life is undergirded by a kind of public philosophy, that it precedes government and can be corrupted by government, and that it is at risk of being lost (77). The public philosophy that he articulates is not directly linked to his questioning during the 1920s of whether there is a such thing as "the public." The public philosophy he articulates is a basic democratic agreement—the acceptance of a norm—that we will seek to resolve our political differences in a civil way, that we must accommodate different sorts of opinions, that we must commit ourselves to finding basic agreements that lie underneath our pluralism of beliefs.

The arc of Lippmann's writing career reflects an ambivalence both about some core aspects of the Progressive agenda and about the sort of corruption rhetoric that characterized much Progressive writing. While he was dismissive of both the Montesquieuian and the Rousseauian theories of corruption, he did believe that corruption was a problem, and that it was a particular problem in early-twentieth-century America. It is not at all clear that the early Lippmann would have agreed with the elder Lippmann's call for a reinforcement of the "public philosophy." This call, though, has elements of both theories. It precedes government in one sense, namely, by underwriting it, by providing it with the social acceptance and justifying the habits that make democratic government work; but it is not innately human or prepolitical. It could possibly be reconciled with the sort of norms that Montesquieu discusses, although it does not amount to a constitution. Its cure depends not so much on the state as on social institutions. More so than any of the other Progressives, however, Lippmann shows an awareness that the corruption talk of the early twentieth century had taken on a life of its own and could have disastrous results for democratic governance.

More broadly, it is apparent that efforts to lump Lippmann in with Croly and Weyl, as well as with the Progressive politicians, may make historical sense, but, as the summary here shows, such efforts must be tempered with the acknowledgment that Lippmann always seemed somewhat skeptical that more direct democracy, direct empowerment of the public or the mythicized people, would solve the nation's economic or political problems. Arguably the most widely read works by Lippmann today are his works on public opinion. Lippmann wrote these before the advent of scientific measurement of public opinion, but he clearly feared that "the public" could not be accurately measured with such tools, and he worried that no matter how advanced the study of public opinion became, we ultimately would have only a chimera of "the people" to serve as justification for any political project. This is not a view that early social scientists shared, but it is one that has substantial empirical support today. Lippmann's work shows how the extensive deployment of corruption talk was fated to be popular and immediately appealing, yet flawed.

6.4: Progressivism's Decline and Legacy

It would be overstating matters to suggest that Progressivism's decline had to do with the philosophical tensions brought about in the work of Ross, Weyl, Croly, or Lippmann. One can tell a relatively straightforward story about how historical events put Progressivism on the back burner. In the years following the zenith of the Progressive movement, the United States found itself embroiled in a European war; then confronting the largest health crisis the country had ever seen; next, enjoying a period of great postwar prosperity, followed by an unprecedented depression; and then in another war. During this time, political Progressives also re-sorted their partisan allegiances as the Republican Party turned away, at the national level, from some of their goals and the Democratic Party sought to co-opt many Progressives and much of Progressivism into a new political outlook, rebranded by Franklin D. Roosevelt as a new sort of liberalism. Many historical accounts note that the Progressive coalition of Eastern elites and agrarian populists fractured over how to understand these developments.

Apart from the historical events that overtook the Progressive movement, there may also be limits to the Progressive anticorruption agenda that played out in subsequent years. It is common to note that the Progressives' faith in direct democracy did not fit well with their emphasis on empowering experts and insulating administrators from "politics," and also to note that Progressives' tools for more direct democracy often did not lead to what Progressives deemed to be democratic outcomes. This tension was in play well before the Progressive Era had wound down, and it was a pivotal feature in distinguishing Progressives' attitudes toward the presidencies of Theodore Roosevelt and Woodrow Wilson, as well as being a defining feature of Progressive responses to the New Deal Era (see, e.g., Postell 2017, 172–76).

The emphasis on corruption also contained self-limiting features. Theodore Roosevelt noted in 1914 that calls for reform simply wore the people out; in assessing the attitudes of Republican voters, he alleged "the dog has returned to its vomit."[4] In a less pungent analysis, William Howard Taft (1922, 29–32) claimed that the quest for the purification of government would not create a plan around which people might mobilize in the long run. And John Chamberlain (1932, 74), looking back on the corruption scandals of the Harding administration during the 1920s, argued that "corruption won out" because the various strands of Progressivism never were able to coalesce around a defined plan of reform. Furthermore, the belief that conventional politics was by its nature corrupt meant that the Progressives did not engage in institution-building of their own. The most prominent Progressive politicians succeeded in large part due to their personal charisma, not because they had built campaign organizations or other institutional political tools. Thus, even when Progressives had achieved reforms, they were not capable of preventing them from being used by self-interested—that is, potentially corrupt—politicians for their own ends.

Just as Progressive theories about corruption had roots in several different strands of late nineteenth- and early twentieth-century corruption talk, so Progressive corruption talk has continued to shape American political discourse. Our task in the upcoming chapters is to show that, as Lippmann feared, the Progressive understanding of and attitude toward corruption did not go away. Although in our judgment there has not been a comprehensive philosophical effort to define, or redefine, corruption in the years since the decline of the Progressives, there is plenty of corruption talk in American society today, Left and Right, that owes a debt to the Progressives.

6.4a: The Theoretical Legacy

Much of the theoretical legacy of Progressivism has little to do with its emphasis on corruption. One of the most consequential legacies for our purposes is the antipartyism of the Progressive Era. By branding partisan politics as corrupt, Progressivism solidified an enduring American ambivalence about parties and the incentives of partisan politicians. Yet Progressive rhetoric showed that arguments about corruption had the potential to build bridges and to cross party divisions. That is, corruption, in a narrow, transactional sense, can be identified regardless of one's political leanings. It thus has the potential to appeal to citizens regardless of their political outlooks or their political goals. Corruption talk is a means of creating a new, nonideological sort of coalition. One can see this in more recent years in the efforts by anti-Trump Republicans to find common ground with Democrats in developing shared standards by which they might judge contemporary politicians.[5] Given, in addition, enduring concerns about the role of business in society, the threat posed by single-issue groups to government, or other aspects of the relationship between economic development and democracy, one might argue that Progressives provided a template by which one might discuss American democracy without partisanship.

At the same time, it is important to note that the Progressive movement avoided many of the major political conflicts that were to be central to American politics in the twentieth century, and that it took place in an era when parties were less divided than today in political outlook. Even then, the difficulties Progressive Republicans had in accepting efforts by Democrats to engage in their quest—during the Wilson administration, but more evidently during the New Deal era—showed the limits of hope for a bipartisan Progressive agenda. We would contend that there has been no equivalent theoretical effort to conceptualize corruption in the years that have followed the Progressive Era, and that the increased ideological sorting of American elites, if not of all Americans, suggests that Progressive antiparty efforts are unlikely to gain ground as long as Americans are preoccupied by the sorts of issues that now divide parties.[6] In short, antipartyism is an element of Progressive thought that endures across party lines, and the focus on corruption is one lens by which one might evaluate partisanship, but it is hard to do so when parties are as far apart as they have become since the Progressive Era.

6.4b: The Presidential Legacy

A brief return to James Madison and the *Federalist Papers* can help us understand the political novelty of Progressivism. As we have argued elsewhere, Progressive intellectuals were not certain whether to count Woodrow Wilson as one of their own, yet it is evident that his ideas presented a radical break from Madison's view of government structure. Although some of Wilson's ideas were presented before the Progressive movement emerged, they are largely consistent with the ideas of Lippmann, Croly, and Weyl.

From Madison's point of view, a legislature is superior to a single executive, partly in that more views can be represented but also in that the multitude is harder to bribe:

> It could not be presumed that all or even a majority of the members of an assembly would either lose their capacity for discharging, or be bribed to betray, their trust. Besides, the restraints of their personal integrity and honor, the difficulty of acting in concert for purposes of corruption was a security to the public. (Publius, *Federalist* #63)

Madison is also concerned that the people, and not merely their representatives, need limitations: "An institution may sometimes be necessary, as a defense to the people against their own temporary errors and delusions." This makes swiftness of government action a risk, not a virtue, in a constitution system:

> As the cool and deliberate sense of the community ought in all governments, and actually will in all free governments ultimately prevail over the views of its rulers; so there are particular moments in public affairs, when the people stimulated by some irregular passion, or some illicit advantage, or misled by the artful misrepresentations of interested men, may call for measures which they themselves will afterwards be the most ready to lament. (Publius, *Federalist* #63)

Finally, Madison notes that those thinkers who have favored a "simple democracy, or a pure republic" have "found their reasoning on the idea, that the people composing the society, enjoy not only equality of political rights; but that they have all precisely the same interests, and the same feelings in every respect. . . . We know however that no society ever did or can consist of so homogeneous a mass of citizens" (Publius, *Federalist* #10). We select these points from Madison to show the striking difference with Progressivism, especially Wilson's articulation of it.

Even though he believed the Constitution needs drastic changes, Wilson was no revolutionary; like later Progressives he argued that these changes must happen stepwise. He writes in *The State* (1889) that "society, like other organisms, can be changed only by evolution, and revolution is the antipode of evolution" (53). But Wilson argued in *Congressional Government* (1885) that "the more power is divided the more irresponsible it becomes" (155) and "the federal government lacks strength because its powers are divided, lacks promptness because its authorities are multiplied, lacks wieldiness because its processes are roundabout, lacks efficiency because its responsibility is indistinct and its action without competent direction" (167). He complains about the Constitution, "Public opinion has no easy vehicle for its judgments, no quick channels for its action. Nothing about the system is direct and simple. Authority is perplexingly subdivided and distributed, and responsibility has to be hunted down in out-of-the-way corners" (173). Instead, he says, we must become "open-eyed" about the Constitution's "defects" so that we can "make self-government among us a straightforward thing of simple method, unstinted power, and clear responsibility" (173).

By the time the Progressive movement was underway, Wilson had concluded in *Constitutional Government* (1908) that this meant, in part, more presidential as opposed to legislative power, as the president alone can be "spokesman for the real sentiment and purpose of the country, by giving direction to the people. . . . He is representative of no constituency, but of the whole people" (183). A self-governing people, he thinks, is "a people who know their own minds and can get real representatives to express them" (203), but this requires strong leadership unfettered by the Constitution's maze of momentum-killers: "We must think less of checks and balances and more of coordinated power, less of separation of functions and more of the synthesis of action" (201). Democracy, leadership, and scientific administration constitute Wilson's recipe for progress. "All that is wanted is a new, genuine and really meant purpose held by a few strong men of principle and boldness" (208). What was meant to prevent corruption, despotism, and abuse of power in the Constitution was seen by Wilson precisely as corrupting democracy, blocking the public will, and stifling progress. To return to Lippmann's points: Much of the disagreement here hinges on what hopes we might have for "the public" and for scientific administration and what fears we might have of energetic and charismatic leaders of the people.

6.4c: The Rhetorical Legacy

One more direct tie between Progressive corruption talk and the presidency had to do with presidential rhetoric and the role of corruption talk in prescribing good behavior. The speeches of Theodore Roosevelt, for instance, are replete with calls for leadership or good citizenship. In his New Nationalism speech at Osawatomie in 1910, Roosevelt (1961, 37, 39) frames nationalism with reference to a variety of anticorruption reforms. He concludes that the fate of government is not, however, about institutions but about people—the more decent (less corrupt) we are in private life, the better off we will be as a nation. Likewise, in "The Nation and the States," a speech he gave before the Colorado Legislature on August 29, 1910, Roosevelt warns that the three most pressing concerns of the United States are corruption, lawless violence, and mendacity. All of these problems are linked; he warns that "if you fall into the Scylla of demagogism it will not help that you have avoided the Charybdis of corruption and conservatism on the other" (1961, 45). And lest one conclude that Roosevelt's concern here is with corruption only on the part of politicians, he goes on in other speeches to adopt the common Progressive trope that demagoguery is an appeal by corrupt politicians to exercise their power so as to satisfy the corrupt aims of citizens: "Never trust a man who says that he is only a little crooked, and that the crookedness is exercised in your interest. If he will be crooked for you, he will be crooked against you" (146). Although Roosevelt did worry that an excessive focus on corruption risked cynicism, it was his hope that arguments against corruption would also elevate the "civic conscience" (125) and lead people to be more aware of corruption in both public and private affairs.

The effectiveness of such appeals, however, could lead to problems. Robert Wiebe (1967, 292) argues that Progressive language about purity and corruption was easily channeled into jingoism and into advocacy for Prohibition. Otis Graham (1967, 22) makes a similar claim, pointing out that the Progressives had largely ignored matters of race and class, but that it was not a rhetorical stretch to argue that governmental inattention to such things was a consequence of corruption. Hofstadter (1955, 282) calls attention to Woodrow Wilson's association of communism, both foreign and domestic, with corruption. Domestic socialists like Eugene Debs (1918), in turn, also rejected the major parties as being corrupt:

> To turn your back on the corrupt Republican Party and the corrupt Democratic Party—the gold-dust lackeys of the ruling class—counts for something. It counts still more . . . to join a minority party that has an ideal, that stands for a principle, and fights for a cause.

Hofstadter goes on to note (1955, 285) that later Progressives such as Hiram Johnson and William Borah tended to speak of corruption without any real content at all. By the late 1940s, argues Russell Nye (1951, 383–84), politicians such as Henry Wallace, who claimed the Progressive mantle, advocated for a program that had little in common with the historical Progressives yet shared its moralistic language. The Progressive movement either had died or had evolved beyond easy recognition, but its rhetorical style lived on.

6.4d: The Academic Legacy

One of the most consequential legacies of the Progressive Era was its contribution to the development of the social sciences. No doubt political science as a discipline would have developed without Progressivism in politics, but many of the most important early political scientists adopted a research agenda that expressed their sympathy for the Progressive political agenda.

Charles Merriam, for instance, engaged in empirical analyses of the effects of Progressive direct democracy reforms, and he did so with the explicit aim of bridging the gap between reforms and the sort of civic education that people like Lippmann felt were necessary as a second step in reducing corruption.[7] One can place Woodrow Wilson's writings on presidential government and on professional associations in this camp as well. The problem that emerged, however, was that the empirical conclusions of these scholars pointed in two directions: First, the eventual empirical studies suggested that citizens might simply not be capable of the lofty goals the Progressives set for them—or perhaps that when "the people" are more empowered, they generally disappoint Progressives by not fulfilling Progressive desires; and second, the emphasis on science had the long-term consequence of pushing out moral arguments about corruption. Hence, corruption becomes a thing to be studied, not a moral ill (see Seidelman 2015, 61; Ross 1991, 452).

In Dorothy Ross's (1991) account of the development of political science, one can see how this plays out during the middle decades of the twentieth century. Progressive Era political scientists such as Robert Bentley sought to understand politics as a forum for group conflict where self-interest is assumed as the ultimate overriding motivation. By the 1950s, the social sciences had fully adopted a quasi-economic emphasis on measurement, in such a manner that even rhetorical exhortations such as those of Theodore Roosevelt either were beside the point or were to be understood as self-interested efforts to manipulate. "Science," Ross argues, "became increasingly a substitute for political prudence" (334). And this was congruent, of course, with the Progressive desire to empower experts for the sake of scientific administration. In social science, then, one might advocate for scientific reforms that would reduce corruption, but the more one veered into advocacy, especially advocacy for reshaping character, the more one risked being guilty of shoddy social science from an empiricist's point of view.[8] Empirical studies of corruption, then, can be seen both as a legacy of the Progressive Era and as a challenge to the Progressives' goals.

6.4e: Corruption and the Public Mood

Finally, what of the Progressive "mood," as exemplified in our cursory study of literature and popular thought of the era? There are many ways in which one might understand this legacy today. One might, for instance, document the popularity of corruption stories in the popular media—in films or television shows. As tempting as such an effort might be, however, we would call the reader's attention to one tool that social scientists of the last century have provided for us—today we are able to assess public concerns about corruption to a degree that was not possible during the Progressive Era. Despite

Lippmann's caution about the enterprise, public opinion studies—without presuming there is such a thing as a simplified public with a clear will—enable us to measure, in a manner that simply was not possible during the Progressive Era, the level and prevalence of concern about corruption and the various ways in which Americans understand corruption. It is hard to use such studies to draw direct parallels to the Progressive Era. Yet our effort here to show that many Americans were preoccupied with corruption during the late nineteenth century, and our effort to link this to social and economic developments of the time, should make us sensitive to the possibility that this preoccupation waxes and wanes over time and that we can use these fluctuations to understand attitudes toward corruption in the years following the Progressive Era.

6.5: Conclusions

One way of understanding Progressive Era thought about corruption is to focus on a few prior assumptions that seemed to animate much of the movement and that have surfaced repeatedly in our survey above. Corruption finds its source in self-interest, the interests of individuals and groups, as opposed to the public interest. Because times change, and because human beings and human society evolve, we cannot know in advance what progress will contain and what future public interest will require. Because human nature and society evolve, we also cannot have a static constitutional structure; instead, we need to find new ways in new contexts for the people to speak, to direct the course of their own development unfettered by artificial rules meant to divide interests and divide power. The key to progress and to avoiding corruption is to empower the public to identify the public interest and to empower expertise or scientific administration to pursue it. Both of these groups are neutral, unbiased. The public is unbiased because its interest is the public interest, rather than a special interest. Expertise, science, is unbiased, by virtue of its being science. These two groups are thus able to see and seek the public interest disinterestedly, apolitically, and thus it makes sense that these two groups—when uncorrupted—would coincide in their views. This is basically the idea of Rousseau's general will, which rises above the many individual interests precisely by virtue of being general.

The Montesquieuian program, exemplified in the United States by Madison, involves dividing power to prevent despotism, as the ultimate anticorruption program. From the Progressive point of view, the Rube Goldberg machine that is the Madisonian government of checks and balances is itself a petri dish of corruption and a barrier to progress, insofar as the diffusion and limitation of power prevent the public from speaking with one voice and prevent quick and energetic action by leaders in tune with the people. Progressives were inspired vaguely by Rousseau without seeing his ultimate pessimism, his conclusion that uncorrupted government (in his sense of corruption, as government alienated from the general will) is an oxymoron. The Progressives often issued harsh condemnations of the system, expressing a disdain rooted in the assumption that purity of government is possible, the recipe for success being something like the following formula: *Democracy* (in the form of enabling the public to speak more directly and univocally with the help of direct voting and popular leaders) *plus experts* (in the form of scientific administration) *leads to progress.*

One corollary of this is that if democracy and expertise do not yield progressive results—that is, if they fail to produce what the people advocating for progress believe is progress right now—then that is evidence that corruption has spoiled the formula. This may be corruption of the people, which would need treatment through education—perhaps if the people were better educated, they would vote and behave as progress requires. This may be corruption of the experts, who may be bought by special interests. Or perhaps it is a corruption of process. Perhaps some cheating or meddling was involved. We—the authors of this book—fear that one consequence downstream from Progressive-era corruption talk is the assumption that when one loses at the ballot box, corruption in some form is the go-to villain to blame.

In this chapter we have sought to show five things. First, we have sought to demonstrate that the Progressives spoke about corruption differently than did Americans of the eighteenth and nineteenth centuries, who seemed to think of corruption more in terms of European decadence. They also spoke differently than theories of corruption in modern political theory, which were preoccupied with the ways in which governments might be constructed so as to minimize officeholder corruption and abuse of power. Hence, a political movement that took American constitutionalism as something to be radically modified, but not, for pragmatic reasons, abandoned, required a different way of talking about corruption. Second, in spite of this departure from pre-Progressive American corruption talk, many of the motifs in traditional corruption talk that we explored earlier (Chapter 3) are echoed in Progressive rhetoric: that the wages of sin is death, that money is the root of all evil, and that politics and politicians are inherently corrupt. Third, we have sought to demonstrate that the Progressive conception of corruption included a wide range of characteristics and actions, avoiding debates about whether corruption is an individual failing or a governmental failing. It sought to be all of the above. Fourth, we have sought to show the ways in which Progressive corruption talk encapsulated some elements of the Montesquieuian and Rousseauian accounts of corruption. It called for a rethinking of our republican project, suspicious of representative politicians and aiming to align the government with something like a general will, but it did so with pragmatic political tools, tinkering with procedural design. It attempted to use Mender's tools for Purifier's goals. And fifth, we have tried to show that this synthesis was untenable—it resulted in a political project that lacked clear goals and put much of its faith in beliefs about human nature and society, about the public, and about expertise that were not borne out by the results of the Progressive movement's innovations. These problems were apparent to some Progressive Era theorists, but they ultimately were not able to contain the corruption talk they had unleashed.

Different types of corruption talk came together during this era, and they have continued to be refracted in post-Progressive political discourse. It is to these refractions that we now turn.

II

Corruption Talk in Contemporary American Political Discourse

7

Social Scientific Corruption Talk

Social scientific studies of corruption, in contrast to philosophical studies, have demonstrated only limited concern about the definition of the corruption behind their various ways of operationalizing the term. This is in keeping with basic principles of social scientific inquiry. The goal in such studies is to develop tools to measure corruption, requiring perhaps a taxonomy of things that are corrupt but not anything deeper or more precise. In other words, if we simply agree to call a particular behavior or set of behaviors "corrupt," then we can move on to measuring these behaviors. In the same fashion, if we all agree to call a particular arrangement of dinosaur bones a "brontosaurus," we can count the number of brontosauruses we have found, compare variation among the brontosauruses, or otherwise gather information about them. If we subsequently decide to call the brontosaurus something else, this does not negate the information we have discovered.[1] Empirical researchers often view names as arbitrary.

At the same time, in reporting their conclusions, researchers need to choose names that reconnect to how words are otherwise used. Imagine if researchers changed the name "brontosaurus" to "alien," and then reported, to great fanfare, that they have found fossils of sixteen alien specimens. Or imagine, again farcically, a set of researchers identifying love with a particular type of chemical state of the brain; perhaps another group of researchers, years later, "discovers" that "love doesn't exist." Respecting nonscientific language is also important. Empirical social scientific studies of corruption operationalize the term to measure corruption or something like it, and one question is how well this links up with how the word has been used by non-specialists and by previous theorists.

To the extent that corruption research is about corruption prevention, such an operationalization is a necessity. Buchan and Hill (2014, chap. 7) allege this, in addition, to be an outgrowth of the development of the social sciences themselves and their purported mission to facilitate the spread of democracy, capitalism, and other modern political and economic "goods." Johnston (2005, 17–18) lauds the notion that "past debates over corruption—so often hung up on definitions, divided over the question of effects, and mired in paralyzing relativism—have given way to extensive agreement that corruption delays and distorts economic growth, rewards inefficiency, and short-circuits open competition." If research on corruption could reduce corruption, then there is an incentive to assume we know what it is, or at least not to haggle over details, as long as we're more or less playing in the same ballpark.

Social scientific research on corruption, then, emphasizes measurement, it seeks to establish a standard that can be used across various sorts of contexts, and it avoids inquiry into motive or moral character or into notions of what corrupt acts might mean more deeply. Social scientific research on corruption is less about determining what corruption is than about asking questions like these: Where does it happen? Why does it happen? What are interventions that might reduce it?

Empirical corruption research also tends to be comparative. European empirical and historical studies of corruption are perhaps the most developed example of this paradigm. Europe provides an easily comparable set of small nations with slight variations in government, population, and other easily quantifiable independent variables. The major European joint endeavors to study corruption have all made use of these features.

There is somewhat less American corruption research, and the research that exists is not as cohesive or as fully developed as European research. There are several reasons why this might be so. First, it is possible that this is an empirical problem; those who study American politics often resist international comparisons, so the sort of variation important to comparative studies simply may not be sufficiently present. Second, it is possible that this betrays a sort of American triumphalism—perhaps, to the extent that corruption tends to be associated with either "backwardness" or luxury, we simply don't think we are that corrupt. Or third, perhaps corruption research is less useful in the United States than it is elsewhere. It simply seems less feasible to sanction American states or cities for corruption than for the European Union or the World Bank to deny nations access to economic supports or partnerships. The proliferation of studies of corruption within U.S. business firms and of the techniques for penalizing such behavior (e.g., Davis and Ruhe 2003; Warren and Laufer 2009) provides some rudimentary support for this claim—if corruption research can be operationalized to sanction corruption, such research may flourish, but if not, there is less of a point in identifying corruption.

Fourth, and perhaps most consequentially, small fields of study can often be radically reoriented by particular research agendas. If there is little research being done on corruption in the United States, the establishment of one such field of study with a particular focus may reorient the field. External stimuli may be more important in inspiring research in particularly small fields than in larger ones with established researchers who have already developed expertise. On a general level, the impact of Progressivism, which we documented in Chapter 7, may have had an influence on some of the topics of concern to American corruption researchers. More recently, the Supreme Court's establishment of "corruption" as a permissible reason for regulation of campaign spending (which we discuss in Chapter 9) provides a smaller, more focused example.

The intent of this chapter is threefold. First, we present a descriptive analysis of the social scientific study of corruption. That is, it is not corruption itself that serves as our dependent variable, but corruption research, or corruption talk among academic researchers. In order for us to do so, the claims about social scientific research must apply—that is, there must be variation in the dependent variable. Accordingly, we look at variation in the quantity of such research across time and across place, comparing the role of the subject in contemporary social science across the past few decades, and in the United States compared to other nations. We also explore variations within the United States. Second, we compare comparative (largely European) corruption research to American corruption research, keeping in mind some of the norms of scientific research design: Is the methodology appropriate for the problem at hand? Are the terms that are used and the arguments that are made likely to generate high-quality empirical research? Does the research enable us to know more about things that are corrupt? And third, we seek to situate this research within our prior discussion of styles of corruption talk: What does our discussion in Chapter 6 of American Progressive corruption talk say about the trajectory of American corruption research? And what does this corruption research miss when it narrows the meaning of the word to something more operationalizable for research? It seems to us that this favors a Mender's approach by prioritizing discrete acts and agents—as opposed to the disposition, more natural to the Purist, to smell institutional or systemic rot.

To explore these points, both quantitative and qualitative approaches could be helpful. We could enumerate the number of studies of corruption, and we might make some rudimentary claims about their value or their influence. But ultimately a qualitative approach is more fitting; it is, we think, evident that there is much more empirical work on corruption in a comparative context than in the United States, so measuring exactly how much more is not a particularly important endeavor. Asking why, or how, the research differs is ultimately a more interesting question, even if it cannot be definitively answered empirically. Thus, we proceed here to summarize some of the major characteristics in comparative research on corruption, we then measure American research against that body of work, and we close by exploring the relationship between these approaches and the limitations of the style of corruption talk employed in this research.

7.1: On the Quantity of Corruption Research

7.1a: Origins

The study of corruption, as the first half of our book suggests, is many centuries old—far older than the social sciences. Its recent prominence in academic research has been the consequence of several organized efforts. As Michael Pinto-Duschinsky (2012) documents, the International Political Science Association's working group on political finance moved to incorporate the study of corruption into its efforts in the 1970s, culminating in the establishment of a formal research committee on corruption in 1994. During the same time period, the World Bank, the United Nations, and the Organization for Economic Cooperation and Development (OECD) adopted anticorruption resolutions and sponsored research on the subject. A variety of new nongovernmental organizations (NGOs) were formed to study corruption in elections and governance, including the International Institute for Democracy and Election Assistance (IDEA) and Transparency International. Beginning in the late 1990s, the Organization of American States, the Council of Europe, the European Union, and the United Nations all developed anticorruption task forces and recommendations.

Some analyses of this effort have pointed to European scandals in the 1970s and 1980s as catalysts (Kroeze 2016). Other, more cynical approaches have suggested that this is all an effort to make developing nations safe for "transnational capital" (Bratsis 2014). However, both Pinto-Duschinsky (2012) and Holmes (2015, chap. 7) attribute much of the original research to efforts to develop democratic regimes in the post-Soviet states of Eastern Europe. The research has had a snowball effect. Findings connecting corruption to terrorism, drug trafficking, and other organized criminal activities indicated that there were international gains to be achieved from anticorruption efforts and practices. Just as the study of corruption inevitably has moral implications, it is also of pragmatic concern for governments, NGOs, and philanthropic foundations. These pragmatic concerns suggest, however, that research on certain types of corruption, or on certain locales for corruption, will be of more value than others, and that this research may matter not because of its anticorruption goals in themselves but because reducing corruption may have a downstream influence on other social, political, or economic phenomena.

7.1b: Measuring Corruption Research

Given this recent history, it is unsurprising that there is more research on corruption today than there was in previous years. The magnitude of the increase, however, is quite striking, as is the focus of recent work on corruption. To get a sense of the change in corruption research in recent years, consider two examples.

First, Figure 7.1 shows the number of papers presented since 1969 at the annual meeting of the American Political Science Association (APSA). The

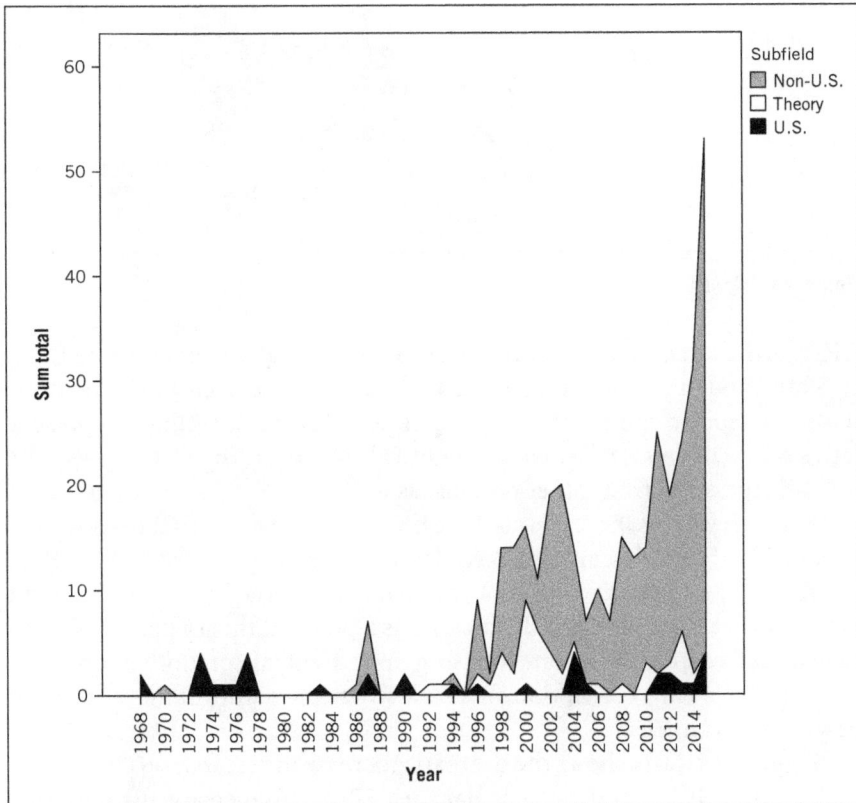

Figure 7.1 American Political Science Association Annual Meeting Papers on Corruption, 1968–2015. *(Source: American Political Science Association Annual Meeting Programs, 1968–2015.)*

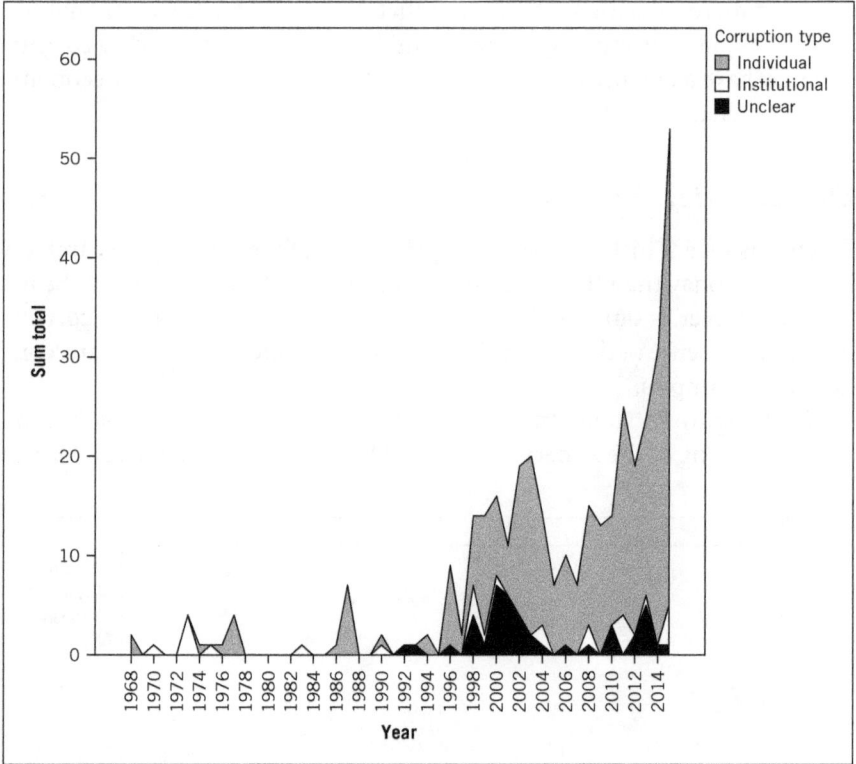

Figure 7.1 *(Continued)*

APSA is the largest national organization of political scientists in the United States, and in recent years the meeting has averaged over 7,000 attendees. It is reasonable to consider the papers presented at that meeting as representative of the interests of American political scientists. The meeting attracts political scientists from other nations, as well.

For each year, we have counted the number of papers with the word "corruption" in their titles, and we have classified each paper, based on the title, abstract, or subsequent publication, as a paper about the United States, about nations other than the United States, or as a political theory paper. We also categorized each paper as one focusing on individual corruption, on institutional or systemic corruption, or as one where the nature of the corruption described was unclear.

Figure 7.1 clearly shows the dramatic increase in research on corruption since the mid-1990s, and in particular since 2010. This increase, furthermore, has almost exclusively been an increase in papers on nations other than the United States. Among papers on corruption presented in 2014 and 2015, China and third world nations were the main subjects of research. There is limited, suggestive evidence that the frequency of papers on corruption is related to events; there was a small spike in papers on corruption in the United States following the Watergate scandal, and recent papers on China may be reflective of the "Tiger Hunt" and other recent anticorruption efforts in Chinese politics as well. Yet there is no single subject that can explain recent changes in political scientists' attention to corruption, apart perhaps from the sort of research infrastructure described above. While the increase is also too substantial to be linked to individual researchers, theme panels on political corruption have been chaired in recent years by officials from the World Bank and other organizations that have worked to develop anticorruption programs. The increase in papers on corruption is, in addition, largely confined to papers on individual officeholder corruption. Many of the political theory papers presented during the 1970s and 1980s considered systemic corruption, and there has been a recent increase in formal theory work on the subject.

Some cautions are required in considering this increase, however. The size of the APSA meeting has increased over this time period as well; the annual meeting program in 1968 was only 39 pages while it reached 247 pages in 2015. Some inflation adjustment may be in order. The timing of the increase in research on corruption, however, does not neatly correspond to a similar growth in the size of the annual meeting; the meeting has grown larger in a roughly linear fashion while papers on corruption grew rather abruptly.

We also did not measure the growth of papers that address subjects related to corruption. Many of the panels that featured papers on corruption also included papers with titles mentioning scandal, clientelism, or patronage. The actual growth in research on things related to corruption may, then, be slightly larger or smaller than what is shown here. We would contend, however, that it is significant that papers explicitly using the term have grown—a major interest here is in what people prefer to call things as much as in what they study.

Second, Figure 7.2 presents yearly totals for corruption research across various disciplines and, within political science, across different regions of the world. The data here come from Harvard law professor Matthew Stephenson's comprehensive bibliography (2016) of corruption research, a bibliography that Stephenson claims is the largest publicly available English-language bibliography on the subject.[2] Stephenson's bibliography includes articles, books, book chapters, technical reports, and unpublished papers. We have taken Stephenson's entries and coded them according to discipline and, within political science, by region, as reflected either by the title of the work or by the title of the journal or edited volume.

This bibliography has been maintained since only 2012, so it is natural that many of the articles in it are relatively recent. Despite this potential for temporal bias, however, Stephenson's bibliography resembles the APSA data

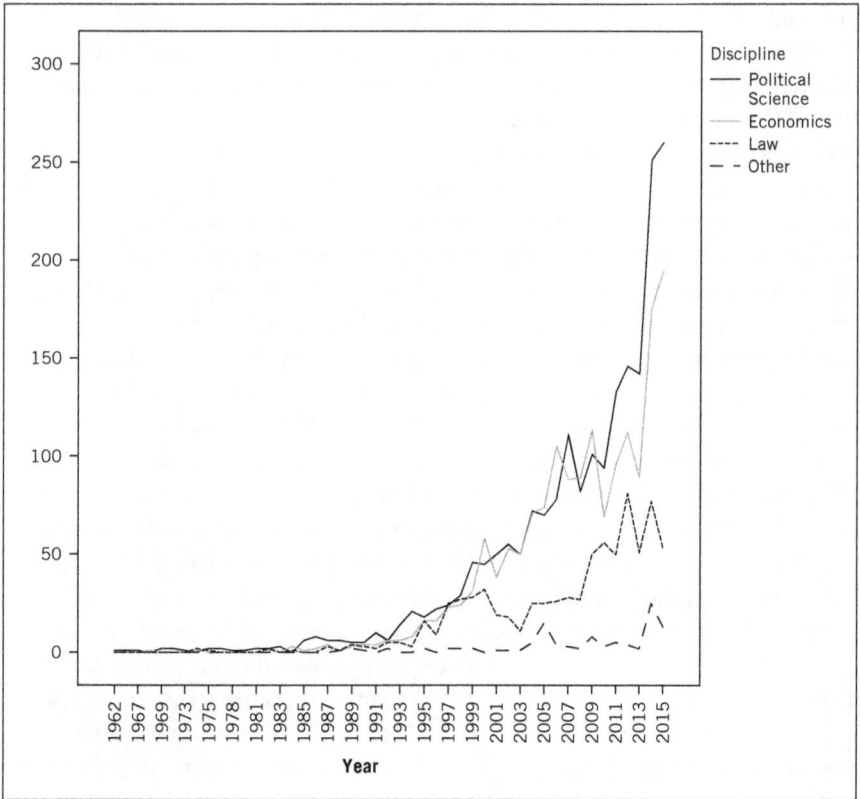

Figure 7.2 Research Articles on Corruption, by Discipline and Regional Focus, 1962–2015. *(Source: Matthew Stephenson [2016] corruption bibliography.)*

quite closely. Like Figure 7.1, this figure shows a remarkable increase in comparative research on corruption, with the most notable increases in research on Europe, Asia, and the developing world. There are more works here on the United States, proportionally, than in the APSA data, but the volume of work on the United States does not noticeably increase across the time period. Even given the potentially selective nature of the data collection here, this correspondence indicates the disconnect between empirical research on corruption and work in American politics.

The data from these two sources are consequential in that they show differences in the development of research agendas. Research on corruption has grown, yet research on American corruption has not. One might contend that this reflects the comparatively low level of corruption that exists in the United States, but the increase in research on European corruption in Stephenson's data renders such a claim suspect—most empirical studies of corruption find the United States to be similar to most Western European coun-

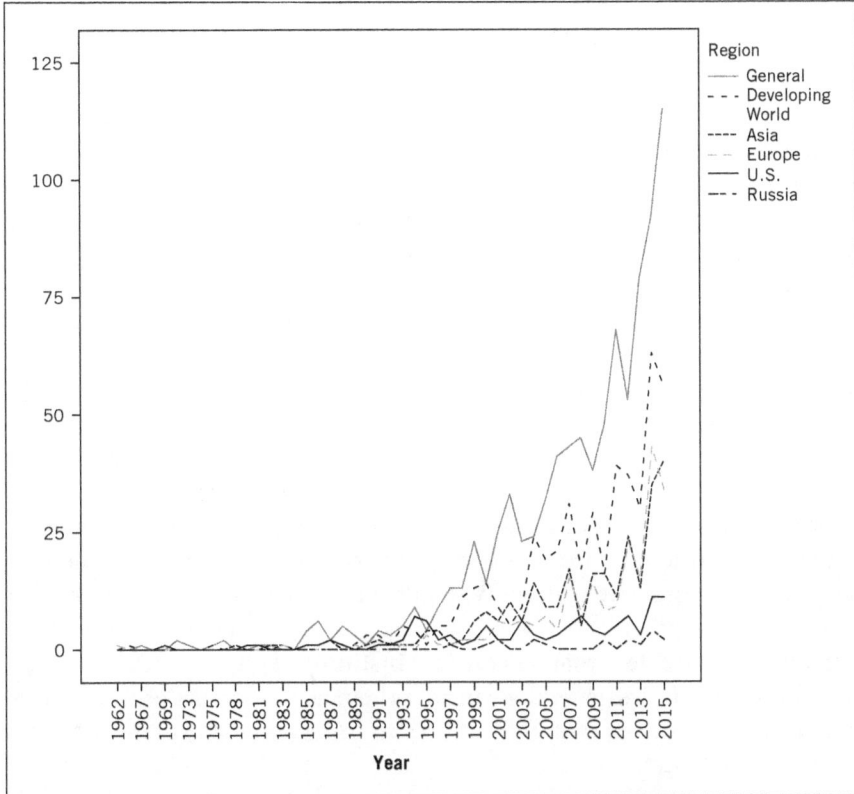

Figure 7.2 (*Continued*)

tries in its level of corruption. It seems safe to infer that American political scientists simply do not have, or have not yet developed, the sorts of tools or research incentives to study corruption. This serves as prima facie evidence of the disconnect we discuss elsewhere: We talk a lot about corruption in the United States, but we're not always certain what we are talking about.

7.2: Methodological Approaches to Corruption

To merely compare the volume of corruption research, however, does not tell us anything about the characteristics of that research. It is important, as well, to consider distinctions in the corruption literature among types of corruption. The most enduring of these is the distinction that tends to be drawn in the literature between institutions and individuals. Using our categories from Chapter 2, this is the distinction between officeholder corruption and an ontological corruption that means the ruin of institutions, such that they no longer function or no longer function as well.

7.2a: Institutional Approaches to Corruption

It is common to divide empirical political science into the study of political behavior or of political institutions. One can conceptualize the study of political behavior as the study of individuals or definable groups of individuals—as inquiry into why people do what they do. Institutions, on the other hand, are formal political structures that can be analyzed independently of the characteristics, traits, or actions of individuals. While institutions necessarily are made up of individuals, we can study them without reference to particular individuals—we can understand changes to the organization, effectiveness, or formal or informal powers of the U.S. Senate, for instance, without reference to the actions, character, or other behaviors of the people who happen to currently be members of the Senate.

Most political research must make reference to both behaviors and institutions. Institutions provide structure, in the form of rules and in the form of behavioral norms or customs that channel political behavior. Yet individual political actions are also taken in pursuit of goals that exist independent of these rules—we seek individual goals such as wealth, happiness, or power, or perhaps collective goals such as justice through our political actions, and to the extent that we consider institutional structures in our pursuit of these goals, we generally consider them as accelerants or hindrances to our pursuits, not as essential features in influencing our preferences regarding these goals.

Where does corruption fit into this schematic between behavioral research and institutional research? Let us first consider the fit between corruption and the study of political institutions. There is no consensus among institutionalists about the appropriate scope of what they study. Some approaches to political institutions concern themselves solely with the formal rules that make up an institution. For such theories, institutions are approached in a value-neutral way—institutions are, as Jean Blondel (2006) puts it, like "big rocks in the landscape." We can't avoid seeing them and working around them, but they don't have the power to change us in morally or politically meaningful ways, at least according to this type of theory. Other modes of institutional inquiry take note of less tangible features of institutions—the networks of individuals that are established within institutional structures, historical understandings of the institution that stand apart from formal rules, or informal customs or ways of being that are a part of our understanding of the institution.

In the case of the study of political behavior, there would seem to be no intelligible way to talk about corruption save for the acts of individuals. Is there a rule that has been broken? If so, and if the rule still stands, then we might posit that a corrupt act has taken place. Yet it is the act, not the rule itself, that is of interest here. If the rule is subsequently modified or changed, then we might take an interest in the act of modifying the rule, but again, we are concerned with behaviors of individuals. We can see and measure things in this approach, but the things we see and measure are considered from a value-neutral attitude.

If, however, we wish to expand our understanding of an institution to include traditions, customs, or ways of doing things, then we have room to talk about corruption more richly—but only if value is "assigned" to those things. Oakeshott (1991, 62–65) contends that institutions cannot be understood without reference to these less measurable features. For Oakeshott, institutions enable our "participation in a conversation"—they provide a language, a common set of reference points, a set of prescribed behaviors that allow our statements to each other to carry meaning. Their very existence implies a normative value; even if we might not fully understand why a particular convention exists, its existence is still valuable to us simply because it allows us understand each other. A lack of respect for these conventions, or a complete dismissal of them, might take place even where no formal rules have been violated, or where formal rule change has taken place through universally accepted means. Such conventions can, perhaps, also change without deliberate choice at all.

An understanding of institutions that proceeds in this manner can allow for the possibility of corruption. Yet the very act of proposing the existence of norms or ideals as a part of our institutions is controversial, and it takes the measurement itself outside the realm of empirical inquiry as conceptualized by contemporary empirical social science. This departure from the methodological assumptions of contemporary social science is perhaps inevitable whenever corruption claims imply a sort of rotting or decay of institutions. To understand this, let us consider two different examples related to the U.S. Congress:

- First, before the advent of inexpensive air travel, it was necessary for members of Congress to remain in Washington, DC, for weeks at a time. During this time, the story goes, cross-partisan socializing was common, and deals were often struck in the wee hours of the morning following drinks at a handful of local bars. As Mann and Ornstein (2012) recount, this tradition largely died out in the 1990s as it became the norm for members of Congress to return home every weekend. A norm was changed. Was Congress corrupted by this change? Was it corrupt before the change? One's interpretation likely depends on one's view of what politics is supposed to be. Political scientists may lament the passing of this era, but it seems unlikely that many American citizens want their members of Congress to spend more time in Washington drinking.

- Second, both chambers of the U.S. Congress have many formal and informal customs regarding how members will speak of and to each other in their remarks.[3] These customs often sound archaic to modern audiences, they likely render floor conversation more boring than it would otherwise be, and they may sometimes impede the exchange of substantive ideas. Yet when given a chance to participate in mock sessions of Congress, many American eagerly adopt such modes of speaking, even when they do not know exactly what to do and even when they cannot fully explain why they are doing so.[4] Here, there is the sort of "flow of sympathy" to which Oakeshott refers, arguably because people sense there must be good reasons for such stilted ways of speaking.

Which, then, is the more essential piece of the institution? And how would we empirically measure its value, the cost of its absence, or the relationship between these intangible pieces of the institution and any potential institutional outputs? Doing so is inevitably a matter of political thought, not merely empirical political science. For example, some scholars have argued that conversational norms perpetuate social inequalities, privilege arguments made by elites who know the conventions, and so forth (Sanders 1997). Yet there is no easy way to prove, by the methods of empirical social science, that this is or is not so.

In sum, then, many institutional approaches to political science provide no particular means by which to quantify corruption or to compare levels of corruption either against some sort of standard or against another institution. Institutional theories that posit the existence of norms as a component of institutions themselves (as opposed to being incidental to the institution, merely an artifact of culture or a behavior engaged in by some but not by others) can aid in the definition of corruption, particularly when coupled with a presumption à la Oakeshott that norms are of value. To summarize, institutional theories present two problems:

(a) The assumption that violation of a norm, not a rule, entails corruption presents measurement problems in that it is harder to quantify norm violations.
(b) Not all norms are of equal value or importance; the very existence of a norm, as well as its overall value and its relative value, are often subject to contestation.

From these problems, it follows that we might establish a list of potentially corrupt acts, of "things like corruption," and measure them with reference to individuals. Some of these acts (bribery, for instance) might uncontroversially be subsumed under a rubric of corruption, while others might be more questionable additions to the list. Or in other words, we can identify the egregious cases, but there is no "bright line" we can use in looking at institutions to distinguish the corrupt from the uncorrupt or to assign gradations of corruptness. In this sense, we would be seeing institutions not as themselves but as collections of individuals.

7.2b: Corruption and Political Behavior

For the most part, contemporary empirical research on corruption measures the prevalence of corrupt acts. Corruption manifested, then, is a form of political behavior. That is, we cannot measure actual corrupt individuals save by their behaviors. We cannot use political behaviors as a means of defining corruption, but if we have a preexisting definition, we can look for behaviors that seem to exemplify parts of this definition. And because the unit of analysis is the act, or behavior, it can only be seen as a sort of officeholder corruption. Even if two or more corrupt behaviors were correlated, or linked, in some fashion, we could not understand them as a form of rot or decay of an institution but only as distinct actions. At most, observing that corrupt acts occur more frequently within particular institutions or settings might inspire us to begin an inquiry into the nature of that institution or setting.

Empirical studies of political behavior tend to fall into three basic categories:

(a) Cross-sectional analyses
(b) Longitudinal analyses (cross-sectional analyses and longitudinal analyses both tend to be quantitative in nature, but may be qualitative)
(c) Case studies (which generally are qualitative)

In the case of corruption research, it seems appropriate to add a fourth category:

(d) Studies of perceptions of corruption

Before we address the findings and the limitations of U.S. corruption research, a few general notes on methodology are in order:

Cross-sectional analyses are appropriate when one wishes to compare instances of a particular phenomenon across different venues. Such studies must be undertaken with an awareness of (or an attempt to analyze) differences among these venues. If, for instance, one wishes to compare the costs of running for legislative office in different countries, one must seek to compare these countries with regard to measurable characteristics of their political systems: the population size of legislative districts, the competitiveness of these districts, restrictions on the raising or spending of money, the nature of the party system, the voting rules in place, and so forth. If one is able to find two countries that are similar according to many or most of these independent variables, a finding of differences (to return to our example here, of differences in the cost of seeking office) might then reflect that something less measurable is operating causally—for instance, that the political culture in these two nations is different.

In the case of corruption, a well-constructed cross-sectional analysis (e.g., Johnston 2005, 2014) might yield insights into either what institutional factors tend to produce or discourage corruption or whether less measurable cultural factors play a role. Such studies require, however, that the dependent variable, corruption, can also be measured, or that a reasonable proxy measure can be used in its place. When done well, such comparative studies can draw upon country-specific case studies in order to provide illustrations of how the cross-national data can be applied or to provide justification for distinguishing country types as Johnston has done. There are numerous technical debates about how to measure corruption and how to account for cultural differences in operationalizing the term, but such differences are to be expected in any sort of cross-sectional analysis.

Longitudinal analyses can be used to control for many of the aforementioned institutional factors by restricting the analysis to one particular country or set of countries and assessing change in the dependent variable across time. Such studies can be used to measure the effects of identifiable events. For instance, a change in party control of government, a change in law, variations in funding for government programs, or the overall economic wellbeing of the nation are all plausible catalysts for changes in the dependent variable of interest. If one wishes to study corruption, one might use any of these variables. It can be difficult, however, to ensure that all relevant changes are controlled for.

A particularly noteworthy example of this approach is the work conducted by the University of Gothenburg's Quality of Government (QOG) Institute. Bo Rothstein (2011b) draws connections between the study of the quality of government and surveys of political trust, civic associations, and social capital. There are three different types of longitudinal studies among the projects pursued within the QOG program. First, some studies have focused upon measurable anticorruption policies, identifying the time of their establishment and setting up before-and-after assessments of corruption allegations or prosecutions (Rothstein 2011a). Second, other studies have sought to compare the correlates of corruption over relatively short periods of time; for instance, in *The Quality of Government* (2011b), the book that summarizes the project, Rothstein describes the relationship between corruption and economic growth, infant mortality rates, or other indicators of well-being during the 1990s. In both of these cases, one might presume that policymakers might be prompted to undertake reforms that have been shown to have results—either in punishing corrupt acts or in reducing their occurrence as a side effect. Such approaches are particularly popular in analyses of the relationship between corruption and civil war or terrorism (see, e.g., Fjelde 2009). And third, some studies take a broader, historical view of the development of political institutions within a particular country and seek to chart changes in corruption that might correspond to such developments. Jan Teorell and Bo Rothstein (2012), for instance, analyze the relationship between the establishment of democratic institutions in Sweden during the eighteenth and nineteenth centuries and political corruption prosecutions. This developmental approach allows institutions to vary across time and presumes, again, that anticorruption efforts are not principally responsible for such changes. Historical studies such as this can help to explain anomalous cases—in the case of Sweden, for instance, they can provide an explanation of how a nation generally held to exhibit low levels of corruption became that way.

Case studies of individual countries, actors, or events can often provide the historical or contextual detail that large-N quantitative studies cannot provide. A well-constructed case study has, of course, a scientific rigor of its own, but the focus on a single case or a small number of cases enables one to draw upon interviews, historical documents, and other forms of "deep description" that can both answer research questions on their own and generate new hypotheses from which one might generalize. Case studies can range from accounts that are largely journalistic in nature to descriptions such as those of the "analytical narratives" project which draw upon formal theory or sophisticated quantitative research to generate and test hypotheses (Bates et al. 1998).

A recent example of a case study–based analysis of corruption is Kelly McMann's (2014) *Corruption as a Last Resort*, which considers political corruption in Kazakhstan and Kyrgyzstan. McMann proposes that many citizens engage in petty corruption as a means of obtaining goods or government services when there are not any alternatives. She draws on interviews and media reports in order to emphasize that the deals most citizens in these countries make are a form of corruption (of which these citizens are clearly aware), yet these transactions are not likely to be decreased by larger anticorruption schemes, such as reducing the size of the government bureaucracy, because they involve necessary governmental functions and happen in a decentralized, largely unmonitored environment. Studies such as this can provide appropriate levels of context for the instances of corruption that they detail, and they can entertain and add to public debate, but assessing the truth behind any generalizations they suggest will prove difficult. One particularly consequential feature of the case study approach, however, is that it can directly engage with the task of defining corruption. That is, particular features of an exchange or behavior can be presented, and the author may explore the nuances of categorizing that behavior and the strengths and weaknesses of various attempts at definition.

Perceptions of corruption do not need to be considered in all behavioral studies; for instance, studies of voting behavior do not require lengthy surveys of what people think voting is. Such a category is relevant, however, in cases where definitions of the term are contested, and it is a means of moving forward without achieving consensus on definition. Studies of racial attitudes, for instance, often begin from the premise that racism might be manifest in a variety of beliefs, attitudes, or behaviors that do not explicitly invoke race. Different types of people hold different beliefs about what racism is, and there is room for debate about whether particular social or political views have a racial component. Similarly, people understand corruption differently, yet just because people believe a particular thing to be an instance of corruption does not make it so. To the extent that the definition of corruption is contested and that corruption itself is not easily measurable, it is appropriate that some studies assess public beliefs. Moreover, a finding regarding perceptions can have merit as both an independent variable and a dependent variable in a variety of contexts. There is, for instance, a long history in American research of measuring the effects that beliefs that politicians are "crooked" have on voting habits (e.g., Dalton 2004) and of measuring the determinants of this belief (e.g., Uslaner 2002). As we shall see, it is also possible to distinguish among people who are susceptible to particular types of perceptions and to give different weight to these views; in the corruption case, perhaps we are more concerned to know whether politically knowledgeable people believe their politicians to be corrupt than whether less knowledgeable people do. Prominent studies of corruption perceptions include Frank Louis Rusciano's (2014) summary of cross-national studies of public opinion about corruption, and the expert surveys conducted by Transparency International (discussed in Montinolo and Jackman [2002]).

The four categories just examined are hardly an original contribution to dividing up social scientific research projects, and they are also not particularly unique to the study of corruption. Many research projects combine more than one of these approaches. Our purpose of distinguishing between them and noting some consequential comparative work, however, is to put U.S.-specific work in context.

7.3: American Corruption Research

As the earlier data show, there has been less research on corruption in the United States, and it is more difficult in the U.S. context to speak of a coherent body of work. This is not a new observation (see Peters and Welch 1978), but it is worth reiterating given the explosion in work on corruption over the past decade. In instances where corruption is studied, as in the case below of congressional scandals, the theoretical touchpoints have tended to be works about Congress, not about patterns of corruption. There have been some instances where researchers who have done primarily comparative work have turned their attention to the United States. Yet, as the following discussion shows, studying corruption in the United States faces limitations, and these limitations have ensured that politicians' references to corruption have far less empirical evidence behind them than do such references in other nations.

7.3a: Cross-sectional Studies

As is the case in comparative literature, many American studies of corruption have sought to compare state governments or municipal governments. For instance, Oguzhan Dincer and Michael Johnston (2015) and Dick Simpson et al. (2015) compare corruption in major American cities, and Adriana Cordis and Jeffrey Milyo (2013) compare federal corruption prosecutions of different types of state or municipal officeholders. This is in keeping, perhaps, with the preoccupations of the Progressive movement; American city and state governments have long been said to be hotbeds of corruption, and thus there has been a long-standing research interest in identifying and measuring this corruption. And just as comparative studies might be able to draw upon imprecise definitions of corruption and yet provide usable information for policymakers, corporations, and the like, so comparisons of American cities or states might yield useful information.

And yet, the same concerns that underpin some comparative research exist within American cross-sectional research on corruption. Many of the studies mentioned earlier draw on criminal prosecutions, which ensures that there is no need for the authors to define corruption; it has been defined by those bringing charges. At the same time, however, a starting point for many of these studies has been to evaluate public stereotypes that particular states or cities—places like Chicago, New Orleans, or Providence—are corrupt. Even when the results do not necessarily support the conventional wisdom about corruption, the conventional wisdom tends to be reiterated and used as a means of drawing hypotheses.

Most consequentially, however, cross-sectional studies of corruption within the United States provide few metrics for evaluating federal politics. Some of the major findings in studies of corruption at lower levels—findings regarding the presence or absence of news media to cover scandals, legislative professionalism, term limits, or city government type—are difficult to apply to federal politics. Some studies (e.g., Cordis and Milyo 2013) have compared federal officeholders to state officeholders, or have compared levels of corruption in the U.S. Congress to those in state legislatures. What one might do with such information, however, is not clear. Is it meaningful to argue that the U.S. Congress should conduct its affairs like the legislatures of less-corrupt states? Are there ethics rules in these states that might be of use in Congress? While it is not uncommon to transfer some lessons from state politics to federal politics—as, for instance, Raymond La Raja and Brian Schaffner's (2016) study of state campaign finance laws shows—it is difficult to control for differences in scale, in the policy domains of states, or in political culture. Even some of the basic findings in the comparative literature on corruption across nations are not easy to use here—one might infer from measurement of corrupt nations that they are bad places to live, but it is less obvious that a corrupt city (e.g., Providence, Rhode Island) or a corrupt state (e.g., Illinois) is similarly a bad place to live, or even if so, whether and how corruption in government contributes much to making it a bad place to live.

7.3b: Longitudinal Studies

Several researchers have also sought to measure patterns in corruption across time. For instance, Michael Genovese (2010) analyzes corruption within presidential administrations across time, and Rodrigo Praino, Daniel Stockemer, and Vincent Moscardelli (2013) analyze the effects of corruption investigations for members of the House of Representatives. Both studies note some of the basic difficulties in measuring changes in levels of corruption across time in U.S. cases.

In the presidency case, Genovese catalogs instances of corruption in different presidential administrations. Is the level of corruption within the executive branch increasing? Overall, the number of corruption allegations for presidential administrations is low, which means that a set of corruption claims may reflect more on the individual president, or on individuals within the executive branch, than on any sort of larger pattern, lapse of accountability, or other governmental failing. There is, in addition, the problem of categorizing events: In the case of President Bill Clinton, for instance, was the president's extramarital affair with a subordinate coworker, or his cover-up of it, an instance of corruption? And there is the problem of responsibility: In instances where corruption at lower levels of the executive branch has been found, is this a sign of presidential ineptitude or perfidy? Even once corruption has been identified, it is not always clear who is corrupt.

The piece by Praino, Stockemer, and Moscardelli (2013) is one of several analyses of scandals in Congress (see also Basinger 2013; Basinger et al. 2014; Groseclose and Krehbiel 1994). Congress has always been a more natural subject of quantitative study than other branches of government, so a finding of variation across time in corruption allegations or prosecutions is perhaps less likely to be a matter of individual idiosyncrasies than would be the case for corruption in other branches. Praino and his colleagues track the number of claims against members filed with the House Ethics Committee or the Office on Congressional Ethics. Here, however, as the authors note, one of the most difficult problems for analysis is changes in the willingness of that committee to entertain claims against members. There are numerous reasons why corruption might go uninvestigated, ranging from intimidation by the allegedly corrupt member or the party leadership to cartel-like partisan agreements not to investigate each other. And there is also the possibility that ethics investigations will be used as a political weapon. In the presidency case, the question of definition arises. Praino and his colleagues are concerned with *scandal*, not corruption. Some scandals involve corruption, some do not. A finding of variation over time can help us to understand, in broad strokes, an empirical fact—that the number and consequences of formal ethics charges against members of Congress change over time. This has something to do with corruption, but it is not the same as measuring corruption in Congress over time.

7.3c: Case Studies

As is the case for the comparative literature, there are many journalistic accounts of instances of corruption in U.S. politics. The sort of comparative case study approach discussed above is rare, however.[5] More common in the U.S. framework are efforts such as those of Dennis Thompson (1993) to develop theories of what corruption is in the American context and then illustrate those theories with reference to particular cases. Thompson has explored lobbying or conflict-of-interest scandals in Congress such as the Keating Five case with an eye toward showing the interplay between individual officeholder corruption and the breakdown of institutional norms. Thompson's research provides much of the grounding for contemporary explorations of the nexus between lobbying or campaign finance practices and individual corrupt acts.

While Thompson's work is perhaps the best-known case of U.S. theory-building regarding corruption, other case study approaches can easily descend into polemic or partisan attacks. Within the context of electoral politics, we suspect this is in part because allegations of corruption can rest on implicit quid pro quo deals that cannot be proven to have taken place (as is the case, for instance, with any connection between campaign contributions and legislative "favors"). As numerous academic (e.g., Holyoke 2014) and journalistic (Kaiser 2009) accounts have noted, it is expected that democratic politicians will be responsive to lobbyists and organized interests, and it is expected that some money will also enter the system without corruption, so explicit proof is rare. This is so, in addition, because if corruption is not the norm, those who have engaged in corrupt practices can hardly be expected to discuss their activities openly. Whereas in the comparative case studies corruption can be so widespread that those who, for instance, pay off bureaucrats for small favors will discuss the reasons why they did so, such cases are rarer in the United States or other Western democracies. Among the most noteworthy exceptions to this are the depositions filed by the defendants in the *McConnell v. Federal Election Commission* (540 U.S. 93 [2003]) case, where proponents of eliminating so-called soft money (or unregulated large contributions to political parties) sought to demonstrate that these contributions were corrupting. Here, a number of major donors to the Democratic Party discussed the return they got for their contributions and their thoughts on the appropriateness of allowing such contributions. These depositions stand out because the alleged corrupters talked about what they had done, but to the extent that we can believe these to be honest statements we must note that the depositions were presented in the hopes of outlawing their contributions (and outlawing politicians' efforts to solicit them).[6]

7.3d: Studies of Perceptions of Corruption

Nathaniel Persily and Kelli Lammie (2004) are among the many authors who summarize Americans' views on corruption. Drawing specifically upon the U.S. Supreme Court's claim that the perception of corruption is a valid reason for regulation of political spending, Persily and Lammie document what they describe as first, the increased belief among Americans that politicians are (or U.S. politics is) corrupt, and second, the lack of correspondence between these beliefs and efforts by politicians to address political spending. Persily and Lammie summarize patterns in Americans' answers to a variety of different public opinion surveys regarding trust in government and beliefs about political malfeasance, but they devote most of their paper to showing trends in Americans' answers to two different American National Election Studies questions: one regarding overt criminality ("Do you think that quite a few of the people running the government are crooked, not very many are, or do you think hardly any of them are crooked?"), and another regarding the goals of politicians ("Would you say the government is pretty much run by a few big interests looking out for themselves or that it is run for the benefit of all of the people?").

Unlike the comparative literature on public opinion about corruption, U.S.-specific studies can at least use comparable language across time and across any potential subgroups. Neither of these questions asks explicitly about corruption, although both questions fit comfortably within most frameworks for understanding what officeholder corruption is. And none provides much indication of what, or who, respondents are thinking about when they think about crooked politicians or the role of "big interests" in politics. It is unrealistic to imagine survey researchers having the ability to ask a detailed set of questions about what people think corruption is. Yet in the absence of such questions, we are left with a battery of questions that reveals quite a bit about the sorts of people who believe that politicians are crooked or that big interests run the government. By and large, the sorts of people who believe this are also people who believe themselves to be disadvantaged by government policy—people whose preferred party is not in power, people who think they pay too much in taxes, people who express a lack of trust not just in politicians, but in other people in general. There is no correlation between political knowledge and perceptions that politicians are crooked or that big interests run government. All of these findings suggest that we can learn a lot about ourselves, or about our fellow citizens, by asking questions about "corruption," but we cannot really learn very much about corruption itself.

A noteworthy exception to this problem is the experimental work of David Redlawsk and James McCann (2005; also McCann and Redlawsk 2006), who conducted a survey experiment listing a set of actions and asking respondents whether they would find these actions to be corrupt. These authors also seek to measure how strongly respondents feel about their judgments—how corrupt they find each act, how angry they would be about it, and whether such acts might sometimes be justified. While this leaves the definition of corruption up to the respondent, it is, more than most other U.S. explorations of public opinion, able to gauge not only what norms citizens hold but what sorts of suspect acts might count as corruption and which might not. The study is also designed to measure differences in expectations—respondents are asked not only about corrupt acts that might be performed by a politician (e.g., offering a no-bid contract to a political supporter) but also about corrupt acts that might be performed by citizens (e.g., falsely claiming eligibility for government benefits). The authors claim that respondents do not hold politicians to a higher standard than they hold citizens. Finally, among the consequential findings in McCann and Redlawsk's 2006 work is that partisanship plays a role in our expectations about who is corrupt (we expect our preferred party to be less corrupt than the opposition), but not in our willingness to see particular actions as corrupt.

7.4: Studying Corruption, and Studying Things That Have Something to Do with Corruption

It is instructive to compare this summary of U.S. literature on corruption with the literature on particular types of potentially corrupt practices (on which activities shade into being "bad"). The summary here of corruption research shows that the American literature is nowhere near as developed as the corruption literature on other countries. Furthermore, when American corruption is studied, researchers often start with the basic theoretical paradigms established in the comparative literature and with examples and images drawn from Progressive Era journalism and political rhetoric.

We do not mean to suggest that there is anything normatively or theoretically wrong with such an approach. Instead, we note only that the methodologies in place for studying corruption and the initial impetus for corruption research (e.g., grant funding, NGO resolutions, intergovernmental research programs) all favor a comparative approach. But this is noteworthy because the foundational concepts for studying many things that are "like" corruption—that are, perhaps, taken as symptoms of corruption as institutional rot or decay—often have their roots in a distinctly American Progressive rhetoric. When corruption is spoken of in politics, it is often connected with areas of study such as campaign or party finance, lobbying and other interest group activity, patronage, or clientelism. While these subjects are not synonymous with corruption and while there are legitimate manifestations for all of these things in politics, this is where we often look for corruption. American theories of political parties, of the role of money in politics, of why and how interest groups gain access to politicians, or of how politicians seek to curry favor among all types of supporters have been widely applied in the study of other nations. Even where U.S. theories do not apply, it is common for researchers to explicitly note why American concepts do not fit the nations they are studying. It is hard to even know where to begin with examples, but one might start with any of the various compendia of comparative work on party finance (Jansen and Young 2011; Boatright 2016) or interest group activities (Beyers, Eising, and Maloney 2010) to see how American practices tend to be linked to other nations' practices and how American paradigms tend to relate to others.

Corruption research—and, perhaps, any sort of social scientific research—is subject to the demands of events in the broader world in which researchers live. In other words, researchers choose particular topics to study based on their own concerns about the world, or perhaps based on the concerns of funding organizations or others who would subsidize research. It is quite possible that contemporary concerns about the consequences of the Trump presidency might encourage further empirical research on corruption, just as the 2016 Trump victory led to an outpouring of research on populism (a subject we discuss in Chapter 11). People see something that they think is corrupt, and they work to understand where that thing came from or how they might address it. American research on corruption may well flourish as researchers turn their attention to the lessons we can learn from the Trump presidencies.

Even if this is the case, however, research that presents corruption as its subject matter will remain restricted to seeing corruption as officeholder crookedness. This is not only a matter of measuring corruption. It is also a matter of the scope of the corruption in question. If corruption also refers to an ontological corruption of institutions, to a rotting, a decay, a contagion, or brokenness of the institutions that structure political lives together, then the measurable phenomena that come from this will not merely be instances of individual corrupt acts. Research on, to name a few things, political polarization, a failure of elected politicians to respond to public sentiment, or gridlock between branches of government all may address symptoms of some sort of broader corruption in the sense of governmental decay or corrosion. Research on declining civic engagement, incivility among citizens, declining public support for government, or rising civic unrest may address a sort of corruption in the sense of decay or dysfunction of the body politic. Research on these subjects will proceed, however, with reference to what is easily measurable. Research on political polarization is research on political polarization, not on officeholder corruption. If students of such matters were to say that they study the corruption of government, this would seem an imprecise and perhaps overly grandiose way to describe that work, given the current colloquial connotations of the term with officeholder malfeasance.

Research programs, incentives, and presumptions about method push the empirical social scientific study of corruption into talk about officeholder corruption, focusing on discrete instances, measurable events. This style of research operationalizes the term to capture individual, transactional officeholder corruption. These forces lend themselves less easily to the study of corruption in a broader sense—corruption as the rotting or corrosion of institutions that are not fulfilling their purpose.

None of this suggests that there is no value, to the academy or to the public, in the study of corruption by empirical social science. There surely is much to be gained by studying, understanding, confronting, and ultimately fixing officeholder corruption. Our argument here, however, is that such research will say little about corruption as rot or brokenness of institutions. It is unlikely to be of use to citizens, or to politicians, who seek to make claims about corruption in that sense. It may mislead us into thinking that the ontological corruption of our institutions—so much a concern in the history of thought about politics—all comes down to corruption in the transactional, office-holder sense. It talks past our fears about our political system or our way of life falling apart. And, as we show in the next three chapters, such fears are, and will continue to be, a regular part of our political discourse.

8

Presidential Corruption Talk

Let us reject the narrow visions of those who would tell us
that we are evil because we are not yet perfect, that we are
corrupt because we are not yet pure, that all the sweat and
toil and sacrifice that have gone into the building of America
were for naught because the building is not yet done.

—RICHARD M. NIXON, STATE OF THE UNION ADDRESS, 1972

Corruption was on the minds of many presidential aspirants in 2016. In an exchange during the February 15, 2016, Republican debate, Senator Ted Cruz sought to position himself as a political outsider, emphasizing stands he had taken in the Senate against Republican orthodoxy:

> When you stand up to Washington, when you honor the promise you made to the men and women who elected you and say enough with the corruption, enough with the cronyism, let's actually stand for the working men and women of this country, Washington doesn't like it.[1]

Cruz contrasted his efforts as a senator to businessman Donald Trump's past financial support for Democratic politicians. Trump responded dismissively:

> Here's a man—Robin Hood. This is Robin Hood over here. He talks about corruption. On his financial disclosure form, he didn't even put that he's borrowed money from Citibank and from Goldman Sachs, which is a total violation. He didn't talk about the fact that he pays almost no interest. He just left it off, and now he's going to protect the people from the big bad banks. Give me a break.

This was not an isolated exchange; Cruz and Trump sparred four other times over the relationship between alleged corruption in federal politics and allegedly corrupt personal behavior. And Trump would go on to make corruption a central theme in his 2016 general election campaign, labeling his opponents "Crooked Hillary" and "Corrupt Kaine," and railing against an allegedly corrupt media and a "rigged" election.

Meanwhile, virtually every Democratic presidential primary debate featured allegations from Senator Bernie Sanders about systemic corruption and about Hillary Clinton's complicity in it as Secretary of State, as senator, and as spouse of former president Bill Clinton. This is shown, for instance, in a March 6, 2016, statement by Sanders:

> Look, we have a corrupt campaign finance system. And what Secretary Clinton is saying and what every candidate who receives from the fossil fuel industry or the drug companies or Wall Street say, not going to impact me. The question the American people have to ask is, why are these people putting millions of dollars into candidates if it's not going to make a difference?

This approach is not original to Sanders. In an October 30, 2007, debate, John Edwards had tried a similar rhetorical tactic:

> What I would say is Senator Clinton just said that she believes we desperately need change in this country, and I agree with that. I actually think we have a system that's broken. It's rigged, it's corrupt, and it does not work for the American people, and it's time we start telling the truth about that. Too much influence from entrenched interests—insurance companies, drug companies, oil companies. Too much influence from Washington lobbyists. And so the question I think that voters have to ask themselves is, do you believe that the candidate who's raised the most money from Washington lobbyists, Democrat or Republican; the candidate who's raised the most money from the health industry—drug companies, health insurance companies; the candidate who's raised the most money from the defense industry, Republican or Democrat; who—and the answer to all those questions is that's Senator Clinton—will she be the person who brings about the change in this country? You know, I believe in Santa Claus, I believe in the Tooth Fairy, but I don't think that's going to happen.

What do these exchanges say about contemporary American politics? Is American politics more corrupt now than in the past? Or are we merely thinking about corruption more? And what do these exchanges say about the strategic use of reference to corruption? Did Republicans talk so much about corruption in 2016 because the issue resonates with conservatives, or rather because they did not hold the presidency? Even if Trump and Edwards are making the same accusations against Hilary Clinton, do we receive their words differently? And finally, did all of these candidates mean the same thing when they talked about corruption? Are there multiple styles of corruption talk, and are these styles shaped by political viewpoint, by political goals, or merely by the candidates' personalities and speaking habits?

In this chapter we explore traditions of "corruption talk" in American presidential politics. We have noted elsewhere that there has been a surge in such talk lately, and we have described two different styles of such talk. In the previous chapter, we noted that focusing on corruption as officeholder corruption, and discussing it with a Mender's attitude, is the preferred mode of academic research on corruption. That is, the strategy is dictated by the goals of that enterprise. Presidents and presidential candidates, however, have more freedom to choose their rhetorical style; their framing of corruption as officeholder malfeasance or as a larger sort of rot or decay besetting our institutions is driven by their political outlooks, by broader trends afoot in society, and by their desire to win or retain office. More so than these other political elites, presidential candidates are strategic: They use language to shape political debate as much as to respond to it. Through the analysis of speeches made by presidents and presidential aspirants, we seek to distinguish between what one might call analysis and strategy. We ask, when presidents and presidential candidates have spoken of corruption, why they appear to have talked about corruption, and what they have meant when they talk about corruption. This chapter shows some of these strategic choices. It also argues, however, that there have been several distinct periods where talk of corruption was a major feature of presidential speeches.

8.1: Two Simultaneous Shifts in Corruption Rhetoric

At various points so far in this book, we have raised the possibility of shifts in what people mean when they talk about corruption. Some studies of political philosophy have remarked upon shifts in the definition of "corruption" at some point in the Middle Ages, while others have remarked upon the adoption in the United States during the Progressive Era of a new and distinctly American understanding of corruption. Our consideration of research on corruption in Chapter 7 noted a tremendous increase in the volume of work devoted to understanding political corruption—a change in both the salience and the science of the subject, if not the meaning of the term. These developments suggest that we might see a change in how politicians understand corruption—sometimes because politicians are responding to changes in language, and sometimes because politicians are helping to shape such changes.

Politicians themselves, however, tend to change their rhetoric strategically. That is, they choose their words in response to changes in the offices they hold, in current events, in the communications technologies they have available, or in the audiences to whom they speak. We consider presidential speeches in this chapter in part because they are broadly comparable over a long period of time. There is, as we document below, a lively research agenda that suggests that the rhetoric of American presidents has shifted, and that studies of presidential rhetoric can yield evidence not only about how the language presidents use has changed but also about how the presidency itself has changed.

The challenge in this chapter is that it is difficult to disentangle the two sorts of changes. A case can be made that corruption came to mean different things and to take on greater salience for American politicians in the early twentieth century; a case can also be made, however, that the role of presidential rhetoric itself changed at the same time. In this section, we document these changes and then sketch the hypotheses one might derive from them.

8.1a: Changes in Corruption Talk, as Seen in Presidential Rhetoric

One way of thinking about presidential corruption talk involves assuming that politicians reflect the values and ideas of the societies in which they live. Changes in the way that presidents and presidential candidates discuss corruption should thus correspond to changes in how society has, or elites within society have, discussed corruption. Such changes may consist of changes in the meaning of the term, in the subjects to which it is applied, and in the frequency with which the term is used.

In Chapter 2, we distinguished between two different attitudes of corruption talk: the Mender attitude, framing corruption as something to repair in order to maintain or restore the health of the system; and the Purist attitude, framing corruption as something to purge, perhaps a rot ruining the system and requiring us to toss the whole loaf. References beyond malfeasance of this or that officeholder, references to corruption as ontological corruption of our institutions or to moral corruption, have obvious rhetorical functions—they can dramatize the sometimes mundane business of governing, and they can add a moral urgency to subjects that might otherwise not appear to be inherently good or evil. Yet these characteristics can also make present political matters seem like intractable problems. Individual corruption and at least some forms of institutional corruption, in contrast, can be related to measurable public policy goals. They can be presented as something requiring housekeeping rather than swamp-draining. If an institution has been corrupted, it (or, usually, its membership) is deemed deficient in comparison to its prior self, and particular reforms might be appropriate to return it to its original, supposedly better form. If the members of Congress have been corrupted by contributions from large corporations, for instance, people may call for a prohibition on such contributions. Similarly, if a corrupt individual action can be identified, legal or political consequences should follow—the action must be prohibited or the individual in question must be sanctioned. While rhetoric pertaining to these types of corruption can be employed to dramatic effect (as perhaps the examples at the outset of the chapter showed), they can also serve much more pedestrian purposes than talk of moral corruption or institutional rot tends to.

These different types of corruption or ways of talking about corruption do not allow us to predict that corruption will be discussed in one way at one time and in another way at another time. Politicians respond to contemporary affairs; as such, things that are undeniably corrupt will take place (and attract public attention) at some times but not others. To take a few obvious examples, we would expect widespread agreement that political scandals, such as the Teapot Dome scandal or Watergate, are examples of corruption, and we would expect politicians to call them that regardless of the politicians' political viewpoint or precise definition of the term. We should see increasing discussion of corruption when there is a lot of it. If presidents' references to corruption are influenced at all by corruption talk in the academy or in legal circles (phenomena we documented in Chapters 7 and 9), we might also see a general increase in references to corruption.

These two potential differences are changes that can be measured over time: Does corruption come to mean different things? Does it get talked about at some times but not others? Yet we should also be sensitive to who is discussing corruption. Two distinctions emerge: To the extent that officeholder corruption in government requires that one actually be in government, a candidate of the party that does not hold power is likely to be more interested in talking about domestic corruption than the candidate of the party in power. Nonincumbents or newly elected presidents, then, should have more to say about corruption than incumbents or candidates of the incumbent party.

Second, differences in the intended meaning of corruption may relate to political outlook or viewpoint. We have already seen this in our discussions of Progressivism and of how corruption is discussed in relationship to election law. The proclivity to discuss corruption in religious or moral terms may be stronger for politicians courting voters who will understand corruption in this way. In contemporary politics, corruption talk may look different among conservative candidates than among liberal candidates. It is difficult in American politics to draw lines between contemporary partisan stances or political worldviews and corresponding views of fifty or one hundred years ago, but we can similarly be aware of whether different politicians of past eras sought to frame corruption in different ways. Or to put things more concretely, differences in how Barack Obama and Ted Cruz talk about corruption may have something to do with liberal and conservative ideas about what political corruption is. Differences in how, for instance, James A. Garfield and Grover Cleveland talk about corruption may likewise have something to do with partisan or worldview differences, but one cannot make direct comparisons or easily identify enduring partisan or viewpoint differences in corruption talk.

To summarize, then, we are looking for changes over time:

1. In response to high-profile instances of corruption
2. As a function of what appears to be a general increase in corruption talk among elites
3. In the type of corruption talk deployed

Also, we are interested in variation across different types of politicians, such as these:

1. Differences in references to corruption according to whether the speaker is of the incumbent party
2. Differences in the type of corruption according to the partisanship or political viewpoint of the speaker

8.1b: Changes in Presidential Rhetoric, as Seen in Corruption Talk

As it turns out, our basic inquiry here dovetails nicely with the central argument that has been made regarding the "rhetorical presidency." In his pathbreaking exploration of the presidents' formal speeches, Jeffrey Tulis (1987) argues that we can understand rhetorical practices as being indicative of the speakers' underlying doctrines of governance. That is, rhetoric matters insofar as it shows us how presidents see their role and how they seek to frame their concerns for the public. Tulis argues, furthermore, that during his presidency Woodrow Wilson fundamentally changed the nature of presidential rhetoric. Prior to Wilson, presidential speeches had been shaped by the founders' concerns about demagogy; the founders were concerned that rhetorically adept presidents would use their skills to confer advantage upon themselves at the expense of the other branches of government. Tulis documents changes in the salience of rhetoric to presidents—since Wilson, rhetoric has been "routinized." Speechwriters and, later, pollsters have tested different types of rhetorical approaches to find which are most effective. The content of presidential speeches has changed as well—as these speeches were now performed before a larger audience, presidents sought to emphasize one-sentence para-

graphs, memorable soundbites, and appeals to passions rather than to reason. This is, for Tulis, exactly what the founders were worried about.

Other scholars have pursued much of the research agenda set forth by
Tulis. In her review essay, Terri Bimes (2009) concludes that evidence in support of Tulis's specific claims has been mixed. There were many instances of
inspirational public rhetoric by nineteenth-century presidents (Teten 2007),
and ultimately variations in rhetorical style may say more about personality
or about the communication options available than about any distinctive view
of the presidency held by Woodrow Wilson. George Edwards (1996), in addition, has concluded that if presidents changed their rhetorical style in pursuit of their own policy goals, they were unsuccessful in doing so. He finds
no evidence that presidential speeches matter in terms of policy outcomes
or public persuasion. Roderick Hart (1987, chap. 2), similarly, shows that the
increase in the number of speeches by twentieth-century presidents correlates with declining presidential success in legislative enactments. David Zarefsky (2004) and Samuel Kernell (1997, 104), however, present a broader understanding of the goals of presidential rhetoric, noting the importance that
language has had in framing causes such as the "war on poverty" or the "axis
of evil." Colleen Shogan (2006) presents a history of moral and religious rhetoric by presidents, linking this rhetoric to the strategic goals of presidents
and the nature of the circumstances they were required to address.

Something definitely has changed in presidential speeches, however. Elvyn
Lim (2002, 2008) argues that presidential speeches have over time come to
express more clearly defined policy agendas; he notes that one characteristic
of the rhetorical presidency has been a growing corps of presidential speechwriters—professional rhetoricians who are skilled at using words to evoke
an emotional response or sell a set of proposals. This is reflected in changes
in presidential language, as presidents after Wilson sought to present inspirational public appeals, increasing their use of words such as "reform," "democracy," "truth," and "ideal" and declining to use words such as "fate" or
"providence." Similarly, Ryan Teten (2003) documents the increasing references to "we" and "our" in State of the Union addresses, concluding that presidents seek to present themselves as leaders of a common public quest rather
than as administrators. This change in rhetoric may be partially a consequence
of a redefinition of the role of the president, as Tulis would have it. As Hart
(2000) points out, this is also a wise campaigning technique; in several of the
presidential elections Hart looks at—most notably, the 1996 election—the vic-
torious candidate was the one who used the most inclusive, active rhetoric.

In fact, Hart presents several different claims about changes in campaign
speech over the past half century. He argues that presidential candidates have
increasingly framed their appeals in a language of "satisfaction, not inspira-

tion"—that is, they promise to placate the desires of the public rather than to enlist them in any sort of cause. He also approvingly reiterates E. J. Dionne's (1991, 317) claim that differences between the major parties in rhetoric have declined as both parties have focused their attention on the same swing voters. It is tempting to brush off Hart's claims by noting that his book's 2000 publication date preceded the highly polarized campaigns of the past six election cycles, as well as the shift in rhetoric, at least on the Democratic side, toward a more movement-oriented approach. Yet Hart does provide compelling evidence that there are major differences between campaigning and governing. While Tulis argues that the lines between governing and campaigning have been blurred for over a century now, Hart's distinctions between speech types, that is, between speeches made through different media, and his attention to the audience for a given speech suggest that we should still try to separate presidential speeches from candidate speeches—even when the candidate in question is an incumbent president.

Although we are not engaged in the sorts of broader explorations of rhetorical tone that Hart, Lim, Shogan, and others provide, their research suggests instrumental reasons why presidents and presidential candidates might change the way in which they talk about corruption. Given what we have said earlier about "corruption" as a moral term, we might expect to see more references to corruption among twentieth-century presidents than among their predecessors. If presidents aim to inspire, then the notion of a common fight against corruption seems like an uncontroversial popular appeal. Similarly, following Lim's logic, we might expect references to specific instances of corruption to increase—overall, but particularly when recent events that might feasibly be labeled as "corrupt" are on the mind of the public. So, in general, over time there should be an increase in references to corruption: references to corruption of the diffuse institutional or moral type, and references to individual corrupt acts.

Finally, we note that the instrumental reasons for discussing corruption should also vary according to the nature of the speech we are looking at. Later in this discussion we document the functions of the different types of speeches we are considering here. A reference to corruption makes more sense for a candidate or a newly elected officeholder than it does for an entrenched one: To the extent that corruption requires a certain amount of power, we would expect that those who do not hold power will be more likely to talk about corruption than those who do hold power. Or at a minimum, those in power should be careful to use the term with reference to other nations or people rather than to their own. We should expect more variation in corruption talk according to the circumstances of the particular president or presidential candidate speaking and according to whether the speech serves a campaigning purpose or a governing purpose.

The literature on presidential rhetoric, then, provides further support for several of the hypotheses listed in the previous section. However, it suggests that such changes stem less from changes in society than from changes in the nature of the presidency itself.

8.2: Data, Method, and Hypotheses

Our data here are drawn from the presidential speeches collected by the University of California, Santa Barbara's (UCSB) American Presidency Project (Woolley and Peters, n.d.). UCSB maintains an online archive of historical data on presidential elections and full-text transcriptions of many different presidential speeches. For the purpose of comparing the rhetoric of presidents and presidential candidates across time, we searched the texts of State of the Union addresses, inaugural addresses, nomination acceptance speeches, and presidential debate transcripts for references to corruption. For each reference, we have identified (a) the speaker, (b) the party of the speaker, (c) whether the speaker was an incumbent president, (d) whether the speaker was an incumbent president seeking reelection, and (e) whether the speaker was a member of the party that currently held the presidency. We have also noted the election cycle and date of each reference.

In the graphs that follow, we simply use raw counts of the number of references to corruption. More sophisticated studies of rhetoric than ours have measured the percentages of speeches with particular words, phrases, or characteristics (e.g., Hart 2000; Lim 2008; Benoit 2014; Shogan 2006; Noel 2013). Given that our concern is with only one word, and given the rarity of that word in discourse overall, we felt it more appropriate to avoid such techniques. We also chose to avoid using words that are similar to "corruption"; we concede that there are references in many of these speeches to corrupt things, or uses of words such as "crooked" or "scandal" that might plausibly serve as synonyms for "corrupt" or "corruption." There are, in addition, some presidential statements that clearly refer to ontological corruption of our institutions—a reviewer of this book suggested Dwight D. Eisenhower's Farewell Address as an example of this—that, again, do not count in our analysis.[2] Our focus here is not on whether presidents and presidential candidates talk about corrupt things but about whether and when they label them as such.

The data sources cover varying time periods, and they do not equally represent the parties over the full time series we consider here. To take the sources one by one:

- The President is required to deliver a State of the Union address, either as a speech or in writing, to Congress each year. We thus can consider references in these dating back to 1789. These reports or speeches differ in length somewhat from one year to the next, but we can take them to be broadly representative of presidential priorities across time. Teten (2003) identifies three distinct periods for State of the Union addresses and shows that they became substantially shorter beginning in 1914, when Woodrow Wilson began the practice of delivering them in person. Since that time, they have been roughly comparable in length. Karlyn Kohrs Campbell and Kathleen Hall Jamieson (1990, 54) describe the goal of the State of the Union address as an "assessment of the current situation"— as an opportunity for the president to identify current challenges and to present specific policy solutions.

- Similarly, all presidents have delivered an inaugural address. The UCSB site provides a histogram showing the length of these speeches, showing that they are relatively similar from one administration to the next, and showing that there is no overall trend toward greater length (Woolley and Peters, n.d.). Presidents have tended to use the inaugural address for different purposes, however, than they have used the State of the Union address. Kohrs Campbell and Jamieson (1990, 16) argue that the inaugural address is designed to unify the nation, and thus it tends to emphasize symbolic statements and avoid policy proposals. Barbara Hinckley (1990) argues that presidents use the inaugural address to situate themselves in a historical context.
- Presidential nomination acceptance speeches are available for each cycle dating back to 1940 (for Republicans) and 1928 (for Democrats), along with an assortment of other acceptance speeches dating back to 1912. It was not common practice for presidential nominees to deliver acceptance speeches before this time; as Hart (2000) recounts, during most of the nineteenth century presidential candidates sought to avoid the impression that they were campaigning for the nomination, and many of these candidates did not appear at the convention at all. There has been less rhetorical analysis of these speeches, but given that they are delivered before the election we can expect a more combative tone than is the case for presidential speeches and expect more variation according to factors such as whether the candidate in question is an incumbent and what the prospects of victory are for the candidate.
- Transcripts are available for general election presidential debates from 1976 through 2016 and for the 1960 election. There was no public expectation before this time that presidential candidates would debate. Primary election debate transcripts are available be-

ginning in 2000. The number of such debates varies substantially across elections; in particular, the number of primary election debates held has increased substantially, from merely four in 2004 to twenty-one in 2016. We exclude the 2020 election because the circumstances of the COVID-19 pandemic limited debates. The length of the debates and the number of candidates also varies substantially across election cycles. The purposes of statements during debates, in addition, vary substantially according to the candidates and the candidates' prospects of victory. Because debates are less scripted affairs, we can expect a mixture of careful use of prepared rhetoric and "sound bites" with more off-the-cuff responses. We should also expect a more limited repertoire of claims—candidate preparation for debates tends to involve the scripting of a small number of basic claims, accompanied by prepared responses to the arguments that opponents are expected to make.

Because of the shorter time series and the year-to-year variability, it makes little sense to consider debate transcripts with transcripts of the other speeches. These debate transcripts do, however, give some insight into how contemporary politicians and political parties differ in their statements on corruption.

The other three speech types, however, can fruitfully be studied as a full time series, with the understanding that the number of available statements increases in the early twentieth century as it becomes the norm for candidates to deliver nomination acceptance speeches. One must use caution in making partisan comparisons over short stretches of this time series; for instance, during the 1932–1952 period of Democratic presidential dominance, there are thirty different Democratic speeches to analyze but only four Republican speeches. Early nineteenth-century speeches, of course, were made in an entirely different party system. Nonetheless, as we shall see, we can still make broad claims about when presidents or presidential candidates discuss corruption, about notable adoptions of the term by one party or candidate, or about different meanings of the term across time. We consider these formal speeches together as a means of maximizing the amount of "corruption talk" we can document. However, we are also sensitive to the different purposes of these different types of speeches, so we present breakdowns by speech type as well.

The nature of the speeches, however, and the literature on them suggest a secondary set of hypotheses—hypotheses not about the nature or prevalence of corruption talk, but about where among presidential speeches it might be most prevalent:

(a) References to corruption should be more common in debates (as debates, by their nature, will feature at least one candidate who is not the president and who is seeking to criticize the status quo) than in presidential speeches.

(b) References to domestic corruption should be less frequent in inaugural addresses, given their ceremonial role in unifying the country, than in more campaign-oriented speeches.

(c) References to corruption in State of the Union addresses should locate that corruption outside of government—in foreign governments or in domestic affairs separable from the administration. Given the alleged proclivity of recent presidents to present "laundry lists" of initiatives in their State of the Union addresses, we might look for references here to transactional corruption, either isolated or systemic, but not necessarily to ontological corruption of our institutions or to moral corruption in the culture.

The appendix to this chapter considers references to corruption in party platforms; we exclude those from the main body of the chapter because these references do not constitute purposive language choices by the candidates.

8.3: Measuring Presidential Corruption Talk

The most complicated task when considering these speeches is to ascertain what presidents or presidential candidates mean when they refer to corruption. In the following discussion we have sought to operationalize the categories we presented above; as in Chapter 7, the categories we use do not precisely map onto the corruption talk styles (again, the Mender's and the Purifier's attitudes) that we discussed in the book's first few chapters. As we argued there, most ways of discussing corruption involve a blending of those styles. We have sought to present discrete categories here, although in many instances there is substantial nuance in the commentary provided about corruption. Our discussion, then, presents several different time series or cross-sectional comparisons, but we do this with the acknowledgment that in many, perhaps most, instances of presidential corruption talk a more complete, more qualitative exploration of the political context of the time, of the rhetorical goals of the particular president in question, and of the nature of the speech itself is not only appropriate but would be more illuminating than simple categorization. We thus present this effort to quantify corruption references as a preliminary step toward a more qualitative exploration of how and why presidential rhetoric regarding corruption has changed.

8.3a: *Speeches by Presidents and Presidential Candidates*

Figure 8.1 shows references to corruption by decade in the three major types of speeches consistently delivered by presidents and presidential candidates over this full time period. The most striking feature of this graph is the dramatic increase in references to corruption during the early 1900s, an increase exclusively driven by President Theodore Roosevelt's adoption of Progressive rhetoric regarding corruption. Roosevelt's references to corruption are, in fact, numerous enough that we give them separate consideration below. Excluding that spike, however, there are still intriguing patterns. Corruption talk was not uncommon in State of the Union addresses before Roosevelt, yet references to corruption in all speech types largely disappeared from presidential speeches in the 1920s, only to rebound in the 1970s. Our claim elsewhere that there has been a growth in interest in corruption in recent years finds some support here.

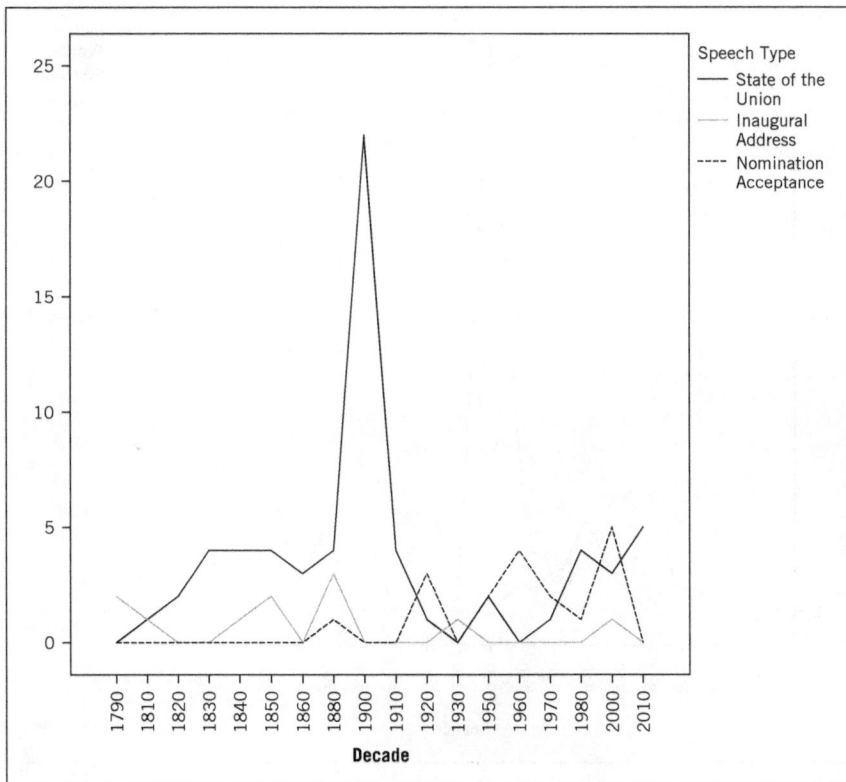

Figure 8.1 References to Corruption by Type of Speech, 1790–2018.
(Source: American Presidency Project, University of California, Santa Barbara.)

The differences among speech types are also notable; inaugural addresses almost never include references to corruption, but nomination acceptance speeches do. This corresponds to claims in the presidential rhetoric literature regarding the purpose of such speeches. Nomination acceptance speeches are a more appropriate forum for attack on one's adversaries than are the other speech types here, and inaugurations tend to be occasions to avoid reference to political disputes and to cast the presidency, instead, in optimistic, inclusive tones.

We are also interested in variation in the type of corruption discussed. For Figure 8.2, we have categorized references according to whether they are to individual corruption, systemic (or institutional) corruption, or corrupt peoples. As in Figure 8.1, it makes sense to look beyond the Progressive Era spike, which is mostly, but not exclusively, about individual corruption. Al-

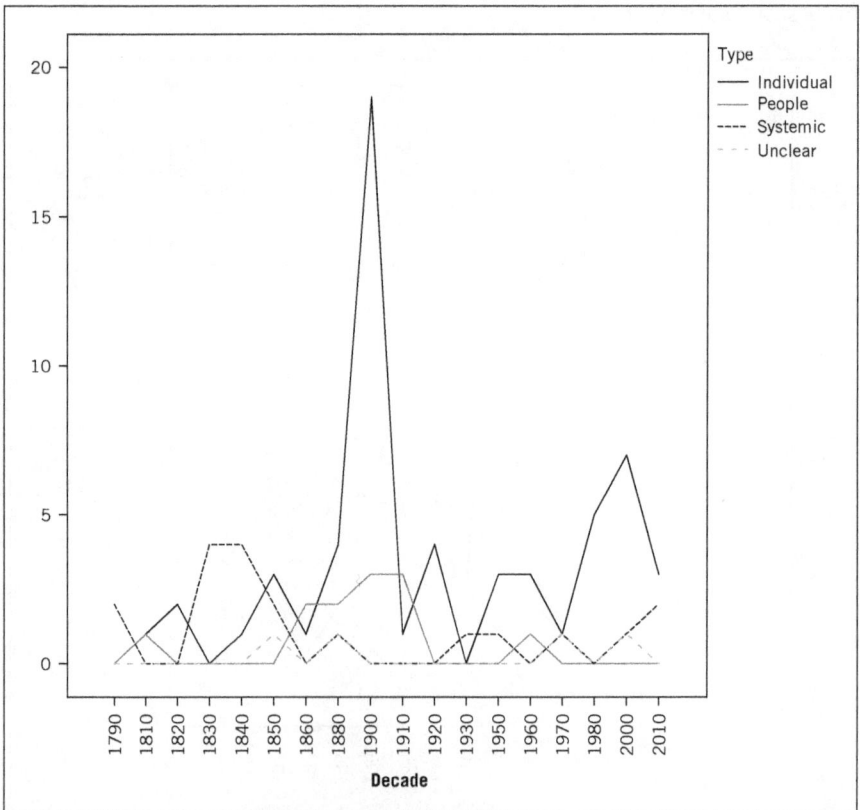

Figure 8.2 Corruption References by Type of Corruption Alleged, 1790–2018.
(Source: American Presidency Project, University of California, Santa Barbara.)
Note: Figure includes references taken from State of the Union speeches, inaugural addresses, and nomination acceptance speeches.

most all of the increase in corruption references in recent decades has involved discussion of individual officeholder corruption. For instance, George H. W. Bush singled out bankers implicated in the savings and loan crisis: "Those who are corrupt, those who break the law, must be kicked out of the business; and they should go to jail." In a list of foreign aid policies, Barack Obama spoke of aiding individuals such as a "young man denied a job by corruption in Guinea." Similarly, Ronald Reagan spoke of aiding "victims of dictatorships that impoverished them with taxation and corruption." The only recent, possible exception is Republican nominee John McCain's rather vague references to running mate Sarah Palin as someone "who's fought corruption."

During the nineteenth century, references to other types of corruption were far more common. For instance, James Monroe stated in his first inaugural address that "it is only when the people become ignorant and corrupt, when they degenerate into a populace, that they are incapable of exercising the sovereignty." Andrew Jackson, in his 1832 State of the Union message, described as corrupting what we would today see as routine congressional behavior (of course, that doesn't mean he was wrong):

Without some general and well-defined principles ascertaining those objects of internal improvement to which the means of the nation may be constitutionally applied, it is obvious that the exercise of the power can never be satisfactory. Besides the danger to which it exposes Congress of making hasty appropriations to works of the character of which they may be frequently ignorant, it promotes a mischievous and corrupting influence upon elections by holding out to the people the fallacious hope that the success of a certain candidate will make navigable their neighboring creek or river, bring commerce to their doors, and increase the value of their property.

It is worth noting that the threat to our constitutional culture that Jackson names here sounds a lot like one that Montesquieu identifies as a typical way republics become corrupt (discussed in Chapter 3). Andrew Johnson, in his 1867 State of the Union message, spoke of corruption in even broader moral terms:

The Union and the Constitution are inseparable. As long as one is obeyed by all parties, the other will be preserved; and if one is destroyed, both must perish together. The destruction of the Constitution will be followed by other and still greater calamities. It was ordained not only to form a more perfect union between the States, but to "establish justice, insure domestic tranquility, provide for the common defense, promote the general welfare, and secure the blessings

of liberty to ourselves and our posterity." Nothing but implicit obedience to its requirements in all parts of the country will accomplish
these great ends. Without that obedience we can look forward only
to continual outrages upon individual rights, incessant breaches of
the public peace, national weakness, financial dishonor, the total loss
of our prosperity, the general corruption of morals, and the final extinction of popular freedom.

Such references—in Monroe's case, to the degeneration of a people; in Jackson's, to what we would today call a particularistic or interest-driven politics;
and in Johnson's, to a disregard for the constitutional limitations on policy—
remain recognizable today. References such as these, all of which seem to us
to suggest an ontological decay of institutions and perhaps moral decay, play
a role in other types of contemporary debates. At least in the realm of official
or quasi-official presidential speeches, however, these older conceptions of
corruption have become rare.

From the mid-nineteenth century to the 1980s it was extremely uncommon for presidents or presidential candidates to attribute corruption to foreign influences or to discuss corruption in foreign countries. The only exceptions were sporadic references to the corrupting power of communism,
such as Harry S Truman's observation that "the rising demand of people ev-
erywhere for freedom and a better life may be corrupted and betrayed by the
false promises of communism." Since the 1980s, however, most of the increase
in presidential corruption talk has involved references to foreign corruption.
This increase is shown in Figure 8.3. The earlier brief quotes by Reagan and
Obama serve as examples of this tendency. Both George W. Bush and Obama
sought to connect anticorruption efforts to U.S. engagement in Afghanistan
and the Middle East. These references seem directly linked to the growing
international concerns with reducing corruption that we discussed in Chapter 7. Obama's final presidential reference to corruption, in his 2011 State of
the Union address, is virtually a direct reference to the international anticorruption effort: "Around the globe, we're standing with those who take responsibility, helping farmers grow more food, supporting doctors who care for
the sick, and combating the corruption that can rot a society and rob people
of opportunity."

There is evidence, then, that presidential corruption references have increased, that these references are now generally about individual officeholder corruption, and that they often locate this corruption in places other than
the United States. It is difficult, however, to simply use a count of references
to make meaningful statements about differences between incumbents and
nonincumbents or between Democrats and Republicans. At times there are
statements that might accord with this pattern—for instance, Ronald Rea-

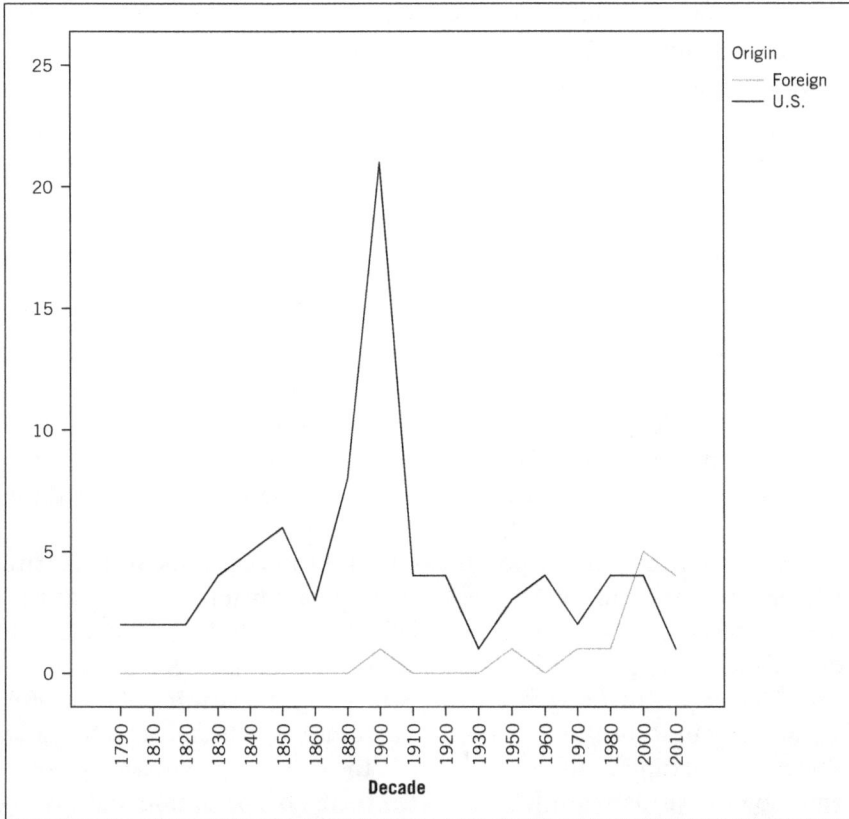

Figure 8.3 References to Corruption by Origin, 1790–2018. *(Source: American Presidency Project, University of California, Santa Barbara.)*
Note: Figure includes references taken from State of the Union speeches, inaugural addresses, and nomination acceptance speeches.

gan spoke of corrupt welfare recipients, while Democratic candidates and presidents did not. Still, there are too few such references overtly attributable to viewpoint differences to comprise a pattern.

It is also difficult to connect corruption talk to particular corrupt events. The reference by George H. W. Bush to corruption in the savings and loan crisis is obviously tied to an event that unfolded during his presidency. The same might be said for Warren G. Harding's commentary on corruption and prohibition, Dwight Eisenhower's discussion of corruption and racketeering, and allegations by Andrew Jackson and James K. Polk of corruption regarding the Bank of the United States. On the other hand, some of the most obvious instances of government corruption go without direct mention here. Neither Harding nor his opponents used the term in discussing the Teapot Dome scandal, and people did not generally think of the Watergate scandal or the

Bill Clinton–era sex-and-coverup scandals as having anything to do with transactional officeholder corruption.[3] Some readers might see Richard M. Nixon's rather hypothetical reference in his 1972 State of the Union address to corruption and political compromise (quoted at the beginning of this chapter) as a defense against the Watergate accusations. One might see his 1972 nomination acceptance speech as a similar sort of vague defense:

> It has become fashionable in recent years to point up what is wrong with what is called the American system. The critics contend it is so unfair, so corrupt, so unjust, that we should tear it down and substitute something else in its place.

However, Nixon had also spoken of corruption twice in his 1968 nomination acceptance speech (albeit in a different sense, in reference to "filth peddlers," "narcotics peddlers," and "merchants of crime"). Perhaps he just liked the word.

This bit of mind-reading points to one of the major problems that arise in developing an account about presidential corruption talk. It is hard to separate rhetorical styles from events and political strategy. Do presidents seek political gain through branding their adversaries, whether domestic or foreign, as "corrupt"? In doing so, are they stretching the meaning of the word? And are they in fact thinking about what it means to brand something or someone as corrupt? And, particularly in the case of contemporary presidents, how do we distinguish between the theory of corruption that a president or presidential candidate may hold, on the one hand, and a lazy speechwriter's rhetorical flourish on the other?

One thing that is clear here, however, is that American political incumbents are generally loath to see corruption as a form of institutional decay or rot that poses any sort of threat to the legitimacy or quality of the American constitutional system. As the people in charge of that government, it may be natural for them to avoid such formulations; either they would be implicating themselves or they would be suggesting that there is little they can do to contain, reduce, or eliminate corruption. Still, the lack of such references today—and their occasional appearance in presidential rhetoric of the nineteenth century—suggests that when American politicians and their critics talk about corruption, they are indeed talking about two very different things. As we see in the next section, this is illustrated in recent presidential debates.

8.3b: Presidential Debates

The three sources of data discussed above are all carefully prepared speeches; whether they were delivered in the modern era, where presidents and presidential candidates are aided by a bevy of paid speechwriters, or in an era where the task of writing fell more on the individual speaker, they all have in common the presumption that the speaker worked to make a relatively clear rhetorical or even philosophical statement about corruption. Debates, however, are different. The references to corruption in debates are not entirely unscripted; for many candidates, the exact same formulations of corruption references are used across multiple debates. Bernie Sanders referred to corruption twenty-one times in the 2016 Democratic primary debates; all of them are essentially the same: some variant of "We have a corrupt campaign finance system where millionaires and billionaires are spending extraordinary amounts of money to buy elections."

A virtue of looking at debates, however, is that they do contain what appear to be less scripted allegations of corruption (as the Donald Trump quote at the outset of the chapter may show), and they feature more variety within the two parties. Particularly in primary election debates, which feature many candidates with a factional following but no realistic hope of actually becoming president, there is much more variation in the type of corruption discussed and the particular thing that is being called corrupt. General election debates, on the other hand, do not feature very many references to corruption, and when references are made, they are usually references to particular foreign governments.

The UCSB transcripts of debates date back only to the 2000 election for primary debates; they include presidential debates for 1960 and for the 1976 to 2012 elections, inclusive. This time period included substantially more Republican than Democratic debates; the 2012 cycle included no Democratic primary debates, and there were more Republican debates and more Republican candidates in all other cycles save for 2004. Nonetheless, there is simply more discussion of corruption within Republican debates. There is not a single reference to corruption in the 2004 Democratic primary debates. In 2008, a year when both parties had large primary fields, there were twenty-two references to corruption among Republicans but only nine among Democrats. In 2016, numbers were similar (twenty-two for Democrats and twenty-six for Republicans), though all but one of the Democratic references were made by Bernie Sanders (one was by James Webb). Twenty-one Republicans talked about corruption, but only seven Democrats discussed it.

Figure 8.4 shows a breakdown of the types of corruption discussed. Republicans talked about corruption in a number of different senses. It is noteworthy, however, that moral or ontological corruption of our institutions gets so much more attention in debates than it gets in other types of statements by presidents or presidential candidates. This may in part be a reflection of the current political environment but it also appears to be a favorite topic of insurgent or outsider candidates. John McCain made several references to

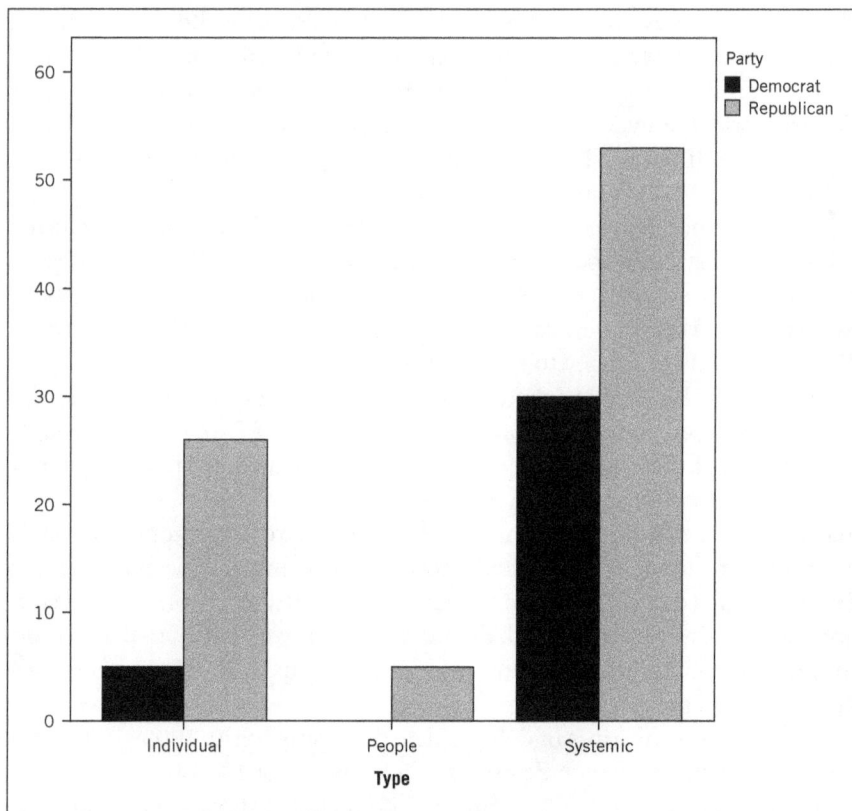

Figure 8.4 Type and Origin of Corruption Referenced by Party, Debates Only, 1976–2016. *(Source: American Presidency Project, University of California, Santa Barbara.)*

institutional corruption in both 2000 and 2008, but most of the discussion of this sort of corruption comes from candidates such as Ted Cruz, Donald Trump, or Bernie Sanders—or if one goes further back in time, Mike Huckabee, Alan Keyes, or Mike Gravel. More conventional candidates, such as the two Bushes, Hillary Clinton, or Mitt Romney, prefer to discuss corruption as an individual criminal act. References to corruption of a people are exclusively the province of social conservatives such as Alan Keyes or Gary Bauer. For instance (to quote a statement by Keyes in the October 22, 1999, Republican presidential primary debate),

> If we abandon our fundamental principles, and we don't have the moral character at the public policy level, then we are setting such a bad example of truth for our children that we should expect their consciences to be corrupted.

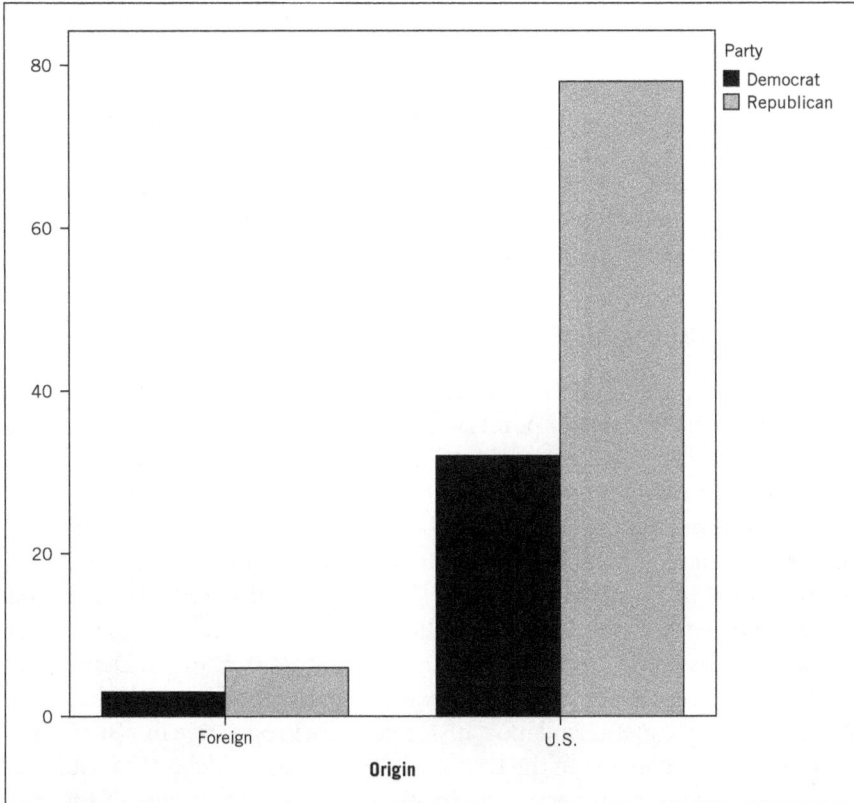

Figure 8.4 (*Continued*)

General election debates are largely devoid of such dramatic rhetoric. George H. W. Bush spoke of corruption and lobbying, George W. Bush discussed corruption in Russia and countries in Africa, Barack Obama spoke of corruption in the Tunisian and Egyptian governments, and Al Gore spoke of placing restrictions on International Monetary Fund loans to corrupt governments. These are all relatively straightforward references to individual, transactional corruption of officeholders. John McCain is the only exception here; McCain spoke more generally about his efforts to fight corruption. Presumably these are references to his work on campaign finance reform, although he did not specify this in his debate comments.[4]

We thus have rudimentary quantitative evidence in support of all of our initial claims except for the hypothesis that corruption references increased when a major corruption scandal had recently taken place. The frequency of corruption references varies according to the type of speech, and the intended meaning of the term changes across time. What these time series cannot tell us, however, is the relationship between presidential discussions of corruption and broader theories about government, whether on the part of the candidates themselves or on the part of their contemporaries. In other words, how deliberate or thoughtful are these references? Are they allusions to a theory of government, or merely a word that gets inserted into speeches for dramatic purposes, or without very much thought at all? In order to provide a closer look at presumed intent, we focus in the next section on what we see as three noteworthy changes in how corruption is discussed.

8.4: Eras of Presidential Corruption Talk

As we have argued in previous chapters, some studies of corruption have sought to identify particular points in time where public discourse regarding corruption changed. For instance, in Chapters 4 and 5 we mentioned one such claim, that for many political theorists the term lost its moral or religious connotations during the late eighteenth century and became a term used to describe instances of inappropriate economic or governmental activity (Buchan and Hill 2014). Similarly, Teachout (2014) and Wallis (2006) have alleged that early American politicians thought of corruption primarily in terms of foreign influence in American government, but that Jacksonian Democrats thought of corruption more as a consequence of the role of wealthy business interests in government. And most histories of the Progressive Era (see Chapter 6) note the expansion of the term to, in the words of Richard M. Abrams (1964, 27), "recognize as corrupt an incredibly varied assortment of conventional acts."

Such arguments suggest that politicians are part of a deliberate effort to change the meaning of words. It would certainly be misleading to allege that all presidential candidates are embarked on such a task. In fact, many of the most consequential presidents (Washington, Lincoln, and Franklin Delano Roosevelt, for instance) rarely or never spoke about corruption. Yet one can identify three such eras in American history where presidents with formidable rhetorical gifts and a well-defined philosophy of government do present lengthy statements on corruption and do appear to be breaking with their predecessors in the way they think about corruption. Two of these coincide with the eras referenced above; below we explore the arguments about corruption advanced by Andrew Jackson and Theodore Roosevelt. Both were clearly successful in reshaping arguments about corruption, as evidenced in part by the enthusiasm with which successors (in these instances, James Knox Polk and Woodrow Wilson) adopted the same framing of the term. To these we would add, however, a third, less complete, reorientation of the term, as advanced by mid- and late-twentieth-century Republicans and shown in the speeches of, among others, Barry Goldwater, Richard Nixon, and Ronald Reagan.

8.4a: The Jacksonian Era: From a Threat
Without to a Threat Within

As several studies of political discourse have noted, discussions of corruption in the early years of the American republic identified corruption with foreign influence in American affairs (e.g., Teachout 2014; Pocock 1975, 52). Among presidential speeches, perhaps the most straightforward example is John Adams's 1797 inaugural address. In an epic 727-word sentence, Adams pledged, among other things, to combat "the profligacy of corruption, and the pestilence of foreign influence, which is the angel of destruction to elective governments." Corruption, in these instances, is not equivalent to foreign influence. Rather, it is endemic to the conduct of foreign peoples. As Teachout notes, the French were seen as a corrupt people because of the luxury of the ruling class, while Great Britain was seen as a corrupt republic in part because of its treatment of its colonies. The conduct of Great Britain, in particular, served as a warning of what an American politics stripped of virtue might become.

If foreign powers had been corrupted, and could consequently corrupt American politics, the manner in which this might be done was not merely through perverting the goals of elected officials. The presumption was not that American leaders were especially vulnerable to bribery or corruption in a transactional sense; after all, these were, for the most part, men of adequate financial means. Rather, their very character—and the character of Americans more generally—might be corrupted. As James Monroe warned in his first inaugural address (1817),

> Had the people of the United States been educated in different principles, had they been less intelligent, less independent, or less virtuous, can it be believed that we should have maintained the same steady and consistent career or been blessed with the same success? While, then, the constituent body retains its present sound and healthful state everything will be safe. They will choose competent and faithful representatives for every department. It is only when the people become ignorant and corrupt, when they degenerate into a populace, that they are incapable of exercising the sovereignty. Usurpation is then an easy attainment, and an usurper soon found. The people themselves become the willing instruments of their own debasement and ruin.

Monroe was the last of the Revolutionary Era presidents, and thus perhaps the last president to effectively invoke ideals of the revolution in describing his view of democracy. For Monroe, as for others of his generation, American institutions provide a bulwark against unrestrained public sentiment.

The corruption of which Monroe speaks is degenerative in nature; the account here is not dissimilar from, for instance, Plato's account of the demise of democracies.

After Monroe, however, discourse around corruption completely changes. Andrew Jackson's State of the Union addresses are full of discussions of corruption; he mentions it in five different messages between 1829 and 1936. Jackson does not ever lay blame outside of government; rather, the problem lies in the character and incentives of those who govern. In his 1829 State of the Union message, he argues that corruption is endemic among long-serving governmental officials:

> There are, perhaps, few men who can for any great length of time enjoy office and power without being more or less under the influence of feelings unfavorable to the faithful discharge of their public duties. Their integrity may be proof against improper considerations immediately addressed to themselves, but they are apt to acquire a habit of looking with indifference upon the public interests and of tolerating conduct from which an unpracticed man would revolt. Office is considered as a species of property, and government rather as a means of promoting individual interests than as an instrument created solely for the service of the people. Corruption in some and in others a perversion of correct feelings and principles divert government from its legitimate ends and make it an engine for the support of the few at the expense of the many. The duties of all public officers are, or at least admit of being made, so plain and simple that men of intelligence may readily qualify themselves for their performance; and I can not but believe that more is lost by the long continuance of men in office than is generally to be gained by their experience.

Jackson's fear is that power and privilege are corrupting even when the officers are not prone to transactional corruption.

In his 1832 address (excerpted earlier in this chapter), Jackson equates what we would today call particularistic or interest group politics with corruption. By 1834, Jackson had taken to pointing directly to the Bank of the United States as a source of corruption, both in a transactional sense ("its corrupt and partisan loans," 1834), and in a more moralistic sense ("it corrupts the sources of the public virtue," 1835). Jackson, it seems, had gone searching for corruption within government, and had found its source. The pattern that emerges in Jackson's speeches largely accords with historians' accounts of Jackson's presidency. Wallis (2006), for instance, presents Jackson as the first candidate whose campaign was presented as a reaction to corruption—an irony, to be certain, given that Jackson worried about corruption in electioneering behavior but was the first president elected after the expansion of the franchise. In his recent biography of Jackson, historian Jon Meacham (2008, 52) also presents Jackson's initial bid for office as a straightforward campaign against corruption "in a broader sense," as a campaign against the corrosion of virtue that ensued when "a few institutions and interests . . . sought to profit at the expense of the whole."

What is striking, however, is not merely that Jackson's addresses reflect the historians' consensus. Rather, it is that subsequent presidential corruption talk reflects Jackson's framing of the subject. From then until the Civil War, all presidential messages also presented corruption as a symptom of either excessive tenure in office or improper financial influence. In some of the more eloquent such references, presidents have managed to do both. In his 1841 inaugural address, William Henry Harrison pledged his support for limiting the president to only one term (and pledged to serve only one term himself), for fear of corruption:

> It may be observed, however, as a general remark, that republics can commit no greater error than to adopt or continue any feature in their systems of government which may be calculated to create or increase the love of power in the bosoms of those to whom necessity obliges them to commit the management of their affairs; and surely nothing is more likely to produce such a state of mind than the long continuance of an office of high trust. Nothing can be more corrupting, nothing more destructive of all those noble feelings which belong to the character of a devoted republican patriot. When this corrupting passion once takes possession of the human mind, like the love of gold it becomes insatiable.

Harrison, of course, contracted pneumonia shortly after giving this speech, and died long before he had a chance to follow through on his pledge.

James Knox Polk, considered in Stephen Skowronek's (1997, chap. 5) history of the presidency to be the "articulator" of Jacksonian politics, spoke of corruption in a manner strikingly similar to that of Jackson. Polk's 1848 State of the Union address contains a lengthy indictment of the now-defunct Bank of the United States ("that dangerous and corrupt institution," "the corrupt power of such a political engine") and a celebration of the ability of the American separation-of-powers system to combat corruption:

> Happily for themselves, the people in framing our admirable system of government were conscious of the infirmities of their representatives, and in delegating to them the power of legislation they have fenced them around with checks to guard against the effects of hasty

action, of error, of combination, and of possible corruption. Error, selfishness, and faction have often sought to rend asunder this web of checks and subject the Government to the control of fanatic and sinister influences, but these efforts have only satisfied the people of the wisdom of the checks which they have imposed and of the necessity of preserving them unimpaired.

If [the president] acts without due consideration, or has been influenced by improper or corrupt motives, or if from any other cause Congress, or either House of Congress, shall differ with him in opinion, they exercise their veto upon his recommendations and reject them; and there is no appeal from their decision but to the people at the ballot box. These are proper checks upon the Executive, wisely interposed by the Constitution. None will be found to object to them or to wish them removed. It is equally important that the constitutional checks of the Executive upon the legislative branch should be preserved.

Somewhat more pedestrian statements by Presidents Fillmore, Pierce, and Buchanan follow the same basic template. Corruption had become a danger from within—a danger brought about by our own laws and institutions, a danger that could only be remedied by citizens' attention to the failings or the overreach of their elected officials. Though Jackson himself is known as the first populist president, the era of presidential corruption talk he inaugurates is remarkably Montesquieuian.

8.4b: Reconstruction Interlude

The Civil War brought about a handful of instances where presidents sought to cast opposition to union or reconstruction as instances of corruption. It is perhaps noteworthy that Abraham Lincoln never referred to corruption in his State of the Union messages or in his inaugural addresses; this fits with what Shogan (2006, 96–113) describes as Lincoln's deliberate choice of "moral restraint"—of avoiding moral language in explaining his justification for emancipation and Union war activities. In the previous section, we quoted from Andrew Johnson's 1867 State of the Union address his grim prediction of what failure in reconstruction would look like. Johnson there spoke of the prospect of "continual outrages upon individual rights, incessant breaches of the public peace, national weakness, financial dishonor, the total loss of our prosperity, the general corruption of morals, and the final extinction of popular freedom." In their study of presidential rhetoric, Kohrs Campbell and Jamieson (1990, 88, 164) refer frequently to Johnson's often harsh rhetoric, and they suggest that it was the cause and consequence of some of the trouble he faced in his dealings with Congress. This raises the prospect that Johnson framed the potential failure of his agenda in such dramatic terms in part as a ploy for staving off the attacks he would face.

Johnson would not, however, be the only Reconstruction Era president to link corruption to postwar conditions. James A. Garfield's references to corruption also single out Southern state governments; his nomination speech (1880) includes a condemnation of suffrage restrictions:

> The most serious evils which now afflict the South arise from the fact that there is not such freedom and toleration of political opinion and action that the minority party can exercise an effective and wholesome restraint upon the party in power. Without such restraint, party rule becomes tyrannical and corrupt. The prosperity which is made possible in the South, by its great advantages of soil and climate, will never be realized until every voter can freely and safely support any party he pleases.

In his 1881 inaugural address Garfield followed up this speech with a similar statement against "corruption and fraud in the suffrage" and a prediction that "if that generation comes to its inheritance blinded by ignorance and corrupted by vice, the fall of the Republic will be certain and remediless."

Although his tenure in office was short, Garfield had far more public sympathy when he took office than did Johnson. He ran for president as an outsider, a reluctant candidate who was untainted by the infighting that had plagued the Republican Party during the 1870s (Millard 2011). Yet if Johnson and Garfield sought to establish a link between corruption and matters of race and reconstruction, they were unsuccessful. During the decades following the Civil War, most other presidents (Rutherford B. Hayes, Chester Arthur, and Grover Cleveland) tended to speak of corruption in reference either to patronage politics or to powerful economic interests such as "the railroads."

8.4c: Theodore Roosevelt and Progressive Corruption Talk

There was substantial debate among Progressive Era thinkers—and there remains substantial debate among historians today—about whether Theodore Roosevelt was a leader among Progressives or a shrewd politician who merely followed the lead of Progressives. Corruption references in Roosevelt's speeches do accord with many of the observations about Progressivism that were noted in Chapter 6. It makes sense, however, to view Roosevelt not simply as an exemplar of Progressive corruption talk but as, in a couple ways, a successor to Jackson. Roosevelt, like Jackson, framed his presidency as a response to corruption. Like Jackson, he changed the meaning of the term for subsequent presidents. It is harder to analyze Roosevelt's views, however, in part because he had so much to say about corruption, and also because he talked about it in so many different ways—though he seems to discuss only officeholder, transaction corruption. Unlike Jackson, he did not speak about corruption in the Montesquieuian idiom of constitutional principles and limitations of power.

In his 1903 State of the Union address (his second one as president) Roosevelt mentions corruption thirteen times, in a variety of different senses. The following passage, presented without any ellipses, illustrates the prominence that the word played in his speeches:

> Corruption strikes at the foundation of all law. Under our form of government all authority is vested in the people and by them delegated to those who represent them in official capacity. There can be no offense heavier than that of him in whom such a sacred trust has been reposed, who sells it for his own gain and enrichment; and no less heavy is the offense of the bribe giver. He is worse than the thief, for the thief robs the individual, while the corrupt official plunders an entire city or State. He is as wicked as the murderer, for the murderer may only take one life against the law, while the corrupt official and the man who corrupts the official alike aim at the assassination of the commonwealth itself. Government of the people, by the people, for the people will perish from the face of the earth if bribery is tolerated. The givers and takers of bribes stand on an evil pre-eminence of infamy. The exposure and punishment of public corruption is an honor to a nation, not a disgrace. The shame lies in toleration, not in correction. No city or State, still less the Nation, can be injured by the enforcement of law. As long as public plunderers when detected can find a haven of refuge in any foreign land and avoid punishment, just so long encouragement is given them to continue their practices. If we fail to do all that in us lies to stamp out corruption we cannot escape our share of responsibility for the guilt. The first requisite of successful self-government is unflinching enforcement of the law and the cutting out of corruption.

In subsequent speeches, Roosevelt spoke about corruption slightly less, largely recycling claims from the 1903 speech. He also, however, gradually formed a more coherent stance on what corruption represents. In the 1903 speech, corruption is cast in profoundly evil and irredeemable terms—worse than thievery, as wicked as murder, and so forth. By his 1904 State of the Union message, he similarly, but with less elaboration, had taken to noting that corruption was indefensible:

> There is no enemy of free government more dangerous and none so insidious as the corruption of the electorate. No one defends or excuses corruption, and it would seem to follow that none would oppose vigorous measures to eradicate it. I recommend the enactment of a law directed against bribery and corruption in Federal elections.

Corruption is also, however, fundamentally alien to American norms of governance, in Roosevelt's framing; those who would corrupt politics stand outside of government and cannot be reasoned with. He noted in the 1904 speech that corruption is not uncommon in other nations, but that such is not the case for

> a people like ours, which in spite of certain very obvious shortcomings, nevertheless as a whole shows by its consistent practice its belief in the principles of civil and religious liberty and of orderly freedom, a people among whom even the worst crime, like the crime of lynching, is never more than sporadic.

Striking somewhat of an isolationist tone, Roosevelt argues that the first priority for Americans is to eliminate corruption here, where it is more controllable and less endemic. He believes, like the Jacksonians, that the cure is vigilance on the part of citizens: We must all watch for corruption. Unlike the Jacksonians, however, Roosevelt also calls frequently for legislative solutions. This tendency to seek legislative remedy for social ills is often said to be a characteristic of Progressives. Kohrs Campbell and Jamieson (1990, chap. 4), however, emphasize that State of the Union addresses are essentially about enunciating legislative goals. Hence, this tendency may be more a matter of the speech venue than of Roosevelt's strategic vision. In any case, Roosevelt's rhetoric is more Purifier than Mender. Moreover, he plays on themes we spoke of in discussing Rousseau (Chapter 5): that corruption threatens the legitimacy of the government because it separates the government from the will of the people, which is its sacred duty to represent.

Roosevelt's idea of what actually constitutes corruption is somewhat more pedestrian than these rhetorical flourishes would indicate, with a nonexclusive focus on officeholder corruption. He connects it to a variety of acts, including misappropriation of funds by government agencies, campaign-related quid pro quos, corporate lobbying, and such. The action is less exciting than is the attribution of blame. By his 1906 State of the Union address, Roosevelt had taken to personifying someone he referred to as "the corruption-ist." This personification further established corruption as something imposed on government and the people from without:

> The plain people who think—the mechanics, farmers, merchants, workers with head or hand, the men to whom American traditions are dear, who love their country and try to act decently by their neighbors—owe it to themselves to remember that the most damaging blow that can be given popular government is to elect an unworthy and sinister agitator on a platform of violence and hypocrisy. Whenever such an issue is raised in this country nothing can be gained by flinching from it, for in such case democracy is itself on trial, popular self-government under republican forms is itself on trial. The triumph of the mob is just as evil a thing as the triumph of the plutocracy, and to have escaped one danger avails nothing whatever if we succumb to the other. In the end the honest man, whether rich or poor, who earns his own living and tries to deal justly by his fellows, has as much to fear from the insincere and unworthy demagog [sic], promising much and performing nothing, or else performing nothing but evil, who would set on the mob to plunder the rich, as from the crafty corruptionist, who, for his own ends, would permit the common people to be exploited by the very wealthy. If we ever let this Government fall into the hands of men of either of these two classes, we shall show ourselves false to America's past. Moreover, the demagog and the corruptionist often work hand in hand.

Here, corruption is the consequence of either the corruptionist, who seeks wealth by letting the rich engage in plunder at the expense of the poor, or the demagogue, who seeks power by letting the people plunder the property of the rich; the two are indistinguishable, in moral terms, and both betray the American way.

Roosevelt recycled this basic claim linking demagoguery to corruption for the remainder of his presidency, in 1908 labeling demagogues "corrupt creatures who introduce blackmailing schemes to 'strike' corporations, and all who demand extreme, and undesirably radical, measures, show themselves to be the worst enemies of the very public whose loud-mouthed champions they profess to be."[5] The idea here, as elsewhere, suggests that some manifestations of corruption can be remedied by legislation, but the intent in many cases seems beyond public policy—corruption entails a willingness to deceive in order to advance one's own ends, to advocate for ostensibly public-minded causes for selfish reasons of wealth or power. In his famous "New

Nationalism" speech delivered in Osawatomie, Kansas, in 1910, Roosevelt urges a balanced approach to restraining both business corruption and mob violence; he also links the corruption targeted during his administration to the exploitation of natural resources and to the efforts by Southern plantation owners to preserve slavery prior to the Civil War. Combating corruption, Roosevelt concludes, requires an admission that the checks and balances established by the Constitution have not always been adequate in restraining special interests.

Roosevelt's arguments may strike modern readers as being somewhat overwrought, but as with Jackson's claims, they set a template for how corruption would be addressed by subsequent presidents. It demands a legislative solution, although such a solution may not be entirely adequate. It is something inimical to American democracy, and it is foreign or alien to the extent that it is accepted, or at least more prevalent, elsewhere, but it is not literally foreign. That is, corruption is not a manifestation of foreign powers meddling in American politics, but it is something introduced by those who have no respect for American political values.

Roosevelt's verbiage is also remarkable because his State of the Union addresses were presented in written form; it was not until the presidency of Woodrow Wilson that the State of the Union address became the public speech that it is today. Woodrow Wilson adopted much of Roosevelt's Progressive agenda, also calling for a variety of laws to rein in what he viewed as corrupt practices and decrying conventional types of transactional corruption within government. Wilson also, however, shared Roosevelt's idea that corruption resulted from a sort of influence of alien customs and ways. Consider, for instance, this excerpt from his 1915 State of the Union address:

> There are some men among us, and many resident abroad who, though born and bred in the United States and calling themselves Americans, have so forgotten themselves and their honor as citizens as to put their passionate sympathy with one or the other side in the great European conflict above their regard for the peace and dignity of the United States. They also preach and practice disloyalty. No laws, I suppose, can reach corruptions of the mind and heart; but I should not speak of others without also speaking of these and expressing the even deeper humiliation and scorn which every self-possessed and thoughtfully patriotic American must feel when he thinks of them and of the discredit they are daily bringing upon us.

Here, Wilson is not talking about measurable, transactional corruption, and he is not talking about self-interest. Rather, this is a moral corruption, an un-

American betrayal of one's citizenly loyalties. Suspicions like these were certainly heightened in the context of World War I, which had begun abroad but had not yet drawn the United States in.

Warren G. Harding, in his 1922 State of the Union address, would go on to use similar language projecting otherness in talking about those who engaged in corrupt profiteering as a result of Prohibition, casting them as people who would be complicit in "the humiliation of our people before the world." Al Smith, the 1928 Democratic presidential nominee, also addressed the corruption brought about by Prohibition, but he sought to link it to business practices and governmental practices. The corrupt bootlegger was equivalent to the corrupt businessman, who prioritized favoritism or cronyism over the national good. In addition, for Smith, returning to a pre-Progressive and more Montesquieuian theme, presidents who sought to legislate rather than to enforce the laws were also corrupt. Both Harding and Smith use the term "corruption" broadly, as did Roosevelt, and they link it not so much to self-interest as to interests or beliefs that run contrary to American values. In such hands, the term maintains its utility as a rhetorical and legislative tool naming officeholder corruption, but it signifies also an antidemocratic and un-American disposition, shared typically by foreigners, criminals, businesses, and politicians.

8.4d: Contemporary Conservative Corruption Talk

We have a smattering of corruption references once the Progressive Era had wound down. Although most are about individual crimes by businessmen or politicians, the term is occasionally used (as discussed above) to describe the influence of Soviet communism. What is striking about the years following the Progressives, however, is the absence of any partisan disagreement about what corruption is—or, perhaps, what sort of corruption should be of concern to us. From the late nineteenth century through the 1950s, Democrats and Republicans both cast corruption as largely an individual failing, a consequence of some combination of private interest influence and the removal of governmental officeholders from democratic control. In this regard, the post-Progressive consensus is like the post-Jacksonian consensus; as we have shown, Democrats, Whigs, and later, Republicans all accepted the Jacksonian formulation. This post-Progressive consensus appears to break down, however, in the 1960s. During that decade Republican politicians, or at least some Republican politicians, begin to frame urban disorder as an instance of moral corruption as well as ontological corruption of our culture and institutions, brought about by liberal policies regarding crime and "the welfare state."

Political theorist David Ricci (2011, 2016) has argued that the major rhetorical difference between American conservatives and liberals today is that conservatives tell stories and liberals don't. Successful conservative politicians have used accepted values to frame their policies, often by drawing our attention to individuals or historical events that illustrate their fears and hopes. Returning to the "progressive" label, today's liberals, by contrast, have tended to adhere to more academic or technocratic language, arguing for incremental improvements without clearly articulating where these improvements are leading us. They have tended to fall prey to a "laundry list" approach, listing a set of ideas (some controversial, some not) without linking them together or organizing them in a narrative intended to inspire. Students of recent presidential speeches can easily summon images of Bill Clinton's exhaustive list of priorities in his 1996 nomination speech or Barack Obama's enumeration of policy goals in the State of the Union addresses of his second term. Even when such goals might be unreachable (as one might argue Obama's goals, given Republican opposition, were), they drew applause at the time. Yet it is hard, today, to remember anything from these speeches as vividly as, for instance, Obama's well-known keynote speech at the 2004 Democratic Convention or Bush's post–September 11 speeches.[6]

Ricci's argument can easily be applied to presidential speeches, as well. The corruption rhetoric of 1964 Republican nominee Barry Goldwater is unlike anything a presidential candidate had said before him:

> Rather than useful jobs in our country, people have been offered bureaucratic "make work," rather than moral leadership, they have been given bread and circuses, spectacles, and, yes, they have even been given scandals. Tonight there is violence in our streets, corruption in our highest offices, aimlessness among our youth, anxiety among our elders and there is a virtual despair among the many who look beyond material success for the inner meaning of their lives. Where examples of morality should be set, the opposite is seen. Small men, seeking great wealth or power, have too often and too long turned even the highest levels of public service into mere personal opportunity.

Goldwater links corruption among political elites to urban violence, governmental largess, ethical disorientation, and the emerging unrest of the 1960s—the implication being that all of these are features of a broad falling apart, a corruption of our institutions, morals, and culture. Richard Nixon would go on, in his 1968 nomination speech, to again identify moral corruption as a problem besetting the urban poor, brought about by criminal villains and misguided liberal policies:

I pledge to you that the new Attorney General will open a new front against the filth peddlers and the narcotics peddlers who are corrupting the lives of the children of this country. . . . Time is running out for the merchants of crime and corruption in American society.

And Ronald Reagan's State of the Union addresses take aim at corruption in the programs designed to provide money for the poor; in 1982 he noted that "corruption has permeated virtually every area of the Medicare and Medicaid health care industry," which resulted in a program where "available resources are going not to the needy, but to the greedy." In 1983, he made essentially the same argument about the Food Stamp Program:

Our standard here will be fairness, ensuring that the taxpayers' hard-earned dollars go only to the truly needy; that none of them are turned away, but that fraud and waste are stamped out. And I'm sorry to say, there's a lot of it out there. In the food stamp program alone, last year, we identified almost $1.1 billion in overpayments. The taxpayers aren't the only victims of this kind of abuse. The truly needy suffer as funds intended for them are taken not by the needy, but by the greedy. For everyone's sake, we must put an end to such waste and corruption.

Our intention here is neither to question nor to assert the veracity of these claims but to note that they were relatively unprecedented among presidential speeches, and that they are quite different from the claims of Democratic politicians of the era and of more "establishment" Republican politicians such as George H. W. and George W. Bush. Other references to corruption during this era tend not to be rhetorical in nature. They tend to indict particular already-prosecuted individual criminal acts or, more commonly, foreign governments. McCain, the lone exception, spoke frequently, albeit in rather ambiguous terms, about his efforts to pursue campaign finance and lobbying reform in Congress—his is a corruption that has little to do with anyone outside of government or its petitioners, and is in many ways a throwback to the Progressive uses of the term, as shown in his 2008 nomination acceptance speech: "We lost the trust of the American people when some Republicans gave in to the temptations of corruption." Contrast this with Nixon's later corruption references, in his 1972 campaign, which are actually denials—he argues that we should *not* be so cynical as to brand such legally permissible practices as corruption.

We have noted the diversity of corruption references on display in Republican presidential primary debates over the past twenty years. Given that we have debate transcripts for only the past few decades (and, for that matter, have had only presidential debates), it is not really fair to use these transcripts to argue that contemporary Republican politicians use "corruption" differently from their predecessors. Yet the same sort of factional divisions among Republicans that are on display in the speeches summarized above are evident in the debates. "Establishment" Republicans such as Bush or Romney do not speak frequently of corruption, and when they do they talk about it as a phenomenon happening somewhere else. It is the minor candidates, such as Alan Keyes, Gary Bauer, Orrin Hatch, and Rick Santorum, who use the term frequently, and often in expressing concerns for moral failure and cultural decay. When Republican candidates in 2000 argued that Bill Clinton's administration was corrupt, they were not referring to financial misdeeds, interest group influence, fundraising practices, the misallocation of cabinet funds, or anything else that might square with a textbook definition of officeholder corruption; rather, they were referring to Clinton's sexual escapades.

The common denominator among these politicians (and, to be fair, among Democratic candidates such as Bernie Sanders and John Edwards, both of whom were quoted earlier in the chapter) is not merely partisanship but the coincidence of political viewpoint and rhetorical style. Oliver and Rahn (2016) define populist rhetoric (a rhetoric that conventional wisdom holds is shared by all of these candidates) as a rhetoric that is, at its core, *about* corruption:

> Its goal is restorative, replacing the existing corruption with a political order that puts people back in their proper place and that is more faithful to their longings and aspirations. Its worldview is apprehensive, suspicious of any claims to economic, political, or cultural privilege; for populists, the good is found in the common wisdom of the people rather than the pretensions of the expert.

This rhetoric is simple and direct in nature, as Nixon's campaign speeches were alleged to be, and it is explicitly moral in nature. To circle back to Ricci's argument, it is also about telling stories, not about enumerating policy goals. This type of rhetoric tends to present corruption as a form of institutional rot or decline, and the corruption is not merely transactional, officeholder run amok. Though Reagan the Mender does want to cut and add better procedures, in general, with this type of rhetoric, there is no presumption that specific policy tools are sufficient to fix or mend the things that have been corrupted. In this case, what is needed is, in addition, a return to principles, both constitutional and cultural. Rhetoric such as this also tends to be vague and grandiose, even when individual examples are provided. For instance, to quote 2016 Republican nominee Donald Trump, the final entrant in our dataset here:

> I have no patience for injustice, no tolerance for government incompetence, no sympathy for leaders who fail their citizens. When innocent people suffer, because our political system lacks the will, or the courage, or the basic decency to enforce our laws—or still worse still, has sold out to some corporate lobbyist for cash—I am not able to look the other way, and I won't look the other way. And when a Secretary of State illegally stores her emails on a private server, deletes 33,000 of them so the authorities can't see her crime, puts our country at risk, lies about it in every different form and faces no consequence—I know that corruption has reached a level like never ever before in our country.

The first Trump presidency certainly generated much talk of corruption, from Trump's supporters and from his opponents. It has since become apparent that Trump's style of corruption talk has taken root; it is not uncommon to find news articles that discuss efforts by lesser politicians to emulate Trump's style (e.g., Herndon 2019). This was the case for prior presidents, such as Jackson and Roosevelt, who tried to make corruption a major campaign issue. If those two presidents' experiences offer any guidance, it is also likely that subsequent presidents might adopt Trump's corruption rhetoric as well.

8.5: Making Sense of Presidential Corruption Talk

Politicians—at the least, the politicians who hold or aspire to the office of the U.S. presidency—occupy a sort of middle ground in their discourse regarding political corruption. By this we mean that politicians are more rhetors than philosophers. They do not attempt to use their public speeches to establish truths or prove theories. They seek to persuade or to justify their actions. At the same time, political rhetoric is not entirely devoid of eloquence or careful theorizing. Many of the politicians quoted here were learned men, well versed in the matters treated in the previous chapters of this book. Even when politicians consciously sought to portray themselves as commoners, their language choices were made deliberately by the candidates or by professional speechwriters, by people who could have spoken more eloquently if they had wanted to, and who had a detailed knowledge of the effects of different words. There is certainly room for variation in the skill of the politicians we have considered here, or in the degree of idiosyncrasy—as we have noted a few times, some of the references to corruption may simply be a function of one politician, or one speechwriter, who liked to use the word.

We contend, however, that for the most part corruption talk for politicians is deliberate and conforms to predictable patterns. In this chapter we have sought to show this in two ways. It is, first of all, used in the context of the speech goals of the politicians. Certain types of speeches, such as nomination speeches, serve as appropriate venues for discussing corruption, while others, such as inaugural addresses, are not appropriate venues for corruption talk. Politicians outside of government also have more reason to talk of corruption than those with a stake in defending the status quo. Second, what we have proposed as the major eras in American corruption talk have been characterized by the rise of political movements that sought to disrupt the status quo. They reflect moments in American history when corruption had become a major subject of public concern, and they sought to use this concern as a means of delegitimizing opponents and legitimizing themselves. Although it is beyond our mission here, we would draw the reader's attention to the correspondence between these eras and the periodicity schemes in major works on presidential history such as those by Tulis (1987) and Skowronek (1997). We have rather tentatively proposed that we are currently at an odd point in American history, where there has been an increase in corruption talk but not yet a shift in paradigm to the degree that Jacksonian Democrats and Progressives posed. This sort of unfinished shift corresponds, in turn, to the contemporary confusions over what feels like an incipient political realignment.

We must remember, however, that politicians operate within the bounds of a language and a theoretical frame that they do not control. In addition to having opinions about what is good and bad, what should be hoped and feared for their country and the world, politicians in general seek short-term advantage and power, not a fundamental rethinking of our relationship to political institutions. Larger theories of corruption—as ontological ruin of our institutions, as moral decay, or as malfeasance of an officeholder within an institutional role—are not subjects that politicians in general have the power or desire to elucidate. Instead, presidential rhetoric tends to reflect the larger patterns in how corruption talk has evolved.

In this regard, political rhetoric about corruption is fundamentally different from other types of contemporary corruption talk that we discuss here: The veracity of politicians' corruption claims is less relevant. To call something "corrupt" when it undeniably is not would perhaps be a bad rhetorical strategy, but beyond that, truth and falsehood are not the most useful criteria for evaluation of presidential corruption rhetoric. In our other explorations of contemporary corruption talk—in social science, legal research, and journalism—the question of whether the things said to be corrupt really are corrupt, or of whether the concept has been decently clarified, is far more relevant. As we are reminded by ancient philosophers, the reasoned pursuit of truth is not particularly relevant to the goals of the rhetor.

APPENDIX: CORRUPTION REFERENCES IN PARTY PLATFORMS

We consider party platforms separately from presidential speeches and presidential candidates' speeches. We do this because party platforms do not necessarily represent the precise views of the presidential candidates, and because they tend to be written by committees and thus are perhaps less rhetorically significant.[7] Despite these drawbacks, party platforms can still provide us with information about the role that views on corruption play in the policy goals of the parties. They can, as well, serve as a counterpoint to the rhetorical stylings of the candidates—they help us to see whether corruption really was a concern of the parties, or whether "corruption" was simply a favorite word for the candidates or their speechwriters.

Earlier we presented several claims regarding the rationale for mentioning corruption in presidential speeches. We call attention to three of these here. First, we noted that candidates of the incumbent party should be less concerned about corruption than candidates of the opposition party; although our conclusions in this regard were mixed, we still expect this relationship to hold for party platforms. Second, we hypothesized that references to corruption should increase in the years immediately following high-profile instances of corruption. Again, our results here were mixed, but given that party platforms tend to serve as a document of the successes or failures of the past administration, we expect that such references should be present here. And third, our qualitative look at corruption talk by presidents and presidential candidates suggested several distinct eras; we look for similar divisions here.

We again use the party platforms compiled as part of the University of California, Santa Barbara (UCSB) presidency database. The UCSB collection of platforms dates back to 1840. It includes all major party platforms since that time, along with the platforms of several consequential third parties, including the Populist Party (1892), the Progressive Party (1912, 1924), the American Independent Party (1968), the States' Rights Party (1948), the Constitutional Union Party (1860), and the Southern Democratic Party (1860). We include these third-party platforms in our analysis. The length of party platforms varies over time; although we have not sought any sort of "inflation adjustment" here, platforms are on average about five times as long today as they were during the nineteenth century.[8] We exclude 2020 because the Republican Party did not adopt a platform.

To explore patterns in party platforms, we again tally references to corruption according to incumbency and party. We present a summary of corruption references according to incumbency status in Figure 8.5. For reading convenience, we present references first by year and then by decade. The yearly results show the election cycles where corruption was particularly important (or at least frequently mentioned) in the party platforms, while the results by decade give a somewhat smoother measure of trends across time.

It does seem clear from both graphs in Figure 8.5 that opposition parties are more likely to discuss corruption than are incumbent parties. There have been some individual elections where this was not the case, but the decade averages show it to be true for almost all decades except the last three. To some extent the variation is a function of the inclusion of third parties—the Progressive Party, for instance, was coded as an opposition party here and referred to corruption several times in both of its platforms. Opposition parties also made frequent reference to scandals in the incumbent party's administration. Democrats referred to the scandals of the Harding administration, for instance; the 1952 Republican platform identified several instances of corruption during the Truman administration; and Democrats referred to corruption in the wake of the Watergate scandal. Incumbent parties did not necessarily address these same instances of corrup-

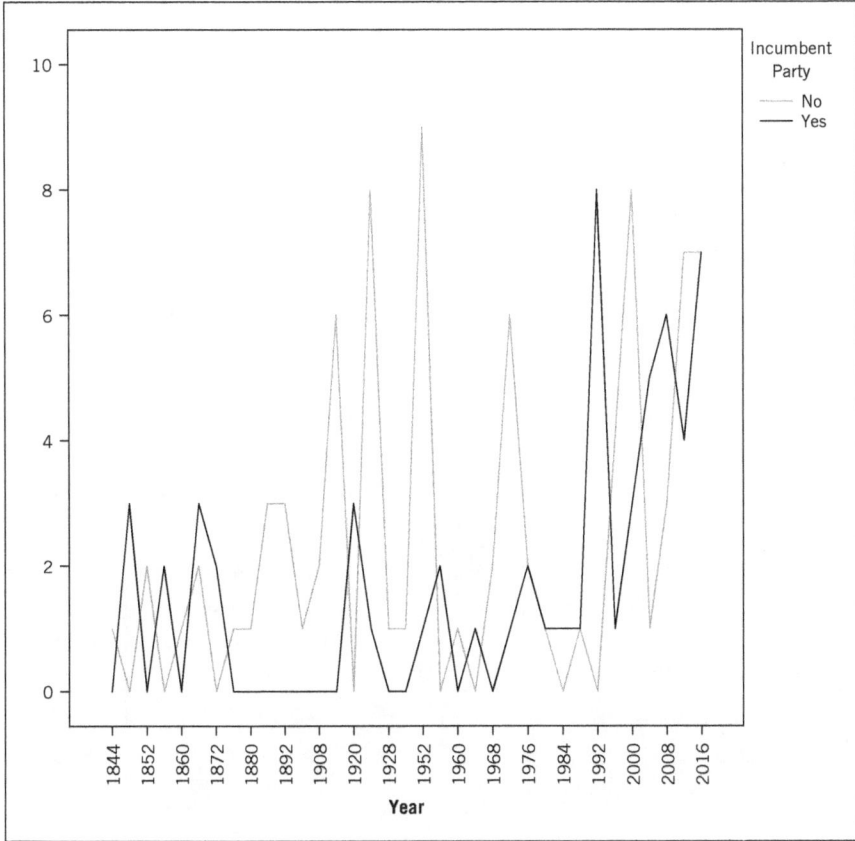

Figure 8.5 Corruption References in Party Platforms, 1840–2016, by Incumbency Status. *(Source: American Presidency Project, University of California, Santa Barbara.)*

tion; in some cases, however, they sought to break with past administrations. The 1868 Republican platform effectively disowned Andrew Johnson's administration, alleging that "the corruptions which have been so shamefully nursed and fostered by Andrew Johnson call loudly for radical reform." And during eras of divided government, it is common for the party that holds the presidency to brand the party that holds Congress to be corrupt, as Republicans did during the 1980s and in 1992.

Figure 8.6 shows differences by party, again presenting them according to election year and incumbency status. The results here are perhaps somewhat surprising; Republican platforms really did not talk very much about corruption in their Progressive Era platforms. Democrat platforms were much more attentive to the subject at the time. Republican platforms referred much more frequently to corruption during the 1950s—an era where the presidential candidates largely ignored it, other than a few references to racketeering in Dwight Eisenhower's State of the Union addresses—and from the 1990s onward.

The party time series suggest two things. First, they call attention to idiosyncrasies on the part of platform writers and presidents. The lack of corruption talk in Republican

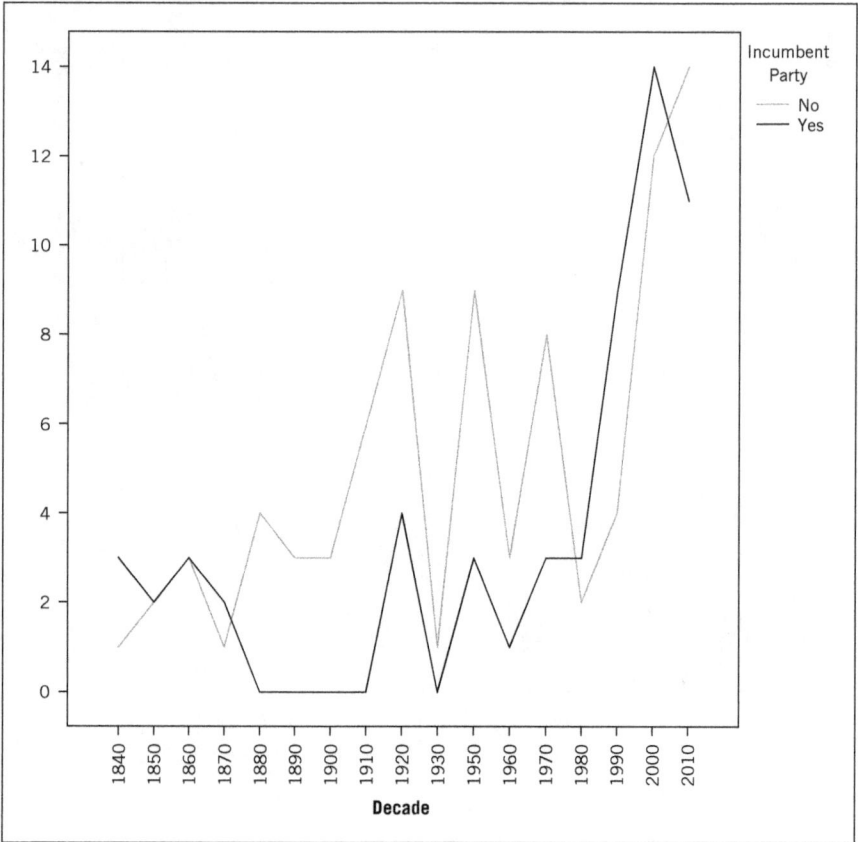

Figure 8.5 (*Continued*)

Party platforms may suggest that corruption was a preoccupation of Theodore Roosevelt, but not necessarily of the mainstream of his party; or rather, perhaps his base was more responsive to such talk than was the party committee that drafted the platform. And the 1992 surge in corruption references in the Republican platform corroborates contemporary claims that that year's Republican platform committee was somewhat more radical than the party as a whole (Fine 1994; Maisel 1993). George H. W. Bush did not speak frequently about corruption either as a first-time presidential candidate or as an incumbent president.

Second, and perhaps most consequentially, the platforms show the distinctiveness of contemporary corruption talk. Of the three eras we have just discussed, the platforms are unable to shed light on the Jacksonian era (although Democrats did refer frequently to the corruption of the National Bank during the 1840s and 1850s); the surge we identified under Theodore Roosevelt is unmatched in the platform data; but our claims about a contemporary increase are clearly borne out here. Even when one considers the increase in platform length, the increase in corruption references since the 1980s is still striking. Although Democrats are complicit in this, it is largely a function of a more aggressive message about corruption on the part of Republicans. This increase is particularly striking

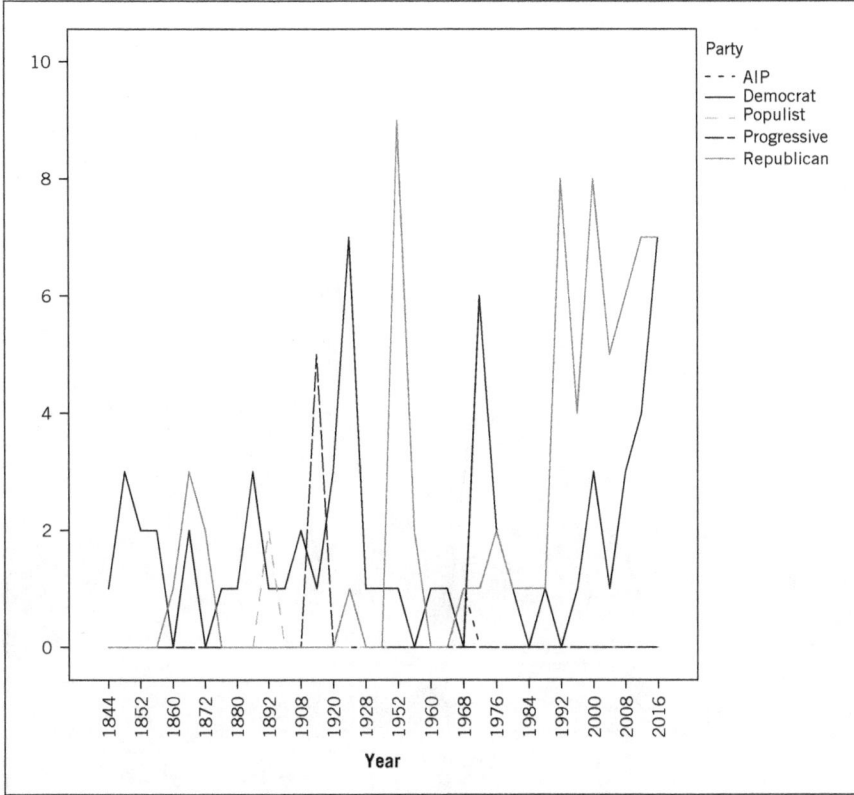

Figure 8.6 Corruption References in Party Platforms, 1840–2016, by Party.
(Source: American Presidency Project, University of California, Santa Barbara.)

given that it takes places both when Republicans are in opposition and when they hold the presidency. The nature of recent corruption references also corresponds to the party differences we noted earlier; for instance, both parties referred to corruption seven times in their 2016 platforms. All seven Democratic references were to foreign governments, while only three Republicans references were to foreign governments. The other four Republican references were to alleged cronyism in the Obama administration; corruption in Fannie Mae and Freddie Mac; corruption in the National Popular Vote Initiative (and its relationship to alleged voter fraud); and corruption among Democratic mayors and city councilors, particularly those of the District of Columbia. A similar distinction prevails in comparing most of the platforms of the 1990s and 2000s, although Republican concern with foreign corruption was somewhat higher during the George W. Bush administration.

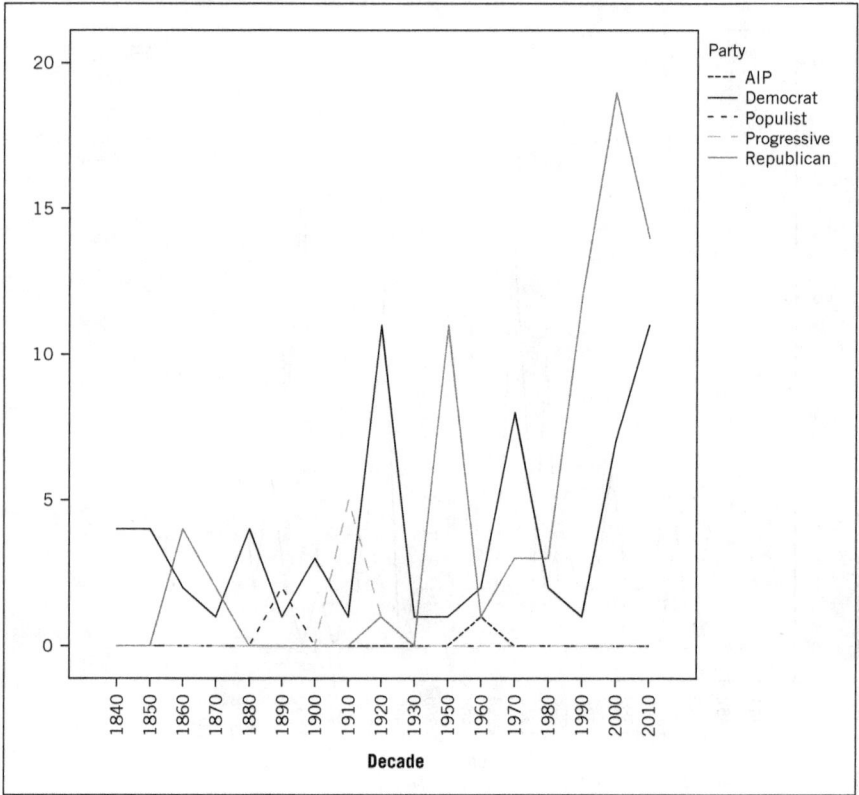

Figure 8.6 (*Continued*)

9

Corruption Talk and Political Reform

The U.S. Congress has been the site of several ostentatious displays of corruption over the past two decades.* There have certainly been, as well, many more mundane instances of things that look kind of corrupt—implicit quid pro quo deals where contributions were made with the expectation that a politician would grant some sort of nonofficial access or favor, or instances where a member of Congress chose to remind a constituent or an interest group of actions voluntarily taken for their benefit.

A couple of decades ago, one of the two of us (Rob) spent a couple of years working as a staff member in the U.S. House of Representatives. Congressional staff members receive relatively low salaries (which is part of why they tend to leave Congress after a few years to work for lobbying firms), and at least during the 1990s they tended to supplement their incomes with a variety of free handouts. During that time, Rob received numerous perks—Baltimore Orioles tickets, lobbyist-sponsored trips to Florida and Las Vegas, and free beer most Friday afternoons. He reasoned that this was not corrupt because he had little influence over his boss—if he did not respond to these gifts by actually doing, or promising to do, favors for the lobbyists in question, he had not been corrupted.

---

* This chapter is adapted from "The Poverty of 'Corruption': Confusions and Disagreements about the Rotten in Politics," in *Corruption and Governmental Legitimacy: A Twenty-First Century Perspective*, edited by Jonathan Mendilow and Ilan Peleg, 287–308. © 2016 by Rowman & Littlefield. Reproduced by permission of Rowman & Littlefield.

The theoretical import of Rob's experience is summarized by Richard Hall (1996) and by Hall and Frank Wayman (1990). Hall contends that interest groups in the United States rarely engage in direct bribery or corruption, but that repeated interactions between legislators and lobbyists prompt legislators to take lobbyists' claims more seriously and sympathetically, and at the least to think carefully before taking steps to attack them. This can have pernicious results; for instance, Hall shows that legislators who had been lobbied by the dairy industry were, statistically, less likely to propose legislation harmful to the dairy industry, even though he could not show that this lobbying influenced actual voting behavior.

Was Rob corrupted by the perks he received? He would say no, and surely no court would punish him. Yet they did make him feel a little bit bad—like he was getting away with something. It seems reasonable to conclude that legislation to limit the ability of lobbyists to offer such perks might be appropriate. Congress has, in fact, done this sort of thing several times—limiting the value of what lobbyists can give members of Congress or their staff, or requiring that "junkets" have a clear educational component. Yet when it has done so, it has been criticized for micromanaging the affairs of its members or complicating the sorts of social activities that can lead to the development of trust or camaraderie among politicians. There is no bright line that demarcates corrupt transactions here, in part because we cannot really know whether there has been any sort of implied quid pro quo.

There are also, of course, matters of scale. Are Rob's actions really *that* bad? Perhaps not. But if left unsanctioned, would they lead to worse actions? Are they indicative of some sort of moral rot? After all, "everyone else" does it. There are those who would say yes—and furthermore, there are those who would say that all of us are vulnerable to this sort of slippage.

We present this bit of personal history to show some of the difficulties inherent in developing legal tools to regulate or sanction officeholder corruption. In the previous two chapters, we have seen that academic researchers and politicians have differing abilities to talk about corruption. In the case of politicians, corruption talk is instrumental—politicians have reasons to label certain types of actions, or even certain types of individuals or institutional arrangements, corrupt. They have the motivation to frame their antagonists as corrupt while defending themselves against corruption claims. They cannot, of course, invent a definition of "corruption" out of whole cloth, but they have some latitude in shaping the public conception of corruption, and some politicians have been successful in doing this. Among academics, there is no deep agreement on what corruption is, but there is a general agreement that academics should seek some sort of common understanding. While academics in general are not tempted by instrumental reasons to redefine corruption or to deploy it for their own gain, there are still competing schools of thought.

At first glance, corruption talk in law and legal theory would seem to fall somewhere between the corruption talk of the academic and that of the politician. Even more so than in the descriptive academic literature, legal theorists compete to develop an acceptable definition of corruption and to classify things that fit that definition. They tend to do so, however, with unambiguously political ends in mind. Whereas the analyst of anticorruption policies in developing nations may simply wish to reduce officeholder corruption, in a clear transactional sense, the articulators of legal definitions of corruption that we discuss below are admitted partisans—they seek to develop definitions of corruption that will serve to advantage their preferred political party or even their own political careers or views. Legal theorists such as Lawrence Lessig (who ran for U.S. president) and Zephyr Teachout (who ran for governor of New York and for an open U.S. House seat) are perhaps not describing corruption for personal benefit in the manner that the politicians profiled in Chapter 8 are, but neither are they disinterested observers.

There is, then, a sort of middle ground for those who would make allegations about corruption. Yet corruption definitions in law are distinct from academic or political ones because of the legal consequences for those who are alleged to be corrupt. One may lose public standing or credibility if one is the subject of a political or academic corruption allegation, yet a legal determination of corruption carries with it civil or criminal penalties (and almost certainly the end of one's career). A legal definition of corruption, then, requires an establishment of criteria by which the allegation can be proven. It is this characteristic that has caused some of the greatest controversy, both within the scholarly community and within the courts themselves.

In this chapter we take a somewhat different approach than we have in previous chapters. We do not purport to provide any sort of metric regarding changes in the use of the term "corruption" in legal discourse or in court decisions. Such a metric would perhaps be possible to develop, but we are not convinced that it would yield anything substantially different than what we have seen in the previous chapters. What interests us here, instead, is that it seems that over the past twenty years or so the American legal community has been embroiled in a larger debate about what corruption is.

Here we provide a more detailed explanation of the role that corruption talk plays in one aspect of American constitutional law—namely, in judicial decisions and legal scholarship regarding the role of money in political campaigns. We consider two related contemporary instances of corruption talk in the United States: the establishment of a research program on corruption undertaken by Harvard University's Edmond and Lily Safra Center for Ethics from 2009 to 2014, and the effort by legal scholars to develop a more expansive definition of corruption so as to respond to the narrow quid pro quo definition at the heart of the Supreme Court's *Citizens United v. Federal Election Commission* (558 U.S. 310 [2010]) decision. Perhaps because the court has highlighted the threat of corruption, both of these efforts, though largely led by lawyers and legal scholars, aim to expose types of alleged corruption not captured by the word in its narrower legal or criminal senses as currently understood. At the same time, these two efforts implicitly assimilate these other phenomena to criminal corruption, and the new, broader sense of corruption they are forging seems to exploit the connotations of the narrow legal or criminal sense of officeholder corruption.

Richard Briffault (2011) suggests that these efforts aim to "dejudicialize" political finance—to reclaim from the courts a degree of democratic control over our politics and to bring our politics in line with the norms and values he believes are expressed in the Constitution. Political finance is certainly not the only arena of political contestation where advocacy groups have voiced frustration about legal obstacles to reform, and it is not the only issue where there is a purported distance between how the judicial branch reads the Bill of Rights and what popular majorities might support. And it may make sense that, when talking about such matters, legal scholars would naturally use legal language and concepts. Yet, this strategy strikes us as wrong-headed. If the point really is to increase democratic control over judges, then perhaps we should be discussing constitutional adjustments, like strengthening Congress or state legislatures or populist referenda and initiatives, and this should apply to many issues (e.g., guns, immigration, abortion, civil forfeiture, and civil immunity), not merely to campaign finance. It seems inadequate to the purported problem to adopt legal language if one wishes to wrest this particular conversation, as well as political decisions generally, away from the lawyers. If corruption is indeed a serious problem in contemporary politics, and if people do not generally mean criminal, officeholder corruption when they say this, then we should talk about it more broadly, without shoehorning it into the Supreme Court's category of corruption merely to get around the court's interpretation of the First Amendment.

Lessig's and Teachout's endeavors are parallel. Using mostly historical arguments about earlier attitudes toward gifts and lobbying, Teachout attempts to broaden the legally relevant definition of corruption, to make it about institutional rot caused by influence. Lessig, likewise, proposes to broaden the legally relevant definition of corruption, again by focusing on influence. Lessig's program goes wider, taking a theory of corruption he derived from analyzing one sphere of society (elections) and then applying it to other areas, such as corporate support for scientific research, banking laws, and other activities that are not strictly political. If one wishes to broaden a term, it is natural to look beyond the phenomena that prompted this course of action, as a means of legitimating the enterprise to one's self and others. Yet, as Underkuffler (2013) argues, there is a reason why the legal conception of corruption is narrow. While there are clearly many rotten things afoot in the United States and the rest of the world, the idea that a word can simply be redefined to advance one's goals is, as we argue below, objectionable.

The previous chapters lead us to a few conclusions about corruption that are relevant to this particular inquiry. First, as we have shown in Chapter 3 in our discussion of motifs in corruption talk, "corruption" is a loaded word. Claims about crooked acts can often imply a deeper or broader moral, cultural, or institutional decay, and can trigger fears of system-wide ruin, fall, decline, sickness, and even death. Second, as we have sought to show in our discussion of academic research on corruption, the precise definition of the term—even in its narrowest application to officeholders—is in dispute. Third, corruption is in some ways what public opinion researchers refer to as a "valence issue."[1] Although it is not (as per the first characteristic, moral) easily scalable (as valence issues such as competence, integrity, honesty, and so forth are), like these examples, it transcends differences of political viewpoints. No one, Left or Right, advocates for corruption. If a behavior can be labeled as corrupt, political foes can join in their condemnation of it. In a political environment as polarized as that of the contemporary United States, such an opportunity for common ground is not to be taken lightly. Although the efforts we reference in this chapter originate from the political Left, it is important to note that corruption has been central to political arguments, both theoretical and practical, among American conservatives as well. A shared language regarding corruption poses the tantalizing possibility of a policy agenda that can avoid the partisan gridlock that has characterized so much of American politics over the past two decades.

All of this poses problems for those who would develop legal arguments about corruption. Some recent American efforts have, as we demonstrate below, sought to recast legal but distasteful (or degrading) activities as corrupt or corrupting in a legally relevant sense, playing on the criminal connotations of the word. Such a focus risks politicizing criminal corruption, thereby casting into doubt the things that have not been contested. In other words, if corruption becomes a matter of partisan or ideological contestation, this can render suspect any research into the bright-line cases of officeholder corruption (scholarship we profiled in Chapter 7); it can even make us more cynical, less vigilant when clear examples of officeholder corruption appear in our politics. Such an effort can also risk turning matters of scale (such as political contributions or lobbying restrictions in the political world, limitations on grant-supported research in academia, or gift-giving and its concomitant attached strings in virtually every walk of life) into categorical sins, and distorting political, ethical, or moral decisions by trying to turn them into legal ones. We concur with Robert Mutch (2014, 184, 192, 198) that much of what gets subsumed by contemporary American corruption talk is properly political; it reflects enduring disagreements about American values that cannot be adjudicated by the courts.

In our consideration here of corruption in American election law, we seek to illuminate what we see as underlying philosophical problems with existing corruption claims in legal theory, problems that render the definitional attempts inconsistent and that hinder constructive discourse about the underlying problems that have prompted contemporary American "corruption talk." Accordingly, in this chapter we describe the contours of contemporary corruption talk regarding elections and we outline some problems with this talk as philosophical project and rhetorical tool.

9.1: Corruption and American Election Law

Within the domain of American campaigns, the contemporary era of "corruption talk" can be traced back to the Supreme Court's *Buckley v. Valeo* (424 U.S. 1 [1976]) decision and to three conceptions of corruption that have dominated American political discourse since that time. While these conceptions have been intertwined with the debate over money in politics, the stakes here and the formulation of them are somewhat larger. Nonetheless, let us start with the court.

9.1a: The Political Story

In *Buckley,* the Supreme Court famously protected political spending as a form of speech under the First Amendment of the Bill of Rights and responded to recently passed campaign finance legislation by declaring that the prevention of "corruption or the appearance of corruption" was the only legitimate reason for restrictions on such speech; it declared that other plausible goals (such as equality, limiting the influence of money, or preventing dominant voices from crowding out a diversity of voices) were not constitutionally permissible rationales for limiting speech.[2] There, and in subsequent decisions, the court went on to clarify the form of corruption that they deemed relevant, limiting it to instances of direct quid pro quo corruption—that is, instances where the corrupt action was by an individual politician. The court would go on in its later campaign finance decisions to largely abandon its concern about the *appearance* of corruption.[3] The problem here was that if we regard the public as the ultimate arbiter of what appears to be corrupt, then virtually any governmental action is suspect—surveys have shown not only that most Americans (and residents of other nations, as well) believe politicians to be corrupt but also that no change in election regulation has any effect on that belief (we take this up in the next chapter). The appearance of corruption is ubiquitous and stubborn, so there is not much that government can do to make itself appear less corrupt. Thus, the rationale for limiting political spending has been narrowed to preventing officeholder corruption in the criminal sense, and that requires showing criminal intent. This is a high bar, and it pushes a wide range of morally corrupt acts, and acts corrosive to our institutions, outside of the scope of criminal sanction.

The court's definition has been adopted and elaborated upon by antiregulation writers such as Bradley Smith (2001) and John Samples (2006). It presents a view of a legislature not as an institution but as a collection of individuals; to make a claim that a legislature is corrupt in the relevant sense, one would have to demonstrate that many, if not all, members of that institution are corrupt. Only defined acts of officeholder crookedness, not moral rot or institutional erosion, are in play here. Since this time there have been two plausible responses by those unhappy with *Buckley*: to challenge the idea that corruption is what matters, or to challenge the court's law-centered definition of officeholder corruption. While both approaches have proven rather futile, to date, for advocates of regulation, there is ample history to suggest that the second approach seems more plausible if one's goal is to win in the courts. It is not uncommon for the Supreme Court to judge legislation unconstitutional but then to go on to counsel Congress on how it might achieve similar ends by slightly adjusting its means.[4] Proponents of the most comprehensive post-*Buckley* campaign finance legislation, the Bipartisan Campaign Reform Act (or BCRA, also called the McCain-Feingold Act), did just this, making direct reference to the prevention of corruption and assembling a lengthy record of statements by political contributors on the potentially corrupting nature of their activities.[5] There is, perhaps, something fundamentally disingenuous in presenting such comprehensive legislation as an anticorruption measure, but the court's rules were clear.

The so-called new corruption arguments that were presented in the legal community in the 1980s and 1990s sought to present an alternate understanding of corruption that allowed for prophylactic measures—efforts to prevent harm to an institution itself by making it clear that suspect individual transactions are prohibited.[6] Under this understanding of corruption, proof of a quid pro quo transaction is not required; if the practices of an institution are deemed by the public to be corrupt, then this is ample reason to take steps to prevent such practices from happening. Instances of quid pro quo corruption can still be identified and punished, but laws that remove the temptation to engage in such corruption—laws that, for instance, limit contacts between legislators and lobbyists or limit unregulated contributions—can be implemented without proof that corruption has occurred as a result of such actions or would occur in the absence of regulation. Note that this type of legislation avoids the court's First Amendment–based concerns, because such laws limit transactions between parties, not freedom of speech or the press. Many prophylactic measures of this nature have been quite popular with the public. *Citizens United v. Federal Election Commission*, however, did reject one prophylactic measure: the limitations on independent expenditures—that is, on spending to support political speech by groups independent of parties and particular politicians. The court held that "influence, gratitude, or access," which may result from such spending, do not constitute corruption in the criminal officeholder sense that the court holds to be relevant for limiting political speech protected under the First Amendment.[7] As long as no explicit agreement has been made between the spender and the politician, such independent expenditures are not corrupt. This holding has established an almost insurmountable barrier for those who would allege corruption in campaign financing. At the same time, there remain many limits on gifts and contributions to officeholders, and more easily identifiable instances have shown that the obvious examples of criminal, officeholder corruption stand far outside of conventional political squabbles.

9.1b: Bigger than Politics

The issues at stake here go beyond campaign finance law, however, or at least they have been framed in such a manner that they purport to be about something broader. In the past several years, a growing number of writers on the Left (mostly) and the Right have sought to articulate a broader argument about corruption, one that incorporates elements of moral rot or ontological decay of institutions. While the court may have inspired some of this, one might contend that the court is no longer the intended audience of this discussion. And although the principals in this discussion have mostly been law professors, the argument is hardly a legal one. It has sought to tap into larger American concerns—it is not merely that our politicians might be beholden to lobbyists or wealthy donors, it is that Americans have become increasingly disenchanted with politics, that America's standing on a variety of cross-national indicators of well-being has fallen, and that our government seems less capable of addressing problems today that it was in prior decades. If we called these circumstances a "corruption of democracy" or something of that sort, most people would understand our meaning, but, as earlier chapters have shown, this is a different sort of corruption. Our government might be increasingly corrupt in this ontological sense—that is, maybe it isn't working well—even if the previous level of criminal, officeholder corruption isn't bad or getting worse. After all, officeholder corruption isn't the only way that a constitutional system or a moral culture could fall apart.

It seems to us that there are currently three different theories of corruption on the loose in American politics, all of which incorporate the concepts of institutional decay or rot to some extent, and all of which rely on influence being the source of that rot or decay. None of these aligns with the interests of the court; although the court perhaps instigated the corruption debate, its definition is sufficiently minimalist that there have been few serious efforts to elaborate upon it.

The most prominent theory of corruption today is associated with Harvard law professor Lawrence Lessig (2012), who has sought to articulate a theory of what he alternately refers to as institutional corruption or "dependence corruption." According to Lessig, individual corruption is essentially a quid pro quo exchange in which a public official seeks some sort of personal benefit in exchange for provision of a private benefit to someone outside of government, whereas institutional corruption occurs when a system tends to promote private interests due to influence, rather than deals. Institutional corruption in Lessig's framing is not an overtly moral failing; rather, it is characterized by improper dependence. That is, contemporary social science might predict that self-interested politicians seek to stay in office, and in doing so they provide benefits to voters or blocs of voters. There is nothing noble in this, but if we are told that this is the way things work, and if we believe that votes are a means of ensuring accountability, this may not seem corrupt because we can reasonably hope it conduces, more or less, to the common good. If, on the other hand, government officials are dependent upon something other than votes—"funders," perhaps—for their well-being, and are providing benefits to funders rather than more generally to voters, then the institution is not dependent in the manner that we want it to be. The institution is corrupt, regardless of the culpability of individual members in corrupt deals. Individual politicians might all regret this occurrence, and they might even speak out against it, but they nonetheless will need to cater to donors rather than voters (perhaps rationalizing that they remain better or more ethical than those who might replace them). An institution can be corrupted, for Lessig, when its members are influenced improperly, even if we cannot punish individual members for corrupt deals.

Lessig has openly drawn upon the work of Dennis Thompson (1987, 1995, 2002, 2013), but there is a crucial difference. In his early work on ethics in Congress, Thompson (1995) sought to distinguish between individual corruption, in which a legislator exchanged favors for personal benefit, and institutional corruption, in which a legislator exchanged favors for political benefit (for example, an endorsement in an upcoming election or support for another bill). Thompson argued that institutional corruption is ultimately more difficult to identify and prosecute, insofar as it often does not yield corrupt results and is not always easily distinguishable from accepted behavior. He insists, however, that instances of institutional corruption in his sense are individual acts that are "mediated" by the practices of the institution. Institutional corruption may bring the norms and practices of the institution into question, but for Thompson it is ultimately an action of individuals (whom he lists in an appendix to his book). Lessig, on the other hand, although he reiterates (Lessig 2013) Thompson's distinction, emphasizes that he does not wish to single out individuals. It is the institution of Congress, itself, that is corrupt. In *Republic, Lost*, Lessig writes the following:

> This corruption has two elements, each of which feeds on the other. The first element is bad governance, which means simply that our government doesn't track the expressed will of the people. . . . The second element is lost trust: when democracy seems a charade, we lose faith in its process. (2012, 8–9)

It is hard to imagine listing the perpetrators of this corruption—which is much of Lessig's point. It seems almost unfair, if this is the general state of things, to single anyone out. Yet the loss of faith here is a process that, once set in motion, is difficult to prosecute, measure, or contain.

The turn in Lessig's story is necessary because he is not talking only about Congress and he is not talking only to the court. He is not interested in a legal case, but in fostering dialogue. He makes this explicit in his Randy L. and Melvin R. Berlin Family Lectures, delivered in 2014 and 2015 at the University of Chicago. There, he summarizes much of the research that he and others pursued at the Safra Center, where he served as the director from 2009 to 2015. He proposes a definition of corruption as "influence, within an economy of influence, that weakens the effectiveness of an institution, especially by weakening public trust of that institution." It seems to us that Lessig here believes he is still using the word "corruption" in the same sense we use it when we talk about corruption of officeholders when they are bribed. Yet, in fact, he is talking more broadly about the ontological corruption of an institution—when it ceases to function as well as was originally intended. Of course, in that case, influence should not be part of the definition. Influence by funders is one thing, but not at all the only thing, that can weaken an institution, preventing it from functioning as well as it should. Whatever one thinks of the specifics of this definition (we consider these specifics later), the intent here is clear—it can be applied, as Lessig proceeds to do, to a variety of different types of institutions, including the academy, the financial industry, and the media. There is no pretense that we are telling the Supreme Court who is corrupt; the intention, rather, is to develop a unified theory. Lessig clearly does document, both here and in the Safra Center work, a variety of ills that have befallen these institutions. Yet, as with government, the extent to which these ills constitute corruption according to Lessig's definition is determined by what he takes to be the purposes of the institutions in question and the government's appropriate dependency relationship with these institutions.

The other principal articulator of this expanded theory of corruption has been Fordham University law professor Zephyr Teachout.[8] In *Corruption in America*, Teachout connects contemporary disputes over money in politics to the historical treatment of corruption in American political thought. Like Lessig, she argues for a more expansive view of corruption, beyond the criminal sense, but unlike Lessig, she explicitly grounds this view in historical references to corruption in eighteenth- and nineteenth-century American thought. Teachout notes that American corruption talk during that period had to do with the perversion of discourse that might occur, for instance, if foreign interests were able to insert themselves into American politics; this account is largely consistent with our discussion in Chapter 8 of presidential corruption references of that era. The corruption involved here is one of duplicity, in that the influences behind a particular argument would not be known, and, as in Lessig's theory, one of improper dependency. While Teachout distinguishes corruption from dependency, she concludes that improper dependency can lead to corruption (of an institution or of a people), and that one solution to this is "bright-line" prophylactic laws, which both deter corrupt behavior and send a clear signal about the "moral weight" of the law itself.

Neither Lessig nor Teachout disputes that individual, or venal, or quid pro quo corruption exists, but both emphasize that that is not what they are talking about—and moreover, in Teachout's case, that that is not what the Founders were talking about when they talked about corruption. Teachout's more historical approach calls our attention to differences between contemporary corruption talk and the American reference points we often use in that talk, but it is, like Lessig's theory, an attempt to reintroduce and expand the concept for use in contemporary politics. It is important to note that in this latter regard, Lessig (2015) and Teachout (both of whom have a long track record of advocacy for Left-leaning Democratic candidates) have actively sought out areas of agreement with conservative writers such as Jay Cost (2015) and Peter Schweizer (2015). As Teachout, in particular, shows, the Left in no way owns the idea that political institutions can be corrupted.

A second, opposing theory of corruption is offered by Cornell law professor Laura Underkuffler. In *Captured by Evil*, Underkuffler (2013) provides a survey of definitions of corruption in theoretical and empirical research. She concludes that references to corruption virtually always are used to make moral judgments about an individual's character. It is a moral, dispositional concept, and as such is unsuitable for use in law. Committing a corrupt act makes one a corrupt person. The moral taint associated with corruption suggests that one is unsuited to engage in politics or public life at all—one's actions simply cannot be trusted. Such corruption certainly exists, but for Underkuffler the accusation of corruption must be used sparingly. If corruption implies "evil," one is effectively banishing one's antagonist from the political sphere when one levels the accusation. Furthermore, the institutional argument runs into problems here: Can an institution be evil, or captured by evil, without the individuals within it being so? Is it possible to sustain Lessig's individual/institutional distinction, where he effectively argues that "the institution is evil but its members are not"? Underkuffler's argument at a minimum provides enough historical detail to convince us that there the connotations of talking about corruption are at odds with Lessig's task and render that task objectionable.[9] Ontological corruption of an institution does not suggest evil; instead, it suggests reduced effectiveness (in Lessig's word) or reduced ability to perform its function well. Such corruption can be based on moral or officeholder corruption, but need not be. The evil connotation that Underkuffler spells out connects to moral corruption specifically.

Underkuffler's notion of individual corruption as "captured by evil" is not the court's notion of individual corruption; quid pro quo corruption applies to particular actions, but it is not dispositional. Underkuffler's notion of individual corruption requires no quid or quo; there are people who would engage in quid pro quo corruption, but for her concept to apply it does not matter if they actually have. There are, furthermore, people who engaged in minor instances of individual corruption but have revealed themselves as the sort of people who would do far worse if they could get away with it. Lessig (2013) responds, essentially, that this sort of criticism of projects like his is too easy; he refers, tartly, to "the simple, self-righteous pleasure of an Underkuffler. The self-righteous pleasure that knows evil when it sees it." But this is unfair. She is simply arguing that the word connotes characterological evil and thus we must be cautious about deploying it as a legal concept.

A third theoretical approach to corruption, this one not from law professors, is presented in the work of Bruce Cain (2015, chap. 7) and Nancy Rosenblum (2008). Neither Cain nor Rosenblum bills their efforts as being exclusively about corruption, and neither disputes the notion that there is a difference between institutional and individual corruption. Both share a broader theoretical orientation that Cain identifies as "reform pluralism." In Cain's argument, however, there are in fact a number of different ways to talk about corruption. There is room for talk of a "corruption of democratic ideals" (which is what he takes Lessig to be talking about), there is room for talk of inappropriate dependence (which is what Lessig takes himself to be discussing), and there is also room for talk of corruption as a "debasement of public deliberation" in which self-serving arguments are deceptively framed as appeals to public ideals. Likewise, Rosenblum catalogs the various ways in which "corruption" is used as an umbrella term to cover "implicit understandings, ambiguous favors, and political advantage." This is definitely part of the idea of officeholder corruption, and we should not be surprised that the criminal concept of corruption is narrower than this—after all, criminal law requires worse acts and clearer criteria than many of our everyday concepts allow. Yet, this vagueness is a problem for the way we talk together because the audience for corruption talk maintains the sort of "gut" response to the word that Underkuffler (2013, 212) describes.

Cain's argument is also taken up by La Raja and Schaffner in their argument for strengthening the capacity of political parties to influence elections. For La Raja and Schaffner (2015, 152), there is a trade-off to be made between addressing corruption and addressing political polarization; one cannot do both, and given the ambiguity of the term "corruption," it can be applied to all manner of political ills. The anticorruption agenda, however, has focused so narrowly on the allegedly corrosive effect of money in politics that it has crowded out concerns such as "fairness, stability, and accountability," concerns that are not easily reconciled with existing campaign finance regulation proposals. Even if the court does not see these as legitimate reasons to abridge constitutional rights, they can still serve as rationales for some types of laws structuring campaigns and elections, and they are, in addition, valid starting points for political conversation.

Unlike Underkuffler, and like Lessig, however, a pluralist theory of corruption would emphasize that political actors are, at least in part, self-interested—and if that alone constituted corruption, then it would be plausible to argue that we are all a little bit corrupt. Cain and Rosenblum both prescribe aggregation by way of institutions as a means of combating corruption; the premier aggregative institutions in American politics are, and always have been, political parties and reputation-bearing interest groups.[10] Only such organizations, which persist from one election to the next, can provide the accountability that is essential for democratic choices to mean anything. A pluralist would not bear a prejudice against political parties or interest groups as corrupt, but rather would suggest that these things be strengthened. Rather than being inherently corrupt, these institutions are legitimate influences within an economy of influence that flourishes with plurality rather than purism.

There is a perhaps unintentional irony to the development of recent arguments about corruption. As Teachout notes, and as Wallis (2006) documents, the story about corruption propounded by moral reformers during the nineteenth century was the one most likely to emphasize corruption as a process of historical decay—it posited an uncorrupted American ideal rooted in the founding, in Christian values, or in the agrarian, antebellum

American ideal, and it presented early-twentieth-century America with political machines and vote-seeking career politicians as a corruption of that ideal. It posited a path toward making America great again. The Progressive argument about corruption may, as we noted in Chapter 6, have been inspired by similar circumstances, but it took aim at individual politicians and posited prophylactic measures—primary elections, the Australian ballot, and so forth—as means of preventing individual corruption. In some ways the contemporary alignment has matters backward; it is self-styled modern progressives (with a lowercase "p") who have championed the nineteenth-century conservative view, albeit without as clear a historical reference point from which we have fallen, and it is today's conservatives who have argued that individual corruption is the major subject of concern (with the caveat that prophylactic measures have been shown not to work very well).

To summarize, the contemporary legal discussion about corruption can be understood in part as a response to the U.S. Supreme Court, but it implicitly acknowledges that the court is not listening, and that the appropriate audience is someone else—the legal advocates of tomorrow, one's base of supporters, the funders of one's research agenda, members of the opposing party, or simply the public. It is easy to conclude that the institutional corruption argument championed by Lessig is "winning"—it has yielded the books that have sold the most copies, one finds its echoes in the 2016 and 2020 presidential campaigns of Donald Trump and Bernie Sanders, and it has the clearest political implications, and yet its implications are not reflexively partisan in nature. But this facility is, for those who articulate opposing views, precisely the problem. The fact that this definition does not appear to "fit" our background assumptions about all that corruption is (even if the Supreme Court's narrow criminal definition does not, either) and the fact that it purports to be a redefinition of a previous concept, or at least a rediscovery of a lost concept, highlights the difficulty of talking about corruption clearly and fruitfully.

9.1c: The Court Throws Down the Gauntlet

There is, of course, a lot of jurisprudence regarding corruption that is not merely about campaign finance or the lobbyist-legislator relationship; the Underkuffler book has a detailed critique of much of this material. Yet one somewhat larger Supreme Court decision that came on the heels of the *Citizens United* case and its subsequent elaborations[11] vividly shows the difference between "corruption" as officeholder crookedness, as a predicate for criminal punishment, and "corruption" as a general sort of institutional or moral decay. In April 2016 the court heard the case of *McDonnell v. United States* (579 U.S. ___ [2016]). The case concerned federal corruption charges made against former Virginia governor Robert (Bob) McDonnell. McDonnell and his wife Maureen had had ongoing discussions with the CEO of Star Scientific, a Virginia-based company that had hopes of gaining the governor's support in testing and marketing a nutritional supplement derived from tobacco. Jonnie Williams, the CEO in question, had given or loaned the McDonnells the equivalent of $175,000 during the time he was seeking state support; his gifts to the family included, among other things, an interest-free loan, designer clothing, and a Rolex watch. Mrs. McDonnell had directly requested some of these gifts, allegedly without her husband's knowledge or consent. The governor had arranged meetings for Williams with various government officials, had hosted events where Williams could meet others in the state government, and had directed his subordinates to talk with Williams and to promote research studies on the drug. McDonnell was convicted of corruption and bribery in a jury trial in Federal District Court; he appealed, arguing that the jury had been given overly broad instructions by the government about what constituted corrupt behavior.

All of this, the Supreme Court admitted, looks rotten—and it could serve as evidence that there *might* be some sort of corrupt quid pro quo agreement. "There is no doubt," the court concluded, "that this case is distasteful; it may be worse than that." And yet the court ruled 9–0 in favor of overturning McDonnell's conviction. "Our concern," the court went on, "is not with tawdry tales of Ferraris, Rolexes, and ball gowns." The court had, essentially, three major claims about why McDonnell's actions were not corrupt in a legally relevant sense. First, there was no explicit "quid" here—gifts were requested and received by the McDonnells, and favors were requested by Johnson, but the two were not linked. The favors were not requested in exchange for the gifts, nor were the gifts requested with any explicit promise of governmental action. Second, there was no measurable "quo." The things McDonnell did, even if they were on some level encouraged by Johnson's gifts, were not "official acts" of a government official. Elected officials can meet with whomever they please, can make phone calls, can encourage subordinates to look into things, but absent a direct exhortation to do something, or an official governmental action for which they are responsible (e.g., issuing an order), they have not acted in the role of governmental official. And third, it is in fact the job of lobbyists to lobby, and the job of elected officials to try to do things for their constituents, whether they have contributed money or not. Who is to say whether Virginia would have smiled upon the development of tobacco-based supplements absent all of Johnson's gifts? The supplements were, after all, made in Virginia, making them provided jobs for Virginians, and they have perhaps done some good for their users. Should Star Scientific actually be at a disadvantage compared to the producers of other Virginia-based products because their CEO has been friendly with the governor? The system may be rotten, but that does not mean that its inhabitants are crooked.

So, corruption here cannot be proven because there was no explicit quid pro quo—just gifts received and favors done. And yet this is the sort of corruption that politicians rail against—the cozy relationships between politicians and special interests, and wink-and-nod dealings. One could argue that it would be malpractice for people engaged in political corruption to announce what they are doing, and it would also likely be unnecessary. In the movies, for instance, corrupt deals are always described euphemistically—as favors that may or may not ever be repaid. The court has, perhaps, a valid point—even in cases like this, it is hard to develop a rule that defines corruption criminally in a way that will not be overbroad or will not deter some perfectly legal behaviors, or the opposite—too narrow, allowing a lot of scuzzy behavior we wish we could get rid of. It is as if the court is saying, however, that it is ultimately not their job to do away with the broader sort of problems that Lessig, Teachout, and many other critics of financial shenanigans in government decry and that those problems do not justify overriding their reading of First Amendment rights. The problems seem not to be problems of corruption in the legal sense of the term, so the solution won't be found in a redefinition of corruption in the legal sense. Those concerned with addressing those problems must find other ways to address them within the domain of politics and policies.

9.2: Confusions

As we have sought to demonstrate in the earlier chapters of this book, many philosophical accounts understand human corruption as a turning away of agents from their proper ends or function, for the sake of serving other, often lower and more selfish, goods, or of pursuing a partial interest rather than a common good. This general framework can encompass a wide variety of actions, but often it is not the action itself that is of deepest concern. Although the legal category targets, as it must, particular criminal acts, the reason citizens take single acts of criminal corruption so seriously is that we see them as indications of something less isolated and more damaging. We tend to see them as the tips of icebergs, portending who-knows-how-big of a problem. A single crooked act implies moral or institutional rot; the question is whether we talk about the act or about its implication. This conception of corruption throws into relief two central areas of confusion in contemporary corruption talk: the relationship between the corruption of individual officeholders and institutions, and the definition of what an institution is for.

In this section, we focus on Lessig's (2013) definition of institutional corruption. He tells us, for example, that he doesn't mean "Type 1 corruption," which is basically bribery. Instead, he means "Type 2," which he calls "dependence corruption," and which he emphasizes as an institutional problem rather than an individual problem. "In this second sense of corruption, it is not individuals who are corrupted within a well-functioning institution. It is instead an institution that has been corrupted, because the pattern of influence operating upon individuals within that institution draws them away from the influence intended" (231). In the Berlin Lectures, he defines institutional corruption as follows: "Institutional corruption is manifest when there is a systemic and strategic influence which is legal, or even currently ethical, that undermines the institution's effectiveness by diverting it from its purpose or weakening its ability to achieve its purpose, including, to the extent relevant to its purpose, weakening either the public's trust in that institution or the institution's inherent trustworthiness" (Lessig 2014). There, again, he emphasizes that institutional corruption does not involve corruption of individuals within the institution.

One common response to distinguishing between institutional corruption and individual corruption in this way is what one might call the "McConnell Paradox." During the debate over what was then known as the McCain-Feingold campaign finance reform bill, and would later become the Bipartisan Campaign Reform Act, Senator Mitch McConnell took issue with the claim that the bill would combat corruption. "How can there be corruption if no one is corrupt?" McConnell asked. "That's like saying the gang is corrupt but none of the gangsters are."[12]

The McConnell Paradox is easy to explain away if we see institutional corruption as a form of ontological corruption rather than as a form of officeholder corruption. Recall our distinctions between ontological, moral, and officeholder corruption in Chapter 2. Institutions—like everything else—can be corrupted in the sense of decay, get damaged, or come to ruin. Things fall apart. And what this means is that the institution does not function or does not function as well as the type of thing it is, with the ends and purposes that define it. There are many things that could cause an institution to become dysfunctional, and officeholder corruption is one of them. If even one or a few key officials within an institution are bribed or extorted away from fulfilling their roles within the institution, then the institution would no longer fulfill its function, or will not fulfill it as well as it should. And if many or all officials act corruptly in their institutional roles, so much the worse for the institution's mission.

While officeholder corruption can lead to the ontological corruption of the institution, many other things can, also. An institution that is not well structured, for example, might have many conscientious professionals working within it, and yet it may not do much at all toward its institutional ends. Further, an ill-conceived organizational structure or changes in technology or in cultural context might, for example, undermine an institution's ability to serve its mission. The global COVID-19 pandemic, for example, destabilized many institutions, destroyed their ways of operating, and brought many to ruin. These are all forms of ontological corruption of institutions—but they did not come about through officeholder corruption of the people within them.

To get around this conceptual concern of ours, perhaps Lessig's point could be recast as follows: Democratic institutions can undergo a kind of ontological corruption, undermining the quality of their functioning, when some people have too much influence, and other people have not enough influence, even though this influence does not amount to corruption of the officeholders. We would agree with this version of the claim, with two important caveats about how Lessig develops his case.

First, we would then want to discuss more deeply what purposes democratic institutions properly serve, and how a pluralism of influences can be protected (rather than erased into the Manichean dichotomy of "the people" and "the Funders"). It is an easy rhetorical claim to make, that democracy should track the will of "the people," but it is also inadequate for serious thought about the common good, once we recognize the legitimate diversity of standpoints among voters, as well as their fluidity.

Second, the pernicious influence of some Funders is not the only thing that can undermine an institution's fitness for fulfilling its mission. Yet, Lessig insists on focusing not only on influence—in fact, on "strategic" or intentional influence especially of money—but also, he allows, on ideology. Yet, the definition of institutional corruption offered by Lessig should not single that out as somehow uniquely threatening. Moreover, the definition he offers relies on the connotations that officeholder corruption has with bribery. It is as though he is saying that institutions have been bribed even while their members have not been—and that, we think, doesn't make sense. It would make more sense for him to claim that there is indeed a kind of (noncriminal) officeholder corruption undergirding Type 2 or institutional corruption, given his claim that this type of corruption relies on the officeholders within the institution being turned away from their proper purpose by bad influences.

Lessig's point, boiled down, is that democratic institutions should "track the express will of the people," but they are not doing this well because of the influence that "the Funders" have. Without using the word "corruption" and offering a new type and definition of it, without engaging in the tradition of Progressive corruption talk, his point would be clearer but also less compelling. He would not have had an anticorruption research program in the sense that would be easily recognizable by his audience, including those in the audience who might have wanted to fund research programs against criminal corruption.

Lessig makes frequent reference to replacing criminal quid pro quo standards with a certain type of influence. While an honest politician will indeed avoid any quid pro quo agreements, no politician can avoid influence—indeed, multiple influences from myriad sources. The Lessig definition nods to this fact by specifying the corrupting influence as occurring within "an economy of influence." The phrase implies that politicians, and other institutional agents, operate within systems of people creating and trading influences. Yet, at other times, he operates with a dichotomy between the "express will of the people" and "the Funders," as though instead of democracy working through a play of many influences, we had a clear demarcation between the general will and private interests. The influences that Lessig's definition labels as corrupting, the influences that allegedly entwine politicians in institutional corruption, are those that "weaken the effectiveness of the institution." This specification does little to reduce the elusiveness of what counts as improper influence, since it leaves out the crucial empirical task of determining the conditions under which an institution operates most effectively and the conceptual and normative task of determining what ends the institution should serve.

To be applied clearly, Lessig's definition requires that we identify for any institution what its purposes are and which sources and degrees of influence on its agents are helpful for these purposes and which are not. Yet, while improper influence is meant to be illuminated by the purposes of our public institutions, those purposes are often just as elusive and contested as the idea of undue influence. Thus, ultimately, Lessig's definition of institutional corruption is unilluminating outside a discussion of these institutional purposes. Second, governmental institutions in our democratic republic seem designed to respond to this human situation of lack of clarity and of agreement about ultimate purposes of our most important institutions. They do this by allowing—within a constitutional framework that imposes limits as well as creating places for debate and decision—the play of influences in the country to determine the particular purposes to be sought. This is what politics is. Thus, ultimately, the definition of institutional corruption seems either to shortchange, or to simply challenge, the constitutional framework as a framework for politics, which involves contesting opinions, competing influences.

9.3: Conclusions

We do not mean to say here that rhetorical arguments about corruption of our institutions are wrong, only that they should be understood for what they are. Corruption is a much bigger and broader concept than the politically convenient parallel with bribery would suggest. There are many valid reasons why Americans might consider demanding changes in our campaign finance laws, including the desire to change the balance of influences on their representatives. Many of the specific reform proposals that are offered by Lessig and others are, when shorn of their "corruption" framework, welcome and entirely valid additions to our political discussion. The question is not whether we should have a serious discussion about reform but, rather, what sort of frame we should use in that discussion. As we have sought to document above, we find the "corruption" frame to be weak as a premise for any sort of legal theory to reply to the court's interpretation of the First Amendment, because it is beside their point, and we find it weak as a rationale for political reform, because it is misleading given how people connect political corruption and bribery and because it seems to define a principal task of politics and political representatives as corrupt—the need to discern the common good through the pluralism of influences and interests.

Lessig closes *Republic, Lost* with a summary of "conventional" proposals—clean elections, overturning *Citizens United*, having more primary challenges—and a pair of much more sweeping, radical ideas: a call for the president to demand substantial congressional reform,[13] and a call for a new constitutional convention, a refounding. Lessig fits into the Progressive legacy of American corruption talk in which corruption, rhetorically deployed, becomes the rationale for proposing very specific changes to how we structure our political life together. Some of those changes seem like minor and moderate tweaks to better channel the will of the people, while others would alter something that is constitutionally fundamental. Moreover, his new definition of institution corruption is reminiscent of Ross's definition of "new sins" (Chapter 6) that our society needs to respond to with some radical changes. We suggest, instead, that officeholder corruption is an old sin. Not only is bribery old, but so is the corruption that happens when politicians cannot distinguish between healthy and unhealthy influences on their character and viewpoint. Ontological corruption of our institutions is, likewise, an old problem, as is the difficulty of designing a democratic system that absorbs and manages a plurality of influences rather than dreaming of a romanticized and simplistic "will of the people."

Many similar, useful terms and frames have been presented in looking at the role of money and self-interest in politics. Corrosion, distortion, influence, and other terms have been used without either the conceptual problems or the pretense that a grand theory is being developed. There is no reason not to continue to employ such terms. Veteran campaign finance lawyer Robert Bauer (2015) has written about the unprecedented nature of contemporary campaign expenditures and the novel role of large campaign donors, while at the same time making it clear that "corruption" has nothing to do with his description. As we have seen, Mutch, La Raja and Schaffner, and Cain also take up this basic point; there is much that one might object to in contemporary politics, but that does not make those things instances of officeholder corruption. Subsuming them under that rubric weakens the term and confuses the issue for only a short-term, rhetorical advantage. Whether one agrees with the sentiments of these pieces or not, regardless of whether the language chosen in them was adopted with the same concerns in mind that we have, they show that we can have a heated discussion about what American politics and our public purpose more broadly should be, without distorting—some might say corrupting—our language to shoehorn our political proposals into the Supreme Court's concern about the criminal corruption of officeholders.

10

How the American Public Thinks about Corruption

n many ways, the 2016 presidential election was about corruption. Both of the major party nominees were accused of being corrupt, and in the two parties' primaries, corruption was a frequent subject of discussion. Republican nominee Donald J. Trump accused Democratic nominee Hillary Clinton and her running mate Tim Kaine of corruption, he criticized primary opponents Marco Rubio and Ted Cruz of participating in a corrupt political system, and he pledged that if he were elected he would "drain the swamp," rid Washington of corruption and cronyism. Many election observers also raised questions of corruption in their discussions of Trump's prior business activities and his failure to release his tax returns. Meanwhile, Senator Bernie Sanders frequently labeled the American campaign finance system corrupt and criticized Clinton of corruption for her role in it. If the system appears corrupt, then anyone who has excelled in the system seems vulnerable to such accusations, without much more evidence than that.

While it might be easy to write off these claims as mere campaign rhetoric, a case can also be made that the candidates were responding to public concerns. In the 2017 Edelman Trust Barometer survey (taken in October and November of 2016), voters were asked whether they were fearful about the state of America at the moment (Edelman Staff 2017). Of those surveyed, 67 percent of Trump voters and 45 percent of Clinton voters said that they were fearful. When asked what it was that they feared, one-third of voters listed corruption as one of their greatest fears. And this fear was bipartisan— 34 percent of Trump voters and 29 percent of Clinton voters made reference to corruption. This was the most commonly cited Democratic fear, and it was the fourth most commonly cited Republican fear—behind immigration, globalization, and eroding social values. The Trust Barometer results were often drawn upon in 2016 to explain differences in worldviews among Trump and Clinton voters, but the results indicate that Americans of all political orientations are anxious about corruption.

Then again, however, these results do not tell us very much about what voters think corruption is. One might argue that, because this survey was taken during the election, voters were thinking about the character of the candidates and about specific actions they had taken—that is, about officeholder corruption. That is, there was a Democratic narrative about the questionable business practices of Donald Trump, and a Republican narrative about the Clinton Foundation or about Hillary Clinton's actions in the past. Voters might also have been concerned about moral corruption or civilizational decline. Trump's crowds sometimes chanted "Lock Her Up," implying a belief that Clinton was corrupt in the sense of having criminally misused her institutional power. The success of Trump's slogan "Make American Great Again," in contrast, shows something deeper and vaguer: a worry about it all going downhill. One might argue that little has changed since then—that the Democrats' story about Trump remained the same in 2020 and 2024, while Republicans raised a host of questions about the use of power by Joe Biden and his family. One might also contend that these concerns, so prominent in 2016, were based on a more general concern about corruption as moral or institutional rot, cultural or civilizational decay: about eroding democratic norms, the influence of money in politics, the dysfunction of bureaucracy or of Congress, or the insulation of political elites from the mass public.

The conception of corruption that citizens use is important for two reasons. First, if there is public concern about corruption, one would hope that politicians recognize this concern and take steps to address the problem. But what exactly are the problems that need addressing? The ambiguity of the word, the vagueness of the fears themselves, makes discerning that difficult. Second, as we noted in Chapter 9, perceptions of corruption have at times been presented by the courts as justification for legislative action. Restrictions on campaign contributions, for instance, were held by the Supreme Court in *Buckley v. Valeo* to be justified on the grounds that citizens might perceive large contributions to be corrupting. Yet if voters are in fact concerned about something less politically tractable than discrete instances of officeholder corruption—for example, corruption as a decline in democratic competence, in civilizational flourishing, or in public morality—these problems (or perceived problems) may well be beyond policy.

We begin this chapter with a summary of prior public opinion research on corruption. We then present two different frames for understanding citizen views about corruption: One such frame or attitude—that of the Mender—tends to focus on corruption as officeholder crookedness and weakened institutional structure and rules, as a matter of individual or group failure to comply with decent constitutional laws and established norms of political behavior. The second frame or attitude—that of the Purist—picks up on our discussion of corruption as a broad societal falling apart, moral disorientation, and institutional failure. We draw on several surveys, the 2014 Cooperative Congressional Election Study (Fowler 2017) and two different modules from the General Social Survey (Smith et al. 2018) in the late 1980s and 2000s, to distinguish among different types of survey questions about corruption. For each, we explore characteristics of citizens who are prone to see corruption in social or political matters. We close with some thoughts on how we might use these patterns to understand the corruption rhetoric of contemporary politicians. Our results show that both of the styles of corruption talk are represented in citizens' beliefs about corruption, but that there are identifiable differences in the types of citizens who employ each type of corruption talk. Different audiences are ripe, it seems, for different types of corruption talk.

10.1: Asking People about Corruption

To reiterate, the term "corruption" is sufficiently complex that it is difficult to know exactly what respondents are thinking about when they are asked about corruption. In addition, however, it is difficult to understand what sort of scale citizens use in considering corruption—what is "a lot" of corruption, and how might one separate economic corruption from political corruption in considering public opinion? A recent survey of attitudes in the United States and Latin America illustrates this; respondents were asked whether a military coup would be justified "when there is a lot of corruption" (Feierhard, Lupu, and Stokes 2018). Over 25 percent of U.S. respondents (a number that includes 25 percent or more of Democrats and of Republicans) responded in the affirmative. Is this troubling? It depends on what citizens think corruption is, and what "a lot" of corruption would look like. As we see below, corruption, despite its central role in political debates, remains an elusive concept, but it has been treated very differently in U.S. and international survey research. Comparative surveys have, for the most part, treated corruption in a more careful fashion than have exclusively American surveys, and these studies are important for us in establishing hypotheses about what the term means to the public.

10.1a: Asking Americans about Corruption

Most empirical survey work on corruption in the United States has relied upon the American National Election Studies (ANES) questions about politicians. Since 1958, the ANES has contained a small battery of questions regarding trust in government. None of these questions specifically ask about corruption, but they address adjacent concepts. Respondents have been asked about the role of special interests ("Would you say the government is pretty much run by a few big interests looking out for themselves or that it is run for the benefit of all the people?"), about how wisely the government uses tax money, and, perhaps of most relevance, whether politicians are "crooked" ("Do you think that quite a few of the people running the government are crooked, not very many are, or do you think hardly any of them are crooked?"). Studies specifically addressing perceptions of corruption, such as the study by Persily and Lammie (2004), have drawn on these time series, and in particular on the "crooked" question, to explore the determinants of perceived corruption. As with virtually all measures of trust in government, each of these questions shows a gradual decline, and these questions show also a growing belief that politicians are "crooked." For instance, in 1968 only 25 percent of respondents responded that "quite a few" politicians are crooked, but 64 percent gave this response in 2012; 19 percent of the 1968 respondents said that "hardly any" politicians are crooked, but merely 4 percent have this response in 2012. Persily and Lammie contend, however, that this change does not seem to be a response to any identifiable instances of corruption—for instance, they claim not to see a noticeable effect from Watergate, from the various campaign finance or investment scandals during the Clinton administration, or from any other discrete event. Instead, perceptions of corruption correlate highly over time with presidential approval and with the performance of the economy. At an individual level, a belief that politicians are crooked correlates positively with libertarian attitudes and negatively with social trust, and seems unaffected by level of knowledge.[1]

A belief that politicians are crooked might seem a reasonable proxy for asking directly about corruption, although the term "crooked" would seem to invite the respondent to think about discrete instances of transactional corruption. The fact that it correlates highly with generalized mistrust of others suggests that people do not always make this distinction, however. One might criticize this question, as well, for the potentially outdated language—how often do people use the word "crooked" in conversation today (putting aside our frequent use of it in this book about some forms of officeholder corruption)? We are not confident that citizens simply equate the two things. At best, this term certainly captures one type of corruption, and is perhaps less ambiguous than the term "corruption" itself is.

It is hard to ask people how they define corruption; some studies have asked politicians to choose among different definitions (Peters and Welch 1978), while others (e.g., McCann and Redlawsk 2006) have asked the public to choose whether they are more worried about corruption in different spheres of society (e.g., about corrupt politicians versus corruption in the private sector). Yet in these cases corruption either remains undefined or is defined in a way that clearly limits it to individual criminal actions.

To address these problems, Jeffrey Milyo and David Primo (2020) placed a series of questions in the 2012 and 2016 Cooperative Congressional Election Studies (CCES). They provide respondents with a series of nine different reasons why a politician might support a policy that is not supported by the voters, and they ask respondents to place each scenario on a scale from "definitely not corrupt" to "definitely corrupt." These scenarios include (in descending order of the level of perceived corruption) personal gain, promises made to contributors, campaign contributions, interest group support, pressure from party leaders, making the other party look bad, gaining favorable media coverage, personal conviction, and acting in the best interest of the country. A majority of respondents claimed that all but the last two are corrupt (4 or 5 on the five-point scale). Corruption, as used commonly, can encompass many behaviors that are entirely legal, and many behaviors that arguably correspond with how democratic politics tends to work or is even supposed to work. On the other hand, there are gradations here—respondents were more inclined to label as corrupt actions with financial motivations (whether personal or in the form of campaign contributions) than actions with motivations relating to advancing one's career or aiding one's reelection prospects. Moreover, this seems justified according to officeholder corruption understood simply as a turning away from one's institutional purpose—in this case, doing what is in the best interest of the country. Like Persily and Lammie, however, Milyo and Primo note that these perceptions seem untethered from knowledge. They concur that these findings suggest that political reforms are unlikely to influence public perceptions of the prevalence of corruption.

In addition, no prior studies have found that beliefs about corruption are shaped by partisanship. Milyo and Primo take this to be evidence that the public is not responding to recent events. Few corruption questions are, however, specific to individual politicians or candidates. The standard formulation of corruption questions—referring to politicians, or government administrators—is sufficiently vague that perhaps citizens do not find cause to reflect on particular instances of corruption. The paucity of American surveys on corruption, however, also makes it difficult to correlate corruption claims with particular events. A 2009 survey that asked questions about corrupt politicians found that perceiving higher levels of corruption is correlated to higher likelihood of participating in politics; the author argues that this contradicts conventional wisdom that corruption prompts political disengagement, but that this also suggests that citizens may take out their frustrations on particular politicians or their parties when there is widespread corruption (Kelly 2016).

10.1b: Comparative Studies of Public Opinion on Corruption

In contrast to the American work, comparative studies of corruption have tended to do two things: to compare perceptions of corruption within a country with other measures of country corruption, such as expert surveys, or to explore the relationship between perceptions of corruption and personal experiences with corrupt governmental actors. The aim here is in part, like the American work, to determine how accurate public perceptions are, but the focus is less on response to specific reforms than it is on whether there is a sort of culture of corruption in the nations surveyed. As in the American case, some comparative studies (e.g., You and Khagram 2005) find correlations between socioeconomic status and perceptions of corruption, with respondents of higher socioeconomic status (SES) perceiving less corruption.

On balance, these studies present a mixed view of the accuracy of public perceptions. Rusciano (2015) finds that public perceptions and expert perceptions are positively correlated across countries and across time, suggesting that the public is aware of general changes in the level of corruption. Johnston (2014, 218) disagrees, arguing that at the individual level, perceptions of corruption tend to reflect political orientations, suggesting that public perceptions are not responsive to empirical events (see also Davis and Ruhe 2003). Ray Fisman and Miriam Golden (2017, 33–34, 72) concur, cautioning that the wording of individual questions in most comparative surveys transforms enough over time that claims about change are harder to justify. They argue, furthermore, that the instances of corruption one might confront are different enough across countries that measuring perceptions becomes problematic for the same reason as the "crookedness" question in the United States— we simply cannot know what respondents are thinking about.

The most comprehensive study on the topic, however, looks at individual-level determinants of perceived corruption. Natalia Melgar, Maximo Rossi, and Tom Smith (2010) do find that public perceptions and expert perceptions are positively correlated across countries. However, they find a strong relationship between socioeconomic status and social connectedness and perceived corruption: Women perceive higher levels of corruption than men; public sector employees perceive lower levels of corruption than private sector employees or the self-employed; married people perceive lower levels than unmarried people; and church attendance, income, and education are all negatively correlated with perceived corruption. When put together, these findings indicate either that people who are more politically engaged are less likely to believe there is a lot of corruption, or that the politically engaged are the "winners" in corrupt systems.

The most common finding in comparative studies, however, is that there is little relationship between perceptions of corruption and firsthand experiences of corruption (see, e.g., Rose 2015). This suggests, perhaps, that corruption talk by politicians is more influential than personal experience. The reason why this is discussed in comparative studies but not American studies may be that in some of the countries surveyed corruption is much more common, more part of the way of life, than in the United States—if a person finds it necessary to pay a bribe to a public official regularly, as is the case in some countries, that person has good reason to believe that there is corruption. If the nature of corruption is a bit less personal—as in the United States, for instance, where concerns include the types of subjects in the 2020 work by Milyo and Primo (such as pressure from interest groups or party leaders)—one would expect respondents to be more influenced by media accounts, politicians' speeches about corruption, or other secondhand sources.

If this is the case—and this is admittedly a leap beyond the findings in existing public opinion work—then we have a bit of a conundrum. The people who are most likely to hear politicians talk about corruption are, one would assume, the people who pay more attention to politics—the more educated, the more politically active, or the more socially connected. Yet these same people are less inclined to believe that there is much corruption. The factors contributing to how one perceives corruption seem complicated and overlapping—and, we suspect, not explainable in any simple way.

These two literatures suggest that we might profitably consider public attitudes toward corruption in two different ways. First, we might set aside our concerns about the content of the term and simply look for cross-sectional or cross-temporal patterns in beliefs about corruption, whatever it is. What types of citizens are likely to believe that there is substantial corruption, and how do these perceptions vary over time or in relationship to particular events—such as a change in which party controls government, or in the behavior of governmental officials? And second, how might we categorize different questions about corruption? Do some questions seem likely to elicit responses about particular politicians and actions, and do others seem to suggest a general state of human affairs? Do responses to these types of questions vary in the same fashion, or do they seem to capture the beliefs of some types of respondents in one formulation while describing others' views in another?

Distinguishing between such types of questions is complicated by the questions we have available. Apart from the ANES questions—which, again, seem to us problematic in that they do not use the term "corruption"—no reliable time series question about what corruption is has been asked in the U.S. context over the past decade. Instead, the best data we have comprise survey responses from three different surveys that seem to show the effects of these two frames. We are interested here in whether different types of citizens use different types of attitudes in thinking about corruption.

10.2: Three Snapshots of Public Opinion on Corruption

10.2a: American Public Opinion on Political Corruption, 2014

First, let us consider one recent study of the ethics of politicians. This survey presents corruption in a broad sense that seeks to measure the amount of corruption without providing any clear definition of what corruption is. The 2014 Cooperative Congressional Election Study (CCES) included a module of questions designed by a team from Wesleyan University to elicit responses about the relationship between respondent partisanship and perceptions of congressional polarization (Fowler 2017; Dancey and Sheagley 2018). This was a 1,500-person module that included several questions on citizens' evaluations of their legislators and their legislators' voting behavior. Among the questions asked of respondents was whether they agree or disagree with the statement "Politics in the United States is fundamentally corrupt." Respondents were given a seven-point scale to indicate their level of agreement or disagreement. Although this question was not central to the various analyses that the survey team conducted, it has the virtue of being much broader than corruption questions tend to be. It is about politics, not politicians, and it does not single out politicians or provide any particular context for what sort of corruption is being discussed.[2] It thus serves as a good starting point.

So many respondents view politics as being corrupt that it is difficult to identify meaningful differences according to any sort of respondent characteristics. Of the respondents, 79.2 percent claimed that they agree to some extent (categories 5–7), and 35.4 percent said that they "strongly" agree; a mere 6.2 percent of respondents said that they disagree (categories 1–3). This overwhelming response makes it difficult to assess meaningful variations. There are no significant differences by political party, by respondent ideology, or by many of the customary demographic variables one might use (gender, race, marital status, geography, and so forth). To put matters bluntly, pretty much everyone in the United States believes that politics is corrupt.

One striking feature about these data, however, is that by many measures, those most attuned to politics are in fact more likely to perceive corruption than are those who are less interested in politics. Measurements of corruption on this seven-point scale are positively correlated with political interest ($R^2 = .184, p < .001$). Other factors that are known to be predictive of political interest and knowledge are also positively correlated with perceptions of corruption; family income and voter registration status, for instance, also correlate positively with a greater perception of corruption. Roughly 81.5 percent of registered voters believe government is at least somewhat corrupt, as opposed to 70.3 percent of those who are not registered. The major outlier here is age—older respondents are slightly less likely to see government as being corrupt than are younger respondents.

Some caution should be exercised in interpreting these relationships, since for the most part the lower categories (that is, those that include people who disagree with the claim that government is corrupt) remain constant throughout, and the variation here is in the percentage of respondents who choose the middle category as opposed to the higher ones. Given that it can be difficult in survey research to disentangle middle-of-the-road responses from "don't know" responses, it may simply be that those with less political engagement or knowledge of political current events are simply less likely to make claims about government corruption than are those who are more engaged or knowledgeable.

These responses show that a significant percentage of Americans believe that politics is corrupt. We cannot know from this survey how and why this perception has changed over time, but it does indicate that a large percentage of Americans is willing to use the term and that usage of the term is not necessarily a matter of political disaffection, disengagement, or self-interest. If it is the case that this study has captured an enduring belief about corruption—as opposed to being a short-term response to political events—then it suggests that we can profitably compare narrower sorts of corruption questions to see if there are different types of corruption perceivers. We turn, then, to two other sets of survey questions.

10.2b: Attitudes about Corrupt Politicians, 2000–2016

The General Social Survey, or GSS—like the ANES, an academic survey fielded for several decades that asks identically worded questions over long periods of time—has occasionally included a battery of questions on corruption. There is no consistent time series regarding corruption perceptions on the GSS, as there is on the ANES, but the GSS has two different sets of questions on corruption that are useful for our purposes here. These two sets map nicely onto the distinction drawn earlier between different attitudes toward corruption.

In the 2006 and 2016 GSSs (Smith et al. 2018), respondents were asked three questions about corrupt politicians:

1. In your opinion, about how many politicians in America are involved in corruption?
2. And in your opinion, about how many government administrators in America are involved in corruption?
3. In the last five years, how often have you or a member of your immediate family come across a public official who hinted they wanted, or asked for, a bribe or favor in return for a service?

In the 2004 and 2014 GSS (Smith et al. 2018), respondents were asked a question about corrupt governmental administrators, similar to question 2:

4. How widespread do you think corruption is in the public service in America?

And in the 2000 GSS, respondents were asked whether they agree or disagree with the following statement about the role corruption plays in government activities:

5. To get all the way to the top in America today, you have to be corrupt.

While these questions are by no means identical, they all ask respondents about the prevalence of individual acts of corruption—or, in the case of question 3, about their own experience with corruption. These are questions about corruption as officeholder crookedness.

Question 3 here closely resembles some questions from the comparative work noted above (e.g., Johnston 2014; Melgar, Rossi, and Smith 2010; Rose 2015; Rusciano 2015); one plausible goal here is to explore the relationship between personal experience of corruption and perceptions about how widespread corruption is. All of these questions provide five scalable responses, ranging, for instance, in the case of questions 1 and 2 from "almost all" to "almost none" and in question 5 from "strongly agree" to "strongly disagree." Implicit in each is a basic derivative claim: that an uncorrupted state of affairs would be one in which all politicians or other government officials did not engage in individual acts of corruption. The precise conception of corruption is not made clear in the question, but it seems that each question prompts consideration of discrete acts.

It should first be noted that in the instance where questions were asked across two separate studies, there is little variation across time in responses. For question 2 (on corrupt government administrators), 33.4 percent of the 2006 respondents argued that "quite a lot" or "almost all" are corrupt, while 34.7 percent said so in 2016. For question 1, 43.7 percent of the 2006 respondents fell into these categories, while 42.6 percent did in 2016. These similarities indicate that there is little harm in combining responses across years.

Table 10.1 shows responses to these five questions; we have collapsed the original five categories down to three for ease of presentation. The percentages here are much lower than those in the CCES module, indicating either that the different scale (five-point versus seven-point) pushes respondents to provide different sorts of answers or that these questions capture only some of the individuals who believe "politics is fundamentally corrupt," in the

TABLE 10.1 SELECTED GENERAL SOCIAL SURVEY (GSS) "CROOKEDNESS" CORRUPTION RESPONSES

Question	Year	Response Options	
In your opinion, about how many politicians in America are involved in corruption?	2006 2016	"Quite a Lot" or "Almost All"	43.2%
In your opinion, about how many government administrators in America are involved in corruption?	2006 2016	"Quite a Lot" or "Almost All"	34.0
How widespread do you think corruption is in the public service in America?	2004	"A lot of people are involved" or "Almost everyone is involved"	29.6
To get all the way to the top in America today, you have to be corrupt.	2000	"Agree" or "Strongly Agree"	17.1
In the last five years, how often have you or a member of your immediate family come across a public official who hinted they wanted, or asked for, a bribe or favor in return for a service?	2006 2016	"Quite often" or "Very often"	1.8

Source: General Social Surveys (Smith et al. 2000, 2004, 2006, 2016).

words of the CCES. Unsurprisingly, the two questions about individual corruption in government are highly correlated ($R^2 = .748$, $p < .001$). And the number of citizens reporting firsthand experience with corruption is vanishingly small and uncorrelated with the other questions about perception.

There is sufficient variation in these responses that we can learn a bit more about who sees corruption in these questions than was possible for the CCES data earlier. Table 10.2 shows some of the statistically significant correlations for each question. We explored variation here according to age, education, sex, marital status, income, partisanship, political engagement, political knowledge, and ideology. There is no relationship at all for several of these—sex and marital status have nothing to do with perceived corruption, and race correlates with only two of the five.

Of course, we cannot directly compare these responses to those of the 2014 CCES module. It seems apparent, however, that the questions here, because they are more focused on individuals, elicit a lower number of responses alleging corruption. In contrast to the CCES findings, most indicators of political engagement, knowledge, and efficacy are negatively correlated with perceived corruption. For the most part, the correlations here suggest that citizens of higher socioeconomic status tend to believe that there are fewer instances of corruption. The question about bribes is somewhat of an outlier in relation to the other questions, given the smaller number of people who have experienced corruption firsthand, yet the correlations suggest that the more vulnerable are more likely to experience corruption. While the CCES questions (Fowler 2017) backed up the findings by Kristin Kelly (2016), showing that people who pay more attention to politics are more likely to

Question	Positive Correlations	Negative Correlations
TABLE 10.2 SIGNIFICANT CORRELATES OF GSS "CROOKEDNESS" CORRUPTION QUESTIONS		
In your opinion, about how many politicians in America are involved in corruption?	Ideological Extremity	Education Political Efficacy
In your opinion, about how many government administrators in America are involved in corruption?		Education Political Efficacy
How widespread do you think corruption is in the public service in America?	Conservatism Ideological Extremity	Education Income Political Efficacy
To get all the way to the top in America today, you have to be corrupt.	Racial Minority	Age Conservatism Education Income Political Efficacy Republican Religiosity
In the last five years, how often have you or a member of your immediate family come across a public official who hinted they wanted, or asked for, a bribe or favor in return for a service?	Age Conservatism Racial Minority	Education Income Political Efficacy
Source: General Social Surveys (Smith et al. 2000, 2004, 2006, 2016).		
Note: All correlations listed are significant at $p < .05$.		

think political corruption is a problem, here the question seems to be tracking a disaffection with and disengagement from politics.

There are, however, two unusual features of this table. First, question 5, on whether one must be corrupt to get ahead in America, correlates with religiosity and race in a way that the remaining questions do not. People who are more religious are less likely to believe that corruption is required to succeed. Non-white respondents on the other hand, are more likely than white respondents to believe that one must be corrupt to succeed. This is perhaps less a question of observation and more a question of optimism and a feeling that the social context supports one's efforts toward success; it is also less evidently about politics than are the other questions.

Second, what these surveys categorize as political ideology also plays an intriguing role in the responses to these questions. Table 10.3 shows the V-shaped relationship between ideology and perceived corruption. In most of these question formulations, the extremely liberal respondents and extremely conservative respondents are more likely to believe government officials to be corrupt. The exception here is the question on whether one must be corrupt to get ahead; here, liberals are more likely to agree than are conservatives. These patterns present a different picture than do the correlations in

TABLE 10.3 IDEOLOGICAL EXTREMITY AND BELIEFS ABOUT CORRUPTION AS CROOKEDNESS

Respondent Ideology	Has R Seen Public Official Asking for a Bribe in the Last Five Years?	A Person Must Be Corrupt to Get to the Top in America	How Many Politicians Are Involved in Corruption in America?	How Many Government Administrators Are Involved in Corruption in America?	How Widespread Is Corruption in Public Service in America?
Extremely Liberal	1.45	3.33	3.59	3.40	3.51
Liberal	1.24	3.61	3.31	3.12	3.11
Slightly Liberal	1.21	3.61	3.17	3.03	3.08
Moderate	1.22	3.60	3.33	3.15	3.18
Slightly Conservative	1.17	3.73	3.23	3.01	3.15
Conservative	1.17	3.71	3.26	3.13	3.40
Extremely Conservative	1.26	3.77	3.44	3.21	3.78
Total	1.22	3.63	3.30	3.13	3.22
N	2,759	1,134	2,713	2,692	1,156

Source: General Social Surveys (Smith et al. 2000, 2004, 2006, 2016).

Note: Numbers shown are mean responses. All responses are scaled 1–4; for all but the "must be corrupt to get to the top" question, higher scores indicate stronger agreement. For the other questions, higher scores indicate greater perceived corruption.

Table 10.2; in some public opinion studies, those who identify themselves as "very liberal" or "very conservative" are often found to be more politically engaged and would thus be expected, based on what we have seen in Table 10.2, to have greater trust in the political system and to see less corruption. Here, however, it seems that the more ideological respondents are more likely to allege corruption. It is not, then, liberalism or conservatism that makes the difference; it is, according to the GSS, ideological extremity on both sides that makes a difference. Perhaps this implies that those with more intense or less mainstream political positions are more likely to take on a politics of faith, the attitude of the Purifier, and are more likely to see corruption because they are less invested in the status quo. The attitude of the Mender is naturally more moderate and such persons are less likely to see instances of corruption as tips of icebergs for systemic rot.

It is, finally, important to note that partisanship or beliefs about the party in power are not significant for any of these questions, save for the question on whether one must be corrupt to succeed. Respondents' opinions of the party that holds the presidency or of the president himself were not significant here, and given that the questions here covered a range of different administrations (a Democratic president and a Republican president, unified government and divided government, and a Democratic Congress and a Republican Congress), it seems evident that respondents are not using the questions on corruption to express their views about any individual politician.

These questions mostly focus on officeholder crookedness, on individuals, and on instances of rule-breaking or norm violation. Some of them could be subject to a broader interpretation, but all invite respondents to consider discrete acts of corruption (except, perhaps, for the outlier, the question about whether one must be corrupt to succeed). The responses to these questions suggest that actual observation of such instances is rare in the United States, but that a large minority of citizens believes that such things are widespread. Such beliefs appear to be a component of a larger political disaffection and disengagement.

10.2c: Attitudes about Corruption as Rot, 1985–2010

Older versions of the GSS contain two questions that clearly tap beliefs about moral corruption. From 1985 through 1998, the GSS asked whether people are good or corrupt; respondents were asked to place themselves on a seven-point scale, where 1 signifies believing that all people are good and 7 signifies believing that all people are corrupt. "Corrupt" here is clearly being used as a synonym for "not good," perhaps for "evil": Attention is not on officeholder malfeasance but on a sort of decay or broad moral failing. On the 1998, 2006, 2008, and 2010 GSSs, respondents were asked whether they agree or disagree with the statement that "An immoral person corrupts society." Respondents were given four options: strongly agree, agree somewhat, disagree somewhat, or strongly disagree. This question invites respondents to comment on the contagiousness of corruption; while corruption is not presented as being evil in the same fashion as the first question, we are still moving beyond beliefs about individual corrupt acts. Because these questions were not used on the same GSS, or on the same GSS as the individual corruption questions discussed earlier, we cannot correlate responses. We can, however, explore whether those who see extensive corruption on these questions resemble those who are prone to seeing extensive officeholder corruption.

Responses to these questions, like the individual corruption questions, are relatively stable across time. The percentage of respondents who report believing people are intrinsically evil (categories 5–7 on the seven-point scale) fluctuates between 14.3 percent and 19.5 percent; the overall mean across the nine years the question was asked is 17.1 percent; the number of respondents who placed themselves in the "worst" category—believing all people are corrupt—is 6.1 percent. An average of 59.7 percent placed themselves in one of the three "people are good" categories, and 24.2 percent took a middle ground. The "good" responses fluctuate slightly more across years; the percent who choose the "best" category—believing all people are good—declines from 27.8 percent in 1988 to 14.9 percent in 1998.

Responses to the contagion question—what the GSS terms the "rotten apple" question—follow a similar pattern. Of respondents, 62.2 percent agree, strongly or somewhat, that an immoral person corrupts society. In the 1988 version only 18.7 percent agree strongly, while in the 2010 study 24.5 percent agreed strongly. The number in the "disagree strongly" category correspondingly declines from 18.9 percent to 12.2 percent. This provides some evidence that respondents became more cynical over time. In the lone year that the two questions were asked together, the responses were correlated (R^2 = .195, p < .001).

What sorts of respondents are likely to identify moral corruption in these two formulations? Both questions correlate with religiosity to a much greater degree than do the individual corruption questions; the respondents who identify as more religious are more likely to believe that people are corrupt or that immoral behavior corrupts society. Age, income, and education are negatively correlated with a belief that all people are corrupt, and racial minorities are more likely to believe that people are corrupt and that immoral behavior corrupts society. Most responses to the political efficacy questions are uncorrelated with beliefs about moral corruption.

Table 10.4 shows the relationship between beliefs about moral corruption and beliefs about political ideology. Whereas the responses to the individual corruption questions suggested that those at the extremes are more suspicious of individual corruption, here only one extreme group—the very conservative—stands out. This group is significantly more likely than others

TABLE 10.4 IDEOLOGICAL EXTREMITY AND BELIEFS ABOUT CORRUPTION AS ROTTENNESS		
Respondent Ideology	Does an Immoral Person Corrupt Society?	World Image: Man Is Good vs. Man Is Corrupt
Extremely Liberal	2.34	3.26
Liberal	2.48	2.93
Slightly Liberal	2.36	3.11
Moderate	2.28	3.07
Slightly Conservative	2.26	3.10
Conservative	2.12	3.33
Extremely Conservative	1.84	3.83
Total	2.27	3.13
N	8,065	11,254

Source: General Social Surveys (Smith et al. 1985–1998, 2006–2010).

Note: Numbers shown are mean responses. Responses to the "immoral person" question are scaled 1–4, where lower scores indicate a stronger belief that immoral people corrupt society; responses to the "good vs. corrupt" question are scaled 1–7, where 7 indicates a stronger belief that all people are corrupt.

TABLE 10.5 SUMMARY OF PATTERNS IN CORRUPTION PERCEPTIONS		
Corruption Type	Variables of Interest	Direction of Relationship
Prior Research	Political Engagement	Conflicting
	Education	*Negative*
	Income	*Negative*
	Religiosity	*Negative*
CCES General Corruption Question ("Politics in the United States is fundamentally corrupt.")	Political Engagement	Positive
	Age	*Negative*
	Education	Positive
	Income	Positive
GSS Transactional Corruption ("Crookedness")	*Political Engagement*	*Negative*
	Education	*Negative*
	Income	*Negative*
	Ideological Extremity	Positive
GSS Moral Corruption ("Rot")	Age	Positive
	Education	*Negative*
	Income	*Negative*
	Conservatism	Positive
	Religiosity	Positive
Note: All correlations listed (righthand column) are significant at *p* < .05.		

to believe that corruption is contagious and that people are intrinsically corrupt. Ideology is also uncorrelated with the characteristics just stated; in a variety of different regression specifications (not shown), age, income, education, race, religiosity, and conservatism are all significant, although collectively they explain only a small amount of the variance.

We cannot know from the GSS questions how related these two sets of beliefs about corruption are, but these responses suggest that two different attitudes about corruption are in play. Table 10.5 illustrates this pattern. Here, the clusters seem evident. Comparative research has shown that perceived corruption is largely a consequence of disengagement from the political system, but cross-national studies indicate that people have relatively accurate understandings of the level of corruption in their own countries. The low level of personal experience with corruption in the United States suggests that perceived corruption is more likely to be a consequence of alienation than of personal experience with corruption.

In both Table 10.4 and Table 10.5, those with more extreme views and those who are less connected to the political system tend to harbor beliefs that individual politicians are often corrupt or crooked. That is, a belief that there is widespread officeholder corruption or crookedness seems correlated inversely with political trust. On the other hand, a belief that there is widespread moral corruption or rot appears to be more a function of conservatism and religiosity. This is intriguing in part because in comparative studies, religious observance is taken to be a sign of social connectedness, and hence something that would reduce perceived corruption. Religiosity has different consequences for how Americans think about corruption, it would seem, than it does for survey respondents in other countries.

10.3: Discussion and Conclusions

One big pattern in these surveys is relatively straightforward: Large majorities of Americans believe that politics is corrupt. Somewhat smaller majorities think that a large number of individual politicians are corrupt and/or that large numbers of government administrators are corrupt. A sizable minority of Americans believes that corruption is endemic in society—that most people are corrupt and that corruption is contagious. Yet many questions remain about what motivates these beliefs.

These findings are certainly not dispositive. We have shoehorned the data into the categories we use elsewhere in our study, and some readers might quarrel with the categorization. We would benefit from more survey research regarding public understandings of corruption. But the data show that citizens are not all thinking about the same thing when they think about corruption, and that people take on different attitudes toward corruption. The characteristics of the people who are suspicious of governmental corruption by officeholders are not the same as the characteristics of those who think moral corruption is widespread in society. Different clusters of corruption perceivers exist, then, according to whether they focus on officeholder corruption or on moral corruption. We also see some evidence here that, across these clusters, the more intense someone is in their political viewpoint (along the lines of the politics of faith we discussed in Chapter 4), the more they perceive corruption. Perhaps moderates tend to take on the attitude of the Menders, and see politics as less corrupt, since they are more invested in institutions. Finally, although some American and foreign studies have found that people generally know what they are talking about—that in places where corruption as officeholder crookedness is rampant, the well-educated and politically aware tend to see this corruption—in the United States it is those who are most estranged from the political system who are most likely to believe the system or its officeholders to be corrupt. It would make sense, then, that a different type of corruption talk would be used by, and would appeal to, those who are more estranged from the status quo and the mainstream.

There are other limitations to the data here as well. We cannot rule out the possibility that the different time periods of the studies are in part responsible for the different results. This is an important consideration with regard to contemporary American politics. While our results indicate that right now there is a larger audience on the political Right for talk of corruption as moral rot, we should not presume that this is an enduring feature of that sort of framing. It is easy to see how a disenchantment with contemporary culture might be characteristic of a certain sort of conservatism. Yet we have also noted in Chapter 5 that this style of corruption talk can be found in Rousseauian philosophy—a philosophy that is by no means owned by contemporary conservatives—and we have noted in Chapter 6 that American Progressives also engaged in this sort of corruption talk. We return to this concept in Chapter 11 when we discuss the relationship between populism and corruption talk.

As matters stand today, however, those on the Far Left and the Far Right tend to believe that individual, transactional corrupt or crooked acts are widespread. In contrast, those on the Far Right but not on the Far Left are inclined to see society and human affairs as being morally corrupt—to see society as being in a process of decay or rot. This is an important distinction. First, there has been a substantial amount of research exploring political polarization in the American electorate. Although not all political scientists agree that mass polarization has taken place (in contrast to elite polarization, which clearly has), mass polarization would, according to our data here, lead to greater public suspicion that politics is corrupt and that politicians (presumably, those on the other side) are engaging in corrupt actions. In contrast, beliefs about corruption as moral rot should not be affected nearly as much by polarization; these beliefs should affect primarily those who move rightward. Either scenario suggests, however, that a movement to the extremes will result in greater suspicion about the actions of politicians.

Second, the data here corroborate arguments we have made in the previous chapters of this book—not all corruption rhetoric is the same; politicians will talk about corruption differently depending on who their target audience is, and citizens will hear corruption references differently depending upon their own characteristics, the frames they use to understand corruption, and the style of corruption talk they tend to engage in or listen to.

This is an argument that could be made about many words that get used in politics. To return to our discussion of Michael Oakeshott (1996), different political styles have different rhetorics, different meanings that they attach to words. "Corruption" is just one such word. Political language is a signal to the public about the speaker's larger plans and views. This poses a problem for social scientists and for others who would seek to establish empirically verifiable facts about the world. Surely there are politicians who violate the law, who enrich themselves at public expense, who do other things that could reasonably be described as corrupt, and certainly we need a way to talk about such things—about how to punish them and how to prevent such things from happening. The danger presented by "corruption talk," however, is that it fails to provide enough precision, and as a consequence politicians wind up talking past each other, fueling confusion and ideological conflict.

11

A Conclusion of Sorts

Corruption Talk and the Current Political Moment

In this book, we have suggested that two dominant types of corruption talk have been in play in American political discourse, and in political discourse broadly: the Purifier's corruption talk and the Mender's corruption talk.* These come with certain normative and exhortative styles. Any accusation about corruption is embedded in a particular language or linguistic style and within certain assumptions about what the institutional situation is and what it should be. The listener to or audience for political corruption talk will detect implications about what should be done with the corrupt actor or in response to the corrupt group. As the names imply, the Purifier's corruption talk—often a jeremiad against the illegitimate system—exhorts toward expulsion, dismantling the power structures, starting over with the right people, policy, and goals, whereas the Mender's corruption talk exhorts to fixing the problem, mending the institution.

A reference to one's antagonist as "corrupt" is suggestive of what we, the community, should do. Just as sexual references, insults, or racial aspersions are often reliant on context and on the listener understanding the ambiguous language and style of the speaker, so too might an allegation of corrup-

---

* This chapter is adapted by permission from two sources. From "Populist Corruption Talk," published in *Mapping Populism: A Guide to Understanding and Studying Populism*, edited by Majia Nadesan and Amit Ron, 176–84. ©2020 by Routledge. Reproduced by permission from Taylor & Francis. Adapted by permission from Springer: "Corruption, Populism, and Sloth," published in *Democracy, Populism, and Truth*, edited by Mark C. Navin and Richard Nunan, 47–59. ©2020 by Springer Nature.

tion be presented as a matter-of-fact observation, but it is often more of a call to action. Especially in circumstances where there has been some documented corrupt act, a reference to corruption on the part of, for instance, a member of the ruling elite or upper economic class or a member of a particular ethnic group can prompt the listener to associate corruption with that group even without the speaker directly saying so. A crooked action can be framed publicly as a symptom of a deeper sort of rot or contamination emanating from a dangerous source. For this reason, corruption talk can serve as a way for political speakers to play on stereotypes or stoke prejudice without explicitly attacking the groups the audience sees as, perhaps by their nature, corrupt.[1]

What normative and exhortative claims does corruption talk generally make? The obvious one, of course, is that corruption is bad—that it is something to minimize, perhaps to quarantine, or at least to avoid. Not every book or article about corruption shares this assumption; for instance, some studies allege that a certain amount of corruption can be beneficial—that it can be a means of cutting through bureaucratic red tape (McMann 2014). Some studies of corruption note that "corruption" is an umbrella term that includes many different types of activities, and not all of these behaviors are equally bad. For example, in his history of nepotism, Adam Bellow (2003) acknowledges that nepotism is often seen as a form of corruption, but he argues that nepotism is not always a bad thing and that it is in many ways a normatively better practice for societies than are other practices commonly understood as corrupt. Still other arguments about corruption contend that there are trade-offs one must make, and that a single-minded quest to reduce or eliminate corruption can have side effects that are worse than the corruption that is targeted in these efforts (e.g., Euben 1978, Rose-Ackerman 1999). There is, however, a sort of naughtiness involved in such efforts: Could it really be that corruption is good? Books like Bellow's, or even more academic efforts like Susan Rose-Ackerman's, read the same way that defenses of smoking, or of eating lots of chocolate, do: We are amused by the breaking of a taboo, but we don't really come away convinced that corruption is benign. At most, we are convinced that something often labeled corrupt isn't, really, or that we would do better to tolerate a little of something not-so-great than to try to stamp it out. As interesting as this devil's advocate view of corruption is, and as valid as their underlying point is, this scholarly contrarian point of view hasn't weakened the moral judgment or the exhorting force expressed in public corruption allegations or assumed by everyday audiences of corruption talk.

When they do not seek to upend conventional wisdom, treatises on corruption often end with a set of recommendations on how to combat corruption. These are noble gestures, and when recommendations such as these are made by people who have spent their lifetimes documenting, prosecuting, or studying criminal behavior, we hope that they have some effect. But we (the authors of this book) are not such people. Our goal in this chapter is not to offer any cures for corruption. This book, after all, focuses on corruption *talk*. The default assumption and implication whenever anyone accuses anyone else of corruption, and even when scholars are doing research on it, are that that allegedly corrupt person or behavior is bad and that such persons and behavior should be punished and avoided—corruption talk suggests that we, the speakers and hearers, should respond.

Corruption talk, we think, generally has one of two functions: When one frames corruption in the Purifier's mode, perhaps as something like rot or disease, the rhetorical force tries to delegitimize institutions or power structures, to excommunicate, or to cast out groups; on the other hand, when one frames corruption in the Mender's mode, perhaps something more analogous to weeds in a garden, the rhetorical force pushes toward modifying behaviors, to punishing particular malefactors, and to repairing our shared enterprises. In this chapter, we put this within the framework of contemporary politics, describing the Purifier's mode as a component of populist political discourse that seeks to remake or purify institutions radically, while describing the Mender's mode as a component of a more traditional pluralist politics that takes place within strong institutions.

Here we explore corruption talk using the categories of populism and pluralism—terms used often today to discuss our political moment, but not only our moment. Both of these political styles consider corruption as an evil, but not the same sort of evil. In the populist framing, corruption claims are about otherness or belonging; the corrupt are alien, contaminating, in some way, to "the people" as they are defined, usually only implicitly, by the populist speaker and the audience. The corrupt either are foreigners in a literal sense or they are deserving of being cast out because alien to our values. In the pluralist framing, we find allegations of corruption to be akin to allegations of sloth, a slothfulness about one's professional duties and about the overriding ends of the institution—the corrupt actor has failed to fulfill their duty because they have lost interest in it, and so have substituted other interests. A corrupt agent should be held responsible, but the precise reasons for this are different from those that are alleged in the corruption talk of the populist, and the practical implications are different. The garden needs to be weeded, but there is no group that needs to be cast out. Instead, we need to call people back to the shared project.

We speak here of populism and pluralism, avoiding simply talking about progressivism, liberalism, and conservatism. Populism and pluralism cut across these political outlooks. We have noted in the empirical chapters of this book (particularly Chapters 8 and 10) that contemporary U.S. Democrats and Republicans seem to have different targets or to mean different things when they talk about corruption. This is, we would argue, a passing circumstance and does not necessarily say anything about the core principles or constituencies of either party or the enduring characteristics of liberalism, progressivism, or conservatism.

We proceed here as follows: First, we outline the logic of the populist/pluralist distinction, drawing on similar distinctions made by Michael Oakeshott and Margaret Canovan. Then we summarize the strong relationship between populist rhetoric and corruption talk in the Purist mode. Next, we examine the more implicit relationship between pluralism and corruption talk. We move from there to suggest a way to frame officeholder corruption as a daughter of sloth, as a moral failing that Menders can condemn within the framework of an inclusive but cautious pluralist politics.

11.1: A Return to Oakeshott's Distinction

In Chapter 4, we discussed Michael Oakeshott's distinction between the politics of faith and the politics of skepticism. To briefly recap, these styles loosely map onto the philosophical frameworks we explored early in this book via Rousseau and Montesquieu and to our distinction between Purifier and Mender corruption talk. It would overly simplify the arguments of Rousseau and Montesquieu to retrospectively categorize these philosophers as, respectively, a populist and a pluralist, or as theorists of faith and skepticism. Yet the parallels are there. What is most consequential for us in Oakeshott's argument is that these two styles of politics—the politics of faith and the politics of skepticism—employ different ways of talking. Political words tend to be ambiguous, carrying related but distinct connotations and valence for audiences that differ in political outlook. Oakeshott gives several examples, including *war, peace, freedom, free, democracy, liberal, reactionary, progressive, treason, traitor, security, justice, order,* and *toleration.* He doesn't include *corruption,* but he could have. Those who speak within different political styles will employ these words with different aims in mind. They will, he continues, occasionally provide (ornamental, or potentially unnecessary) modifiers—"social justice," as opposed to simple "justice," for instance—to distinguish a reference within one style from another and to make it clear to the audience which style one is speaking in.[2] There is no neutral meaning beneath these terms that we can separate out, only the shared kernel of meaning concretized differently in the twin contexts. And, importantly, there is for Oakeshott no possibility that social scientists might develop a normatively neutral language, terms reduced to some empirical content alone, for developing a scientifically grounded shared understanding of the final and full truth behind any of these terms.

In this chapter we explain how different styles of corruption talk map onto Oakeshott's dichotomy. We are aided in doing so by Margaret Canovan's 1999 essay, "Trust the People? Populism and the Two Faces of Democracy." Given current concerns about the rise of populist politics in the United States and elsewhere, Canovan's argument has served as a touchstone for those who would try to situate populism within contemporary political belief systems. In this essay, Canovan rephrases Oakeshott's dichotomy; she speaks of the "redemptive" and "pragmatic" faces of politics, building on Oakeshott's politics of faith and skepticism while adjusting it as well. Redemptive democracy, she argues, is essentially populist. It has what might be noble goals, at least for Rousseau-influenced political philosophy: It seeks the romantic goal of self-actualization of the people, solidarity, and overcoming alienation. Genuine rule by the people is vaguely salvific. Canovan goes on to list several features of populism and populist rhetoric that echo Oakeshott's description of the politics of faith (we return to these shortly). In the case of populism, she goes further than Oakeshott in listing actual politicians and political events as examples.

Canovan's pragmatic democracy, like Oakeshott's politics of skepticism, builds and operates through institutions. One might find in it a sort of conservatism, but one might just as easily find a sort of pluralist institutionalism of the kind that animates the work of many contemporary American empirical political scientists—people such as Bruce Cain, Thomas Mann and Norman Ornstein, or Larry Bartels. These writers tend to focus their work on the consequences of the decline of formal institutions (e.g., Congress, parts of the federal bureaucracy) or mediating institutions (e.g., political parties, the media), and on the inability of citizens to make intelligent political decisions absent the structure that these institutions provide. Yet Oakeshott's own discussions of institutions address something broader or deeper than this or that institution; he is concerned with tradition, or contingent heritage, "participation in a conversation," or a "flow of sympathy" (Oakeshott 1991, 99–131). In his commentary on Oakeshott's place in the study of institutions, R. A. W. Rhodes (2006) emphasizes that the key concept here is *examination* or awareness. Institutions, in Oakeshott's sense, are pieces of traditions that are known to be such, as opposed to folklore or unexamined habits. We know they are there, and we consciously recognize at least some of the goods they help us achieve.

That pragmatic democracy works through institutions exposes it to corruption and to allegations of corruption by populist movements. Populism is a style, not a set of political beliefs or principles. Depending on the context, depending on the particular elite or establishment that a populist movement accuses and challenges, populism can adopt—often fervently—a commitment to different beliefs, policies, and principles. Likewise, a pragmatic form of democracy is no belief system; the things that one might be pragmatic about depend on context. Pragmatic democracy aspires to make things work, to peace, moderation, and stability of a polity made of different groups with different interests. People operating within it might be animated by the spirit of collegial contest and negotiation, wanting to get the compromises made so the next deal can go forward and things keep working. When such politicking is devoid of faith, it degenerates. According to Canovan, "Pragmatism without the redemptive impulse is a recipe for corruption" (1999, 11). She continues, "Democracy requires a kind of 'halo of sacred authority' such that if it becomes clear that those involved see in democracy nothing but horsetrading, they, and eventually the system itself, are liable to lose their legitimacy" (11). While populism purified of a pragmatic, negotiating spirit cannot get anything done in the long run, a pragmatic democracy too skeptical of principles loses a sense of its raison d'être. It becomes ripe for corruption and for accusations of corruption by a populist movement, which promises to heal the felt alienation between the ways things really work and the ideal that genuine rule by the people would make real. Just as for Oakeshott a politics of faith and a politics of skepticism are both necessary aspects of political life and cannot meaningfully exist by themselves without destroying the polity, so according to Canovan, the redemptive and pragmatic aspects of democracy call each other into existence: "Although these are opposed, they are also interdependent" (9).

11.2: Populism and Corruption

We know a fair amount about the "style" of the populist, and we are able to comment a bit on the consequences of populist allegations of corruption. It is difficult to articulate exactly what corruption is for the populist, although we think that this difficulty is a natural consequence of a useful and often strategic vagueness on the part of populist rhetors.

11.2a: Populism, Ideology, and Political Style

A central debate in the study of populism has to do with the question of whether populism is an ideology in the sense of contemporary empirical social science—that is, is populism a relatively coherent network of beliefs and values animating political behavior? Within the American context, populism is often framed as a sort of minor ideological variant. In two-dimensional renderings of economic and social cleavages, populism tends to be defined as an ideology that blends economic progressivism (that is, a preference for greater governmental involvement in the economy) and social conservatism (greater government regulation of social practices). It is, in such conceptualizations, the polar opposite of libertarianism, which prescribes a government that abstains from intervening in economic or social matters. Some contemporary empirical studies of increasing populism (e.g., Steger 2017; Carmines, Ensley, and Wagner 2017) describe populism in this fashion. Seeing populism as mere advocacy for a pattern of policies strips it of some of its obvious attitudinal content, however. While this renders it more amenable to measurement, such a description misses much of the nature of populist leaders and the people to whom they appeal—there is nothing inherent in a bundle of policy preferences that has obvious links to the sort of demographic, sometimes demagogic appeals associated with actual populists in history.

Most contemporary comparative work on populism, in contrast, has concluded that it is not a set of beliefs or policy preferences at all; instead, it tends to be framed as parasitic upon a wide range of possible host parties, ideologies, or institutions. This is Canovan's position, which we share: "The values that are populist also vary according to context, depending upon the nature of the elite and the dominant political discourse. . . . Attempts to define populism in terms of any such ideology fail, because in another context the antielitist mobilization concerned may be reacting to a different ideological environment" (1999, 4). Ernesto Laclau (2005, 76) contends that populism contains a "leveling instinct" that has no content of its own but absorbs existing ideas from the Left and the Right. Cas Mudde and Cristobal Kaltwasser (2017) assert that populist politicians attach to a "host party," which they abandon at some point once they have established a following. Similarly, Müller (2016) argues that populism tends to "colonize or occupy the state"—a successful populist will "hollow out" political institutions to get them to work for the populist's own ends. Hence, political movements as diverse as the American populists of the late nineteenth century; Latin American strongmen such as Hugo Chàvez or Evo Morales; European totalitarian leaders; mid-century American politicians such as George Wallace, Richard Nixon, and Ronald Reagan; and more recently, the politicians Bill Clinton, Ross Perot, and Donald Trump tend to be subsumed under the category of populists. It can become difficult, however, to separate instances of populism from examples of particularly charismatic politicians or from examples of politicians whom the theorist does not like.

This generally pejorative framing of populism is insufficient, however, to clarify its aspirations. Populism is said to be a form of identity politics in which "the people" is appealed to in an anti-elite, perhaps radically egalitarian way. In fact, "the people" that the populist speaks of—that is, the human beings whom the populist counts as being authentically part of "the people"—is constituted by not being the elite that the populist targets. Populism reliably appears at moments of democratic alienation—at times when political or economic elites appear to have become removed from the public, when policy debates have become divorced from public concerns, when the wealthy's immunity from many common hardships is too flagrantly displayed, or when the relationship between elected officials and their purported core constituencies has become tenuous. Abby Inness (2017) argues that this is particularly the case when parties of the Left become involved in promarket activities. The emergence of new technologies (especially such new mass communication technologies as radio in the 1930s or Twitter in the 2010s), economic crises, and surges in immigration have all been said to correlate with populist success (Grzymala-Busse 2017).

All of these claims indicate that even though we perhaps know a popu-list politician when we see one—that is, to take the U.S. example, we know that Donald Trump is different from most other Republican politicians and we question his commitment to any set of ideological positions—there is a certain elusiveness to our labeling of populists. What does it mean to say, for instance, that Trump and Bill Clinton are both populists? Michael Kazin (1995, 271) argues that populism is merely a marketing strategy—a way that politicians of any sort can learn to talk. It may be that populism entails a lan-guage that makes reference to "the people," but it seems to do so by targeting an antagonist, and not all politicians have the desire or ability to construct the sort of threat, real or imagined, that populist politics requires. The theo-ries that reject the notion that populism might be a set of policy preferences tend to conclude that it is a style, and that it is a style that exists within a sort of framework or axis in opposition to other styles.

What is it that makes populism a "style"? An important marker of pop-ulism, it seems to us, is its language. Just as Oakeshott (1996) notes that the politics of faith has its own language, so most treatments of populism have emphasized the ways in which language serves as a marker of populism. Pop-ulist language tends to be "low"—to deliberately seek to appeal to the com-mon person (Ostiguy and Roberts 2016). "Low" discourse consists of simple, direct language; of unambiguous and simple adjectives to describe things; and, most importantly, of black-and-white moralistic framing of political and social phenomena. This sort of formulation serves not only to ensure that the populist speaks in terms that their audience understands but also as a means of discrediting elite discourse. Complex or morally equivocal descrip-tions of matters may seem a deliberate attempt by elites to hide their true motives. As Canovan (1999) puts it, "Populists claim that all this complexity is a self-serving racket perpetuated by professional politicians, and that the solutions to the problems ordinary people care about are essentially simple" (6). Oliver and Rahn (2016) summarize populist rhetoric as including "peo-ple-centered" language, references to nationalism, "we/they" talk, and con-spiracy theories. We might add that populist discourse on the Left, rather than referring to nationalism, more often refers to "the people" as opposed to "the bankers," "the funders," or "the 1%." In both cases, the populist leader not only proclaims a faith in the people and a promise to fight for them but also with populist language invites them to see this leader as one of them, not part of the elite. The people, in exchange, are asked to put their faith in the leader.

Kazin (1995, 16) provides numerous other common themes in populist rhetoric that are of relevance to us here. Populist rhetoric relies frequently on demonization or character assassination. Such attacks often include animal metaphors (octopus, pig, dog) and even sometimes a questioning of one's opponent's heterosexuality or masculinity. If the elite are targeted rhetorically as not one of "the people," it seems a short step to say that they are not persons. Insinuations that one's opponent is gay, or comparisons of political opponents to prostitutes, are also not uncommon. Satire, sometimes in the form of parables or crude cartoons, has often accompanied populist appeals. Such efforts can be used to effectively link together opponents who have no common political agenda. On the flip side, the promises of populist leaders tend to be presented in simple, noble terms. At its best, Kazin argues, populism expresses an optimism that a lost version of what a nation or a people is can be recovered through the removal of a particular malefactor.

We might add that this simple, noble language appears in both Left and Right populism—often on the Right in terms of nostalgia, rejection of some recent or impending change, and promise of a recovery, and on the Left in terms of utopia, acceptance of some enlightened new policy, and hope for a promised land in which "the people" have what the elite have hoarded. In both cases, the populist tends to cast some group as an elite, as greedy masterminds, as parasites opposed to the people—for example, to the real workers or to the authentic Americans.

11.2b: Populist Corruption Talk

What distinguishes populist rhetoric talk from mere marketing, it seems to us, is the "othering" that is involved in populism. Corruption talk accomplishes this purpose in two important ways.

First, corruption talk is an effective means to delegitimize one's opponents, to insert moralistic language, usually without directly singling out specific actions of one's opponents. It is a way to insinuate that individual corruption is a manifestation of a deeper rot. Donald Trump's references to corruption, documented in Chapter 8, are examples of this. They are not meant to be verifiable claims; rather, they seek to extrapolate the alleged transgressions of Hillary Clinton, Peter Strzok, James Comey, Robert Mueller, or whomever the antagonist of the moment is into a broader systematic critique. Catherine Stock's (1996, 56) observation that late-nineteenth-century American populists tended to equate corruption with "bigness" is another such example; large, complex organizations, corporations, or bureaucracies tend to obscure their inner workings and thus may well conceal cases of individual corruption. It is not difficult to go from alleging that corruption exists within such large organizations (because, after all, it probably does) to arguing that the entire organization is corrupt or in some way foreign to the American way of life and antagonistic to the genuine good of the people. Indeed, the mere size of a corporation or the mere quantity of wealth of an individual seems to provide evidence, to the populist, of systemic corruption. One example might be taken from the following quotation of Bernie Sanders (2018, 104): "Globally the top 1 percent owns more wealth than the bottom 99 percent of the world's population. In other words, while the very, very rich become much richer, thousands of children die every week in poor countries around the world from easily prevented diseases, and hundreds of millions live in incredible squalor. Inequality, corruption, oligarchy, and authoritarianism are inseparable. They must be understood as part of the same system, and fought in the same way." Here, the implication is that rich people are responsible for the death of children, and then attention is turned to the whole ball of wax, the entire system, which must be fought. And Müller (2016, 23–24) provides two fascinating instances of populist references to corruption from the other extreme: the occasional use by American "birthers" of the term in their allegations that Barack Obama was not born in the United States, and the equation by the Hungarian right-wing Jobbik party of government officials' corrupt acts and the criminal actions of the Roma, or gypsies. In both cases, corruption is clearly linked to foreignness, or to alleged deceptions perpetrated by foreigners. In these latter cases, "the people" gets defined ethnically, as opposed to, for example, economically or religiously. In all these cases, simple moralistic language is deployed to identify an opponent as corrupt and as symbolic of the corruption of the whole system, without, however, specifying any verifiable actions of those opponents.

In all of these examples, an allegation of corruption is a clear dismissal of the right of the corrupt actor to engage in a political contest. The corrupt here are framed as being evil, yet there is no specific clarity to the claim.[3] That is, it is not necessary to explain what the corrupt have done or to explain why the people or the institution is corrupt, and in some instances the association with another purportedly foreign or corrupt actor or group removes the need for explanation. When the content of the corruption is specified, it is sometimes a clear instance of transactional corruption—misusing public powers or resources for private gain—but in many instances it is merely conventional politics. While the corruption that is alleged need not be illegal, the word casts the activity as immoral, even evil, and as a betrayal of the people.

Second, and more consequentially, populist corruption talk elides many of the distinctions we have drawn earlier in this book between individuals and institutions, between moral and legal transgressions. Consider just two of the examples of populist rhetoric that Michael Kazin provides, both Left-populist, proto-Progressive figures:

> Corruption dominates the ballot box. The people are demoralized. The newspapers are subsidized or muzzled. The urban workmen are denied their right of organization for self-protection. A vast conspiracy against mankind has been organized on two continents and is rapidly taking possession of the world. (Ignatius Donnelly, 1892, quoted in Kazin 1995, 28)

> The struggle is between the farmers and their friends on one side and on the other side corruption and robbery, supported by its tools, paid agents, and sympathizers. (A. C. Townley, 1915, quoted in Kazin 1995, 68)

The precise nature of the corruption being discussed here is economic, and both instances are clearly populist. In both, corruption itself is personified and set in opposition to the people—in the Donnelly case, to the workers, and in the Townley case, to the farmers. Both groups have friends or allies as well, and the speakers flag themselves as such. There is no particular corrupt act that is of concern in either quotation; instead, corruption is a force, and it stands opposed to the people.

Vague allegations like these do not lend themselves to verification or falsification. There may be actual, indisputable instances of corruption motivating populist corruption claims, but they need not be remarkable ones. The populist style uses these instances insinuatingly, to paint with large brush strokes over whole institutions or demographic groups. The calling out of an instance of corruption can taint a wide range of similar practices or individuals. It can magnify the importance of a relatively inconsequential or irrelevant event. As Jason Stanley (2015, 42) points out in his study of propaganda, a true claim (the example Stanley uses is an American politician observing that there are Muslims present in the community) can take on ominous overtones when presented to an audience that is likely to see such claims as a call to action. Similarly, frequent observations that a relatively routine act of corruption has occurred within government can magnify the implications of that act.

Populist rhetoric implies that corruption is bad in part because of its fellow travelers, or because of the kinds of people who tend to act corruptly. If "good" people, one of "us," were to engage in similar types of corrupt practices, they might be let off the hook simply because they do not have these same sorts of associations with suspect groups. Similarly, if a person of a particular group—a foreigner, a member of the governing elite, a financier or "funder," a member of the opposition party or of a middleman minority—is exposed as corrupt, a reference to this corruption embedded in a discussion of other actions of that group insinuates that that group itself is corrupt. Accordingly, an instance of corruption on the part of one member of the group renders other statements, or policy positions, of others in that group suspect. For Stanley (2015, chap. 4), the populist's identification of opponents with things they deny being—for example, Barack Obama as a Muslim, or Dick Cheney and his advisors as Straussians—ultimately serves to question their sincerity, even their identity. This plays into a fear that our institutions have been hijacked by some suspect group with its own agenda now working, surreptitiously, against the people. Corruption here appears as infiltration, infection.

11.2c: Consequences

There are essential reasons why populism is a perennial phenomenon in democracies and is perennially failing to live up to its promise, thus making way for other populists, as Canovan (1999) explains: "In so far as populism exploits [the] gap between promise and performance in democracy, there is no end to it. For if a populist movement is so successful in appealing past the established political forces that it actually gets into power, its own inability to live up to its promises will be revealed, offering scope for further populist appeals to the people" (12). Although Canovan doesn't reference Rousseau here, her reasonings are reminiscent of points discussed in our chapter on Rousseau. She continues:

> Clearly, in so far as democracy's promise of popular power is made good, this can be done only through institutions that make that power effective and lasting. But entwined with the redemptive strand of democracy is a deep revulsion against institutions that come between the people and their actions, and a craving for direct, unmediated expression of the people's will. . . . Democracy can be a very powerful form of government insofar as it does have the legitimacy of being recognised as our government. But to work as a government, it has to take institutional forms that are very far removed from spontaneous popular expression. (1999, 13)

Critics of populism often point to the failings of populists in office as a necessary consequence of populist rhetoric.

If one comes into office denouncing political insiders, it can be difficult either to make the transition to becoming a successful insider or to maintain one's image as an outside crusader. If one comes into office without a clear set of principles or a strategic plan, the plan one adopts may either collapse because of its own incoherence, or the populist may merely adopt existing elite policies and make them the populist's own. In the former case, some populists in office have alleged that they do not actually wield full control; the system itself is corrupt, the power of office is not what it should be, or unelected, shadowy figures (the "deep state," perhaps) secretly continue to control the levers of power and undermine their effectiveness. In the latter case, populists must work to separate elites from their policies; it is not the policies pursued by elites that were wrong; rather, the problem was that elites pursued them for corrupt reasons. In either case, corruption of others tends to remain a concern of populists once they have achieved power and they must attempt to protect themselves from the same corruption talk they hurl at others.

On an immediate level, the moral ills of populist corruption talk are clear—the need for a scapegoat can easily lead to the targeting of unsympathetic groups, the unfair persecution of political opponents, or attacks that undermine important institutions. Various populist movements have labeled foreigners, immigrants, gays and lesbians, and other vulnerable groups as corrupt, as well as middlemen (especially middlemen minorities), strike breakers ("scabs"), or capitalists. More commonly, ruling elites and the generators of elite ideas (bureaucrats, academics, the wealthy) are labeled as corrupt. There is a thin line between, on one hand, the common, low-grade, and unremarkable public hostility toward government employees or the rich and, on the other hand, the labeling of bureaucrats or financiers, as a class, as corrupt. And there are, of course, plentiful documented incidents of actual corruption among such groups. Populism, as most studies note, tends to develop because of real problems, because of gaps between elite politics and public sentiment, because the establishment within institutions has failed to respond sincerely or quickly enough to problems experienced by the publics of those institutions. The hollowing out of government institutions, the undermining of trust in government, and a decline in citizens' willingness to entertain policy ideas as sincere and disinterested pieces of public discourse might seem to be reasonable responses to poor governmental performance. Yet, studies of populism argue, these developments often tend to encourage, rather than discourage, corruption.

Populists in office also, it has been noted, often practice the same corruption—or even more overt corruption—than did the "corrupt" elites they sought to replace (e.g., Moffitt 2016). Whereas populists tend to deride the corruption inherent in the routines of transactional politics, they are often less competent at such politicking. At the same time, they are able to engage in more brazen corrupt acts, in part because they can simply argue that all politicians do what they are doing but that they are at least being honest about what they are doing and are at least representing and fighting for "the people."

There are positive aspects to populist corruption talk, however, and it may not become demagogic. There are moments when nation-building may require that some practices be figuratively cast out, their motives described as suspect. Early American writers tended to frame corruption as a European problem (see Teachout 2014, 18). The values of the British and the French threatened the American political project, and were thus branded as corrupt. The fact is, these values may well have been corrupt. But even apart from this, it seems appropriate for a new nation to separate itself from other nations, especially those that had previously colonized it. The British and French were hardly vulnerable minorities, so the most obvious dangers in populist corruption talk do not necessarily apply, but the two nations could be understood as elites. Some of the more positive accounts of populism note that it appears to be self-limiting—that it cannot succeed in the absence of actual corruption, and that throughout most of history, populist leaders have given way to institution-building successors. Populists, in this optimistic account, remind us eventually of our need for strong political institutions, while also potentially undermining or refreshing some political institutions that may not be functioning well. According to Canovan (1999), "populism is a shadow cast by democracy itself" (3). While its dangers are evident, it may serve a homeostatic function within democracy by calling democracy back to its principle of serving the people. "Pragmatism without the redemptive impulse is a recipe for corruption" (11).

11.3: Corruption as Sloth

Much venal corruption springs obviously, and superficially, from greed, resentment, or the desire for status or power. The populist casts the depth motivation of officeholder corruption as betrayal and malice—the corrupt agent is an enemy of the people; the corrupt institution is aiming for interests of some other group, not for the good of the people. Though democratic government can work only through institutions, these are, as Canovan argues convincingly, permanently susceptible to falling away from the animating and legitimating impulse of the redemptive face of democracy. They are also, even when operating well, susceptible to populist broadsides, because they are institutions, intermediaries—the people cannot in fact rule directly. We would like to suggest a different way of framing the origins of corruption.

An alternate way of describing corruption—a way that is in keeping with the skepticism described by Oakeshott or the pragmatism described by Canovan or the appreciation of institutions typical of pluralism—is to view the origin of corruption in a sort of sloth. Of course, much sloth does not lead to criminally corrupt actions, yet to have behaved slothfully is to have engaged in a culpable neglect of one's proper role. That is, individuals can be held responsible for forgetting the purpose of their institutions and forgetting the importance of their jobs within those institutional purposes. Sloth, however, is unusual among the capital sins in that it has also historically been seen as a sort of disease, akin to depression—that is, we can become slothful not out of evil intent, but simply because we have failed to combat its onset. The opposite of sloth in an officeholder is a kind of professionalism.

To see what we mean here, however, a brief summary of the history of the concept is in order. Sloth stands out today as one of the more perplexing of the vices. In his essay on the subject, Evelyn Waugh (1962) refers to it as "the most amiable of weaknesses"; in the New York Public Library series of books on the deadly sins, playwright Wendy Wasserstein (2005) extols the benefits of sloth; she advertises her book as an essay on "sloth—and how to get it." Contemporary uses of the term tend to equate sloth with laziness, often analogizing it to the behavior of the animal that bears the same name; with a sort of boredom or lack of purpose; or with sadness or depression. Sometimes all three are combined: Aldous Huxley, for instance, saw sloth as a "mixture of boredom, sorrow, and despair." These understandings of sloth tend to miss or downplay normative problems—as Huxley goes on to point out, boredom or sadness may be good in that they can prompt people to change their circumstances, or to use their state of mind as a prompt for unconventional or creative thinking. Yet these all represent, according to Siegfried Wenzel's (1967) history of the concept, a failure of secular writers to grasp the depth of this term, which was once fundamentally spiritual.

The original Greek word for sloth, *acedia*, is perhaps best translated as "absence of care." Acedia may be prompted by one's external surroundings; it was referred to as the "noonday demon" that tended to strike monks in desert cloisters, driving them to neglect their prayers and their earthly duties. Yet medieval writers such as Evagrius and John Cassian emphasize the intentionality here. Cassian classified sloth as a sin because it entailed a *willful* laziness—a decision not to care. In this sense, one can be slothful and yet still active; the activities in question, however, are not generally meaningful or important ones. Sloth might entail rote reenactment of past activities, or a preoccupation with insignificant ideas or activities. It entails a sort of emotional distance from one's duties, or even one's activities generally, a resistance to feeling joy or sorrow. A host of religious writers have written evocatively about this condition; John Buchanan describes it as an inability to engage in "vital occupations," and Josef Pieper argues that it entails a refusal to affirm one's own being and dignity, one's *telos* or proper activity (Kathleen Norris 2008, 114, 143, 179). Petrarch described sloth as a reluctance to be cheered up, a bitterness, and a weariness of godly things (Wenzel 1967, 160).

Far from seeing sloth as benign, then, medieval Christians saw sloth as one of the most dangerous faults—one of the seven "deadly" sins. Cassian subsumed a wide range of vices under the concept of sloth as its daughters or natural consequences, including idleness, restlessness, rudeness, and inquisitiveness. Medieval penitential manuals, likewise, tended to list many different types of sloth. Sloth is particularly dangerous because it can facilitate other sins—a person who is slothful is not vigilant about recognizing the good or bad in others' actions, or in the person's own. Sloth can also overtake a person slowly, without an awareness of it. Think about, for example, when we turn to our cell phones to avoid having to do something better, more important, but harder and less pleasant. This habit of turning away from one's situation and neglecting one's job in that situation, this habit of doing something else that feels more rewarding in the short term, is slothful.

Some, however, might want to see sloth more in medical or psychological terms than in spiritual or ethical ones. The original association of acedia with dry desert climes, as well as the physical manifestations of it, suggest a range of simple cures. If sloth is prompted by one's surroundings, move. If the slothful appear idle, they should get some exercise. If the slothful appear sad, they should try therapy or medication. None of these prescriptions addresses the soul, which may be why today we tend to think of sloth, when we think of it at all, not as sloth but as depression—more as a disease or a condition than a sin. Wenzel (1967) argues that the church's reclassification of acedia from a temptation of the devil to a temptation of the flesh ultimately led to a failed secularization of acedia, a term that lost its coherence and relevance and, as a consequence, gradually "disintegrated into its components" (181).

Yet when the term "sloth" is used more precisely today—and it sometimes is—it carries with it a host of political implications. Uses of the term in the more popular media are rare, although George Will had a habit of using it to discuss Donald Trump's behavior during Trump's first term in office.[4] Jean Bethke Elshtain's (2000, 77–84) discussion of acedia calls attention to its resultant "acquiescence in the conventions of one's day" and "refusal to take up the burden of self-criticism." For Elshtain, pride and sloth are linked—those who too readily accept the status quo and their role in it are guilty of both pride (about their past doings) and slothfulness (regarding their present actions, as well as the actions of others). Early-twentieth-century sociologist Robert Park contended that today sloth is manifested in urban thrill-seeking behavior (Park and Burgess 1925; for discussion see Lyman 1978); other writers have echoed Park's contention, noting variously that mindless consumerism or mindless adventurism can be manifestations of sloth. There is, according to these accounts, a growing unreality to our practices, an unseriousness about what is important, one best understood in terms of this old vice.

A larger concern of contemporary authors has been the link between sloth and extremism. Contemporary philosopher Lars Svendsen (2005), for example, emphasizes that extremism can be an attractive antidote to boredom, and the diminution of care about moral matters can make extremism even more possible. Stanford Lyman (1978) contends that a common theme in the works of Max Weber, Bruno Bettelheim, Albert Camus, and Hannah Arendt has been the link between sloth and its daughter boredom, on the one hand, and extremism or violence, on the other. He goes on to write, from a very 1950s perspective, that "acedia has played a role in bringing to power the most terrible of regimes—we are just now seeing the relationship between apathetic voters, social anomie, lonely crowds, rootless masses, etc., and their support for illiberal politics" (Lyman 1978, 48).

Lyman's characterization is important, whether or not it goes too far, in that it reinforces Oakeshott's distinction, with which we began. The style of the politics of faith seems to lend itself to the type of corruption talk populists use. Populists see in the establishment, in the institutions and their workaday procedures, a corruption of betraying the people, serving the interests of other, perhaps shadowy groups. The style of the politics of skepticism seems to lend itself to a more staid corruption talk in order to diagnose the problem with institutions based on the idea of sloth—even if that word is not often used. Oakeshott notes, as does Canovan, that the politics of skepticism, or the pragmatic face of democracy, can become stale, can degenerate into rote procedures, into plays and deals within the system, forgetful of principles, neglecting their ultimate purpose. If the institutions are in general solid but in need of maintenance and some attentiveness, if individual agents are falling occasionally into frivolous misuse of their offices or into outright officeholder corruption, it would make sense that this would result from their inattentiveness to their duties—either an inattentiveness from boredom, or from distraction by other things, or by the avoidance of difficult issues and challenging tasks because wrestling with them would disrupt smooth functioning and a comfortable status quo. If this—and not a shadowy conspiracy against the people—is the depth course of corruption within otherwise beneficial institutions, what would be required is piecemeal fixes and a reminder to officeholders of the importance of our responsibilities, rather than a cleansing of contaminating groups or a dismantling of rotten power structures.

If one of the evils prompted by a politics of faith is a sort of ideological extremism, one of the evils prompted by a politics of skepticism can be a lack of care for what is an unthinking acquiescence to social norms and rituals that are no longer working or that we have come to recognize as not as good as they could be. We can be tempted to other sins simply because we are not attentive to what we are doing and what we are supposed to be doing. Alternatively, however, the torpor into which we sink can prompt the rise of populist movements, and can bring about an unthinking and indiscriminate will toward destruction of all of our norms and patterns. In this fashion, corruption of the slothful variety can actually encourage populism and foster the sort of corruption talk endemic to populism.

11.4: Where Social Scientific Research Fits

Given the empirical focus of the middle chapters of this book, we wish to note where social scientists, and perhaps academics in general, are disadvantaged in the current political moment, and how they are disadvantaged by our framing of corruption in this chapter more broadly. It is easy to see why empirical work on corruption has little to do with the populist tradition. We have noted that populism itself is difficult to study empirically. Similarly, populist allegations of corruption tend to be imprecise and only tenuously related to clearly measurable instances of criminal corruption; a distancing of elites from the masses may be a measurable phenomenon, but it is not generally part of empirical measures of corruption. The phenomena that tend to abet populism may be discrete and measurable instances of corruption, but they need to indicate widespread or systemic corruption, and populist leaders themselves, as we have noted, tend to engage in corrupt behavior of their own. Populism, then, may not necessarily reduce corruption, as an empirically measurable phenomenon, but perhaps may substitute one group of corrupt political actors for another.

It would also make sense that the general distrust of elites that characterizes populism would, in addition, lead populists to dismiss scientific methods of studying corruption. Populist leaders tend to be dismissive of academic research. This may be in part because of its limited utility in pursuing their goals, but it may also have to do with the elite status of the researchers themselves. Highly educated people tend to be enmeshed within the political elite in most democratic societies, so populist opposition toward bureaucracy and toward the unelected experts also is easily transferred toward academics or toward the sorts of NGOs and international agencies that study corruption. For the populist, the very institutions and conventions of research into corruption and tools for combating corruption may seem corrupt in themselves.

It is equally difficult, however, to reconcile social scientific research on corruption with the "corruption as daughter of sloth" framing. This is so for two reasons. First, empirical work on corruption avoids the sorts of normative questions that are central to both types of discourse. A basic premise of contemporary social scientific work is the emphasis on description rather than on ethical judgment. While scholars interested in documenting corruption may be inspired by a desire to limit corruption, they must separate their normative goals from their efforts to describe—and, as we have seen, they often wind up developing explanations about why a certain level of corruption may facilitate certain social goals or about why an effort to entirely eradicate corruption may not be cost-effective. Such explanations presume a consensus that corruption should be limited, but the scholars are not able to explain "scientifically" why this is so. This research occurs within inherited professional practices, and within organizations that are funded by government or philanthropy for certain purposes. Corruption of those practices, corruption of those institutions, would undermine the empirical research—yet such research cannot interrogate or affirm their own normative conditions. This is not a criticism of those practices or institutions, but rather a request that they notice their lack of self-sufficiency both practically and philosophically.

Second, corruption tends to take root in part because of a forgetting about or a confusion about what is being corrupted. The very nature of sloth is a lack of attention to one's role or purpose, or to the purpose of the institutions in which one operates. The establishment of a referent—of an uncorrupted or pure exemplar of what has been corrupted—is also an endeavor for which scientific research is ill-prepared. This type of research into corruption of officeholders in our institutions makes sense only when the research is enriched by other types of reflection and research—that is, by conversations about what our officeholders are supposed to do and how our institutions are supposed to operate in service to the common good.

11.5: Conclusion

It would be a bit presumptuous to end this book with a bold normative claim about how we *should* talk about corruption. We (the authors of this book, that is) have no hope or ambition to alter the ways in which corruption tends to be framed in political discussions. We wrote this book not to change corruption talk, but because we find it interesting. We do wish to conclude, however, with a suggestion that we all might add something to balance corruption talk. More about its opposite: professionalism.

Professionalism itself is a kind of immunization that protects officeholders from temptations of corruption. Professionals recognize their responsibility as fiduciary, knowing that their offices are matters of trust in which they are to serve a good that is not simply their own. That recognition provides some internal resistance when the opportunities arise for officeholders to use their office as leverage for goodies or as platforms for self-promotion. Moreover, professionalism of its officeholders can help keep an institution on track, on topic, pointing in the right direction. Professionalism refuses to simply punch the clock or do as it is told. Thus, professionals genuinely concerned about doing their job, serving the goods that their jobs are meant to serve, can hold an institution's feet to the fire, resisting its decline into staleness and sloth. A professional remembers that an office or a job does not exist for the benefit of the officeholder. Instead, someone with the virtue of professionalism can ask these questions—and can answer thoughtfully: Why does my job exist? What good does this institution, and my role within it, do?

Notes

CHAPTER 1

1. The United States consistently ranked between the fifteenth and the eighteenth least corrupt nations (among 175) in Transparency International's corruption perception index between 1995 and 2014. By "newsworthy event" we suggest that a scandal of the magnitude of Watergate might have provided a short-term spike in attention to corruption. We would contend that nothing in the United States over this time period happened (the Clinton impeachment notwithstanding) that would singlehandedly reach such a level.

CHAPTER 2

1. All Bible quotes in this chapter are from the King James version.

CHAPTER 3

1. Carlin said this many times, as a quick YouTube search will reveal.
2. See, in particular, Part II, chaps. 24 and 29, of *Leviathan*.

CHAPTER 6

1. For the original quote, see Theophilus Parsons (1859, 378).
2. See J. O. Hertzler (1951) for a full summary of Ross's career.
3. See David Levy (1985, 190–91) for more on this point.
4. Quoted in Nancy Rosenblum (2008, 202).
5. See, for example, David Frum (2018, x–xi).
6. For a summary of literature on this general point, see Morris Fiorina (2017).
7. See, for example, Charles Merriam (1908); for discussion, see Raymond Seidelman (2015, 11).
8. See Ralph Boots (1927) for such a critique of Merriam.

CHAPTER 7

1. As parents of young children today are likely aware, the dinosaur known in the 1970s as Brontosaurus was reclassified in 1994 as a subspecies of Apatosaurus, and was returned to its classification as Brontosaurus in 2015. In other words, the Brontosaurus ceased to exist for twenty years as a category, but, of course, the actual dinosaur bones remained.

2. Matthew Stephenson, personal communication, December 21, 2015.

3. For instance, members may not address each other directly, but must address their comments to the Speaker or the Chair. They may not refer to each other by name, but with reference to their home state (e.g., "the gentleman from Ohio"). And they may not speculate about each other's motives—for instance, by claiming that another member has lied. For details, see House Parliamentarian's Office (2023).

4. See, for instance, Edward M. Kennedy Institute (n.d.).

5. Exceptions include Peter DeLeon (1993) and Edward Glaeser and Claudia Goldin (2006).

6. See Trevor Potter (2006).

CHAPTER 8

1. This, and all subsequent presidential and presidential candidate quotations, are taken from the University of California, Santa Barbara database described below (Woolley and Peters, n.d.).

2. This is the case for two reasons—first, because we have sought to use comparable speeches for each president, and thus have not systematically looked at Farewell Addresses, and second, because Eisenhower never actually uses the word "corruption" when he discusses the increased role of the "military-industrial complex" in American government and economics.

3. To be more accurate, no one makes these connections at the time these events are still fresh in the public memory. In a Democratic primary debate in late 1999, Al Gore attributed his early interest in politics to his concern over the corruption displayed in the Watergate scandal.

4. McCain was presumably referring to his work on campaign finance reform legislation. Few Republicans supported the specific reforms McCain advocated; hence, McCain may have been seeking to capitalize on his image as a reformer without reminding audiences of which specific reforms he had championed.

5. See Colleen Shogan (2006, 67) for a discussion of the "radicalism" of this particular address.

6. Although, as noted in the discussion of Karlyn Kohrs Campbell and Kathleen Hall Jamieson's (1990) argument, the rhetorical purposes of these speeches are quite different than are those of State of the Union addresses.

7. For discussion of the platform writing process and its relationship to presidential campaigns, see Terri Susan Fine (1994, 2003), David Karol (2009), and L. Sandy Maisel (1993). For a discussion with specific reference to the importance of the language of party platforms, see Gwendoline Alphonso (2015).

8. A graph of average platform length is available from the American Presidency Project (Woolley and Peters, n.d.).

CHAPTER 9

1. Valence issues, as articulated by Donald Stokes (1963), are issues where all voters share an ideal point; such issues include honesty, competence, or morality. Stokes presents these as a contrast to positional issues (such as abortion or gun control), where there is disagreement and where politicians arrange themselves on competing sides.

2. *Buckley v. Valeo*, 424 U.S. 1, 25 (1976).

3. One could make this claim about the *Citizens United* decision, but also about corruption language in *Federal Election Commission v. Wisconsin Right to Life, Inc.* (551 U.S. 449 [2007]); *Davis v. Federal Election Commission* (554 U.S. 724 [2008]); and *McCutcheon v. Federal Election Commission* (572 U.S. 185 [2014]).

4. See, for instance, Justice Scalia's majority opinion in *California Democratic Party v. Jones* (530 U.S. 567 [2000]), where the court rejected California's blanket primary law yet instructed the state on how to write a new, constitutionally permissible law that essentially created the same system.

5. See the various depositions pursuant to the BCRA challenge, *McConnell v. Federal Election Commission*, 540 U.S. 93 (2003).

6. See, for example, Joshua Rosenkranz (1999).

7. *Citizens United v. Federal Election Commission*, 558 U.S. 310, 359 (2010).

8. For an excellent journalistic account of the relationship between Teachout's work and Lessig's work, see Jill Lepore (2014).

9. As to empirical evidence, one might imagine some sort of effort to scale corruption punishments as, for instance, John Peters and Susan Welch (1978) have done.

10. That is, well-known groups that expect to remain active across multiple elections. See Robert G. Boatright (2016).

11. For example, *McCutcheon v. Federal Election Commission* (572 U.S. 185 [2014]), which lifted the aggregate limit on individual political contributions, and *American Tradition Partnership, Inc. v. Bullock* (567 U.S. 516 [2012]), which prohibited the state of Montana from arguing that the state's history of corrupt practices in the mining industry served as justification for restricting corporate spending.

12. See Alison Mitchell (1999).

13. The precise proposal here is difficult to summarize succinctly. Lessig proposes a "regent president" who will take office and refuse to sign any legislation until Congress radically reforms itself. This proposal is not entirely dissimilar to the concept (in Thompson 1995, 135) of ethics tribunals, or having an outside organization enforce anticorruption standards upon an institutionally corrupt body that is unable to do so itself. One might even trace this idea to Rousseau's description of tribunals in *On the Social Contract*.

CHAPTER 10

1. The ANES political knowledge index measures the correct answers to a range of questions about government, including which party had the most members in the House and in the Senate, who the Speaker of the House is, who the chief justice of the Supreme Court is, and who the vice president is.

2. However, given that the full survey module includes several questions about legislative voting and interest group influence, it is possible that respondents may be primed to think about corruption in such terms.

CHAPTER 11

1. We draw upon work by Jason Stanley (2015, chap. 4) in making this point.

2. This is our example (drawing on our observation of the language of contemporary campus debates), not Oakeshott's.

3. This is why contemporary theorists Russell Muirhead and Nancy Rosenblum (2019, 8, 25) quarrel with the notion that Trump is in fact a populist; they prefer to see his language as an example of what they call "the new conspiracism."

4. A sample quote: "It is urgent for Americans to think and speak clearly about President Trump's inability to do either [x or y]. This seems to be not a mere disinclination but a disability. It is not merely the result of intellectual sloth but of an untrained mind bereft of information and married to stratospheric self-confidence" (Will 2017).

References

Abrams, Richard M. 1964. *Conservatism in a Progressive Era: Massachusetts Politics, 1900–1912*. Cambridge, MA: Harvard University Press.

Achen, Christopher H., and Larry M. Bartels. 2016. *Democracy for Realists: Why Elections Do Not Produce Responsive Government*. Princeton, NJ: Princeton University Press.

Aesop. 1909. *Folklore and Fable*. Edited by Charles W. Eliot. New York: P. F. Collier and Son.

Alphonso, Gwendoline. 2015. "From Need to Hope: The American Family and Poverty in Partisan Discourse, 1900–2012." *Journal of Policy History* 27 (4): 592–635.

American National Election Studies (ANES). n.d. Available at https://electionstudies.org/.

American Political Science Association. Various dates. *American Political Science Association Annual Meeting Program*. Washington, DC: American Political Science Association.

Aquinas, St. Thomas. 1949. *On Kingship*. Translated by Gerald B. Phelan. Toronto, Canada: Pontifical Institute of Medieval Studies.

———. 2006. *Summa Theologiae*. Edited by Brian Leftow and Brian Davies. New York: Cambridge University Press.

Aristotle. 1984. *The Politics*. Translated by Carnes Lord. Chicago: University of Chicago Press.

Azari, Julia, and Marc J. Hetherington. 2016. "Back to the Future? What the Politics of the Late Nineteenth Century Can Tell Us about the 2016 Election." *Annals of the American Academy of Political and Social Science*, no. 667, 92–109.

Basinger, Scott J. 2013. "Scandals and Congressional Elections in the Post-Watergate Era." *Political Research Quarterly* 66 (2): 385–98.

Basinger, Scott J., Lara M. Brown, Girish J. Gulati, and Douglas B. Harris. 2014. "Counting and Classifying Congressional Scandals." In *Scandal! An Interdisciplinary Approach to the Consequences, Outcomes, and Significance of Political Scandals*, edited by Alison Dagnes and Mark Sachleben, 3–28. New York: Bloomsbury Press.

Bates, Robert H., Avner Greif, Margaret Levi, and Jean-Laurent Rosenthal. 1998. *Analytical Narratives*. Princeton, NJ: Princeton University Press.

Bauer, Robert. 2015. "The New Donors." *More Soft Money Hard Law* (blog). Available at http://www.moresoftmoneyhardlaw.com/2015/04/new-donor/.

Bellow, Adam. 2003. *In Praise of Nepotism: A Natural History*. New York: Doubleday.

Benoit, William B. 2014. *Political Election Debates*. Lanham, MD: Lexington Books.

Beyers, Jan, Rainer Eising, and William A. Maloney. 2010. *Interest Group Politics in Europe*. London: Routledge.

Bierce, Ambrose. 1999. *The Devil's Dictionary*. New York: Oxford University Press.

Bimes, Terri. 2009. "Understanding the Rhetorical Presidency." In *The Oxford Handbook of the American Presidency*, edited by George C. Edwards III and William G. Howell, 208–31. New York: Oxford University Press.

Blondel, Jean. 2006. "About Institutions, Mainly, but Not Exclusively, Political." In *The Oxford Handbook of Political Institutions*, edited by R. A. W. Rhodes, Sarah A. Binder, and Bert A. Rockman, 716–30. New York: Oxford University Press.

Boatright, Robert G. 2016. "Campaign Finance Law and Functional Differentiation among Nonparty Groups in the United States." In *The Deregulatory Moment? Comparative Perspectives on Changing Campaign Finance Laws*, edited by Robert G. Boatright, 71–104. Ann Arbor: University of Michigan Press.

Boatright, Robert G., and Molly Brigid McGrath. 2020. "Corruption, Populism, and Sloth." In *Democracy, Populism, and Truth*, edited by Mark C. Navin and Richard Nunan, 47–59. AMINTAPHIL: The Philosophic Foundations of Law and Justice Series, vol. 9. New York: Springer. Available at https://doi.org/10.1007/978-3-030-43424-3_4.

Boots, Ralph S. 1927. "Review of Charles E. Merriam, *Four Party Leaders*." *American Political Science Review* 21 (2): 450–52.

Bratsis, Peter. 2014. "Political Corruption in the Age of Transnational Capitalism." *Historical Materialism* 22 (1): 105–28.

Briffault, Richard. 2011. "On Dejudicializing American Campaign Finance Law." In *Money, Politics, and the Constitution: Beyond* Citizens United, edited by Monica Youn, 173–94. New York: Century Foundation Press.

Buchan, Bruce, and Lisa Hill. 2014. *An Intellectual History of Political Corruption*. London: Palgrave Macmillan.

Cain, Bruce E. 2015. *Democracy More or Less: America's Political Reform Quandary*. New York: Cambridge University Press.

Caine, Stanley P. 1974. "The Origins of Progressivism." In *The Progressive Era*, edited by Lewis L. Gould, 11–34. Syracuse, NY: Syracuse University Press.

Canovan, Margaret. 1999. "Trust the People? Populism and the Two Faces of Democracy." *Political Studies* 47 (1): 2–16.

Carmines, Edward G., Michael J. Ensley, and Michael W. Wagner. 2017. "The Role of Populists in the 2016 US Presidential Election and Beyond." Paper presented at the State of the Parties Conference, University of Akron, Akron, OH, November 9–10, 2017.

Chamberlain, John. 1932. *Farewell to Reform: The Rise, Life, and Decay of the Progressive Mind in America*. New York: John Day.

Chayes, Sarah. 2015. *Thieves of State: Why Corruption Threatens Global Security*. New York: W. W. Norton.

Chernow, Ron. 2017. *Grant*. New York: Penguin.

Cooper, James Fenimore. (1838) 1981. *The American Democrat*. Indianapolis, IN: Liberty Fund.

Cordis, Adriana, and Jeffrey Milyo. 2013. "Measuring Public Corruption in the United States: Evidence from Administrative Records of Federal Prosecutors." Unpublished manuscript.

Cost, Jay. 2015. *A Republic No More: Big Government and the Rise of American Political Corruption.* New York: Encounter Books.

Croly, Herbert. 1915. *Progressive Democracy.* New York: Macmillan.

———. 1919. *The Promise of American Life.* New York: Macmillan.

Dallinger, Frederick. 1897. *Nominations for Elective Office.* Cambridge, MA: Harvard University Press.

Dalton, Russell J. 2004. *Democratic Challenges, Democratic Choices: The Erosion in Political Support in Advanced Industrial Democracies.* New York: Oxford University Press.

Dancey, Logan, and Geoffrey Sheagley. 2018. "Partisanship and Perceptions of Party-Line Voting in Congress." *Political Research Quarterly* 71 (1): 32–45.

Dante Alighieri. 1995. *Dante's Inferno.* Edited and translated by Mark Musa. Bloomington: Indiana University Press.

Davis, James H., and John A. Ruhe. 2003. "Perceptions of Country Corruption: Antecedents and Outcomes." *Journal of Business Ethics*, 43, 275–88.

Debs, Eugene V. 1918. "Canton Speech." In *Debs and the War*, edited by Eugene V. Debs. Chicago: National Office of the Socialist Party.

DeLeon, Peter. 1993. *Thinking About Political Corruption.* Armonk, NY: M. E. Sharpe.

Dewey, John. 1927. *The Public and Its Problems.* New York: Swallow Press.

Dincer, Oguzhan C., and Michael Johnston. 2015. "Measuring Illegal and Legal Corruption in American States: Some Results from the Edmond J. Safra Center for Ethics Corruption in America Survey." Cambridge, MA: Edmond J. Safra Center, Harvard University.

Dionne, E. J. 1991. *Why American Hate Politics.* New York: Simon and Schuster.

Dobel, J. Patrick. 1978. "The Corruption of a State." *American Political Science Review* 72 (3): 958–73.

Dreiser, Theodore. 1912. *The Financier.* New York: Harper and Brothers.

———. 1925. *An American Tragedy.* New York: Horace Liveright.

Du Bois, W. E. B. (1903) 1909. *The Souls of Black Folk.* Philadelphia: A. C. McClurg.

Duneier, Mitchell. 2016. *Ghetto: The Invention of a Place, the History of an Idea.* New York: Farrar, Strauss, and Giroux.

Edelman Staff. 2017. "Edelman Trust Barometer." Chicago: Daniel J. Edelman Holdings. Available at https://www.edelman.com/trust/2017-trust-barometer.

Edward M. Kennedy Institute. n.d. "The Senate Project." Boston: Edward M. Kennedy Institute. Available at https://emkinstitute.org/the-senate-project/.

Edwards, George C. III. 1996. "Presidential Rhetoric: What Difference Does It Make?" In *Beyond the Rhetorical Presidency*, edited by Merlin J. Medhurst, 199–217. College Station: Texas A&M University Press.

Ellis, Joseph J. 2000. *Founding Brothers: The Revolutionary Generation.* New York: Vintage.

Elshtain, Jean Bethke. 2000. *Who Are We? Critical Reflections and Hopeful Possibilities.* Grand Rapids, MI: Eerdmans.

Euben, J. Peter. 1978. "On Political Corruption." *Antioch Review* 36 (1): 103–18.

Farr, James. 1989. "Understanding Conceptual Change Politically." In *Political Innovation and Conceptual Change*, edited by Terrence Ball, James Farr, and Russell L. Hanson, 24–49. New York: Cambridge University Press.

Feierhard, German, Noam Lupu, and Susan C. Stokes. 2018. "A Significant Minority of Americans Say They Could Support a Military Takeover of the U.S. Government." *Washington Post*, February 16, 2018.

Filler, Louis. (1939) 1976. *Crusaders for American Liberalism: The Story of the Muckrakers.* University Park: Pennsylvania State University Press.

Fine, Terri Susan. 1994. "Proclaiming Party Identity: A View from the Platforms." In *The State of the Parties: The Changing Role of Contemporary American Parties*, 2nd edition, edited by John C. Green and Daniel M. Shea, 265–74. Lanham, MD: Rowman & Littlefield.

———. 2003. "Party Platforms as Tools of Presidential Agenda Setting." *White House Studies* 3 (2): 199–211.

Fiorina, Morris P. 2017. *Unstable Majorities: Polarization, Party Sorting, and Political Stalemate.* Stanford, CA: Hoover Institution Press.

Fisman, Ray, and Miriam A. Golden. 2017. *Corruption: What Everyone Needs to Know.* New York: Oxford University Press.

Fjelde, Hanne. 2009. "Buying Peace? Oil Wealth, Corruption and Civil War, 1985–99." *Journal of Peace Research* 46 (2): 199–218.

Forcey, Charles. 1961. *The Crossroads of Liberalism: Croly, Weyl, Lippmann, and the Progressive Era, 1900–1925.* New York: Oxford University Press.

Fowler, Erika Franklin. 2017. "CCES 2014, Team Module of Wesleyan University (WES)." Harvard Dataverse, V1. Available at http://dx.doi.org/10.7910/DVN/NIU9IT.

Frederick, Peter. 1976. *Knights of the Golden Rule: The Intellectual as Christian Social Reformer in the 1890s.* Lexington: University Press of Kentucky.

Friedrich, Carl J. 1972. *The Pathology of Politics.* New York: Harper and Row.

Frum, David. 2018. *Trumpocracy: The Corruption of the American Republic.* New York: HarperCollins.

Genovese, Michael A. 2010. "Presidential Corruption: A Longitudinal Analysis." In *Corruption and American Politics*, edited by Michael A. Genovese and Victoria A. Farrar-Myers, 136–76. Amherst, NY: Cambria Press.

George, Henry. (1896) 1946. *Progress and Poverty.* New York: Robert Schalkenbach Foundation.

Glaeser, Edward L., and Claudia Goldin, eds. 2006. *Corruption and Reform: Lessons from America's Economic History.* Chicago: University of Chicago Press.

Graham, Otis L. 1967. *An Encore for Reform: The Old Progressives and the New Deal.* New York: Oxford University Press.

Groseclose, Timothy, and Keith Krehbiel. 1994. "Golden Parachutes, Rubber Checks, and Strategic Retirements from the 102nd House." *American Journal of Political Science* 38 (1): 75–99.

Grzymala-Busse, Anna. 2017. "Global Populisms and Their Impact." *Slavic Review* 76 (S1): S3–S8.

Hall, Richard L. 1996. *Participation in Congress.* New York: Cambridge University Press.

Hall, Richard L., and Frank W. Wayman. 1990. "Buying Time: Moneyed Interests and the Mobilization of Bias in Congressional Committees." *American Political Science Review* 84 (3): 797–820.

Hart, Roderick P. 1987. *The Sound of Leadership: Presidential Communication in the Modern Age.* Chicago: University of Chicago Press.

———. 2000. *Campaign Talk: Why Elections Are Good for Us.* Princeton, NJ: Princeton University Press.

Herndon, Astead W. 2019. "How Trump's Brand of Grievance Politics Roiled a Pennsylvania Campaign." *New York Times*, March 15, 2019.

Hertzler, J. O. 1951. "Edward Alsworth Ross: Sociological Pioneer and Interpreter." *American Sociological Review* 16 (5): 597–613.

Heywood, Paul M., ed. 2014. *Routledge Handbook of Political Corruption*. New York: Routledge.

Hinckley, Barbara. 1990. *The Symbolic Presidency: How Presidents Portray Themselves*. New York: Routledge.

Hobbes, Thomas. 1994. *Leviathan*. Edited by Edwin Curley. Indianapolis, IN: Hackett Publishing.

Hofstadter, Richard. 1955. *The Age of Reform: From Bryan to F.D.R.* New York: Knopf.

Holmes, Leslie. 2015. *Corruption: A Very Short Introduction*. New York: Oxford University Press.

Holyoke, Thomas T. 2014. *Interest Groups and Lobbying*. Boulder, CO: Westview Press.

House Parliamentarian's Office. 2023. *Constitution, Jefferson's Manual, and Rules of the House of Representatives of the United States, 118th Congress*. Washington, DC: US Government Printing Office. Available at https://www.govinfo.gov/content/pkg/HMAN-118/pdf/HMAN-118.pdf.

Howe, John R., Jr. 1967. "Republican Thought and the Political Violence of the 1790s." *American Quarterly* 19 (2): 147–65.

Howell, William G., and Terry M. Moe. 2016. *Relic: How Our Constitution Undermines Effective Government*. New York: Basic Books.

Inness, Abby 2017. "Draining the Swamp: Understanding the Crisis in Mainstream Politics as a Crisis of the State." *Slavic Review*, 76, 30–38.

Jansen, Harold J., and Lisa Young, eds. 2011. *Money, Politics, and Democracy*. Vancouver: University of British Columbia Press.

Jefferson, Thomas. (1780) 1998. *Notes on the State of Virginia*. Edited by Frank Shuffleton. New York: Penguin Classics.

John of Salisbury. 1990. *Policraticus*. Edited by Cary J. Nederman. New York: Cambridge University Press.

Johnston, Michael. 2005. *Syndromes of Corruption: Wealth, Power, and Democracy*. New York: Cambridge University Press.

———. 2014. *Corruption, Contention, and Reform*. New York: Cambridge University Press.

Kaiser, Robert G. 2009. *So Damn Much Money: The Triumph of Lobbying and the Corrosion of American Government*. New York: Vintage.

Kant, Immanuel. 1983. *Perpetual Peace and Other Essays*. Edited by Ted Humphrey. Indianapolis, IN: Hackett Publishing.

———. 2002. *Groundwork for the Metaphysics of Morals*. Edited by Allen W. Wood. New Haven, CT: Yale University Press.

Karol, David. 2009. *Party Position Change in American Politics*. New York: Cambridge University Press.

Kazin, Michael. 1995. *The Populist Persuasion: An American History*. New York: Basic Books.

Kelly, Kristin J. 2016. "Political *Quid pro Quo* and the Impact of Perceptions of Corruption on Democratic Behavior." *Election Law Journal* 15 (2): 160–74.

Kernell, Samuel. 1997. *Going Public: New Strategies of Presidential Leadership*. 3rd edition. Washington, DC: Congressional Quarterly Press.

Key, V. O. 1956. *American State Politics: An Introduction*. New York: Knopf.

Klein, Jacob.1969. "The Problem of Freedom." *Bulletin of St. John's College* 12 (1): 21–25.

Kohrs Campbell, Karlyn, and Kathleen Hall Jamieson. 1990. *Deeds Done in Words: Presidential Rhetoric and the Genres of Governance.* Chicago: University of Chicago Press.

Kroeze, Ronald. 2016. "The Rediscovery of Corruption in the 1970s and 1980s." In *Corruption and Governmental Legitimacy: A 21st Century Perspective,* edited by Jonathan Mendilow and Ilan Peleg. Lanham, MD: Lexington Books.

Laclau, Ernesto. 2005. *On Populist Reason.* New York: Verso.

Lansing, Michael J. 2015. *Insurgent Democracy: The Nonpartisan League in North American Politics.* Chicago: University of Chicago Press.

La Raja, Raymond J., and Brian F. Schaffner. 2015. *Campaign Finance and Political Polarization: When Purists Prevail.* Ann Arbor: University of Michigan Press.

Lepore, Jill. 2014. "The Crooked and the Dead: Does the Constitution Protect Corruption?" *New Yorker,* August 25, 2014.

Lessig, Lawrence. 2012. *Republic, Lost.* New York: Twelve Books.

———. 2013. "Institutional Corruption." Edward J. Safra Research Lab Working Paper 1, Harvard University, Cambridge, MA.

———. 2015. "Democrats Embrace the Logic of *Citizens United.*" *Washington Post,* May 8, 2015.

Levy, David W. 1985. *Herbert Croly of the New Republic: The Life and Thought of an American Progressive.* Princeton, NJ: Princeton University Press.

Lim, Elvin T. 2002. "Five Trends in Presidential Rhetoric: An Analysis of Rhetoric from George Washington to Bill Clinton." *Presidential Studies Quarterly* 32 (2): 328–66.

———. 2008. *The Anti-Intellectual Presidency.* New York: Oxford University Press.

Link, Arthur S. 1954. *Woodrow Wilson and the Progressive Era.* New York: Harper Torchbooks.

Lippmann, Walter. 1913. *A Preface to Politics.* New York: Henry Holt.

———. (1914) 1961. *Drift and Mastery.* Englewood Cliffs, NJ: Prentice Hall.

———. (1921) 1965. *Public Opinion.* New York: Free Press.

———. (1925) 1993. *The Phantom Public.* New Brunswick, NJ: Transaction.

———. 1931. *A Preface to Morals.* New York: MacMillan.

———. 1936. *The Good Society.* New York: Little, Brown.

———. 1955. *The Public Philosophy.* New York: Mentor.

Locke, John. 1988. *Two Treatises of Government.* Edited by Peter Laslett. New York: Cambridge University Press.

Luther, Martin, and John Calvin. 1991. *Luther and Calvin on Secular Authority.* Edited by Harro Höpfl. Cambridge University Press.

Lyman, Stanford M. 1978. *The Seven Deadly Sins: Society and Evil.* New York: St. Martin's.

MacGilvray, Eric. 2011. *The Invention of Market Freedom.* New York: Cambridge University Press.

Machiavelli, Niccolò. 1950. *The Prince and the Discourses.* Edited by Max Lerner. New York: McGraw-Hill.

———. 1985. *The Prince.* Translated by Harvey C. Mansfield. Chicago: University of Chicago Press.

———. 1996. *Discourses on Livy.* Translated by Harvey C. Mansfield and Nathan Tarcov. Chicago: University of Chicago Press.

Maisel, L. Sandy. 1993. "The Platform-Writing Process: Candidate-Centered Platforms in 1992." *Political Science Quarterly* 108 (4): 671–98.

Mandeville, Bernard. 1924. *Fable of the Bees.* Oxford: Clarendon Press.

Mann, Thomas E., and Norman J. Ornstein. 2012. *It's Even Worse than It Looks*. New York: Basic Books.

———. 2016. *It's Even Worse than It Was*. New York: Basic Books.

Marsiglio of Padua. 1993. "The Defender of the Peace." In *Readings in Medieval Political Theory 1100–1400*, edited by Cary J. Nederman and Kate Langdon Forhan, 173–299. Indianapolis, IN: Hackett Publishing.

McCann, James A., and David P. Redlawsk. 2006. "As Voters Head to the Polls, Will They Perceive a 'Culture of Corruption?'" *PS: Political Science and Politics* 37 (4): 797–802.

McCarty, Nolan, Keith E. Poole, and Howard Rosenthal. 2006. *Polarized America: The Dance of Unequal Wealth and Riches*. Cambridge, MA: MIT Press.

McCraw, Thomas K. 1974. "The Progressive Legacy." In *The Progressive Era*, edited by Lewis L. Gould, 181–201. Syracuse, NY: Syracuse University Press.

McCurry, Justin. 2019. "Hundreds of North Korean Execution Sites Identified, Says Rights Group." *The Guardian* (London), June 11, 2019.

McMann, Kelly M. 2014. *Corruption as a Last Resort*. Ithaca, NY: Cornell University Press.

Meacham, Jon. 2008. *American Lion: Andrew Jackson in the White House*. New York: Random House.

Melgar, Natalia, Maximo Rossi, and Tom W. Smith. 2010. "The Perception of Corruption." *International Journal of Public Opinion Research* 22 (1): 120–31.

Merriam, Charles. 1908. *Primary Elections*. Chicago: University of Chicago Press.

Millard, Candice. 2011. *Destiny of the Republic*. New York: Doubleday.

Miller, Seumas. 2011. "Corruption." In *The Stanford Encyclopedia of Philosophy* (Spring 2011 Edition), edited by Edward N. Zalta. Available at http://plato.stanford.edu/archives /spr2011/entries/corruption/.

Milyo, Jeffrey D., and David M. Primo. 2020. *Campaign Finance and American Democracy: What the Public Really Thinks and Why It Matters*. Chicago: University of Chicago Press.

Mitchell, Alison. 1999. "Republicans Pillory McCain in Debate over Soft Money." *New York Times*, October 15, 1999.

Moffitt, Benjamin. 2016. *The Global Rise of Populism*. Palo Alto, CA: Stanford University Press.

Montesquieu, Charles de Secondat. 1989. *The Spirit of the Laws*. Edited by Anne Cohler, Basia Miller, and Harold Stone. New York: Cambridge University Press.

———. 1999. *Considerations on the Causes of the Greatness of the Romans and Their Decline*. Translated and with an Introduction and Notes by David Lowenthal. New York: Hackett Publishing.

Montinolo, Gabriela R., and Robert W. Jackman. 2002. "Sources of Corruption: A Cross-Country Study." *British Journal of Political Science* 32 (1): 147–70.

Moore, R. Lawrence. 1974. "Directions of Thought in Progressive America." In *The Progressive Era*, edited by Lewis L. Gould, 35–53. Syracuse, NY: Syracuse University Press.

More, Thomas. 2016. *Utopia*. 3rd edition. Edited by George M. Logan. Translated by Robert M. Adams. Cambridge: Cambridge University Press.

Morlan, Robert L. 1955. *Political Prairie Fire: The Nonpartisan League, 1915–1922*. Minneapolis: University of Minnesota Press.

Mudde, Cass, and Cristobal Rovira Kaltwasser. 2017. *Populism: A Very Short Introduction*. New York: Oxford University Press.

Muirhead, Russell, and Nancy L. Rosenblum. 2019. *A Lot of People Are Saying: The New Conspiracism and the Assault on Democracy*. Princeton, NJ: Princeton University Press.

Müller, Jan-Werner. 2016. *What Is Populism?* Philadelphia: University of Pennsylvania Press.

Muller, Jerry Z. 2002. *The Mind and the Market.* New York: Alfred A. Knopf.

Mutch, Robert E. 2014. *Buying the Vote.* New York: Oxford University Press.

Noel, Hans. 2013. *Political Ideologies and Political Parties in America.* New York: Cambridge University Press.

Norris, Frank. 1899. *McTeague.* New York: Doubleday.

———. 1901. *The Octopus.* New York: Doubleday.

———. 1903. *The Pit.* New York: Doubleday.

Norris, Kathleen. 2008. *Acedia and Me.* New York: Riverhead Books.

Nye, Russell B. 1951. *Midwestern Progressive Politics: A Historical Study of Its Origins and Development, 1870–1950.* East Lansing: Michigan State College Press.

Oakeshott, Michael. (1962) 1991. *Rationalism in Politics and Other Essays.* Indianapolis, IN: Liberty Fund.

———. 1996. *The Politics of Faith and the Politics of Scepticism.* New Haven, CT: Yale University Press.

Oliver, J. Eric, and Wendy M. Rahn. 2016. "Rise of the *Trumpenvolk*: Populism in the 2016 Election." *Annals of the American Academy of Political and Social Science*, no. 667, 189–206.

Ostiguy, Pierre, and Kenneth M. Roberts. 2016. "Putting Trump in Comparative Perspective: Populism and the Politicization of the Sociocultural Low." *Brown Journal of World Affairs* 23 (1): 25–50.

Östlund, Ruben, dir. 2014. *Force Majeure.* Copenhagen, Denmark: Beofilm.

Park, Robert, and Ernest W. Burgess. (1925) 2019. *The City.* Chicago: University of Chicago Press.

Parsons, Theophilus. 1859. *Memoir of Theophilus Parsons, Chief Justice of the Supreme Judicial Court of Massachusetts.* Boston: Ticknor and Fields.

Persily, Nathaniel, and Kelli Lammie. 2004. "Perceptions of Corruption and Campaign Finance: When Public Opinion Determines Constitutional Law." *University of Pennsylvania Law Review*, no. 158, 119–80.

Peters, John G., and Susan Welch. 1978. "Political Corruption in America: A Search for Definitions and a Theory, or If Political Corruption is in the Mainstream of American Politics Why Is It Not in the Mainstream of American Politics Research?" *American Political Science Review* 72 (3): 974–84.

Phillips, David Graham. 1906. "The Treason of the Senate." *Cosmopolitan Magazine* 40 (5).

Piketty, Thomas. 2013. *Capital in the Twenty-First Century.* Cambridge, MA: Harvard University Press.

Pinto-Duschinsky, Michael. 2012. "Preface." In *Money, Corruption, and Political Competition in Established and Emerging Democracies*, edited by Jonathan Mendilow, vii–xv. Lanham, MD: Lexington Books.

Pizan, Christine de. 1994. *The Book of the Body Politic.* Edited by Kate Langdon Forhan. New York: Cambridge University Press.

Pocock, J. G. A. 1975. *The Machiavellian Moment: Florentine Political Thought and the Atlantic Republican Tradition.* Princeton, NJ: Princeton University Press.

Postell, Joseph. 2017. *Bureaucracy in America.* Columbia: University of Missouri Press.

Potter, Trevor. 2006. "*McConnell v. FEC* Jurisprudence and Its Future Impact on Campaign Finance." *University of Miami Law Review*, no. 60, 185–200.

Praino, Rodrigo, Daniel Stockemer, and Vincent G. Moscardelli. 2013. "The Lingering Effect of Scandal in Congressional Elections: Incumbents, Challengers, and Voters." *Social Science Quarterly* 94 (4): 1045–61.

Publius. (1787) 1961. *The Federalist Papers.* Edited by Clinton Rossiter. New York: Mentor Books.

Redlawsk, David P., and James A. McCann. 2005. "Popular Interpretations of 'Corruption' and Their Partisan Consequences." *Political Behavior* 27 (3): 261–83.

Reisert, Joseph R. 2003. *Jean-Jacques Rousseau: A Friend of Virtue.* Ithaca, NY: Cornell University Press.

Reynolds, John F. 2006. *The Demise of the American Convention System, 1880–1911.* New York: Cambridge University Press.

Rhodes, R. A. W. 2006. "Old Institutionalisms." In *The Oxford Handbook of Political Institutions,* edited by R. A. W. Rhodes, Sarah A. Binder, and Bert A. Rockman, 90–108. New York: Oxford University Press.

Ricci, David. 2011. *Why Conservatives Tell Stories and Liberals Don't: Rhetoric, Faith, and Vision on the American Right.* Boulder, CO: Paradigm Press.

———. 2016. *Politics without Stories: The Liberal Predicament.* New York: Cambridge University Press.

Robinson, Marilynne. 2019. "Is Poverty Necessary?" *Harper's Magazine,* June 2019.

Roosevelt, Theodore. 1961. *The New Nationalism.* Edited by William E. Leuchtenberg. Englewood Cliffs, NJ: Prentice Hall.

Rose, Jonathan. 2015. "Corruption and the Problem of Perception." In *The Routledge Handbook of Political Corruption,* edited by Paul M. Heywood, 172–82. New York: Routledge.

Rose-Ackerman, Susan. 1999. *Corruption and Government: Causes, Consequences, and Reforms.* New York: Cambridge University Press.

Rose-Ackerman, Susan, and Tina Søreide, eds. 2011. *International Handbook on the Economics of Corruption.* London: Edward Elgar.

Rosenblum, Nancy. 2008. *On the Side of the Angels: An Appreciation of Parties and Partisanship.* Princeton, NJ: Princeton University Press.

Rosenkranz, E. Joshua, ed. 1999. *If Buckley Fell: A First Amendment Blueprint for Regulating Money in Politics.* New York: Century Foundation Press.

Ross, Dorothy. 1991. *The Origins of American Social Science.* New York: Cambridge University Press.

Ross, Edward Alsworth. 1907. *Sin and Society.* New York: Houghton Mifflin.

Rothstein, Bo. 2011a. "Anti-Corruption: The Indirect 'Big-Bang' Approach." *Review of International Political Economy,* 18 (2): 228–50.

———. 2011b. *The Quality of Government: Corruption, Social Trust, and Inequality in International Perspective.* Chicago: University of Chicago Press.

Rothstein, Bo, and Aiysha Varraich. 2017. *Making Sense of Corruption.* New York: Cambridge University Press.

Rousseau, Jean-Jacques. 1964. *The First and Second Discourses.* Edited and translated by Roger D. Masters and Judith R. Masters. Boston: Bedford/St. Martin's.

———. 1978. *On the Social Contract.* Edited and translated by Roger D. Masters and Judith R. Masters. Boston: Bedford/St. Martin's.

———. 1985. *Considerations on the Government of Poland.* Translated by Willmoore Kendall. Indianapolis, IN: Hackett Publishing.

———. 1997. *The Social Contract and Other Late Political Writings.* Cambridge: Cambridge University Press.

———. 2009. *A Discourse on Political Economy*. Reissue edition. Oxford: Oxford University Press. First published in 1755.

———. 2012. *Rousseau: The Basic Political Writings*. 2nd edition. Edited by Donald A. Cress. Indianapolis, IN: Hackett Publishing.

Rusciano, Frank Louis. 2014. "The Meaning of Corruption in World Opinion." In *Corruption in the Contemporary World*, edited by Jonathan Mendilow and Ilan Peleg, 27–46. Lanham, MD: Rowman & Littlefield.

———. 2015. "The Dynamics of Changes in Corruption Measures Over Time." Paper presented at the IPSA RC20 Conference on Party Finance and Political Corruption, Aix-en-Provence, France.

Samples, John. 2006. *The Fallacy of Campaign Finance Reform*. Chicago: University of Chicago Press.

Sanders, Bernie. 2018. *Where We Go from Here*. New York: St. Martin's.

Sanders, Lynn. 1997. "Against Deliberation." *Political Theory* 25 (3): 347–76.

Schweizer, Peter. 2015. *Clinton Cash: The Untold Story of How and Why Foreign Governments and Businesses Helped Make Bill and Hillary Rich*. New York: Harper.

Seidelman, Raymond. 2015. *Disenchanted Realists: Political Science and the American Crisis*. 2nd edition. Albany: State University of New York Press.

Shakespeare, William. 1993. *The Yale Shakespeare*. Edited by Wilbur L. Cross and Tucker Brooke. New Haven, CT: Yale University Press.

Shklar, Judith N. 1969. *Men and Citizens: A Study of Rousseau's Social Theory*. New York: Cambridge University Press.

Shogan, Colleen J. 2006. *The Moral Rhetoric of American Presidents*. College Station: Texas A&M University Press.

Simpson, Dick, Thomas J. Gradel, Melissa Mouritsen, and John Johnson. 2015. "Chicago: Still the Capital of Corruption." Chicago: University of Illinois at Chicago, Department of Political Science. Available at https://pols.uic.edu/wp-content/uploads/sites/273/2018/10/ac_corruptionrpt8.pdf.

Sitaraman, Ganesh. 2017. *The Crisis of the Middle-Class Constitution*. New York: Alfred A. Knopf.

Skinner, Quentin. 1989. "Language and Political Change." In *Political Innovation and Conceptual Change*, edited by Terrence Ball, James Farr, and Russell L. Hanson, 6–23. New York: Cambridge University Press.

Skowronek, Stephen. 1997. *The Politics Presidents Make*. 2nd edition. Cambridge, MA: Harvard Belknap.

Smith, Bradley A. 2001. *Unfree Speech*. Princeton, NJ: Princeton University Press.

Smith, Tom W., Michael Davern, Jeremy Freese, and Michael Hout. 2018. General Social Surveys 1972–2016 [machine-readable data file]. Chicago: NORC.

Stanley, Jason. 2015. *How Propaganda Works*. Princeton, NJ: Princeton University Press.

Stearns, Matt. 2007. "Jerry Falwell, 1933–2007." *McClatchy Newspapers*, May 16, 2007.

Steffens, Lincoln. 1957. *The Shame of the Cities*. New York: Hill and Wang. First published in 1904.

Steger, Wayne. 2017. "The Second Great Populist Wave in the Turbulent 2016 Presidential Nominations." Paper presented at the State of the Parties Conference, University of Akron, Akron, OH, November 9–10.

Stephenson, Matthew. 2016. *Bibliography on Corruption and Anti-Corruption*. Available at http://www.law.harvard.edu/faculty/mstephenson/, accessed January 13, 2016.

Stock, Catherine McNicol. 1996. *Rural Radicals: From Bacon's Rebellion to the Oklahoma City Bombing*. New York: Penguin.

Stokes, Donald E. 1963. "Spatial Models of Party Competition." *American Political Science Review* 57 (2): 368–77.

Svendsen, Lars. 2005. *A Philosophy of Boredom*. London: Reaktion Books.

Taft, William Howard. 1922. *Liberty Under Law*. New Haven, CT: Yale University Press.

Teachout, Zephyr. 2014. *Corruption in America: From Benjamin Franklin's Snuff Box to Citizens United*. Cambridge, MA: Harvard University Press.

Teorell, Jan, and Bo Rothstein. "Getting to Sweden: Malfeasance and Bureaucratic Reforms, 1720–1850." Quality of Government Working Papers Series 18, University of Gothenburg, Gothenburg, Sweden, 2012.

Teten, Ryan L. 2003. "Evolution of the Modern Rhetorical Presidency: Presidential Presentation and Development of the State of the Union Address." *Presidential Studies Quarterly* 33 (2): 333–46.

———. 2007. "'We the People': The 'Modern' Rhetorical Popular Address of the Presidents during the Founding Period." *Political Research Quarterly* 60 (4): 669–82.

Thompson, Dennis F. 1987. *Political Ethics and Public Office*. Cambridge, MA: Harvard University Press.

———. 1995. *Ethics in Congress: From Individual to Institutional Corruption*. Washington, DC: Brookings Institution.

———. 2002. *Just Elections*. Chicago: University of Chicago Press.

———. 2013. "Two Concepts of Corruption." Edward J. Safra Research Lab Working Paper 16, Harvard University, Cambridge, MA.

Tocqueville, Alexis de. (1848) 1969. *Democracy in America*. Translated by George Lawrence. New York: Harper Perennial.

Toohey, Peter. 2011. *Boredom: A Lively History*. New Haven, CT: Yale University Press.

Tulis, Jeffrey K. 1987. *The Rhetorical Presidency*. Princeton, NJ: Princeton University Press.

Underkuffler, Laura S. 2013. *Captured by Evil: The Idea of Corruption in Law*. New Haven, CT: Yale University Press.

Uscinski, Joseph E., and Joseph M. Parent. 2014. *American Conspiracy Theories*. New York: Oxford University Press.

Uslaner, Eric M. 2002. *The Moral Foundations of Trust*. New York: Cambridge University Press.

Wallis, John Joseph. 2006. "The Concept of Systematic Corruption in American History." In *Corruption and Reform: Lessons from America's Economic History*, edited by Edward L. Glaeser and Claudia Goldin, 23–62. Chicago: University of Chicago Press.

Warner, Hoyt Landon. 1964. *Progressivism in Ohio, 1897–1917*. Columbus: Ohio State University Press.

Warren, Danielle E., and William S. Laufer. 2009. "Are Corruption Indices a Self-Fulfilling Prophecy? A Social Labeling Perspective of Corruption." *Journal of Business Ethics* 88: 841–49.

Wasserstein, Wendy. 2005. *Sloth*. New York: Oxford University Press.

Waugh, Evelyn. 1962. "Sloth." In *The Seven Deadly Sins*, edited by Raymond Mortimer, 56–64. London: Sunday Times Publications.

Weber, Max. 2004. *The Vocation Lectures*. Translated by R. Livingstone. Indianapolis, IN: Hackett Publishing.

Wenzel, Siegfried. 1967. *The Sin of Sloth: Acedia in Medieval Thought and Literature*. Chapel Hill: University of North Carolina Press.

Weyl, Walter. 1912. *The New Democracy: An Essay on Certain Political and Economic Tendencies in the United States*. New York: Macmillan.

White, William Allen. 1910. *The Old Order Changeth*. New York: Macmillan.

Wiebe, Robert H. 1967. *The Search for Order, 1877–1920*. New York: Hill and Wang.

Will, George. 2017. "Trump Has a Dangerous Disability." *Washington Post*, May 3, 2017.

Williams, Raymond. 1976. *Keywords: A Vocabulary of Culture and Society*. Glasgow: Fontana.

Wilson, Woodrow. (1885) 2005. *Congressional Government*. In *Woodrow Wilson: The Essential Political Writings*, edited by Ronald J. Pestritto. Lanham, MD: Lexington Books.

———. (1889) 2005. *The State*. In *Woodrow Wilson: The Essential Political Writings*, edited by Ronald J. Pestritto. Lanham, MD: Lexington Books.

———. (1908) 2005. *Constitutional Government*. In *Woodrow Wilson: The Essential Political Writings*, edited by Ronald J. Pestritto. Lanham, MD: Lexington Books.

Wittern-Keller, Laura. 2008. *Freedom of the Screen: Legal Challenges to State Film Censorship, 1915–1981*. Lexington: University Press of Kentucky.

Woolley, John, and Gerhard Peters. n.d. American Presidency Project. University of California, Santa Barbara. Available at https://www.presidency.ucsb.edu/.

You, Jong-Sung, and Sanjeev Khagram. 2005. "A Comparative Study of Inequality and Corruption." *American Sociological Review* 70 (1): 136–57.

Zarefsky, David. 2004. "Presidential Rhetoric and the Power of Definition." *Presidential Studies Quarterly* 34 (3): 607–19.

Index

Italicized page numbers indicate illustrations; those with a *t* indicate tables.

Robert G. Boatright is Professor of Political Science at Clark University and Director of Research for the National Institute for Civil Discourse at the University of Arizona.

Molly Brigid McGrath is Professor of Philosophy at Assumption University and Director of the D'Amour Center for Teaching Excellence.

www.ingramcontent.com/pod-product-compliance
Lightning Source LLC
Chambersburg PA
CBHW030643270326
41929CB00007B/185